Generational Dynamics
Forecasting America's Destiny

By:

John J. Xenakis

www.GenerationalDynamics.com

Bookman Marketing
Martinsville, Indiana
www.BookmanMarketing.com

© 2004 by John J. Xenakis. All rights reserved.

No part of this book may be reproduced, stored in a retrieval system, or transmitted by any means, electronic, mechanical, photocopying, recording, or otherwise, without written permission from the author.

ISBN: 1-59453-048-3

xxxx – rev. 01/01/04

Table of Contents

Table of Figures xi

Preface xiv
    Predicting the future xv
    America and the "Clash of Civilizations" xvi
    Limitations of Generational Dynamics xviii
    A Note to Skeptics xx
    Web Site xxi
    Credits xxi

Chapter 1 — Basics and Some Myths about War 2
    Doomed to repeat the same mistakes 4
    The "Generation Gap" and the Generational Cycle 6
    Fault Lines 8
    Fault Lines and Generation Gaps 8
    Crisis, Austerity, Awakening and Unraveling Periods 10
    Example: From Revolutionary War to Civil War 12
    Cause versus Timing of War 13
    Example From Mideast Crisis to Mideast Crisis 14
    American Fault Lines since World War II 16
    How long is an 80-year cycle? 17
        Didn't humans use to have a shorter lifespan? 17
        Merging Timelines 18
    Things happen in their time 19
    Why is war necessary? 20

Chapter 2 — American History 23
    Adjust your point of view 23
    The Colonists versus the Indians — 1675-78 25
    Aftermath of King Philip's War 29

The Great Awakening of the 1730s and 40s 30
The Revolutionary War — 1772-1782... 32
The pursuit of the war.. 35
    Aftermath of the war 36
    The Awakening of the 1820s and 1830s 37
The American Civil War, 1857-65.. 38
    Causes and Timing of the Civil War 40
    Why was there no "Civil War II"?... 41
    Aftermath of the Civil War... 42
    The Awakening of 1890-1920 43
World War I... 44
The Great Depression and the Smoot-Hawley Tariff Act 47
World War II... 50
    World War II without Hitler?... 50
A world with two superpowers... 52
    The Korean War 53
    The Vietnam War 54
    Vietnam Syndrome 55
September 11, 2001 55
The character of a nation.. 56
A brief word about Mexico... 57
The future of the United States 57

Chapter 3 — The Principle of Localization I.. 59
Applying the Principle of Localization... 59
Identity Groups and Fault Line Wars 61
Civilizations and Fault Line Wars 62
The Bosnian Conflict 64
    Why did America support the Bosnian Muslims? 65
    The Character of a Nation.. 66
    What was the "cause" of the Bosnian war?............................... 67

Chapter 4 — The Principle of Localization II 69
"Identity Group Expansion" versus "The Principle of Localization" ... 69
Picking sides in the Clash of Civilizations 70

Forecasting the coming Mideast War and its aftermath 71
   A Brief Historical Analysis 71
   The future in the Mideast 73
   Will this be the clash of civilizations? 74
The Generational Dynamics Forecasting Methodology 76
   Overcoming Forecasting Limitations 76
   Methodology Part I: Historical Analysis 77
   Methodology Part II: Economic Analysis 78
   Methodology Part III: Monthly Current Attitudes Analysis 79
Crisis Wars versus Mid-Cycle Wars 80
Winners and Losers: The process of national transformation 82
   Transformation of the defeated nation 82
   Recognizing the depth of transformation 84
Why wasn't World War I a Crisis War for Germany? 85
A different view of World War I 88

Chapter 5 — Tolstoy's *War and Peace* 89
Why did Napoleon invade Russia? 91
The Russian Background 96
Napoleon's advance to Moscow 98
Momentum Wars: The French reach Moscow 99
The Council of War 105
Moscow and the Destruction of Napoleon's Army 107
Napoleon and Hitler 111

Chapter 6 — Another Great Depression? 114
Irrational Exuberance in the 1990s 115
Investor hysteria 117
Bubbles in American history 119
   Tulipomania 120
   American bubbles 122
Can Federal agencies protect us from a new depression? 123
The "Crusty Old Bureaucracy" Theory 125
What does a "depression" mean for our lives? 127

Chapter 7 — Great Awakenings in World History 128
Understanding Awakenings 128
The Golden Age of Ancient Greece 129
Persian Wars, 510-478 BC 130
The Awakening Period 131
Peloponnesian War, 431-404 BC 133
The spread of Greek Culture 133
The generational analysis 134
Judaism and the Spread of Christianity 134
Judaism and Diaspora 135
A Jewish Homeland 137
King Herod 138
Aftermath of Herod: Jesus Christ and Christianity 139
Converting to a new religion 141
Proselytizing and Non-Proselytizing Religions 141
Top-Down and Bottom-Up Religions 142
The Teachings of Mohammed 143
The early life of Mohammed 144
The Years in Medina (Yathrib) 145
The Conquest of Mecca 149
Aftermath of Mohammed's death 150
Hinduism and the Life of The Buddha 150

Chapter 8 — History of Western Europe 153
Medieval Spain 154
Spain's Anti-Jewish Pogroms of the 1390s 154
The Spanish Inquisition and the Reconquest — 1480s-1490s 155
The Golden Age of Spain and Manifest Destiny 156
Medieval England 159
The Norman Conquest in 1066 160
Civil War, 1135-54 160
War with Normandy and Magna Carta, 1204-15 161
Civil war and war with Wales, 1264-1282 162
Hundred Years' War begins, 1337-47 162
Civil war and Welsh Revolt, 1386-1409 163

Wars of the Roses, 1455-85 164
War with Spain, 1559-88 164
Britain's Great Civil War, 1638-60 165
Aftermath of the Civil War: The Glorious Revolution 165
The Protestant Reformation in France and Germany 167
Religious wars in Germany 167
Religious wars in France 167
Thirty Years' War 168
German Civil War begins, 1618 169
The war expands 170
Aftermath of the Thirty Years' War 171
The War of Spanish Succession, 1701-1714 172
Aftermath of the War of Spanish Succession 173
The French Revolution and Napoleonic Wars, 1789-1815 173
Prelude 174
From Bankruptcy to Waterloo 174
Could the French Revolution have been predicted? 177
Aftermath of the Napoleonic Wars 179
The Revolutions of 1848 179
The Crimean War, 1853-56 181
Wars of German Unification — 1864-1871 181
The future of France and Germany 183

Chapter 9 — Islam versus Orthodox Christianity 184
The World prior to Mohammed 186
The spread of humans and civilizations 187
The rise and fall of the Roman Empire 187
The separation of Orthodox and Catholic Christianity 190
The Rise and Fall of the Muslim empires 191
The spread of Islam 191
The invasions of the Asians 193
The Seljuk Turks 195
The Kingdom of Jerusalem 196
Catholics vs. Orthodox: The Great Schism 196
The Slavs: Russian Orthodox 198

The Ottoman Empire and the fall of Constantinople 199
Russia's Generational Timeline 201
    Livonian War, 1557-82 201
    Russian Conflict Fault Lines 202
    Peasant Rebellions and Church Schism, 1649-71 203
    The Great Northern War, 1700-1720 204
    War with Ottomans and Pugachev's Rebellion, 1762-83 205
    France's invasion of Russia, 1812 206
    Crimean War and Emancipation Edict, 1853-61 206
    Aftermath of the Crimean War and Emancipation Edict 207
    Bolshevik Revolution, 1905-1927 208
    Aftermath of the Bolshevik Revolution 209
    Russia's Future 210
The Ottoman Empire's Generational Timeline 211
    War with the Holy League, 1683-99 211
    War with Russia, 1768-74 212
    Crimean War, 1853-56 and Aftermath 213
    Young Turk Revolution to Destruction of Empire, 1908-1922 214
Zionism and the state of Israel 215
The Future of the Mideast 216

Chapter 10 — History of Asia 217
China 217
    Analyzing China's history 218
    China's past 219
    The White Lotus Rebellion - 1796-1805 221
    First Opium War, 1840-1842 223
    The Taiping Rebellion, 1851-64 224
    Aftermath of the Taiping Rebellion 225
    Why wasn't the Chinese Rebellion a crisis war? 226
    The Nationalist / Communist war, 1934-49 227
    The Great Leap Forward, 1958-60 229
    Tiananmen Square (1989) and Beyond 232
Japan 233
    Commodore Perry and the Meiji Restoration, 1853-68 233

    Japan's Imperialist Period — 1894-1945 234
    Vietnam 235
    Cambodia and Laos 237
    The Future of Southeast Asia 237

Chapter 11 — Trend Forecasting 238
    Types of trends 238
        Cyclic Trends 238
        Growth Trends 239
        Combined Growth / Cyclic Trends 241
    Population Growth 241
        Exponential growth 242
        Thomas Roberts Malthus 245
        Complexity Theory: Why Communism and Socialism must fail .. 246
    Technology Growth Trends 248
        Artificial Light Sources 249
        Speed of combat aircraft 250
        Installed Technological Horsepower 251
        Growth of Computing Power 253
        Sociological changes related to technology 256
    Forecasting Stock Trends 263
        Should stock prices grow exponentially? 263
        Dow Jones Industrial Average 264
        S&P 500 Stock Index 265
        The S&P Price Earnings Ratio 266
        Comparison to 1980s Japanese Nikkei Stock Market Index 268
        Sub-cycles in economic growth 270
        Reflating the Money Supply 271

Chapter 12 — The Next Century 274
    The Singularity 275
    The need for philosophers and theologians 275

Chapter 13 — America's Manifest Destiny and You 277
    What you should do — as an individual 278

    What you should do — as a community leader 279
    What you should do — as a national politician 280

Appendix — List of Crisis Periods 282

Bibliography 285

End Notes 287

Concept Index 297

Colophon 332

Table of Figures

Figure 1 Crisis periods and mid-cycle periods; number of years is approximate 4
Figure 2 Fault lines and generation gaps 9
Figure 3 Mid-cycle austerity, awakening and unraveling periods; number of years is approximate 10
Figure 4 America c 1810 11
Figure 5 America c 1830 12
Figure 6 America c 1850 12
Figure 7 America c 1861 13
Figure 8 Mideast c 1948 14
Figure 9 Mideast c 1952 15
Figure 10 Mideast c 1967 15
Figure 11 Mideast c 2007 16
Figure 12 Crisis and mid-cycle periods; number of years is approximate 17
Figure 13 Two countries on separate timelines 18
Figure 14 The same two countries with merged timelines 19
Figure 15 New England in 1675. The Pilgrims had landed in 1620 at Plymouth Rock, in the midst of the Wampanoag tribe. 25
Figure 16 Map of Europe divided into 50 separate cultural regions 60
Figure 17 The nine major civilizations today* 62
Figure 18 Napoleon Bonaparte 90
Figure 19 Stages in Napoleon's invasion of Russia in 1812*. 96
Figure 20 Moscow is burning 108
Figure 21 Dow Jones Industrial Average — 1896 to 1940 115
Figure 22 Dow Jones Industrial Average — 1896 to 2002 116
Figure 23 Tulips 121
Figure 24 Ancient Greece and Persia, and city-states Athens and Sparta.... 130
Figure 25 Alexander the Great's empire at his death in 323 BC. Alexander spread Greek culture throughout the entire region, affecting the direction of history for centuries. 133

xi

Figure 26 Map of Europe divided into 50 separate cultural regions 153
Figure 27 Population (millions) of England and Wales*, years 1000-2000. . 163
Figure 28 Contemporary rendering of St. Bartholomew's Night Massacre. 168
Figure 29 Rough map of Europe showing main participants in last decade of the Thirty Years' War.. 170
Figure 30 Eastern Europe / Western Asia, showing major Orthodox/Muslim fault line regions: Balkans, Crimea, and Caucasus (mountains). Not shown: Muslim Bosnia, east of Serbia in Balkans................................... 184
Figure 31 The spread of humans from north Africa around the world*...... 186
Figure 32 The nine major civilizations today*. 187
Figure 33 Alexander the Great's empire at his death in 323 BC. 188
Figure 34 Roman Empire at its peak, around 120 AD...................................... 188
Figure 35 Byzantine Empire around 600 AD. The Roman Empire in the West had been completely destroyed by the invading barbarian hordes...... 189
Figure 36 Further spread of Islam... 192
Figure 37 Arrival of Seljuk Turks.. 194
Figure 38 Eastern Europe in 1600 AD 200
Figure 39 Population of China in millions of people* from 200 BC to 1710 AD 219
Figure 40 China and adjoining countries* (modern names and boundaries). Note the regions of the White Lotus Rebellion and the Taiping Rebellion. 222
Figure 41 College student blocks path of a row of tanks in Tiananmen Square in China, 1989 232
Figure 42 French Indochina in the 1880s and 1890s consisted roughly of today's Vietnam, Cambodia and Laos.. 236
Figure 43 Population (millions) of England and Wales*, years 1000-2000, with an exponential trend line. 242
Figure 44 Population of China in millions of people* from 200 BC to 1710 AD 243
Figure 45 Population of China in millions of people* from 200 BC to 1710 AD, shown with logarithmic scale.. 244
Figure 46 This diagram shows how numerous different technologies for artificial light have always been invented at almost exactly the right time*... 249
Figure 47 Top speeds of combat aircraft (bombers and fighters)*............... 250

xii

Table of Figures

Figure 48 Installed Technological Horsepower in the United States, Population of the United States, and Installed Technological Horsepower per Capita♦. 251

Figure 49 The number of transistors per chip for new chips produced by Intel♦. 254

Figure 50 The number of transistors per chip for new chips produced by Intel. This graph is like the preceding one, except that the y-axis has a logarithmic scale. 255

Figure 51 The number of divorces in each year per 1,000 marriages from 1860 to 1988♦. 257

Figure 52 Same as preceding graph, but with logarithmic scale. 258

Figure 53 The number of marriages ending in divorce, 1867 to 1985, based on year marriage was begun♦. 259

Figure 54 Same as preceding graph, but with logarithmic scale. 260

Figure 55 Rate of out of wedlock births for all women, and for black and white women 262

Figure 56 Dow Jones Industrial Average — 1896 to Present, with best-fit exponential growth line. 264

Figure 57 Dow Jones Industrial Average — 1896 to Present (log scale) 265

Figure 58 S&P 500 Real Price Index — 1870 to Present (log scale), with best fit exponential growth line. 266

Figure 59 Historical price/earnings ratio for S&P 500, 1881 to 2002. 267

Figure 60 Japan's Nikkei Stock Market Index, 1973 to 2002 269

Figure 61 Dow Jones Industrial Average — 1896 to Present (log scale) 270

Figure 62 Consumer price index (CPI) from 1870 to present, with an exponential growth trend line. The CPI is 185 in 2003, and 2010 has a trend value of 129. 272

Preface

"I know it's hard on America. And in some small corner of this vast country, in Nevada or Idaho, these places I've never been but always wanted to go, there's a guy getting on with his life, perfectly happily, minding his own business, saying to you the political leaders of this nation: Why me? Why us? Why America?

"And the only answer is: because destiny put you in this place in history, in this moment in time and the task is yours to do."

— British Prime Minister Tony Blair, addressing a joint session of Congress, on July 17, 2003

For the past 60 years, since the end of World War II, America has led the world in seeking freedom and democracy for everyone, in all nations.

The terrorist attacks of 9/11/2001 served to focus and refine this role. As the quote above from British Prime Minister Tony Blair shows, most Americans and many people around the world today see America as having a unique place in history, as having a "manifest destiny" to bring the world from terrorism to freedom and democracy.

The 9/11 attacks profoundly affected America, but it turns out that another change, a generational change, has been occurring in the early 2000s, and this generational change is having an even more profound affect.

Who are the nation's leaders? The President obviously, but there are many others. There are politicians in Washington and in all the state capitals; there are teachers, journalists, businessmen and women, labor leaders, investors, authors, TV script writers, mentors, and so forth, all of whom provide leadership to other people. And the ones who make most of the final decisions are the senior people, the workers in the 55 to 65 age group.

Now, what happens if, by magic, you could change all the country's leaders from being indecisive, conformist and risk-aversive to being assertive and demanding, willing to risk everything for what's right?

Well, that's exactly what's happened in the last few years, and there's nothing magic about it.

The babies born in the 1930s and 1940s were originally called "depression babies," but in the 1950s, *Time Magazine* gave them a new name: the Silent Generation, because they valued conformity and loyalty above all else, and didn't complain about much.

The members of the Silent Generation were too young to fight in the war, so they lived in the shadow of the G.I. Generation, their older brothers and sisters who became heroes who actually fought in the war, and are now called by Tom Brokaw and others "the greatest generation of the 20th century."

Meanwhile, the Silents had to deal with a new generation, the Baby Boomers who were born *after* the war. The Boomers were very sure of themselves, and led the antiwar riots and demonstrations during the 1960s and 1970s, rebelling against their parents in the G.I. Generation. The Silents were sandwiched between these two warring generations, and served as mediators and compromisers.

The G.I. generation were our nation's leaders during the tumultuous days of 60s and 70s. As they retired and died, the Silent generation became the nation's leaders in the 80s and 90s.

Now, in the decade of the 2000s, the members of the Silent generation are retiring and dying, and being replaced as leaders by the Boomer generation.

Now let's repeat the question: What if, by magic, you could change all the country's leaders from being indecisive, conformist and risk-aversive to being assertive and demanding, willing to risk everything for what's right?

Well, that's what's happened, but there's no magic. The indecisive, conformist and risk-aversive Silent generation was leading the nation in the 80s and 90s, and the assertive, demanding, risk-taking Baby Boomers are the nation's leaders today.

That's why the American public is more willing to risk war today for what they know is right: That America must be the country that leads the world from terrorism to freedom and democracy. As the most powerful nation the world has ever known, that's America's manifest destiny.

Predicting the future

Is it possible to predict the future? Yes, of course - we do it every day. But we can only do it for certain things that involve the actions of large groups of people, and usually only approximately.

For example, we can predict pretty reliably that approximately 130 million Americans voters will vote in the 2008 Presidential election, even though we can't predict whether any particular person will vote. That's an example of a prediction that is approximate as to number.

Shortly after 9/11/2001, I became aware of a prediction that America was headed soon for another world war, based on the fact that previous major crisis wars — the Revolution, Civil War and World War II — had all occurred at roughly 80-year intervals. The prediction was made in an oddly named 1997 book, *The Fourth Turning, an American Prophecy*, by William Strauss and Neil Howe.

I decided to do my own research. Was this crystal ball stuff, or was there solid evidence? Did this apply only to America or to other countries as well? Could a solid theoretical framework be developed, or was it all guesswork?

Generational Dynamics and this book are the result. There is solid evidence presented throughout this book. Generational Dynamics evidently applies to every nation and society throughout history. And there's now a full theoretical framework, highlighting its areas of validity as well as its limitations.

America and the "Clash of Civilizations"

In his 1995 book, *The Clash of Civilizations*, Harvard Professor Samuel P. Huntington showed how the Christian and Jewish western civilization appears to be heading for a worldwide conflict with Muslims around the world. The phrase "clash of civilizations" evokes an image of one billion Muslims fighting with one billion Christians and Jews, even though that's not the image that Professor Huntington wished to evoke.

Still, we'd like to know, what *are* the most likely scenarios? What *does* America's manifest destiny means in terms of the "clash of civilizations"?

Nothing ever happens as planned or predicted, but there are some scenarios that are more likely than others are. To arrive at these scenarios requires a basic principle called the Principle of Localization, which is discussed in chapters 3 and 4. This principle shows how particularly violent crisis wars tend to be cyclic, with a roughly 80-year cycle length, but only when viewed and analyzed on a local basis — typically a single tribe, society or nation. These chapters show how the Principle of Localization works with another principle, Identity Group Expansion, described by Professor Huntington in his 1995 book. These two principles can be used together to explain the causes and timing of regional wars, and how regional wars either get extinguished or else expand to larger wars, possibly world wars. They can also be used to forecast the timing of new wars, using the Generational Dynamics Forecasting Methodology. With regard to the "clash of civilizations," this methodology tells us what the most likely scenarios are.

An important part of the theoretical development is to distinguish between crisis wars, the bloody, violent, genocidal wars that occur every 80 years or so, and the numerous other mid-cycle wars that occur all the time. A fascinating illustration of the differences between the two kinds of wars is Tolstoy's description of Napoleon's invasion of Russia in *War and Peace*. This is discussed in chapter 5, along with extracts from the novel.

Generational Dynamics is not just about wars. Every 80-year cycle begins and ends with a crisis war, but midway between the two crisis wars is an awakening, a period of civil unrest, but with a flowering of new ideas and new policies. America's last awakening occurred in the 1960s and 70s, and gave rise to the antiwar movement, the environment movement, antiracial laws, and women's lib.

Chapter 7 discusses some of the greatest awakenings in history — the Golden Age of Greece, the ministry of Jesus Christ, the life of Mohammed, and the life of the Buddha.

Unfortunately, Generational Dynamics has some more bad news for America in the 2000s decade: it's predicting that we're in a new 1930s style Great Depression. This is discussed in chapter 6, and it's discussed again using mathematical forecasting techniques in chapter 11.

The next three chapters provide histories of Western Europe, Eastern Europe and Asia, respectively. Of particular interest is the history of Eastern Europe, which is presented as a centuries-old conflict between Islam and Orthodox Christianity. If we have a new "clash of civilizations," it will probably be related to Eastern European history.

There are many people, especially some Christian fundamentalists, who believe that the next world war will be the end of the world as described in the Bible. Although I don't believe that the next world war will bring the end of the world any more than World War II did, those who do will find plenty of material in this book that will make you feel the end might be coming. War does that to you. However, the next-to-last chapter of this book, "The Next Century", does make some surprising predictions about the world to come.

The last chapter tells what you can do — you as an individual, you as a community leader, and you as a national policymaker.

Limitations of Generational Dynamics

Although this book is written for the general public, there's a fair amount of rigor behind it. My own educational background is in mathematical logic, and so there's an "axioms, proof, theorem" kind of structure in my mind that is presented in the book in an accessible non-mathematical manner.

When I first was developing Generational Dynamics, my original intention was to either validate or refute the generational theory. What I found validated the theory.

If I had found that there were examples in history that violated the generational paradigm, I would have dropped this project very, very quickly. In fact, if it even turned out that the generational theory only applies since the 1500s, as some people claim, that alone would have been enough to cause me to abandon the entire project.

Writing this book has been a fascinating journey for me. Studying and analyzing each new period in history served to refine and clarify the theory, but never to contradict or refute it.

As I was completing the book, for example, I decided to add some material to Chapter 8 (on Western Europe) to respond to the claim by some people that the generational paradigm doesn't apply prior to 1500. I analyzed England's timeline back to 1066 and found, not to my surprise, that the generational analysis clearly applies. I say "not to my surprise" because by that time I'd done so many similar analyses that the surprise would have been if the generational theory were violated. As long as the Principle of Localization (described in chapters 3 and 4) is honored, then the generational paradigm applies to all societies at all times in history.

The general exposition of the theory behind Generational Dynamics is presented in chapters 1, 3 and 4. I've proven the generational methodology almost as a mathematical theory, or as much a mathematical theory as it's possible to have when you're dealing with human behavior.

This approach also permits me to clearly see the limitations of the generational approach.

For one thing, any conclusion or forecast derived from Generational Dynamics must be based on mass population beliefs and attitudes, not the beliefs and attitudes of any particular person or group of politicians. (The example I like to give is the one that I gave above: that I can predict, fairly reliably, that about 130 million people will vote in the 2008 Presidential election, but I can't predict whether any particular person will vote.)

This means that there's no way to forecast terrorist acts. Terrorism is committed by individuals or small groups of individuals, and there's no way to predict the actions of individuals.

Even more important, there's no way to forecast mid-cycle wars. We could have predicted the Civil War and World War II, and we're predicting a new major war in the next few years, but there's no way that I know of, using this or any other methodology, to predict mid-cycle wars like our Korean, Vietnam or Gulf Wars. That's because those wars do not come from the people; instead, they come from the nation's leaders.

Another limitation in Generational Dynamics is that it's a medium to long-range forecasting tool. That means that when a forecast is available, it's a forecast of what our final destination is, but I can't tell you what road we'll take to get to that destination.

Furthermore, it also means that I can tell you what's going to happen within a time range of a "few years," but I can't tell you with any greater precision than that.

This requires a great deal of care in making forecasts to make it clear what's certain and what's uncertain about each forecast. Thus I can forecast, with very great certainty, that there will be a major war engulfing the Mideast, threatening the existence of Israel, as well as the governments of Egypt, Jordan and Syria, resulting in a major transformation of the Mideast, probably with new national boundaries. But when will this war occur? History shows it will be within two or three years after the next generational change occurs. And when is that? I can only guess that it will be signaled by the disappearance of Yasser Arafat from the scene. I have to make it clear that one part of this forecast is certain, but the timing is not nearly as certain.

I'm always looking for ways to enhance the theory so that short-range forecasts can be made more accurate. To this end, I've developed the three-part "Generational Dynamics Forecasting Methodology," which is described in chapter 4 (see p. 76). This part of the theory is still really being developed, but with a year or two of experience, I believe I'll be able to provide improved shorter-range forecasts.

As you read this book, you'll find that everything is explained in terms of the underlying theoretical basis. I don't claim any magical powers or even any great insight. Every statement is explained as common sense, so that the reader can reach the same conclusion by starting from the same principles, and can decide for him or her self the level of certainty to apply to any Generational Dynamics forecast.

In summary, the limitations of Generational Dynamics are as follows:

- Any forecast applies only to large masses of people, never to a particular individual or small group of politicians. Therefore, it's possible to forecast (predict) crisis wars, but it's impossible to forecast (predict) mid-cycle wars or terrorist acts.

- Since it's a medium to long-range forecasting tool, any forecast provides a final destination, but cannot tell you how we'll get to that destination.

- For the same reason, a forecast might be made with a very high level of certainty, except that the timing of the forecast cannot be made with a precision greater than a few years. (However, I'm working on an enhanced methodology to improve short-range timing forecasts.)

If these limitations are kept in mind, the reader should find that Generational Dynamics is an extremely reliable method for analyzing history and forecasting the future.

A Note to Skeptics

I listen to analysts and pundits on TV all the time, and they make typical statements like this: "Let's compare today's stock market to 1991," or, "The last time something like this happened was waaaaaaaaaaaaay back in 1962," or, "Ever since 1945, such and such has always happened." These analysts never go back any earlier, because almost no one is around any longer who *remembers* earlier times.

The skeptics echo those statements, completely ignoring the conclusion of this book: That we're now in a period resembling the 1930s, and nothing that's happened since then is particularly relevant.

The skeptics claim that we *can't* be repeating the 1930s, because "It's impossible." Why is it impossible? "Because the government set up agencies to prevent it from happening again." They say this even though those agencies have already failed: The SEC was specifically created to prevent a repeat of the 1920s stock market bubble that caused the 1930s depression, but the SEC did not prevent the 1990s stock market bubble. (The one difference that people point to is the Fed reflation policy; this is discussed on page 271).

The whole point of this book is that the mistakes of the 1920s and 1930s are being repeated in the decades of the 1990s and 2000s because the people who remember those earlier decades are no longer around. They've retired or died.

So if you want to argue against the conclusions of this book, you have to depend on more than your memory. You have to do the actual research comparing today to the 1920s and 30s.

And when you do that research, as I have, you discover that there really isn't much difference at all.

Web Site

The book web site is at: http://www.GenerationalDynamics.com

Credits

The beautiful cover art was created by the artist Libby Chase, whose work can be found at http://www.libbysgallery.com.

Clip art images were obtained from http://www.budgetstockphoto.com.

Chapter 1 — Basics and Some Myths about War

Those who cannot remember the past are condemned to repeat it.

— George Santayana

Countries go to war all the time, but there are certain wars that are more crucial than others. These are the wars where most of the people feel that their country's existence is at stake, or at least that their way of life is at stake. We call these "crisis wars." The difference between crisis wars and other wars is measured both viscerally and by actions.

America's last crisis war was World War II. Remember how the entire country was traumatized by the attacks of 9/11/2001? There were numerous articles about how children across the country were frightened that similar acts of terror would occur in their cities.

The same was true in WW II. People were terrified during WW II. Americans watched Hitler's armies overrun France, bomb England, and threaten the Atlantic sea-lanes. They had citizen's watches on both coasts with telescopes looking out for incoming bombers. In fact, the west coast actually *was* bombed — Japan put thousands of bombs onto balloons, and sent them into the atmosphere, and about a thousand of them did reach America. These actions were psychologically effective in terrorizing Americans. And let's not forget the effects of the Depression, which caused massive homelessness and added to the feeling of terror at the war.

By the end of WW II, the American population's anger and even desire for revenge was palpable, especially because of news reports of Japanese' brutal treatment of American prisoners, including torture and beatings. Those emotions were captured and conveyed perfectly by President Harry Truman, in his famous speech on August 9, 1945, shortly after destroying the city of Hiroshima with an atomic bomb: "Having found the bomb we have used it. We have used it against those who attacked us without warning at Pearl Harbor, against those who have starved and beaten American prisoners of war, against those who have abandoned all pretense of obeying international laws of warfare. We have used it in order to shorten the agony of war, in order to save the lives of thousands and thousands of young Americans. We shall continue to use it until we completely destroy Japan's power to make war. Only a Japanese surrender will stop us."

There have been numerous wars since then, the major ones being the Korean War, the Vietnam War, and the 1991 Gulf War. But none of these wars terrorized and infuriated the American public the way World War II did. Nobody feared that the Vietnamese would endanger the American way of life, for example.

Furthermore, none of these wars ever had the massive public support that World War II did. Few if any Americans ever questioned the need to send troops to fight Hitler. Today, Tom Brokaw and other call the soldiers who fought in World War II the "greatest generation" of the twentieth century.

In the Korean, Vietnam and Gulf wars, however, many in the public questioned the need for war. Especially during the Vietnam War there was a large, vocal, powerful pacifist (antiwar) movement. In the Gulf War, once we expelled the Iraqis from Kuwait, President Bush bowed to public pressure to bring the troops home without pursuing Saddam Hussein.

It's only today that Americans feel terrorized and infuriated again, as they were in World War II. Americans across the country were traumatized by the attacks of 9/11. Only a very small percentage of the American population opposed the war in Afghanistan or the 2003 war in Iraq. There is a small pacifist movement, but it's almost completely ineffective.

> *It's only today that Americans feel terrorized and infuriated again, as they were in World War II*

Generational Dynamics is based on the observation that although a society or nation may go to war often, these crisis wars, wars that create a visceral feeling of anxiety, terror and fury throughout the population, occur only occasionally. In particular, a crisis war occurs only when the generation of people who lived through the terror and anxiety of the last crisis war retire or die.

This results in a cycle of crisis wars: Since the human lifetime is about 80 years, crisis wars tend to occur every 70-90 years in any society or nation. This chapter presents some basics to show how nations go from one major crisis war to another in roughly 80-year cycles. The number of years is approximate; it's usually 70-85 years, but some cycles run as little as 60 years or as many as 100 years.

This is not a cyclical view of history in the way that Arnold Toynbee and other historians have tried (and failed) to develop, since the cycles do not apply to the entire world, or entire Western world. Generational Dynamics cycles apply only to local regions and nations — as we'll describe in detail in the Chapters 3 and 4 on the Principle of Localization. This makes sense because the visceral feelings of terror and anxiety are local to a particular nation or society.

This chapter illustrates the basic concepts with two examples:

- How America's Revolutionary War (1772-82) led to the Civil War in 1861
- How Mideast fighting in the 1930-40s is leading to a new major Mideast war in the next few years.

Nations and societies go through two types of wars. Each cycle begins and ends with a major war called a "crisis war," a war that traumatizes and transforms the nation. In between crisis wars there may be many "mid-cycle wars," wars in which soldiers die, but otherwise do not transform societies in a major way.

The adjoining diagram illustrates the difference. A cycle begins and ends with a crisis war, separated by a mid-cycle period. Wars that occur in the mid-cycle period are (naturally) mid-cycle wars.

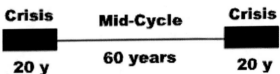

Figure 1 Crisis periods and mid-cycle periods; number of years is approximate

This chapter provides the basics of Generational Dynamics. Later chapters contain a fuller exposition of the theory, as well as dozens of historical examples illustrating the theory.

Doomed to repeat the same mistakes

George Santayana's famous remark, quoted at the beginning of this chapter, states an eternal truth about human beings: humans make the same mistakes over and over throughout history, since they don't remember the past.

In particular, people rarely know much about history before they were born, except for a few basic facts that "everybody" knows.

For example, do you know who controlled Korea during the first half of the 20th century, and why that's crucially important today? Very few Americans have the vaguest idea. (The answer is given elsewhere in this book, at the appropriate place in the text.)

Here's another example, a true/false question: Hitler caused World War II, and if we had killed Hitler in 1935, we could have saved millions of lives. True or false?

Most people would say that's true, forgetting that America wasn't even attacked by Hitler's Germany. We were first attacked by Japan at Pearl Harbor. Hitler never had anything to do with that.

Another question: The Civil War broke out when Abraham Lincoln tried to free the slaves. True or false?

> *The 1960s generation gap was not only not unique in history, it's actually quite common*

Once again, most people would say it's true. In fact, Lincoln never intended to end slavery, and only issued the Emancipation Proclamation under political pressure two years after the Civil War began.

So, what *were* the causes of the Civil War and World War II? Those are the kinds of questions that this book will answer.

We're going to show that major wars happen in their time. Briefly, a major war almost always ends in some compromises, and this creates (or perpetuates) what we call a *fault line* between two groups or nations. A new major war breaks out 70-90 years later over the same fault line. Briefly, the Revolutionary War created a fault line between the North and the South, leading eventually to a Civil War. And the Franco-Prussian war of 1870-71 perpetuated a fault line between France and Germany, leading to World War II.

Why did the Civil War break out in 1861, instead of 1830 or 1890? These issues were always there, so what was special about that particular time? We'll show you.

The "Generation Gap" and the Generational Cycle

Readers who are old enough to remember America in the 1960s and 1970s will be familiar with the phrase "generation gap," which filled thousands of media stories for a decade. It was explained that, for the first time in history, young people were not only not showing respect for their elders, but were actually rebelling against their elders. The explanation was that the Vietnam War was causing this attitude, resulting in the "antiwar movement," the "environmental movement," the "women's lib movement," the "anti-racism movement," and so forth.

Actually, the 1960s generation gap was not only not unique in history, it's actually quite common: It's called an "awakening," and it always happens in every society and nation in every 80-year cycle, midway between two crisis wars.

However, let's dwell on the 1960s for a moment, because the generation gap at that time was truly enormous, as I can illustrate from a few personal anecdotes.

The reason for the generation gap was not the Vietnam War; actually, the generation gap was caused by the Great Depression and World War II. People who lived through that period of horror had very different views of life than those who, like me, were born afterwards.

For example, when my own mother fell ill in 1995, and I was forced to take care of her finances, I was utterly astounded by what I found. She lived on almost nothing. She paid rent for a decent apartment, she paid the electric and phone bills, and she subscribed to *TV Guide*, and that was about it for her regular expenses. Her Depression-era experiences caused her to count every penny as if it were her last. No one born after 1940 would ever live like that — although we may have to learn to as the next few years progress.

I tell this anecdote to emphasize how different people like me, born after 1940, from people who actually lived through the last crisis.

Here's another personal anecdote:

When I was in high school in the 1950s, I wrote a report on political third parties, and I sent away for literature from a whole bunch of them — the Greenback Party, the Prohibition Party, the Socialist Party, and a few others I can't remember. The material was quite hilarious, as I recall, especially the Greenback Party literature that contained a little song about how we should have greenbacks everywhere.

Well, at some point, my father discovered that I had this literature, and he was very concerned. Although he never shouted at me, I could tell that he was very upset. He reminded me that he was an immigrant working for the government in Fort Monmouth, N.J., and that if it became known that his son was in possession of third party literature, he might lose his job. I promised him I would never do it again, but that isn't the end of the story.

A couple of years later, after my freshman year in college, he got me a summer job at his office at Fort Monmouth doing computer work. When I went in for the interview, he cautioned me to confess that I had ordered this literature — in case they already knew — so that there wouldn't be a problem.

I remember thinking how nuts this was — no one could possibly care that I'd sent away for some literature that I didn't even care about except to write a school report, but I did as my father asked, fully expecting the interviewer to simply laugh at the whole thing.

Well, that's not quite what happened. I told the interviewer that I'd ordered this literature, and I wanted him to know. The interviewer looked at me sternly and asked me what it was for. I told him. He asked me a few more questions to make sure that I hadn't completely sold out to the Communists, and then said, "Well, it's OK, as long as you realize your mistake and won't do it again." I agreed, and happily, this bizarre moment ended, we changed the subject and I got the job.

Almost everyone who grew up in the 50s can recount similar stories. Today, looking back, we can only marvel at how enormously our attitudes and world views differ from those who were born earlier.

It's very important to appreciate the enormity of these differences, because in that way can we understand the forces that are leading us to a world war today.

Those of us who were born after 1940 have no personal memory of any of this. We grew up in the 1950s, at a time when the country was celebrating its victories. America had beaten the depression, and American had beaten the Nazis.

To us, the horrors of that period were only a vague story out that our parents bored us with. So what if an uncle died on the beach at Normandy, or if a cousin practically starved to death during the Depression? Doesn't that happen all the time to people in other parts of the world anyway?

We didn't feel any horror. We felt only the exhilaration. We'd beaten the Depression and the Nazis and, to us, not only did we win, but we even won easily and effortlessly, and there really was never any other possible outcome. We won because we were always going to win, and in case another foe comes along, we won't have any trouble winning over them also.

By contrast, our parents lived in constant fear of a new Great Depression, and a new World War (this time with the Communists, rather than the Nazis).

The point is that these generation gaps always happen — in the midst of every 80-year cycle. There is *always* a generation gap between the people of the older generation who lived through the last crisis war (and who fear that it will happen again at any time) and the younger generation born *after* the last crisis war.

Fault Lines

We use the phrase "fault line" as a convenient term to describe the "line" separating two warring groups. We put the word "line" in quotes, because the line is partially imaginary (like the "line" between Catholics and Protestants) and partially physical (like the "line" between France and Germany in World War II).

We use the term "identity groups" to describe the two warring groups, the two groups that are separated by the fault line. Identity groups go beyond geography. For example, there's a fault line today between the Palestinians and the Israelis in the Mideast, and it corresponds roughly to the geographical border of Israel.

However, Arabs and Muslims around the world identify with the Palestinians in the Mideast, and Jews (and many Christians) around the world identify with the Israelis. Thus, there are two identity groups — Palestinians plus Arabs and Muslims around the world, and Israelis plus Jews and Christians around the world — and the fault line separating the two identity groups is partially geographical and partially religious.

Fault Lines and Generation Gaps

Generational Dynamics recognizes two kinds of societal conflicts: conflicts across generational lines, and conflicts across fault lines.

CHAPTER 1 — BASICS AND SOME MYTHS ABOUT WAR

Most people understand fault line conflicts, because they result in real wars. But few people understand generational conflicts because their memories don't go back far enough to understand the generational cycle.

Spend a minute examining the diagram below, which illustrates both fault lines and generational lines. In this diagram,

- The **Fault Line** separates the two identity groups. Conflicts across fault lines are usually wars — from minor wars to all-out crisis wars.

- The **Generation Gap** line separates the generations in both identity groups. Conflicts across generation gap lines are usually riots and demonstrations, rather than wars. Today, this kind of conflict is usually described in the media as "college students rebelling against authority."

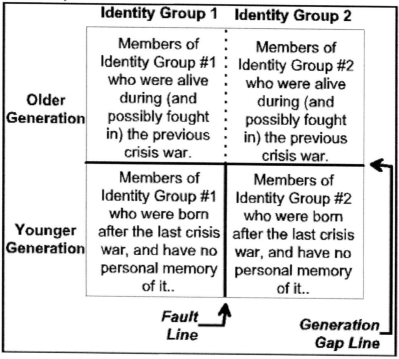

Figure 2 Fault lines and generation gaps

In the diagram, notice that the fault line is illustrated as a solid line on the bottom, and as a dotted line at the top. This is done to illustrate the fact that, even across fault lines, the older generations have much more agreement than the younger generations.

Even if the people in the older generations of two different identity groups "hate" each other, they still have a great deal in common, as a result of having fought a brutal, violent, bloody war with each other. The people in the older generations are more "pragmatic," more willing to compromise, to avoid a renewal of hostilities. And if a new mid-cycle war *does* break out, the people in the older generations limit the violence, since they know each other, and may even have signed a peace agreement together. The people in the younger generation have no such history, and are more idealistic, are more certain of "what's right," and less willing to compromise.

Crisis, Austerity, Awakening and Unraveling Periods

As illustrated in the diagram below, there are roughly 60 years in the mid-cycle period from the end of a crisis war to the beginning of the next crisis period. We break up this 60-year period into three smaller periods, each roughly 20 years long. These three smaller periods are given the names "austerity" (Strauss and Howe call this a "high" period*), "awakening," and "unraveling," respectively.

These names are given for the following reasons:

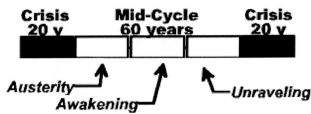

Figure 3 Mid-cycle austerity, awakening and unraveling periods; number of years is approximate

- **Austerity**: The period following a crisis war is a time of great policy confusion for any nation or society, as it tries to recover from the enormous devastation of the war and implement policies that will prevent another similar war anytime soon. The society is united in this desire, and implement austere measures to achieve that goal.

- **Awakening**: When the generation of kids born after the crisis reach college age (17-20), they begin to question and rebel against the austere measures implemented by what is now the older generation.

CHAPTER 1 — BASICS AND SOME MYTHS ABOUT WAR

This is the beginning of the "generation gap." The difference in world view of the younger and older generations is enormous, and this difference leads to riots, demonstrations, and other forms of low-intensity conflict.

In America, the generation of kids born after the last crisis are called "Baby Boomers." In Germany, this same generation was called the "68ers." This is an important generation, because first it leads the awakening period and then, 40 years later, it leads the nation into the next crisis war.

- **Unraveling**: All the compromises that ended the last crisis war and all the austere measures implemented to prevent the next crisis war become unraveled during this period, as the elders who implemented those compromises and measures all retire or die. The generation in power at this point is the generation of kids that were born and grew up *during* the last crisis war. They remember the horrors of the war, but they were too young to have participated in the acceptance of those compromises and austere measures. At times, society itself seems to be unraveling, as it lurches in one direction then another.

Finally, the unraveling period ends when the generation of kids who grew up *during* the last crisis war all retire or die, leaving in charge the generation born *after* the last crisis war — the same generation that rioted and demonstrated during the awakening period.

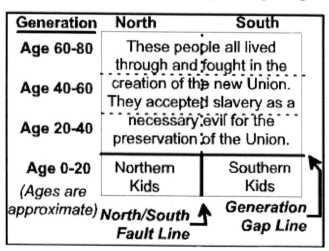

Figure 4 America c 1810

Example: From Revolutionary War to Civil War

Figure 4 illustrates America in 1810, 20 years after George Washington had taken office for the first time as President.

At this time, the fault line between the Northern and Southern states was just beginning to form. The elders in both the North and the South were actually in agreement about the slavery issue — they both viewed slavery as a necessary evil — necessary to preserve the union.

Now let's move ahead 20 years. Figure 5 shows a nation well into the "awakening" period. By this time, the lines of conflict are becoming more sharply drawn — both the North/South fault lines, and the generational lines.

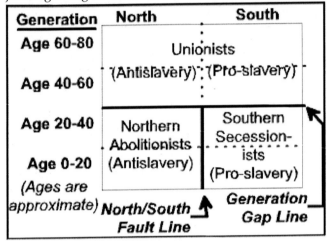

Figure 5 America c 1830

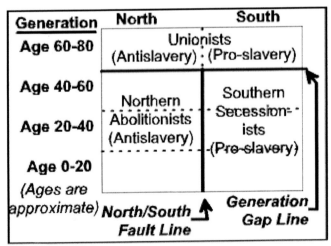

Figure 6 America c 1850

There are three distinct and recognizable groups:

- The antislavery Abolitionists: Gener-

12

ally, the younger generation in the North;

- The **pro-slavery Secessionists**: Generally the younger generation in the South;

- The **Unionists**: Generally the older generation. Some were pro-slavery and some were anti-slavery, but they all considered the slavery issue secondary to preserving the Union.

In 1850, America was into the unraveling period. If you compare Figure 6 to the preceding one, you see that there are far more Abolitionists and Secessionists, and far fewer Unionists. However, the Unionists are still running the nation, since they're the elder statesmen, politicians, journalists and teachers.

The final diagram shows America in 1861,

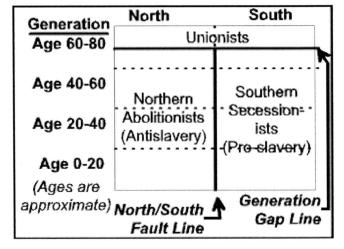

Figure 7 America c 1861

when the Civil War started. At this point, anyone who actually lived through the Revolutionary War was likely to be too old to exert any real influence.

Cause versus Timing of War

Distinguish between two separate things: The cause of the war versus the timing of the war.

- **Cause**: We won't discuss the cause of the Civil War here, except to say that the entire courtly Southern lifestyle, based on large cotton plantations, differed in almost every conceivable way from the Northern world of factory labor. Slavery was a political lightning rod, but it was just one of many, many differences between North and South that led to war across the North/South fault line, and there would have certainly been a Civil War even if there were no slaves.

- **Timing**: Let's suppose that slavery *was* the cause of the Civil War. Then the question still arises: Why did the war take place in 1861? Why not 1830 or 1890? The issues were same, so what was so special about 1861? Generational Dynamics answers that question.

As we study history, we see the following time after time: A crisis war occurs, and ends only when austere compromises are forced on the participants. No one is really happy with the compromises, but no one wants another war either. The compromises finally unravel, and that's the *cause* of the next crisis war. The *timing* of the next crisis war is determined by the timing of when the compromises unravel, and that happens when the final generational change occurs.

Example From Mideast Crisis to Mideast Crisis

Let's now look at an example that concerns all our lives today: The Arab / Jewish fault line in the Mideast.

The Arabs' and Jews' last crisis war occurred from 1936-1949. It started in 1936 as low-intensity violence (riots, demonstrations, rock-throwing, etc.), and became full-scale war in 1948 after the creation of the state of Israel. The war ended in 1949 when compromise was forced on both sides.

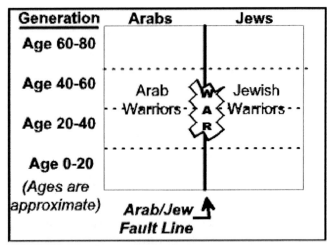

Figure 8 Mideast c 1948

CHAPTER 1 – BASICS AND SOME MYTHS ABOUT WAR

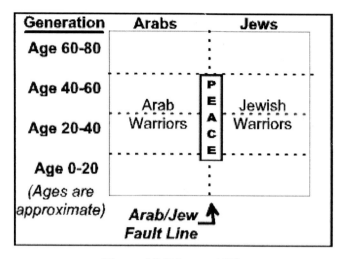

Figure 9 Mideast c 1952

Figure 8 illustrates the Mideast shortly before the end of the last Arab/Jewish Mideast crisis war. At that point, there was no generation gap one either side. Both sides were fighting for survival, and were unwilling to make any compromise or respect any rules of war.

Figure 9 (above) shows the same population shortly *after* the end of the same war. At that point, peace had been imposed. There was still no generation gap, but both sides had accepted the imposed peace.

Now we move ahead to the 1967 midcycle Mideast war (Figure 10). At this point, the generation gap was forming.

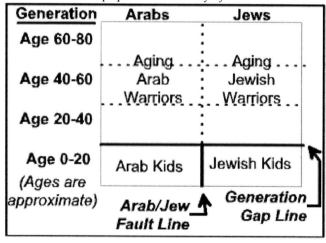

Figure 10 Mideast c 1967

This war was lower in intensity than the wars of the late 1940s, largely because the aging Arab and Jewish warriors were not anxious to repeat the terror of the 1940s.

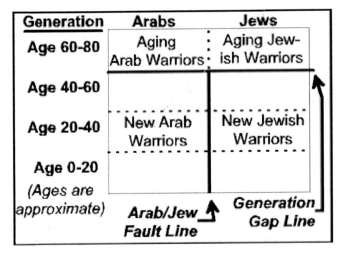

Figure 11 Mideast c 2007

Figure 11 shows the Mideast during the decade of the 2000s. The Arab and Jewish warriors from the last crisis war (especially Ariel Sharon and Yasser Arafat) are in their 70s. A new Mideast crisis war is expected within a couple of years after the generation of aging warriors retires or dies. This could happen at any time, but my expectation is that it will be signaled by the disappearance of Yasser Arafat from the scene.

American Fault Lines since World War II

What have been the fault lines that America has faced since World War II? Several have come and gone, and it's interesting to review the list:

- During World War II, the fault line separated the Allies from the Axis — America, England, France and other democracies and Russia versus Japan, Germany and Italy. Once the war ended, this fault line mostly disappeared.

- A fault line with Communist countries opened with the Bolshevik Revolution in 1917. Even though Russia was an ally in World War II, the fault line persists to this day with other Communist countries: North Korea, China, and Cuba. However, this fault line is not considered important today (except for the South Korea / North Korea fault line).

- Our Korean and Vietnam Wars were really across the Communist fault line.

- A fault line between Western civilization and Muslim civilization has opened up in recent decades, especially in the Mideast, and the next war will probably be across this fault line.

These examples illustrate how fault lines change and redefine themselves with time. Some fault lines last from cycle to cycle (like the fault line between France and Germany for centuries), and others appear and disappear quickly, depending on circumstances.

How long is an 80-year cycle?

This is actually a trick question. While the answer to "Who's buried in Grant's tomb?" is "Grant," the answer to "How long is an 80-year cycle?" is: "It depends."

The basic cycle is shown in the adjoining diagram — with a 60-year mid-cycle period separating two 20-year crisis periods, meaning that it's 80 years from the beginning of one crisis to the beginning of the next.

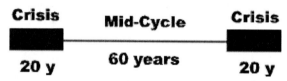

Figure 12 Crisis and mid-cycle periods; number of years is approximate

The reason it's 80 years is because that's the length of a human lifetime. The 60-year mid-cycle period permits enough generations of people to come and go so that the lessons of the last crisis war are forgotten, and a new one can start.

Didn't humans use to have a shorter lifespan?

This is the question that's asked most often, and interestingly enough, the answer is pretty much "No!" That's because we're talking about maximum lifespans, not average lifespans.

80 years appears to be an almost immutable constant. It's true that the average lifetime has increased (because of reduced infant mortality, for example), but the maximum life span seems to have been relatively constant throughout history. For example, during the Golden Age of Greece, Pericles lived 66 years, and Aristides lived 72 years — not quite 80 years, but close enough to make the point.

There are always a few people in each generation who live to be 70-80, and those are the elders who remember the last crisis, and who protect everyone by counseling caution and compromise. It's when the elders of that generation die that society loses all their wisdom at once, and the new crisis begins.

Merging Timelines

One of the important reasons that cycle lengths vary is that two separate regions, on separate timelines for centuries, have a war with each other. There are several possible outcomes, but one possibility is that their timelines will merge.

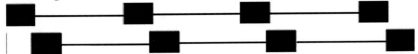

Figure 13 Two countries on separate timelines

Figure 13 is a typical situation. It shows the timelines of two separate regions or countries. Each has its crisis wars at regular intervals, but as long as they don't fight each other, they stay on separate timelines.

However, suppose that the two countries finally have a crisis war with each other. This is what happened, for example, in the 1600s. France and Germany had never had a major crisis war with each other, and were on separate timelines 20 years apart. But they fought each other in the Thirty Years' War that ran from 1618 to 1648.

Figure 14 shows what can happen, and what did happen in the Thirty Years' War. Normally, a crisis war runs about 5 to 15 years long, but the Thirty Years' War began as a German civil war, and continued against France for an additional decade.

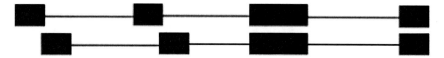

Figure 14 The same two countries with merged timelines

In the case of France and Germany, this pretty much synchronized their timelines for centuries to come. The next crisis war was the War of Spanish Succession, in which they fought each other from 1701 to 1714.

This is only one of many possibilities that occur when two nations on different timelines have crisis wars with each other. In many cases, both countries remain on their separate timelines. This is what happened in the Vietnam War, for example, which was a crisis war for the Vietnamese but a midcycle war for America. Other possibilities will be illustrated throughout this book.

Things happen in their time

Everyone knows that Thomas Edison invented the incandescent bulb in 1879. Suppose that Thomas Edison had never been born. Does that mean we would still be using candles today instead of light bulbs?

The answer is no: If Edison hadn't invented the incandescent bulb, then someone else would have invented it shortly thereafter. There were several other inventors working on the same problem at the same time, and one of the others would have gotten the patent if Edison hadn't. One of the others, Joseph Swan, actually invented an improved light bulb, with the result that Edison and Swan went into partnership together.

The point is that the electric light bulb was invented at exactly the right time. It was exactly at that time that the "ingredients" for the light bulb were available — the right kind of electrical current, the right kind of filament, the right kind of container, and so forth. The light bulb couldn't have been invented earlier, because the "ingredients" weren't yet available; it wouldn't have invented later, because once the "ingredients" were available, somebody would have invented the light bulb. Edison got there first.

Here's another question: Suppose Martin Luther King had never been born. Does that mean that the civil rights laws would never have passed?

Once again, we can say with certainty that other black leaders would have led the fight at that time. This time, the "ingredients" were a new Baby

Boomer generation that was increasingly impatient with their parents' insistence on discriminatory laws, the same generation that created the antiwar movement, the environmental movement, the women's lib movement, and so forth. Martin Luther King came along at just the right time to take advantage of this new generation, and if he'd never been born, someone else would have done the same.

Thomas Edison and Martin Luther King were *agents* or *catalysts* for events that were going to occur anyway at about the same time. By this, I mean absolutely no disrespect for either Edison or King. I'm simply saying that there were many contemporaries of each man who would have stepped to the plate and done the job *at about the same time* if Edison and King, respectively, had never been born.

Many people have difficulty believing this. They believe that Thomas Edison, personally, was necessary for the invention of the light bulb, and Martin Luther King, personally, was necessary for the passage of civil rights laws.

Those are the people who will have difficulty understanding this book. They will not believe that the Civil War would have occurred without Abraham Lincoln, or that World War II would have occurred without Hitler. These people do not understand why wars are necessary and inevitable. These people have not learned the lessons of history. If you're one of these people, you might want to give this book to someone else.

> *It's actually mathematically provable that wars are necessary.*

Why is war necessary?

Pick any day of any year in the last century, and the chances are that 20-40 wars were going on in the world on that day.

Now, if there are that many wars going on all the time, why do some people find it so hard to believe that wars are necessary and inevitable? Why do so many people have a romantic notion that we can all avoid wars if we just reason together?

It's actually mathematically provable that wars are necessary. You can prove mathematically that the worldwide birth rate grows faster than the rate at which new sources of food are developed. Therefore, people must eventually starve — unless they are killed by war or disease.

In fact, those are the three ways that nature provides to kill people when there are too many: famine, disease and war.

Nature provides us with a powerful sex drive to guarantee that we'll have children — too many children. Nature also provides humans with a powerful desire for war at the right time.

This may surprise you, but America is in one of those times right now. As of this writing, American has just been prosecuting two different wars, one in Afghanistan and one in Iraq.

Of course, we have wars all the time, but there's something different today, and this is the point: The American public is ready, willing and anxious to pursue these wars, as justice and retribution for the 9/11 attacks. President Bush has openly adopted a new policy of "preemption," permitting America to take military action against a country that is only *a threat* to American citizens, and the American public overwhelmingly supports this policy. The antiwar movement has been silenced — not by the government, but by open hostility to it by ordinary Americans.

This is new: When Islamic fundamentalists bombed New York's World Trade Center in 1993, killing or wounding over a thousand people, no wars were declared, and the public outcry would have been enormous if there had been.

Things happen in their time, as we've said, and this is the time that America is headed for a new major war. Americans want justice and retribution.

This change of attitude is coming from the American people. If Al Gore were president, instead of George W. Bush, the same thing would be happening, because Americans' attitudes would have changed in exactly the same way no matter who became President.

What we will show is that there's a very good reason why Americans' attitudes have changed in this way, and it has nothing to do with today's politicians. We will show that Americans' attitudes changed because, around the year 2000, the generation of people who had grown up during World War II all retired or died at roughly the same time.

We'll show that this risk-aversive generation of people who grew up during World War II guided us through decades of international policy, keeping us from taking unnecessary chances. As older workers, these people were our politicians, journalists, teachers, and mentors, and thanks to their caution and risk-aversion, we took few risks as a nation.

We'll show that once they were replaced, *en masse*, by a new generation, the Baby Boomers who grew up *after* World War II, things changed. We'll show how this new generation of politicians, journalists, teachers and mentors is much less risk-aversive and cautious, willing to take much greater risks. We'll show how this change of generations will now lead us to the major war.

If you'd like an explanation that's just a little too simple, here it is: Getting revenge is an elemental human desire, as powerful an emotional force as sex. When any major crisis war ends, it's out of exhaustion. The side that lost wants revenge, but the people who lived through the war realize that revenge will have to wait. It waits until the people who lived through the war are gone. That creates a roughly 80-year generational cycle. This simple model will be refined and expanded in the chapters that follow.

> *Pick any day of any year in the last century, and the chances are that 20-40 wars were going on in the world on that day.*

Chapter 2 — American History

O thus be it e'er, when free men shall stand
Between their loved homes and the war's desolation;
Blest with vict'ry and peace, may the heav'n rescued land
Praise the Power that hath made and preserved us a nation!
Then conquer we must, when our cause it is just,
And this be our mot-to, "In God is our trust!"
And the star-spangled banner in triumph shall wave
O'er the land of the free and the home of the brave.
— Stanza 4, *The Star Spangled Banner*,
Francis Scott Key, 1814

If you're an average American, you know almost nothing about American history, and may not even know the difference between the Civil War and the Vietnam War. In fact, that's why there are generational cycles in history: most people have almost no knowledge of events that occurred before they were born, and so repeat mistakes of an earlier generation.

On the other hand, it you're reading this book, then you probably know more about history than the average.

This chapter is written to provide new information to you, no matter which of those two categories you're in.

The chapter reviews and analyzes American history using the generational (80-year cycle) methodology. This methodology provides a way to gain a new overview of American history, if this is your first exposure, and it provides additional insights and perspectives if you're already a student of history.

Adjust your point of view

A book on history will almost always center on the nation of the author, and this book is not a major exception. But if you really want to understand the workings of history, you have no choice but to expand your scope of interest, and sometimes move the center of the universe away from your own nation to some other nation — at least temporarily.

Here's the basic arithmetic: In the 15,000 or so years of recorded history, there have been thousands, or tens of thousands, of individual tribes or societies formed by primitive men and women moving from place. Today, there are about 250 nations, comprising about 9 major civilizations* (Western, Latin American, African, Islamic, Sinic, Hindu, Orthodox, Buddhist, Japanese.

Now here's one more indisputable fact: In that same 15,000 years, the amount of land available on earth has remained relatively unchanged, despite the fact that these tribes and societies all had a tendency to grow and become more populated.

How did we go from tens of thousands of tribes to such a small number of nations and civilizations, living on earth with a constant amount of land? Sometimes tribes would combine via a friendly merger, but the answer, in almost all cases, is through war. Two tribes grow larger and larger, they bump into each other trying to occupy the same farmland or hunting lands; they may try to coexist for a while, but eventually they settle it with a war. The victors keep the land in dispute, and not infrequently murder all the men in the defeated tribe and rape all the women, unless some more agreeable settlement can be reached first.

Most history books treat these wars as somewhat random events that occur from time to time in different places.

Our approach is quite different, since we're analyzing history from the point of view of generational cycles. We see two tribes or societies compromising with each other, or at worst having only small wars, as long as possible, as long as most decision makers still remember how awful the last big war was; when the new generation comes in, then there's another big war.

So let's start with American history, and let's look at it in a new way. The major wars were not random events, but were great periodic events, influenced by events that were remote in both time and place.

As you study this, don't just think of yourself as an American. Think of yourself as an American sometimes, but at other times an Indian, a Brit, a Northerner, a Southerner, a Japanese, or a German. Try to understand the point of view of each of these people, and ask yourself what motivated them to go to war.

CHAPTER 2 – AMERICAN HISTORY

The Colonists versus the Indians — 1675-78

The most devastating war in American history was the Civil War, but the most devastating war in New England's history occurred about 100 years before independence between the colonists and the local Indian tribes. This war cast a shadow that lasted until the American Revolution, and had an enormous influence on events leading all the way up to the Revolution.

The standard America-centric view of this war is as follows: The colonists and the Indians got along pretty well until the colonists started taking too much valuable farming and hunting land. There was a devastating war in the years 1675-76, just one of many wars that the colonists, and later the "white man," used to steal land from the Indians.

That's an interesting political point of view, and it's true in a sense, but it doesn't provide any real understanding unless we expand the scope of our vision a little bit.

In the year 1600, throughout what is now the United States, there were some 2 million Indians within 600 tribes speaking 500 languages*. What happened, starting at that time, was a "clash of civilizations" between European culture of the colonists

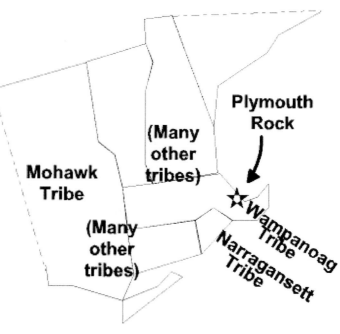

Figure 15 New England in 1675. The Pilgrims had landed in 1620 at Plymouth Rock, in the midst of the Wampanoag tribe.

and the indigenous culture of the Indians. These cultures were so different that haven't yet merged even today, inasmuch as many Indian tribes still live separately on reservations. It's ironic that the American "melting pot" has merged so many cultures, but has not yet entirely merged the preexisting Native American cultures.

Most history books treat "the Indians" as a monolithic group, as if they spoke with a common voice and common intent, but that's far from the truth. There were undoubtedly many brutal wars among the 600 tribes of the time. What would have happened if no colonists and no other outsiders had come and intervened in the life of the Indians? What would have happened? There's no way to know, of course, but it's likely that one or two of the tribes would have become dominant, wiping out all the other tribes in numerous wars. That's the nature of human societies: As they grow larger and run into each other, they go to war, and the dominant societies survive.

For the purposes of our story, we're going to focus on just three of those Indian tribes: The Wampanoag tribe that occupied what is now southeastern Massachusetts (where Plymouth Rock is) and the Narragansett tribe that occupied what is now Rhode Island, and the Mohawk tribe (part of the Iroquois) of upstate New York.

> *The victors keep the land, murder the men, and rape the women*

There is some historical evidence that a major war among these tribes had occurred in the years preceding the colonists' arrival[*] at Plymouth Rock, probably in the 1590s. The Wampanoag and the Narragansett tribes were particularly devastated and weakened by that conflict.

So, when the pilgrims arrived at Plymouth Rock in 1620, in the midst of the Wampanoag tribe, they had little trouble developing a pleasant cooperative relationship. The Wampanoag Indians were in an awakening period, and they taught the colonists how to hunt and fish[*], and in autumn of 1621, they all shared a Thanksgiving meal of turkey and venison.

Most significant was the colonists' early "declaration of independence." Before the colonists landed in 1620, they signed the Mayflower Compact, where they agreed that they would be governed by the will of the majority. This laid the framework for the view that neither the king nor parliament had any say in colonial government. And why would they need the King anyway? After all, they could provide for themselves, and they were friendly with the Indians.

This friendliness extended to trade. Before long, there was a mutually beneficial financial arrangement between the Indians and the colonists. The colonists acted as intermediaries through whom the Indians developed a thriving business selling furs and pelts to the English and European markets, and they used the considerable money they earned to purchase imported manufactured goods.

There were two particular Indian chiefs who are important to this story: one is a father and the other is his son, who took over when the father died in 1660.

The father's name is Massasoit, chief of the Wampanoag Indians, the Indian tribe most familiar to the Massachusetts colonists.

We have no way of knowing Massasoit's history. He was born around 1580, and so he must have been alive during the devastating war with the Narragansett. In fact, since he became Chief, he may well have been a hero who fought in the war in his teen years. With his personal memory of the devastating results of the last all-out war, he would not want to go through another war again unless absolutely necessary.

We have no way of knowing the details of what the Indian tribes had fought over, but chances are it was over what most wars are fought over — land. Each tribe wanted the best hunting, fishing and farmland for its own use. But Massasoit maintained friendly relationships with the colonists because of the financial benefits, and because he was a wise, elder leader who didn't want another big war in his lifetime.

Several dramatic changes occurred in the 1660s, when Massasoit died. "The relationship between English and Native American had grown inordinately more complex over forty years*," according to Schultz and Tougias. "Many of the important personal ties forged among men like Massasoit and Stephen Hopkins, Edward Winslow, and William Bradford had vanished. The old guard was changing on both sides, and with it a sense of history and mutual struggle that had helped to keep the peace."

Massasoit was replaced as Chief by his oldest son, Wamsutta — who died under mysterious circumstances that were blamed on the colonists. The younger brother, Metacomet, nicknamed King Philip by the colonists, became Chief.

Things *really* began to turn sour in the 1660s for another reason: Styles and fashions changed in England and in Europe. Suddenly, furs and pelts went out style, and the major source of revenue for the Indians almost disappeared. This resulted in a financial crisis for the Indians, and for the colonists as well, since they were the intermediaries in sales to the Indians.

But that's not all. Roughly 60-70 years had passed since the end of the last tribal war. The Mohawk War (1663-80) began, and created pressure from the west. The colonists were establishing ever-larger colonies in the east. In this pressure cooker atmosphere, the Wampanoag tribe, led by a young chief anxious to prove himself, allied with their former enemy, the Narragansett tribe, to fight their new enemy, the colonists.

One of the most fascinating aspects of history is how two enemies can carry on a brutal and almost genocidal war, and then, 80 years later, can be allies against a common enemy. This appears to be the way things are going today with our old World War II enemies, Germany and Japan, and it's certainly true of protagonists in the most destructive war in American history, the Union and the Confederacy in the Civil War.

In this climate of general war tensions and financial distress, we see the same pattern for how a major war occurs: There's a generational change, then a period of financial crisis, then a series of provocative acts by both sides, each of which is a shock and surprise to the other side, and calls for retribution and retaliation.

It's important to understand the role of all three of these elements. In particular, without the generational change, the provocative acts are met with compromise and containment, rather than retribution and retaliation.

> *Massasoit must have fought in a major war with another tribe in the 1590s*

This is particularly important in understanding what's going on when one side is provocative and the other side is compromising. This often means that the generational change has occurred on the first side, but not yet on the second.

In our own time, the 1993 bombing of the World Trade Center was a provocative act by Islamist extremists, but was met by no more than a criminal trial for the perpetrators; the 9/11/01 attack was met with a war against Afghanistan.

The actions of the colonists, in the face of provocations by the Indians, seemed to display a similar range of goals. In the 1660s, perpetrators were brought to trial, and executed if found guilty of the most serious crimes.

The trial process was brought to a head in 1671, when King Philip himself was tried for a series of Indian hostilities, and required by the court to surrender all of his arms; he complies by surrendering only a portion of them.

After that, the trial process seems to have fallen apart, as the colonists began to lose their patience and willingness to compromise. Trials were still held, but they became mere provocations: they were kangaroo courts with the results preordained, and the Indian defendants were always guilty.

These provocations kept escalating, until King Philip's War began with Philip's attack on the colonists on Cape Cod.

The war was extremely savage and engulfed the Indians and the colonists from Rhode Island to Maine. There were atrocities on both sides, and the war ended with King Philip's head displayed on stick. His wife and child were sold into slavery.

This was the most devastating war in American history on a percentage basis, with 800 of the 52,000 colonists killed. (It was devastating for the Indians as well.)

Aftermath of King Philip's War

If you want to start understanding how one world event sequences to the next, you have to start examining each event in the light of its position within the 80-year cycle.

> *This was devastating: 800 of 52,000 colonists killed*

Let's take a lighter example, the Salem Witch trials of 1692. Overall, 150 witchcraft subjects were jailed, the result of a frenzy that grips the town after a group of young girls feign hysteria and accuse a family slave of bewitching them.

If you forget about the previous major war, you would think that the only explanation is that someone had poisoned the water. But in fact, Salem was located in the heart of the battlefields of King Philip's War, which had ended only 14 years earlier. It's likely that in 1692 there were few males above age 30. In those austere, heavily religion-conscious times, the concerns about witches represented the same overreactions to anxieties that Communist blacklists represent following World War II.

The Salem Witch trials provide a weird but relevant example that helps us understand what life must have been life following King Philip's War — and any crisis war. Those who lived through it are always into setting rules. The ones who survive always feel guilty and angry. Why didn't I protect my family better? Why didn't we live somewhere else where we would have been safer? Why wasn't I a more religious man, so that God wouldn't have punished me (and us) this way? Why weren't English soldiers here to defend us?

That brings us back to the Mayflower Compact, signed in 1620, which guaranteed that local government would be independent of the English Crown. The colonists had thought they would build their new community without outside interference, with their own rules and their own self-government.

After the war, they felt forced to acquiesce completely to English rule. All home rule was dissolved and Governors would be appointed from London. British troops would protect the colonists from the Indians and the French, and colonists would pay taxes to the Crown in return.

Isn't that eerie? Those were all the things that caused trouble later, and led to the Revolution.

And that's how one crisis war leads to another. When one war ends, outsiders often impose compromises to prevent the war from repeating. Those compromises only last so long, and often end up being the root causes of the next war.

The Great Awakening of the 1730s and 40s

After every crisis war, there's always a generation gap that causes social turmoil about halfway to the time of the next crisis war. The turmoil is caused by rebellion against authority — those too young to remember the war rebel against the austere rules imposed by those who lived through the war.

Many people believe that the social turmoil of the 1960s and 70s, with the antiwar movement, the environmental movement, the women's lib movement, and so forth, was unique in American history. But nothing could be further from the truth.

The social turmoil that occurred in the 1730s and 40s was so great, history has given it a name, "The Great Awakening in American history."

For our study of the cycles of history, the actual details of both the wars and the awakenings are not as important as the simple fact that they occurred. Nonetheless, we look at a few of the details in order to gain insight into how the cycles of history work.

The great compromise of the crisis of the late 1700s was that the colonists were forced to cede political control to the English Crown, since the colonists needed the protection of the British army from the French and the Indians. This was a serious issue, since England was at war with France and Spain throughout many years of mid 1700s, and North American often became a battlefield.

Closely related to political control was religious control. The official religion in England was, well, the Church of England, which was supported by and closely tied to the English government. It was called the Anglican Church in the colonies.

The Anglican Church never did have much success in establishing religious control in the colonies, as congregations of Puritans, Presbyterians, Congregationalists, Baptists, Quakers and many other religions sprang up in the colonies from the beginning, and had to compete with one another for followers.

Starting in the 1730s, something brand new came about — something we recognize today in the form of "televangelists." Various preachers went from city to city, telling thousands of rapt listeners that they would be punished for their sinfulness, but could be saved by the mercy of an all-powerful God. To take one example, John Wesley, born in 1703, created the Methodist religion, and traveled on horseback throughout the country for years, stopping along the way to preach three or four sermons each day.

> *The Great Compromise was that the colonists accepted political control by the Crown*

As we go from crisis war to crisis war, we'll see that there's always an "awakening" midway between two crisis wars. This happens because a crisis war creates a "generation gap" between people who lived during the war and the kids who were born afterwards.

The traumatized older generation tries to impose controls on the kids, so that "nothing like that will ever happen again." The kids, who have no personal knowledge of the war's horrors, rebel against the controls.

The Great Awakening of the 1730s and 1740s was not just a religious revival; it was also an act of rebellion against the older generation that favored control by the British in return for protection. By rejecting the Anglican Church, the colonists were symbolically rejecting British control.

The Revolutionary War — 1772-1782

All the contradictions and compromises that were forced upon the colonists following the devastation of King Philip's War came to a head in the Revolutionary War. In particular, the taxes that England had levied against the colonies to pay for protection from the Indians and the French led to colonist demands for "No taxation without representation!", the catchphrase for pre-Revolutionary days.

If, as this book claims, major world events can be measured in 80-year cycles, why did 100 years pass between King Philip's War and the Revolutionary War?

The 80-year period is, of course, an estimate, and we could simply end discussion by saying that the interval we're discussing here was simply a little longer than average.

Still, it's interesting to analyze the situation, because there's valuable insight to be gained from understanding why the 80-year cycle was lengthened to 100 years.

The main factor was that England was on a different timetable. England had not experienced King Philip's War. Instead, England had been in a major war against its perennial enemy, France. That war, called the War of Spanish Succession (see page 172), was extremely brutal, and took place in Europe from 1701 to 1714. Following that war, England and France didn't fight another war until the 1790s, after the French Revolution. In between, England and France fought a number of mid-cycle skirmishes in other locations, including the colonies, but without having a serious crisis war.

So, the other factor delaying the American Revolution was the fact that the danger presented to the American colonists by the French and the Indians was quite real. Although England and France had temporarily ceased active warfare on the European continent, the two countries were still fighting proxy wars in America and India.

The largest of these wars in America occurred when the French formed an alliance with the American Indians, with the purpose of driving the English out of North America. The French had formed outposts in Canada, and south along the Mississippi River. The Seven Years' War ensued (known in America as the French and Indian War), from 1756 to 1763. France was decisively defeated not only in America but also in India, leaving England as the preeminent power in the world, by the time the two countries signed the Treaty of Paris in 1763.

Returning now to the question of why the Revolutionary War seems to have occurred some 20 years later than its "scheduled" time in the 1750s, we see that the colonists still desperately needed English protection from the French in the 1750s, and would not have wanted to risk a separation at that time. Without the French, the American Revolution might indeed have occurred 20 years earlier.

Once the Treaty of Paris was signed, the colonists were no longer in any danger from the French, and generational forces began to take hold. The English were, quite simply, no longer needed. The colonists grew increasingly hostile to English control, and especially objected to taxation without representation.

The British had other motivations. As soon as the treaty with France had been signed, they moved to consolidate their control over America as a British colony. In particular, the Sugar Act and Currency Act of 1764 were imposed in order to prevent the colonies from trading with any foreign country except through England as an intermediary. The Stamp Act of 1765 was enacted to recover at least a fraction of the money England had to spend to maintain its military forces in the colonies.

> *The colonists needed England's protection from the French until 1763*

These moves by England hardly seem unreasonable. The colonies were expensive children, and like a parent expecting his children to pay a little rent, England had a right to expect the colonists to pay for a portion of the cost of protecting them.

But the pressure for revolution had been building for a long time. The Stamp Act was particularly galling. All printed documents, including newspapers, broadsides and even legal documents, had to have stamp affixed, with the cost of the stamp being paid to England.

An underground terrorist group called the Sons of Liberty was formed. This group used violence to terrorize Stamp Act agents and British traders in numerous towns. However, violence was rare: colonial opposition was designed to be non-violent. The colonies formed a "Stamp Act congress" to call for repeal. English imports were boycotted.

Since this was a mid-cycle time period for England, the English sought merely to contain the problem and compromise. As a result, the Stamp Act was repealed by 1766.

However, England was still trying to find a way to collect revenue from the colonies without engendering riots, but they never succeeded. In 1767, England passed the Townshend Acts, imposing further taxes on goods imported to the colonies. Four more years of increasingly virulent protests force England to repeal the taxes in 1771.

There's no question that England was doing everything it could to compromise and contain the situation.

When occasional violence broke out, it was contained. In the most well known incident, the 1770 Boston Massacre, where British soldiers fired into a crowd and killed five colonists, two of the soldiers were tried and convicted, and tensions were relieved again.

By 1771, all taxes had been repealed except a tax on importation of tea, and even that tax was often evaded. From a purely objective view, the colonists really had few major grievances at this time.

As we've previously said, three factors are required for a major crisis war to break out: a generational change, then a period of financial crisis, then a series of provocative acts by both sides, each of which is a shock and surprise to the other side, and calls for retribution and retaliation.

The financial crisis occurred in July 1772, when the English banking system suffered a major crash[*]. Many colonial businesses were in debt to the English banks, and were suddenly unable to obtain further credit, forcing them to liquidate their inventories, thus ending their businesses. Business conditions only improved with the start of the war. We'll discuss this particular financial crisis further in chapter 6.

There's always an event that seems to electrify a society, leading up to a major war. Previous similar events have no major effect, but some particular new event causes a reaction way out of proportion to its seeming significance.

In May 1773, The English Parliament passed a new Tea Act, and in December 1773, a group of Boston activists dumped 342 casks of English tea into Boston Harbor.

This was simply another round of the same dance — a new tax and a non-violent response. There was no reason for it to end any differently, except that now the country was in the middle of a financial crisis.

The response, known as the Boston Tea Party, has become world famous. It was so electrifying at the time that it surprised and shocked both the colonies and England. After that, one provocation after another on both sides finally led to war.

CHAPTER 2 — AMERICAN HISTORY

The furious English Parliament passed a series of "Coercive Acts" to dismantle the colonial Massachusetts government, close the port of Boston, and control the hostilities. This was tantamount to a declaration of war. With positions on both sides becoming increasingly hardened, war was not far off.

Hostilities actually began in April 1775, when the colonial minutemen attacked the British forces following the midnight ride of Paul Revere. The separation became official on July 4, 1776, when the Continental Congress endorsed the Declaration of Independence.

The war continued until November 30, 1782, when American and British representatives signed a peace agreement recognizing American independence.

The pursuit of the war

> *The British faced a very strong anti-war movement*

The Revolutionary War was a crisis war for the colonies, but it was a mid-cycle war for England. This makes a big difference in the pursuit of a war. The Americans fought the war with great ferocity; the English fought the war halfheartedly.

(Think of our own war in Vietnam, where the North Vietnamese fought fiercely and won, while the American public supported the war halfheartedly.)

The American forces, under George Washington, fought for six years under the most brutal conditions. In a letter requesting more provisions, Washington wrote, "For some days past, there has been little less than a famine in camp. A part of the army has been a week, without any kind of flesh, and the rest for three or four days. Naked and starving as they are, we cannot enough admire the incomparable patience and fidelity of the soldiery...."

They could easily have given up at any time, and the country would have returned to being a British colony. But sheer momentum, sheer determination, kept the American forces going to victory.

The British should have won. They had many more soldiers and vastly greater provisions. But they didn't have the ferocity that the Americans had.

In passing the Coercive Acts of 1774, England was effectively declaring war on the colonies, but doing nothing to prepare for the war. In fact, England did nothing to strengthen its forces in America that year, and even actually reduced the size of its Navy*.

According to British General John Burgoyne, writing from Boston in 1775, "After a fatal procrastination, not only of vigorous measures but of preparations for such, we took a step as decisive as the passage of the Rubicon, and now find ourselves plunged at once in a most serious war without a single requisition, gunpowder excepted, for carrying it on."

Once the war began, there was a strong anti-war movement of sorts in England*. The King had difficulty recruiting soldiers, and largely employed German mercenaries (Hessians) to fight against the Americans. A loud, vocal English minority denounced the entire war, and called for withdrawal.

England's time was not 1776. England's next major crisis began in 1793, with France and the French Revolution, and then England fought with great ferocity. That will be discussed in chapter 8.

Aftermath of the war

The end of the Revolutionary War didn't mean the end of the American crisis. There were still grave doubts as to whether the Union could survive. The colonies had formed a very weak Confederation, which left each former colony largely autonomous, adopting its own currencies, taxes, laws and rules. The economy suffered a major recession in 1786, resulting in severe acts of terrorism by bankrupt farmers and businessmen — acts that couldn't be controlled since the terrorists could not be pursued across state lines because there was no federal army. The crisis did not end until 1790, after the Constitution was ratified and George Washington became president.

We'll soon be jumping ahead to America's next great crisis war, the Civil War, but before we do that, we have to tie those two great wars together. And indeed, they are tied together by a single divisive issue: slavery.

The United States of America was formed because of a compromise that permitted slavery to exist in the South, though it was made illegal in the Northern states. This compromise in 1776 was necessary to form the nation in the first place, but it almost destroyed the Union in 1861. That's usually how any society goes from crisis war to crisis war. There may be other wars in between, but the crisis wars are usually tied together by a great compromise of some kind — a compromise that ends one crisis war falls apart decades later and becomes the cause of the next crisis war.

The Awakening of the 1820s and 1830s

The Republic of the United States of America was a "great experiment." Today we take our Republic for granted, but nothing like it had ever been tried before. Europe was filled with interlocking monarchies that started to come unraveled by the French Revolution that began in 1789, and thinkers were heavily influenced by the American Constitution in devising their own republics.

However, the usual "generation gap" that follows a crisis war was created. We've already discussed the transition from the Revolutionary war to the Civil War (see p. 11), so here we'll fill in some additional details.

The people who were involved in the creation of the Union considered it to be very fragile, and not certain to survive. This was the "older generation," people who witnessed the creation of the Union, spent the remainder of their lives doing everything in their power to hold the Union together.

However, those doubts about the Union were not shared by those born after 1790 or so. To the "young generation," the Union was a *fait accompli*. They had no personal experience of the doubts that the Union could be created, and so they took the Union for granted. As a result, their concerns turned to new areas.

These concerns blossomed in the awakening (and the social turmoil) of the 1820s and 30s, when this new generation grew into adulthood. Women's rights began to be seriously addressed at this time. And, as with the previous awakening, there were heavy religious overtones, with many evangelists holding "revivals," telling people how to revive their sinful souls from damnation.

However, the greatest turmoil arose out of the slavery issue. Slave rebellions began to develop, especially in those parts of the South where blacks outnumbered whites. The fiercest was the 1831 revolt led by black slave Nat Turner, who had been born in 1800. Turner's rebellion resulted in the deaths or massacres of dozens of whites and blacks, until Turner himself was hanged several weeks later.

As I study the events leading up to each cataclysmic war in the cycles of history, I always get the feeling of a kind of "pressure cooker" of resentment and anger building up over decades of time, until finally the pressure cooker explodes into war.

It's hard not to feel this pressure cooker effect in reading about the abolitionist movement of the first decades of the 1800s. The Northern abolitionists became increasingly determined to see slavery abolished, and the Southerners became increasingly defensive and less willing to compromise their need for black slaves to harvest cotton.

In the midst of it all were the Unionists, the cautious men on both sides of the slavery issue who wanted to compromise and contain the problem. These were mostly people in the older generation, born before 1790. Some supported slavery and some opposed slavery, but all of them made slavery secondary to the most important goal of all: Saving the Union.

As the people in the older generation retired or died, the new generation, which took the Union for granted, began to assume power. Some in the new generation supported slavery, and some opposed slavery, but these people were different: For them, the Union was a given, and there was no more important issue than slavery itself.

The American Civil War, 1857-65

As long as the older generation held power in Congress, compromise was king. And the lengths to which the Congress went to maintain the compromise would be considered almost comical, if they weren't about such a serious subject.

The juggling game that went on was to keep the number of "slave states" equal to the number of "free states." As states were added to the Union throughout the early 1800s, this balance had to be maintained. Thus, the "Missouri Compromise" of 1820 admitted Missouri as a slave state, simultaneously with Maine as a free state. The huge Louisiana Purchase was split into slave and free regions.

Other artifices were used as well. In 1836, the House of Representatives adopted a "gag rule," which prohibited discussion of any bills that involved the issue of slavery in any way. This gag rule continued through 1844.

The last great Unionist Senator was Henry Clay. Born in Virginia in 1777, he spent his entire life in efforts to preserve the Union. He sponsored and brokered compromise after compromise to keep the slavery issue contained. Indeed, the last great speech of his career, given to the Senate in 1850, urged a major compromise that included admitting California to the Union as a free state. He was joined in this effort by a fierce opponent, the vehemently anti-slavery Massachusetts Senator Daniel Webster, born in 1782. They were fierce political opponents and both great orators, but in March 1850, they stood together to support one more major compromise to preserve the Union. These are the kinds of compromises that are standard fare during an "unraveling" period. These men both died in 1852, and there were no further "great compromises."

For the next few years, the slavery issue was contained. One event of note was the formation of a new third party — the Republican Party — in 1854, to promote abolition from a political point of view. For the next century, the Republican Party would be identified as the anti-slavery party, and the Democratic Party would be stigmatized as the party sympathetic to slavery.

As we've previously said, three factors are required for a major crisis war to break out: a generational change, then a period of financial crisis, then a series of provocative acts by both sides, each of which is a shock and surprise to the other side, and calls for retribution, justice and retaliation.

The financial crisis occurred in August 1857, when the New York branch of the Ohio Life Insurance and Trust Company failed. Almost 5,000 businesses failed in the resulting Panic of 1857. This primarily affected the industrialized North, since the South's cotton was still in demand, and increased the North's resentment against the South and against slavery. The depression in the North continued well into the 1860s, and was one of the primary factors motivating the anti-draft riots in New York City — the riots occurred in high unemployment areas by people who were afraid that freed slaves would take the few jobs they had.

In October 1859, abolitionist John Brown (born in 1800) seized the Federal arsenal at Harper's Ferry in order to protest slavery. His intention was to spur a massive slave insurrection or even a civil war that would end slavery[*]. (Incidentally, this was similar to the reason Osama bin Laden gave for the 9/11 terrorist attacks: To provoke a worldwide war between Muslims and the infidels.) He was tried for criminal conspiracy and treason, convicted and hanged. This sequence of events polarized the entire country, and inspired the Northern troops' Civil War anthem, "John Brown's Body Lies A'mouldering in the Grave." Even today, I've heard southerners refer to John Brown as a "murdering menace to society."

This was not the first violent act committed by abolitionists; in fact, John Brown himself had committed some in the past. But with the national mood transformed by a generational change and a financial crisis, the Harper's Ferry raid electrified the nation, and hardened positions in both the North and the South.

From a purely objective point of view, there's no reason why the election of Abraham Lincoln as President in 1860 should have triggered the Civil War. It's true that he was opposed to slavery, and would never agree to extend it, but he also made it clear that he would not do away with slavery in those states where it already existed. Even after the Civil War started, he wrote that he would abolish slavery if it would save the Union, keep slavery if it would save the Union, or amend slavery if it would change the Union. At some other time in history, compromise might have contained the situation. But now, with a generational change and a financial crisis in play, things deteriorated quickly.

South Carolina voted to secede from the Union right away, in December 1860. By the time of Lincoln's inauguration, on March 4, 1861, seven Southern states had formed the Confederate States of America. The war began on April 12, when South Carolina forces fired on the federal troops at Fort Sumter.

The Civil War was devastating, and filled with atrocities. In the Battle of Gettysburg alone, there were 28,000 rebel casualties and 23,000 Union casualties. All told, there were hundreds of thousands of deaths — a rate of 823 deaths per 100,000 of population, the highest ratio of any war in American history (though only half the rate of the pre-revolutionary King Philip's war).

Causes and Timing of the Civil War

What were the "causes" of the Civil War?

Slavery was certainly a big issue at the time, but it's hard to see why slavery was the *cause* of the Civil War.

After all, Lincoln did not intend to abolish slavery before the war, or even well into the war. Even if he had wanted to, the Congress could not have done it as long as the Southern states were voting. The only reason that slavery was abolished is because the Southern states had seceded and couldn't prevent it.

As I get older, I tend to get increasingly cynical about many things, including the causes of war. I see money as the cause of most things, and great, lofty ideals as mere rationalizations that come after the fact. The Panic of 1857 caused a lot of hardship, and the people of the North and South blamed each other. It's as accurate to say that the Panic of 1857 caused the war, as it is to say that slavery caused the war.

What about timing? If slavery was the cause, why didn't the war occur in 1830 or 1890 instead of 1860?

That's where Generational Dynamics provides an answer. The war occurred in 1860 because that's when the generational change occurred, approximately 80 years after the start of the Revolutionary War.

This shows how causes and timing work together to produce crisis wars.

Why was there no "Civil War II"?

This question, which is rarely discussed, is possibly one of the most important we'll consider. Why didn't the Civil War result in a hostile fault line between the victorious North and the resentful South, ending in a new Civil War 80 years later?

First, it's worth noting that the end of the war did not bring the end of the crisis.

The slaves were freed, but they had no place to live and few rights as citizens. The Reconstruction period was so brutal, it was almost a continuation of the war. Following Lincoln's assassination, President Johnson took political control of some of the Southern states, and kept troops stationed to enforce voting rights for blacks. Southern states continued to resist full integration of the blacks, passing laws that restricted the freedom of blacks.

The South was extremely bitter, not only because emancipation had been forced down their throats, but also because there was so much financial corruption and abuse during the Reconstruction. The Civil War crisis did not really end until 1877, when the last Federal troops policing the South were withdrawn.

There was no "great compromise" coming out of the Civil War. The North achieved all its objectives — the seceding states were forced to return to the Union under the terms specified by the North — including the full abolition of slavery. So why wasn't there a new Civil War 80 years later?

Scholars can debate this question (and, I believe, should debate it more than they have), but in my opinion, it's because of the flexibility of the American constitutional system, especially the Supreme Court.

Many people blame the Civil War on an 1857 Supreme Court decision known as the Dred Scott decision, wherein the Court ruled, in essence, that Dred Scott, a black man, was property and not a human being in the meaning of the Constitution. Many people believe that the Civil War could have been avoided if the Dred Scott decision had been made in the opposite direction.

I don't agree with that view. The Dred Scott case came far too late to have any effect one way or the other on the war.

Nonetheless, the Dred Scott case has served as a permanent reminder to the Justices of the Supreme Court that their highest objective is keep the Union safe. By being an "activist" court at the right times in history, the Court can release some of the pressure leading the country to a new Civil War, or to putting the country in danger in other ways. (My personal belief is that the Court intervened in the 2000 Presidential election for exactly this reason. The back-and-forth lawsuits could have gone on for months, leaving the country with no President at all for several months. The Court learned its lesson from Dred Scott and felt it had no choice but to intervene, and end the Presidential election once and for all.)

Incidentally, there's another example of a Civil War that did not lead to Civil War II: The English Civil War of the 1640s (page 165). The English government became flexible enough to allow for the "Glorious Revolution" of 1689, which permitted a major change in government with no blood shed. England has fought in many wars since then, but never another civil war.

Aftermath of the Civil War

Before 1800, the world's leading industrial power was France. But the Industrial Revolution that took place in England in the late 1700s and early 1800s made that country the leader by 1850. By 1900, the leading industrial power in the world would be the United States. How did that happen?

The industrial revolution jumped from England to America in earnest with the end of the Civil War.

It was a time of *laissez-faire* capitalism, with the public tolerating almost no regulations or restraints on business at all.

This was understandable; after all, slavery had been possible because the federal government had made it possible. The opposite of slavery is freedom, and so the post-war sentiment was that the federal government should not interfere with anyone's freedom. Any regulations or restrictions on anybody would have been just a short step on the slippery slope back to slavery.

The *laissez-faire* atmosphere permitted the accumulation of some great fortunes, especially through the building of the railroads. By 1900, building railroads also created enormous fortunes for people like J. P. Morgan and J. D. Rockefeller, who controlled more assets and had more income than the federal government. Such an idea would be recognized with horror today, but it wasn't even strange back then: it had never been the founders' intentions that the federal government be large or wealthy.

Other inventions dramatically changed American life: Alexander Graham Bell invented the telephone in 1876, and Thomas Edison invented the incandescent light bulb in 1879. Both inventions became quickly very popular, and played major parts in the success of America as an industrial nation.

The Awakening of 1890-1920

Awakenings tend to focus on social issues and social injustice; young people, who do not have personal memory of the previous crisis, rebel against the austere restrictions imposed by their elders whose only motivation is that "nothing like that should ever happen again."

In this case, the austere restrictions were, ironically, almost complete freedom from government: the federal government must never enslave anyone again.

The awakening, then, was led by people who reacted against the injustices of nearly complete freedom from government. (Once again, we can't help but note the irony of this statement.)

These reactions mainly focused on the trade unions (or labor unions). If the government were not going to prevent the capitalists from controlling all the wealth, then the workers would do so through the (often pro-socialist) labor unions. The 1886 labor rally in Chicago's Haymarket Square, in which someone bombed the policemen trying to control the crowd, terrorized the nation's people, and focused people on their grievances.

The extremes of capitalism's order and socialism's terror gave rise to a new movement called "progressivism," under whose banner some reforms were made, including legislation to do these things: provide for rights of workers to join labor unions; break up large businesses with anti-trust or "trust busting" regulations; and make it easier for ordinary citizens to own shares of stock. Other laws provided for consumer protection, women and child protection, and income tax collection. Further changes brought women's suffrage in 1918.

The arts played an important part in this awakening as well. Symphony orchestras and arts museums sprang up in cities around the country, and new architectural ideas of Frank Lloyd Wright and others were used in homes and buildings throughout the country.

World War I

At this point, it's worthwhile to stop and consider why World War I was *not* a crisis war for the United States.

A question is frequently asked: Why is World War II considered to be a crisis war, but World War I is considered to be a mid-cycle war?

WW I was not a major war for the United States. One way that this is indicated is by the number of people killed in battle: The figure as a percentage of population was substantially lower for World War I than for the crisis wars (Revolutionary War, Civil War, WW II), as the following table shows:

War	Pop (M)	Deaths	Deaths Per 100K	Crisis?
King Philip's War (1675-76)	0.05	800	1538	Yes
Revolutionary War (1775-83)	2.5	4,435	177.4	Yes
War of 1812 (1812-15)	9.8	2,260	23.6	
Mexican War (1846-48)	23.2	1,733	7.5	
Civil War (1861-65)	34.4	283,394	823.8	Yes
Spanish-American War (1898)	76.2	385	0.5	
World War I (1917-18)	100	53,513	53.5	
World War II (1941-46)	132	292,131	221.3	Yes
Korean War (1950-53)	151	33,667	22.3	
Vietnam War (1964-73)	203	47,393	23.3	
Persian Gulf War (1991)	249	148	0.1	

However, number of soldiers killed is only one of many considerations in deciding whether a war is a "crisis war" (see page 80). What's the difference?

In our studies, we've found that we can summarize the difference between crisis wars and mid-cycle wars in the concepts of "energy" and "transformation."

I mentioned earlier, in conjunction with the Civil War, that it's possible to feel a kind of "pressure cooker" of resentment and anger building up over decades of time, until finally the pressure cooker explodes into war. If the pressure in the pressure cooker is great, then the country almost explodes into war; otherwise, the country dribbles into war. If a country pursues a war with a great deal of energy, then it's a crisis war; if not, then it occurs at some other point in the 80-year cycle. After the war is over, signs that indicate a major transformation of society are major changes in the way the society is governed, whether national boundaries change or populations are displaced. None of that applied to America and World War I.

America entered WW I only very reluctantly.

America was actually neutral to the war when it first began in 1914, and Americans themselves were often split in their sentiments along ethnic lines. Americans were shocked when the British passenger ship *Lusitania* was sunk by German submarines in 1915, killing thousands of people including 114 Americans, but not shocked enough to enter the war, or to change its neutrality.

President Wilson's own sentiments leaned toward the side of the Allies (England and France) against Germany, but a strong pacifist (anti-war) movement forced him to proceed cautiously. In fact, America continued to provide goods and services to both the Allies and Germany, until it finally entered the war in 1917.

America stayed neutral despite numerous German terrorist attacks on Americans, and against American citizens. German subroutines sank an American freighter, as well as British, French and Italian passenger ships, killing thousands of civilians including hundreds of Americans. A German exploded a bomb in the U.S. Senate reception room. President Wilson's own Secretary of State, William Jennings Bryan, resigned in protest when Wilson merely sent a protest note to the Germans. Bryan then headed a pacifist group that vigorously opposed American's involvement in the war, and used Senate filibusters to prevent America from challenging Germany in any significant way.

In January 1917, Wilson outlined a peace plan, calling for "Peace without victory." Germany's response was to sink several American steamships without warning. Only then did America finally declare war on Germany in March 1917.

Furthermore, WW I didn't really change anything in America. Reparations were imposed on Germany, but they were lifted quickly. The League of Nations was created, but America didn't join.

WW II was very different. We were on the side of Britain before we even entered the war, and we declared war immediately when Pearl Harbor was bombed. America was completely transformed by WW II — in that we accepted the mantle of "policemen of the world." Not only did we form the United Nations and join it, but also we headquartered it in New York. We used the Marshall Plan to help rebuild Europe, and we took over the government of Japan for a few years.

It's this enormous difference in "energy" that separates a crisis war from a mid-cycle war.

Those who remember the Vietnam War remember how divided we were as a country. That was another mid-cycle war for us, and one of the reasons we lost is because we didn't have the energy to support our troops in Vietnam. The North Vietnamese forces were far more energetic than we were because it was a crisis war for them.

Contrast that to America's response when Japan bombed Pearl Harbor — we declared war the next day, and mobilized against Japan and Germany without hesitation. There was a pacifist movement, but it was completely ineffectual.

Contrast it also to America's response to the 9/11/01 attacks. We declared war against Afghanistan within a month, and President Bush is receiving overwhelming public support for military actions there and against Iraq.

Reading the above examples, you begin to see what "energy" means. The United States was not anxious to get into WW I. There was constant dithering and debate, in the face of numerous terrorist acts.

So if WW I was not a crisis war, why do historians why was it called the "war to end all wars" when it happened, and why do historians call it one of the worst wars in history?

The answer is that WW I and WW II are different timelines. WW II was a west European war, while WW I was an east European war.

We'll be discussing World War I in chapter 4, but here's a summary. WW I was a crisis war for several east European countries, two of them in particular:

- Russia transformed completely without even fighting the war to finish. Russia adopted the Bolshevik Revolution, and built the Soviet

Empire as the major communist nation on earth. Russia's experiment with communist lasted for only one 80-year cycle, however; in 1991, the Soviet Union dissolved, and Russia itself has become a capitalist democracy.

- The Ottoman Empire, which was Muslim and had once been the greatest empire in the world, was destroyed. Turkey was formed out of the remains, and several Arab and Muslim countries in the Mideast were formed as well. The Muslim and Arab communities were transformed from a collection of warring tribes into one of the major civilization of the world with a unique identity.

As you can see, what came out of World War I is profoundly affecting the world today. It's possible that America's timeline will merge with the Islamic timeline, and the much-discussed "clash of civilizations" between the West and Islam will be a crisis war for both sides. This scenario will be discussed in chapter 4.

The Great Depression and the Smoot-Hawley Tariff Act

The Great Depression and World War II go together — it's impossible to understand one without the other. We're going to be studying the Great Depression in detail in chapter 6, but for now let's look at its part in leading to World War II.

Research seems to indicate that a financial crisis and a war crisis seem to feed on each other and make each other worse: A financial crisis makes people restless and angry, looking for a scapegoat, for justice and retribution, making a war crisis worse; and a war crisis makes people financially risk aversive, less willing to make purchases and investments, making the financial crisis worse.

There seems to be plenty of evidence that the Great Depression was a major factor in providing the energy for World War II. When a person loses his job or his home, he'll get angry with his former boss or the bank that foreclosed on him.

When a society goes through a recession, the people look to their own government leaders to blame.

When the recession gets very bad, to the point of a depression, then jealousy can set in, and the desire for justice and retribution becomes enormous. A nation might start thinking about how great things are on the other side of the border. This is the kind of thing we've already seen in the Civil War: the Panic of 1857 devastated northern businesses, but hardly had any effect at all on the cotton farms of the south, especially in view of the free slave labor.

When a financial crisis gets so bad that many people are starving and homeless, a war becomes much more desirable. If you're starving you really have nothing to lose by going to war, and becoming a soldier may be the only way to get food and shelter, and to feed your wife and children.

Now let's see how the Great Depression was an integral part of the steps that led to World War II.

Perfectly reasonable acts by one country can be interpreted as hostile acts by another country. Guns and bombs are not needed to create an impression of war.

And if one country's innocent act is a shock to another country and is viewed as hostile by that country, and if the people of that country are in a mood for retribution rather than compromise, than they may well look for a way to retaliate.

In that sense, the enactment of the Smoot-Hawley Tariff Act in June 1930, can be viewed as the first of the shocking, provocative acts that led to World War II.

The Act was opposed by an enormous number of economists as being harmful to everyone, but it was very popular with the public, because of the perception that it would save American jobs. Many in the public believed that the crash had been caused by withdrawal of investment funds by foreign banks, just as many in the public today believe that the Nasdaq crash of 2000 was caused by the illegal or improper actions of CEOs of Enron and other corporations. The public demanded the Smoot-Hawley Act in retribution, just as the public today demands the jailing of corporate CEOs.

Interestingly, the Smoot-Hawley Act is still debated by politicians today, with regard to whether it caused or aggravated the Great Depression or had no effect, with pro-free trade politicians taking the first position, and politicians supporting restrictions on free trade taking the second position.

Those discussions are entirely America-centric because, for the purposes of this book, it makes no difference whatsoever whether or not the Act aggravated the American depression. We're interested in the effect it had on foreign nations.

And the effects were enormous. The bill erected large trade barriers for numerous products, with the intention of saving American jobs. How many American jobs it saved, if any, is unknown, but it virtually shut down product exports to the United States. Both Germany and Japan were going through the same financial crisis America was going through, and they were furious that America as a market was closed to them.

Japan was the hardest hit. The Great Depression was hurting Japan just as much as it was hurting America but, in addition, Japan's exports of its biggest cash crop, silk, to America were almost completely cut off by the Smoot-Hawley Act*. Furthermore, Japan would have been going through a generational change: The country had undergone a historic revolution some 70+ years earlier, culminating in a major change of government (the Meiji Restoration) in 1868, and the people who had lived through that revolution would be dead or retiring by the early 1930s.

So one thing led to another, and in September 1931, almost exactly a year after Smoot-Hawley, Japan invaded Manchuria and later northern China. Britain and American strongly protested this aggression, and Roosevelt finally responded with an oil embargo against Japan.

This is the usual pattern of provocative acts on both sides. America saw Smoot-Hawley as its own business, but to Japan it was a hostile shock. Japan saw the Manchuria invasion as "Asian business," while Britain and America saw it as attacking their own Asian interests. Roosevelt saw an oil embargo as a measured response of containment, while energy-dependent Japan saw it almost as an act of war, eventually triggering Japan's attack on Pearl Harbor in 1941.

Japan wasn't the only country affected, of course. England, Germany, Italy, and many other countries were hit hard by the sudden trade barriers with America. Just like in Japan, nationalistic and militaristic feelings were aroused in many countries.

Germany was especially frustrated. The map of Central Europe had been redrawn some 70 years earlier during a series of wars in the 1860s, culminating in the Franco-Prussian war of 1870, and the unification of Germany in 1871. The Great War (WW I) had been a mid-cycle war for Germany, and had been a humiliating defeat, especially because the American and British led Allies had imposed harsh conditions — the loss of some German-speaking territories, and the payment of reparations. The loss of territories was especially provocative, since it partially reversed the German unification of 1871.

Germany was reaching the point where it was going to explode anyway, when the Smoot-Hawley Act was passed. On top of the reparations, the Act was seen as enormously hostile by the Germans. As in Japan, it gave rise to militaristic nationalism in the form of the rise of the Nazis. Germany remilitarized its border with France in 1936, and then annexed German-speaking parts of Eastern Europe in 1938.

So when did World War II start? It depends on what the word "start" means, but an argument can be made that American had started the war, and that the first act of war was the Smoot-Hawley Tariff Act.

World War II

The Central European wars of the 1860s were renewed in full force when Germany invaded Poland in September 1939, causing France and England to declare war. Japan bombed Pearl Harbor in December 1941, causing America to declare war on the Japan / Germany / Italy Axis.

Russia ended up playing a big part in World War II, but not by choice, since it was a mid-cycle war for the Russians. Still exhausted from World War I and the Bolshevik Revolution, Russian dictator Josef Stalin tried to stay neutral, but was forced into it when Hitler invaded Russia. Ironically, this invasion was Hitler's undoing — the irony being in the fact that Napoleon was similarly undone when he invaded Russia in 1812, in a remarkable war that was also mid-cycle for Russia (see chapter 5).

World War II without Hitler?

Many people believe that Hitler was a unique monster who *caused* World War II. This belief is usually stated as: "If only we had killed Hitler in 1935, then we could have avoided World War II."

In fact, when I discuss this book with people, that's possible the biggest criticism I hear, since this book essentially claims that World War II would have occurred with or without Hitler. "How could World War II ever have happened without Hitler?" people ask.

Well first off, Hitler never attacked America: Japan did. What did Hitler have to do with that?

Second, Hitler didn't even attack Britain and France until they attacked Germany.

Third, the early conflicts of World War II were well under way before Hitler invaded anyone. Japan invaded Manchuria in 1931, and Italy invaded Ethiopia in 1935. Hitler's reoccupation of the Rhineland came later, in 1936, and was standard fare for Europe for centuries.

Fourth, Germany has been having wars with France and England literally for centuries. Hitler didn't cause those, so why should this one be blamed specifically on him?

Fifth, Hitler only assumed absolute power in Germany when a specific generational change took place: the death of the President of Germany, Paul von Hindenburg.

Von Hindenburg was born in 1847, and he'd fought in the convulsive wars of the 1860s that created the German union. He was a national hero, and became President in 1925. It was only on his death in 1934 that Hitler was able to overthrow constitutional government,

Germany was like a pressure cooker, ready to explode. Hitler was the agent that brought about one portion of World War II, but he was not the cause of World War II, or even the cause of Germany's part in World War II. All the factors pushing Germany towards war were in place before Hitler's rise to power.

There's one more question that people ask about Hitler: "But even if you're right and World War II would have occurred anyway, at least someone else wouldn't have committed genocide of the Jews. Hitler was a unique monster to have done that."

Well, if you think that, you're wrong. You may say that Hitler was a monster, and you would be right, but he was far from unique.

Genocide was quite commonplace in European wars, which have seen genocide against Jews, Muslims, Christians, and probably other groups as well. Furthermore, there was a history in particular of genocide of the Jews going back many centuries. Finally, genocide is hardly unique to Germany. Worldwide in the 20th century, there have been close to a dozen cases of genocide where a million or more people have been killed on purpose. Genocide is going on today.

So there's no particular reason to believe that things would have been any different if some other leader besides Hitler had taken over after von Hindenburg died. Hitler was a monster, but he was really just an ordinary monster.

A world with two superpowers

The aftermath of World War II brought a startling change to the Western world.

For hundreds of years, the Western world was dominated by various European powers — Spain, France, Britain or Germany at different times. As a result, the nations of Europe were always poised to fight with one another: on the Continent in crisis wars, and around the world in mid-cycle wars over various colonies.

Following World War II, this multitude of national powers was replaced by just two major superpowers: the United States of America on one hand, and the USSR (Union of Soviet Socialist Republics or Soviet Union for short) on the other hand.

However, the situation was more complex than that because World War II was a crisis war for America and Western Europe, but was a mid-cycle war for Russia. These facts affected the interplay of the two superpowers.

The negotiations to settle World War II involved four nations: America, Britain, France and Russia (the USSR).

The three countries of the west had been through a crisis war, and were willing to accept compromises to end the war, provided that "nothing like this must ever happen again."

Russia was "in a different place." Russia had gone through a huge civil war during the 1920s and 30s, with Josef Stalin's faction winning. This was followed by millions of deaths by starvation and execution as Stalin transformed the country in the world's first Communist nation.

Stalin himself was a highly ideological Communist. He claimed to believe that the world would never be at peace until the entire world was Communist.

Stalin's plan was to convert the world to Communism. So World War II was not a crisis war to him; instead, it was an opportunity to spread Communism to other countries.

The contrast in their attitudes gave Stalin an advantage over the west in negotiations. The West was anxious for Stalin's help against Hitler, so Stalin could manipulate the terms.

Germany and Russia had fought two world wars. Stalin insisted on being given a "buffer region" to protect itself from another war with Germany.

In 1945, Stalin was given control of numerous countries in Eastern Europe on condition that they have free elections. These countries included one-fourth of Germany itself, to be known as East Germany.

Winston Churchill was the first to recognize what was really going on, and that Stalin had snookered the West, when he said, "an iron curtain has descended across the continent." It took another year for the public at large to understand as well.

Stalin intended to use military force in each of these countries and convert it to Communism.

That set the framework for Europe for decades to come. Europe was partitioned into a Western region, consisting of democracies, and Eastern region, consisting of Communist dictatorships, all behind the Iron Curtain.

By commandeering the resources of the East European countries, Russia became a second superpower, alongside the United States.

For decades, the "Cold War" referred to the struggle between Western democracy and Soviet Communism. It was called a Cold War for the obvious reason — the West and the Soviets never actually launched their respective nuclear-tipped intercontinental ballistic missiles (ICBMs).

However, Russia was on an earlier timeline than the West, and so its next crisis began in the 1980s; the Soviet Union dissolved in 1991.

The Korean War

The Korean and Vietnam wars are examples of what I call "momentum wars": They're mid-cycle wars, so they aren't fought with a great deal of energy, but they're fought with the same justification as the preceding crisis war. These wars occur because of the momentum created by the previous crisis war, but the public has no real desire to fight them.

By the late 1940s, the attitude in the West was that it had been snookered twice, by two different violent dictators, Hitler and Stalin:

- In 1938, British Prime Minister Neville Chamberlain had gone to Munich to sign a peace agreement with Hitler. When he returned to London, he announced that he and Hitler had agreed to "peace in our time." It later turned out that on the same day that Hitler met with Chamberlain, he also met with Italy's Fascist dictator Benito Mussolini, and the two had signed a private agreement planning their invasion of England.

- In 1945, Stalin had obtained control over East European countries as a "buffer zone" between Russia and Germany, on condition that free elections be held. It later turned out that Stalin had lied in order to turn these countries into Communist satellites of Russia.

These were bitter discoveries for the generation that had fought a bloody war to save Europe from Hitler. "If only we'd stopped Hitler earlier, if only we hadn't appeased him," the reasoning went, "we might have been able to prevent World War II. Let's not make the same mistake with Stalin."

The first battleground was Korea. Following the war, Russia occupied North Korea and America occupied the South. In 1950, North Korea invaded South Korea under Russian direction. America was committed to stopping Russia before another mistake was made (as mistakes with Hitler and Stalin had been made before). The Korean War ended in a stalemate in 1953.

In the 1950s, it seemed to the people who had fought in World War II that they had defeated Hitler and the Nazis, but were losing to Stalin and the Communists. Even after Stalin died in 1953, the news seemed all bad. China under Mao Zedong had also become Communist, and was allied with Russia. And Russia was continuing to consolidate its hold on Eastern Europe's nations as Communist satellites of Russia.

The Vietnam War

It should now be possible to see the massive generational conflict that occurred in America during the 1960s and 70s, centered on the Vietnam War in Southeast Asia.

The previous crisis war in Southeast Asia had been between the French and the Chinese in the 1880s and 1890s (see p. 235). After World War II, the French were driven out of Vietnam, and Vietnam became partitioned — like North and South Korea — into Communist-controlled North Vietnam and Western-aligned South Vietnam. As in Korea, America intervened to prevent North Korea from conquering South Vietnam.

By the time of the mid 1960s, a generational change had occurred.

I would be surprised if more than 1% of all kids born after 1940 or so had the vaguest idea where Vietnam was, prior to the mid-1960s, or even knew anything at all about Southeast Asia.

This is the heart of the "generation gap" that we've been discussing. The people who had fought with their blood and their lives to stop the Nazis, and didn't want to see anything like that happen again with the Communists, were horrified to see the Communists succeed where the Nazis had failed.

But the kids with no personal memory of WW II felt no such horror. They couldn't see any point in fighting the Vietnam War, and this fomented the intergenerational rebellion that occurred in the 60s and 70s.

Vietnam Syndrome

The heroes who fought in World War II have every reason to feel very bitter about how they were treated. It's true that they returned to parades that glorified them in 1945, but that glory didn't last forever.

The generation of heroes that fought in WW II were tremendously humiliated by the antiwar movement in the 60s and 70s. The older generation was treated as evil incarnate, though their goals were no more venal than a desire to prevent World War III against the Communists. Instead of being praised for this effort, they were disgraced. The natural reaction was, "OK, if you don't want to have any wars, then let's not have any wars."

This gave rise to what was called, "the Vietnam Syndrome," the fear of being humiliated again by another war.

September 11, 2001

By the time of the 9/11 terrorist attacks, the heroes who had fought in WW II were long gone, and the kids who grew up during WW II were mostly dead or retired.

What generation was left in charge? The generation that had rebelled in the 60s and 70s; the generation that had humiliated the previous generation of war heroes; the generation that was sure it knew, better than anyone else, when war was "right" and when war was "wrong"; the generation that had no personal experience with WW II.

This generation had been very well protected by the heroes of WW II, and their wisdom guided the country through decades of danger.

Now we're being guided by people with much less appreciation for the dangers that the world holds — both the dangers of war, and the dangers of failing to stand up to monster dictators. America's destiny for the next decades will be determined by the wisdom of this new generation.

The character of a nation

Just as an individual has a character, a nation also has a character. And just as a crisis can force an individual to change from sinner to saint, or vice versa, a crisis war can cause a nation to change its character in a significant way.

America has changed its character after every crisis war. It's almost as if America has been several different nations. Here's a summary:

- **After Plymouth Rock (1620)**: The colonists were totally independent pioneers, in a new land. They had good relations with the Indians, and expected to live side by side with them indefinitely.
- **After King Philip's War (1675-78)**: The colonists were totally dependent on England for protection from the French and the Indians, and were required to pay taxes.
- **After Revolutionary War (1772-82)**: America was an independent nation with two separate civilizations, one in the North and one in the South.
- **After Civil War (1857-65)**: America was a unified nation, manifesting complete freedom — freedom for individuals and freedom for businesses in a *laissez-faire* economy. America was isolationist, and stayed out of world affairs.
- **After World War II (1929-1945)**: America assumed its place as the greatest superpower in the world, and its place as "policemen of the world," with a manifest destiny to lead the world to freedom and democracy.
- **After WW 2010**: Unknown.

We can only guess what kind of nation America will be after the next world war.

In the worst-case scenario, where America is ravaged by nuclear weapons, disease, and foreign bombs, American might be a beaten nation, no longer a superpower, just struggling for survival.

In the best-case scenario, where America's isolation protects it, as it has before, so that the war never really reaches America's soil, then America may yet again be the world's leading superpower.

A brief word about Mexico

Mexico is not covered elsewhere in this book, but there are some important things about Mexico that Americans need to know.

Mexico's last crisis war was the Mexican Revolution, which began in 1910 with an insurrection against dictator Porfirio Díaz. The insurrection grew into a massive civil war that lasted into the early 1920s.

Today, Mexico appears to have entered a new crisis period, although no new crisis war has occurred yet. The country came through a massive financial crisis it suffered in 1994, but economic problems are still severe, with big areas of poverty and unemployment.

This is important to America because of the number of Mexican immigrants in America, especially in California. Some 10 million of California's 35 million people — almost 1/3 — are Mexican immigrants, 70% of them illegal*. Mexicans in California make far less than native Californians, and use far more in public services, including welfare programs.

The result is that a major fault line has developed between Americans and Mexicans, in California and across the border. In a new Mexican crisis war, the war will almost certainly engulf parts of California, and other southern states may be involved as well.

The future of the United States

A crisis war transforms a country, gives the country a new character, and makes it a different country than it was before the crisis war. World War II transformed America completely, changing it from a laissez-faire economy to a heavily regulated economy, and from an isolationist nation to the Policemen of the World, with things like the United Nations and the Marshall Plan. This 70-80 cycle may well be known in history as "The Golden Age of America."

In the space of a few years, America's role as Policeman of the World has changed from a defensive role to a preemptive role. This is President Bush's stated policy, and it's fully supported by the American people, where it wouldn't have been, just a few years ago.

Generational Dynamics predicts that America is due for a crisis war in the next decade. When will it occur? It will probably be triggered by some other event, such as a Mideast or Korean War.

How will America fare in a new world war? Generational Dynamics predicts that America will be completely transformed. There is no guarantee that America will do well or poorly. But if history is any guide (and it is), then one way or another, America will no longer be Policeman of the World twenty years from now.

Chapter 3 — The Principle of Localization I

As we explained in Chapter 1, the difference between crisis wars and mid-cycle wars is that in a crisis war the population feels a great deal of visceral fear and anxiety that their nation is at stake, or at least that their entire way of life is at stake.

That's why Generational Dynamics does not analyze the actions of any particular leader or any group of politicians; rather, it analyzes and forecasts the actions of large masses of people. For these forecasts to be effective, these people must share a common cultural memory. This means that these analyses and forecasts can only be done for groups of people on a local basis. This leads to what we call the Principle of Localization.

Many historians have attempted to discern cycles in history, and generally, those attempts have failed. Those attempts were essentially misguided because they attempted to identify worldwide cycles or, failing that, cycles that apply to the entire Western world. Such attempts fail because, for example, it makes no sense to believe that a regional war in 17th century Ireland can meaningfully be related to a regional war in China or Africa at the same time.

The reason that Generational Dynamics works is that it does not attempt to define its 80-year cycle as worldwide. Quite the contrary, the cycles we're describing apply only to small regions, albeit regions that have been getting larger over the centuries. This is what the "Principle of Localization" is all about.

In this chapter and the next, we're going to expand the theory of Generational Dynamics in several ways. We'll describe the Principle of Localization, how to tell a crisis war from a mid-cycle or interim war, and how small regional wars expand into large world wars.

Applying the Principle of Localization

Historical scholars who reflexively criticize cyclical theories of history should understand this point about localization. What we're talking about in this book is simple common sense. When a society has a brutal, bloody, genocidal war (a "crisis war"), then the people of that small, local society decide "never again," and are willing to make compromises to avoid a repeat. When the people who remember the war die, then there's another crisis war.

So we're not claiming anything magic here — that a war in one region somehow magically causes a war in another region. What we're claiming is simple human nature.

However, this simple observation has yielded enormously interesting results, and that's what this book is about.

Let's start with the adjoining map, created by Peter Turchin of University of Connecticut for his analysis of the development of Europe over two millennia. In order to do his analysis, he found it necessary to divide Europe into 50 separate geographical units, taking into account both terrain features (mountains, coastlines) and ethnic divisions (language, religion)*, with the result as shown.

Figure 16 Map of Europe divided into 50 separate cultural regions

The Principle of Localization claims that each of these regions has its own 80-year cycle timeline, at least to start with. As the centuries pass, and regions merge, their timelines also merge. Even today, however, not all these regions are completely merged: At the very least, Western Europe, Eastern Europe and the Balkans are still on separate timelines.

Of course, to rigorously test Generational Dynamics, it would be necessary to show that the 80-year cycle applies to each of these 50 regions. That's a very big piece of work. However, in chapter 8 we do trace the timeline of Spain back to the 1300s and of England back to 1066; Spain and England present relatively clean examples because they're both somewhat isolated from the rest of Europe.

Having now explained how local regions must be considered separately, let's now discuss how separate regions still go to war together.

Identity Groups and Fault Line Wars

Few Americans are familiar with the ancient Ibo ethnic group or its distinguished history. Consider a member of this group. He may be an Owerri Ibo or an Onitsha Ibo in the Eastern region of Nigeria. In Lagos, he is simply an Ibo. In London, he is Nigerian. In New York, he is an African. ♦

This example illustrates how the same person is viewed very differently different people. Each of the descriptions — Owerri Ibo, Onitsha Ibo, Ibo, Nigerian and African — identifies this person as part of a group he understands — an identity group.

How should one view the intermittent civil war that's dominated Nigerian politics for decades? To a participant, a war is always an "us" versus "them" kind of thing. To the Ibo man we've been describing, the "us" consists of the Ibo and other tribes in the south and the "them" are the Fulani-Hausa tribes in the north.

To an American, the Nigerian civil war is just a bunch of local tribes fighting one another — just as dozens of local groups fight among themselves around the world at any given time. With so many regional conflicts going on all the time, there's no reason why this particular one should draw the average American's attention.

> *It makes no sense to believe that a regional war in Ireland can meaningfully be related to a regional war in China or Africa at the same time.*

Question: What must change before an American would become interested in the regional war in Nigeria?

Answer: Just point out the simple fact that this is a war between the Muslims in the north and the Christians in the south.

Suddenly, this is a much more important "us" versus "them" war. If you're a Christian, the "us" consists of the Christian fighters, and the "them" are the Muslims; to a Muslim anywhere in the world, these roles of "us" and "them" become reversed.

This simple little use of identity groups turns a simple, unimportant regional war into a portion of a major worldwide war stretching from Africa, through Europe and Asia, into Indonesia.

It's worth pointing out, in passing, that the identity group concept is not new. A marvelous exposition of a related concept will be found in the fourteenth century Arab politician and sociologist, Ibn Khaldun. Khaldun's concept, *asabiya*, measures the cohesiveness or solidarity of a group*. An analysis by Peter Turchin of University of Connecticut shows how Khaldun examined numerous Muslim societies, to find that asabiya is the essence of rendering one group superior to another in war. Khaldun shows that frequently asabiya declines and dynasties disappear four generations after the dynasty is established — thus providing a kind of 14th century basis for the 80-year generational cycle! Turchin's analysis goes on to correlate asabiya to a number of geographical and ethnic characteristics (coastlines, mountains, religion, language, economics). He develops mathematical models that show specifically how Europe was formed into nations, and, in particular, the influence of the Roman Empire.

Civilizations and Fault Line Wars

What are the major civilizations in the world today? Scholars differ, but for our purposes we'll use the collection defined by Harvard Professor Samuel P. Huntington in his book, *The Clash of Civilizations**: Western, Latin American, African, Islamic, Sinic (Chinese), Hindu, Orthodox, Buddhist, and Japanese.

Figure 17 The nine major civilizations today*

Huntington defines a fault line war to be one that takes place between two identity groups from different civilizations. (Since the phrase "fault line" is so compelling and so graphic, we'll use that term to describe other kinds of conflicts as well, such as the fault line between the North and South that led to the Civil War, or the fault line between the French and the Germans that led to numerous wars.)

As a practical matter, it's unlikely that a major fault line war will ever break out between the Latin American and Japanese civilizations. Both of these are purely geographical civilizational designations, and even if we imagine a scenario where some sort of conflict breaks out between these two groups, it's hard to see how it spreads into anything like a world war.

No, the fault line wars that are biggest, bloodiest and longest lasting are between identity groups based on religion. They rarely are settled except through genocide.

Huntington's book describes the potency of religious identity groups, and shows in detail radical leaders on both sides of a regional conflict use religious identities to expand the conflict into other regions sharing the same identities.

Here's how Huntington describes what he calls "the rise of civilization consciousness":

> Fault line wars go through processes of intensification, expansion, containment, interruption, and, rarely, resolution. *These processes usually begin sequentially, but they also overlap and may be repeated. Once started, fault line wars, like other communal conflicts, tend to take on a life of their own and to develop in an action-reaction pattern. Identities which had previously been multiple and casual become focused and hardened.... As violence increases, the initial issues at stake tend to get redefined more exclusively as "us" against "them" and group cohesion and commitment are enhanced. Political leaders expand and deepen their appeals to ethnic and religious loyalties, and civilizational consciousness strengthens in relation to other identities. A "hate dynamic" emerges ... in which mutual fears, distrust, and hatred feed on each other. Each side dramatizes and magnifies the distinction between the forces of virtue and the forces of evil and eventually attempts to transform this distinction into the ultimate distinction between the quick and the dead.

It's important to note that the "processes" that Huntington describes include negotiation, compromise and containment, as well as intensification and expansion. A wide variety of processes are possible, because other nations drawn into a regional battle may be more interested in seeing the battle settled than in seeing it expand.

Good examples of these containment processes are the roles of America and Jordan today in the Mideast conflict between Israelis and Palestinians. Jordan is in the Muslim civilization, and America is in the (Judeo-Christian) Western civilization. Yet, both countries are more dedicated to mediating the conflict than expanding it.

Later, we're going to use the phrase "Identity Group Expansion," referring to the expansion process described above, to refer to the principle that wars expand by rallying other societies or nations in the same identity group.

The Bosnian Conflict

Starting in 1990, a conflict broke out in the Balkan region of Europe. The war was characterized by "ethnic cleansing," mass murder of men who were then buried in mass graves, and mass rape of women, who were thus forced to bear children with the sperm of their conquerors. By 1995, America was sending thousands of troops in a peacekeeping role to end the hostilities.

Huntington provides a lengthy analysis of this conflict, which I'll summarize here. However, my main intent is to identify important aspects of the analysis that Huntington omits, but which can be analyzed using Generational Dynamics.

Imagine a map of Eurasia with three civilizations labeled on it: the Western (Judeo-Christian) on the left, the Orthodox on the upper right, and the Muslim civilization on the lower right. (We're omitting other civilizations for simplicity here.)

> *The major civilizations today are Western, Latin American, African, Islamic, Sinic (Chinese), Hindu, Orthodox, Buddhist, and Japanese*

Now, where do these three huge civilizations meet? The answer is that they meet in the Balkans, with large populations of Catholics in Croatia, large populations of Orthodox Christians in Serbia, and large populations of Muslims in Bosnia and Albania.

Remarkably, these three groups lived together peacefully for decades in the Balkans. In many cases, they were friends and neighbors, living near each other, babysitting for each other's children, often intermarrying - just like any suburban neighborhood in America. That's why it was so remarkable to see how brutal and violent the Balkans war of the 1990s was. It was as strange and unexpected as if the citizens of Stamford, Connecticut, decided one day to rise up and start killing each other.

Huntington details violent acts on all sides, pointing out that the violent acts began with the Albanian Muslims in the late 1970s. By the late 1980s,

Slobodan Milosevic was appealing to Serbian nationalism♦. In a celebration in 1989, Milosevic lead one to two million Serbs to commemorate the 600th anniversary of the 1389 conquest of Serbia by Muslim Turks. This illustrates how the appropriate choice of "us" and "them" can inflame mass passions: it's not Serbs versus Albanians; it's Serbs versus Muslims.

In looking to use Generational Dynamics to enhance Huntington's analysis, we wish to consider two questions:

- Why didn't America, the leading country in Western civilization, simply side with the (Roman Catholic) Croats?

- What were the "causes" of the war? What factors turned friends, neighbors, lovers into genocidal warriors?

Let's look at these two questions.

Why did America support the Bosnian Muslims?

Most Americans know little about the Balkan region of Europe, and yet because of its unique position as the meeting place of three major civilizations, it's one of the most critical regions of the world. It's worth remembering that World War I was the result of identity group expansion of the regional hostilities that broke out in the Balkans in 1914.

Huntington shows how identity groups rallied in the most predictable ways in the Bosnian wars♦: Germany, Austria, the Vatican, other European Catholic and Protestant countries and groups rallied on behalf of Croatia; Russia, Greece and other Orthodox countries and groups behind the Serbs; and Iran, Saudi Arabia, Turkey, Libya, the Islamist international, and Islamic countries generally on behalf of the Bosnian Muslims.

However, America was "a noncivilization anomaly in the otherwise universal pattern of kin backing kin." It should have supported just Croatia, its civilizational relation, but instead it supported *both* the Croatian Catholics and the Bosnian Muslims, siding *against* only the Orthodox Christian Serbs.

I don't think any Americans find it remarkable that we supported both the Croatians and the Bosnians against the Serbs. After all, when Serb president Slobodan Milosevic started implemented his "ethnic cleansing" program, the stories of mass genocide and rape by Serbs horrified Americans, so supporting the Bosnians as well as the Croatians seemed quite natural.

But if that's true, then why was America unique in doing so? Generational Dynamics provides some important insight into this question.

The Character of a Nation

Each crisis war transforms a nation in a new way, and so a country takes on a new character during that 80-year cycle. This character can be entirely civilizational, or it can go beyond the purely civilizational.

The Great Depression and World War II transformed America from a country with a "laissez-faire" economy and a small government to one with a large government and a heavily regulated economy, and from an isolationist nation to "Policeman of the World." More specifically, America transformed itself into "Impartial Policeman of the World," in a sense almost rejecting the civilization paradigm.

This insight is important for policy planners as they try to assess the future "clash of civilizations" between Western and Islamic situations, because it shows that the civilization paradigm isn't monolithic. In other words, when the great "clash of civilizations" arrives, it's not certain that all Muslim countries will stick together on one side, and all Western countries will stick together on the other side.

The easiest way to see this is to note that there have been major intra-civilizational wars in the past — as recently as World War II, when England sided with France against Germany. In the Napoleonic wars, England sided with Germany against France.

Based on history, it seems unlikely that all European countries will be on the same side of a future war, even if we're all from the same Western civilization. Today, we can only speculate, but we have to note that hostile attitudes between America and France have been hardening for some time, and show few of abating.

On the other side, we take note of the fact that Muslim country Iran is run by Islamic clerics, but has a population that regularly engages in large pro-American demonstrations.

What was the "cause" of the Bosnian war?

Huntington analyzes the cause of the Bosnian war in the context of wars worldwide between Muslims and non-Muslims,* and the fact that "as the twentieth century ends, Muslims are involved in far more intergroup violence than people of other civilizations." He considers several reasons — the history of Islam, the difficulty Islam has coexisting with other religions, and "Finally, and most important, the demographic explosion in Muslim societies and the availability of large numbers of often unemployed males between the ages of fifteen and thirty as a natural source of instability and violence both within Islam and against non-Muslims. Whatever other causes may be at work, this factor alone would go a long way to explaining Muslim violence in the 1980s and 1990s."

These factors all explain the causes of the Bosnian and other wars, but they don't explain the timing. All of these factors were true in 1970, 1980, 1990, and 2000, and yet the Bosnian war occurred at a particular time.

The same puzzle occurs with most other wars. You can look at various causes of the American Civil War — differences over slavery, differences in lifestyle, economic issues — but those causes don't explain why the war occurred in 1861, rather than 1850 or 1870.

The answer to these puzzles is explained by Generational Dynamics. The Civil War has previously been discussed at length (pp. 11 and 38), but with regard to the Bosnian War, note the following: The Bosnian war was a replay of the Balkan wars that occurred 80 years earlier. Albanian-Serbian relations degraded throughout the decade of the 1900s, and did again in the decade of the 1980s. Full-scale war broke out in 1912, and again in 1990.

It's true that there were other wars in the region before and since, but none were nearly as transformational. The Kingdom of Yugoslavia was created in 1918, and that was a major transformation. After World War II, Yugoslavia became a Soviet satellite, but remained a single Yugoslav state, without undergoing a major transformation as it had done in 1918. During the years from 1918 to 1990, there were other conflicts and skirmishes in Yugoslavia, but none with enormous transformational impact of the Balkan wars of the 1910s. It was only in the 1990s that a new major transformation occurred, as Yugoslavia itself fell apart.

Finally, with regard to other wars involving Muslims, we note that the entire Muslim world was transformed by World War I, starting with the 1908 coup by the "Young Turks" in Turkey, to the carving up of the Ottoman Empire in the 1920s. It's now 80 years later, and all these wars are being replayed in one way or another — whether it's the intra-Muslim Iran-Iraq war of the 1980s, or the inter-civilizational war in the Balkans of the 1990s.

So Huntington and other historians can identify and discuss the *causes* of the Muslim wars of recent times, and the *timing* of these wars can be explained by the fact that they're occurring one 80-year cycle after World War I.

In the next chapter, we continue to explore this relationship between the causes of a crisis war and its timing, in order to further develop the theory of Generational Dynamics.

Chapter 4 — The Principle of Localization II

This chapter continues the theoretical aspects of Generational Dynamics, by discussing the relationships between fault lines and generational changes.

In particular, in this chapter we want to explore the "clash of civilizations" concept we hear about so much today. This phrase evokes a mental image of a billion Muslims going to war with a billion Westerners. We'll discuss exactly what the "clash of civilizations" means, and what kind of war we can expect.

"Identity Group Expansion" versus "The Principle of Localization"

In the previous chapter, we identified two different principles of war that appear to be somewhat in conflict with each other.

- **Identity Group Expansion** is the process, described by Huntington, by which a small regional war expands into a larger war. Belligerents identify themselves as part of larger rather than smaller groups — e.g., Muslims instead of Bosnians, or Christians instead of Croatians — in order to rally other nations in similar identity groups to their side.

- **The Principle of Localization** is the Generational Dynamics principle that, basically, every war is local, on a timeline which applies to a smaller, rather than a larger identity group. Thus, the Bosnian War of the 1990s is a replay of the Balkans war of the 1910s.

Thus, the first principle seems to imply that wars grow larger, while the second principle seems to indicate that wars are small.

The way to explain this apparent conflict is to go back to square one.

Generational Dynamics predicts a society will go through a transformational crisis war every 80 years or so — the length of a human lifetime. The next crisis war begins around the time that the generation of risk-aversive people who grew up during the previous crisis war retire or die, and thus are replaced as leaders with a generation of people who grew up *after* the last crisis war. Since they have no personal memory of the last crisis war, they do have the same risk-aversiveness, and they take the risks and demand the justice and retribution that lead to a *new* crisis war.

A generational change will have this kind of effect only among a group of people who share the experience of the crisis war as a common cultural memory. That leads to the Principle of Localization, which says that this 80-year cycle applies only within a local region. A region may be small, but it may also be as large as a country like the United States. In cases where multiple political units (of the same or different civilizations) are fighting in the same crisis war, each political unit will have its own separate timeline. 80 years later, the timelines of these separate units may again converge, or they may diverge.

The Identity Group Expansion principle says that wars will expand because other societies or nations will join because they are in the same identity groups as the original belligerents. But this doesn't conflict with the Principle of Localization, because "join" can have many different meanings. Suppose a third nation is part of the same identity group as one of the two belligerent nations in a war. If the third nation's population is entering a crisis period (the generation that grew up during the last crisis war is retiring or dying off), then it may become a full-fledged participant in the war. But if the third nation is in an awakening period, then it may "join" the war simply by local rioting and demonstrations. And if the third nation is in an unraveling period, it may desperately take any policy position it can to force a compromise or contain the problem.

Let's see how these two principles work together to provide answers to the following question: In the "clash of civilizations," which nations will be fighting, and on which side?

Picking sides in the Clash of Civilizations

In the anticipated "clash of civilizations," the Identity Group Expansion principle says, in essence, that Western nations will stick together and Muslim nations will stick together.

However, as discussed in the last chapter, this doesn't mean that all nations in an identity group join in the war; some of them may provide only "verbal" assistance, and others may use their influence to help negotiate a truce.

This observation provides the nexus between the Principle of Localization and the Identity Group Expansion principle: If an identity group ally is a country "scheduled" for a crisis war, then it's more likely to participate in the war; if not, then it may be reluctant to actually fight in the war, or may do so with little energy if it does.

This means that the two sides in the coming clash may not be entirely monolithic — something we already pointed out in the previous chapter (page 66) for a different reason: the character of a nation may go beyond civilizational considerations.

There are over a billion people in each of the Muslim and Western civilizations. The phrase "clash of civilizations" evokes a mental image of a major war with a billion people on each side.

However, we can take the two principles we've been discussing and use them together, in order to forecast which countries are likely to participate on each side of a future clash of civilizations.

Forecasting the coming Mideast War and its aftermath

We don't know today what events will trigger the "clash of civilizations" between Western and Muslim societies, but a good guess would be a new Mideast war. Let's see how a new Mideast war might lead to a worldwide clash.

Let's illustrate how the Identity Group Expansion principle and the Principle of Localization work together to forecast what might happen after a new Mideast war breaks out between Israelis and Palestinians.

We begin with a historical analysis before getting to the actual forecast.

A Brief Historical Analysis

Turkey, Iraq and Jordan (as Transjordan) are three of the countries that were formed from the pieces of the breakup of the Ottoman Empire following World War I. We would expect these three countries to be on the same generational timeline. Furthermore, if a Mideast war broke out between the Israelis and Palestinians, we would expect these three Muslim countries to join in the war on the side of the Palestinians, because of Identity Group Expansion.

However, two issues militate against that conclusion.

The first issue is that there are other identity groups involved. The Turks, though Muslim, are not Arabs, and identify with Western Europeans rather than Arabs on many issues (see chapter 9, page 195, for history). Iraq is a melting pot of various ethnic groups, Arabs, Kurds and Persians, and each of these identity groups has issues that go beyond Islam. And Jordan, of course, is Palestinian Arab. So each of these countries may side with its ethnic identity groups or its religious (Muslim) identity groups. In general, Identity Group Expansion is not always predictable because it's not always certain which of several identity groups a nation may choose.

The second issue is that the timelines aren't completely identical.

Indeed two of these countries are on roughly the same timeline, though with a little bit of divergence. Iran fought in the Iran/Iraq war in the 1980s, and Turkey fought in the civil war with the PKK Kurds from 1984-2000. Both of these wars occurred approximately as expected, around 80 years after World War I.

> *Turkey and Iraq are roughly on the same timeline, and they've completed their new crisis wars*

Thus, Turkey and Iraq are both roughly (but not exactly) on the same timeline, and even more important, they've already completed their new crisis wars, and will not be anxious to fight in a new one, unless they're forced to.

The same might have been true for Jordan, if it weren't for external intervention that occurred starting in the 1930s.

Because of Nazi persecution, European Jews flooded into Palestine in the 1930s. Hostilities between the Palestinians and the Jews began in 1936, and reached a climax in a major war in 1948-49 following the creation of Israel. The crisis war that ran from 1936 to 1949 defines the timeline for the Palestinians and the Israelis.

In the mid 1940s, Jordan's King Abdullah led the way to act as a mediator between the Palestinians and America. He made it clear that Arabs have always lived peacefully with Jews, but now were opposed to huge migrations of thousands of Jews to the Mideast, "not because they're Jews, but because they're foreigners." Abdullah reduced tensions in the area by allowing hundreds of thousands of Palestinians to settle in Jordan, where they automatically became citizens. Later, King Hussein carried on the role of mediator by marrying Queen Noor, an American-born Arab.

Following its mid-cycle "awakening," Jordan took a number of steps to maintain a middle path between America and the Palestinians. It terminated its connection to the West Bank; it stayed out of the Iran-Iraq war, though it officially sided with Iraq as America did; and it made major Parliamentary changes to move in the direction of a "Western-style" democracy.

The future in the Mideast

What will be the causes and the timing of a new Mideast war?

The *causes* will be among those listed by Huntington in the previous chapter (page 66).

The *timing* will be determined by the last crisis war, which occurred in the 1936-49 time frame.

Few analysts seem to have any idea of what's in store in the Mideast. They all look at the 1967 and 1972 wars, as well as the late 1980's intifada, because that's as far back as they can remember, and they say, "Any new war won't be any worse than those."

That's completely wrong. Those were mid-cycle wars, led by veterans of the extremely violent and bloody 1940s wars who were willing to compromise before allowing that much violence to occur again. Those veterans are dying off now, and the next war won't have their influence. Today we're repeating the steps of the early Palestinian-Jewish confrontations in the late 1930s, leading up the extremely violent and bloody wars of the late 1940s. History shows that there's no guarantee that the state of Israel will survive the new wars.

When will the generational change take place?

There's an incredible irony going on in the Mideast today, in that the leaders of two opposing sides are, respectively, Ariel Sharon and Yasser Arafat.

These two men hate each other, but they're the ones cooperating with each other (consciously or not) to prevent a major Mideast conflagration. Both of them fought in the wars of the 1940s, and neither of them wants to see anything like that happen again. And it won't happen again, as long as both of these men are in charge.

The disappearance of these two men will be part of an overall generational change in the Mideast that will lead to a major conflagration within a few years. It's possible that the disappearance of Arafat alone will trigger a war, just as the election of Lincoln ignited the American Civil War. (It's currently American policy to get rid of Arafat. My response is this: Be careful what you wish for.) Most likely, the disappearance of Arafat will lead to increased violence, but not a full-fledged war for a few months.

Will this be the clash of civilizations?

Now let's apply the Identity Group Expansion principle to speculate on how a new Mideast war might lead to a wider war.

None of the following is certain, of course, but we can specify the most likely scenarios:

- The **United States**, as "impartial policeman of the world" will attempt to intervene in the Arab/Israeli battle, probably under the auspices of either NATO or the United Nations. However, once a Mideast war starts in earnest after the generational change has occurred there, it will be almost impossible to stop. America will try to stay neutral, but will eventually be forced to choose sides, and to fight with Israel.

- **Jordan**, like America, will attempt to play a role as an impartial mediator, but from the Arab side. Eventually, they will be forced choose sides, and to fight with the Palestinians.

- **Iraq**, **Iran**, and **Turkey** are all Muslim countries that have already completed their crisis wars. They will be reluctant to enter the war, and because of conflicting ethnic and religious identities (as described above), it's not 100% certain which side they'll be on. Also, it will be a mid-cycle war for them, so there will be opportunities to encourage compromise.

- The fault line in Kashmir between **Pakistan** and **India** is just as serious as the Mideast fault line, with the added certainty that nuclear weapons would be used. It seems likely that the "Identity Group Expansion" principle would work in either direction (Mideast to Kashmir or Kashmir to Mideast), causing a war in either region to trigger a war in the other one.

- **Russia**'s previous crisis war was World War I, where the Russian Empire suffered humiliating losses, leading to an enormous transformation: The adoption of Communism, and the violent suppression of the Russian Orthodox Church. World War II was an awakening period for Russia, and included a partial revival of the Church. (See Russia's history in chapter 9.) Russia's next crisis period began in 1990 with the dissolution of the USSR, and has not yet ended. Russia will come in on the side of India against Pakistan, and against the Palestinians in the Mideast. (Russia has a strong national sense as a protector of Jerusalem: The Orthodox Christian religion was directly established by Jesus' immediate followers; the Catholic religion was only established centuries later. In 1948, Russia was almost the first country in the world to recognize the new state of Israel.)

- **France** and **Germany** will initially join with America in whatever impartial peacekeeping force is set up in the Mideast. When France is finally forced to choose sides, the country's vocal Muslim population makes it possible that it will fight on the side of the Palestinians. There may yet be one more world war between France and Germany.

To repeat, the above scenarios are not certain, but they represent a considerably more textured forecast for the coming clash of civilizations than would otherwise be possible. By using the Identity Group Expansion principle together with the Principal of Localization, we can produce planning information that is more reliable than is otherwise available.

<u>Note:</u> As this book is just being sent to the publisher (August, 2003), we see a trend emerging. American troops are in Iraq, where the people are not anxious for war, but where we're seeing a pattern of worsening terrorist attacks. The evidence appears to indicate that the terrorist attacks are being sponsored by al Qaeda and other Islamic extremist forces outside of Iraq — especially Syria and Saudi Arabia. At the same time, the level of violence in the Palestine region has been increasing, and Arafat appears to be having less control. This is all consistent with the above analysis, indicating that the terrorism in Iraq is related to the coming crisis war in the Israel/Palestine area, rather than to the Iraqi war, and that the Iraqis themselves won't be willing participants unless Iraq itself becomes a theatre of war.

Remember that Generational Dynamics is a medium to long-range forecasting tool, and can only forecast the attitudes, behaviors and actions of large masses of people, not individual politicians or terrorists. Thus, we cannot predict terrorist acts, but we *can* predict a major uprising between Palestinians and Israelis; but even here, we can't predict exact timing. Nor can we predict exact timings for other expected theaters of war: India versus Pakistan over Kashmir, and Korean reunification and war with Japan.

At this writing, Israel and the Palestinian group Hamas are increasing the pace of their mutual attacks, and the Palestinian people are expressing increasing fury. It's increasingly getting the feel of the famous people's uprisings of the past — the French Revolution (p. 173), the Bolshevik Revolution (p. 208) and Mao's Long March (p. 228). This is not a good sign, since all of these uprisings resulted in enormous bloodshed. **End of note.**

The Generational Dynamics Forecasting Methodology

As the world enters a dangerous new era, new methods are needed by policy makers and investors to anticipate attitudes and actions around the world.

The Generational Dynamics forecasting methodology is an experimental forecasting tool that can provide a great deal of information that can't be obtained any other way, as was illustrated by the preceding analysis of the Mideast situation.

Overcoming Forecasting Limitations

However, as we discussed in the Preface, forecasts that are obtained using Generational Dynamics are subject to three limitations:

- Any forecast applies only to large masses of people, never to a particular individual or small group of politicians. Therefore, it's possible to forecast (predict) crisis wars, but it's impossible to forecast (predict) mid-cycle wars or terrorist acts.

- Since it's a medium to long-range forecasting tool, any forecast provides a final destination, but cannot tell you how we'll get to that destination.

- For the same reason, a forecast might be made with a very high level of certainty, except that the timing of the forecast cannot be made with a precision greater than a few years.

The objective of the forecasting methodology is to overcome the last two of these limitations as much as possible. This is done by combining generational forecasts with contemporary data, so that generational changes and the changes in attitudes and beliefs that go along with them can be pinpointed to an exact time.

The methodology has three parts: A historical analysis provides the approximate dates of generational changes; a financial analysis, which provides additional timing information; and a current attitudes analysis, which detects changes in public attitude that signal generational changes.

Methodology Part I: Historical Analysis

An important purpose of the Generational Dynamics methodology is to predict / forecast, with a fair amount of reliability, when and whether a nation or society is likely to go to war, how they'll react to war if war is brought to them, how energetically they'll fight a war, how long the war should last, and how the war, once begun, can be settled or ended.

> *The objective of the methodology is to provide better short-range forecasts*

There are three parts to the methodology, starting with a Historical Analysis of the society or nation.

There are three major reasons why this Historical Analysis is important:

- The Historical Analysis establishes the country's timeline. Simplistically, you could add 80 years to the time of the last crisis war to get the next crisis war; of course, the time between crisis wars is seldom exactly 80 years, but later steps in the methodology will provide more precision.

- It defines the compromises and fault lines that ended the last war. If you can understand those compromises and fault lines, then you can probably understand what's going to cause the next crisis war.

- It establishes the character of the society during the current 80-year cycle. A crisis war performs a kind of societal lobotomy (or a transformation) that defines the character of the society for exactly one 80-

year cycle. That character might be part of the civilizational identity, or it may go beyond or even conflict with the civilizational identity.

Example: The American Revolution and the aftermath that created the United States of America were based on a major compromise involving slavery, with a political fault line between the Northern and Southern states. The Civil War was fought across this fault line about 80 years later.

Example: World War I transformed Russia completely, in the form of the Bolshevik Revolution, into a Communist country. It remained a Communist country for exactly one 80-year cycle, until the Soviet Union dissolved in 1991.

Example: Japan has always had little contact with the outside world for almost its entire history, but became imperialistic for exactly one 80-year cycle after the Meiji Restoration in 1868. After surrendering in 1945, Japan changed, for the next 80-year cycle, to be pacifist.

Methodology Part II: Economic Analysis

There's a romantic notion that people fight wars over grand, lofty ideals. Maybe that's true for some wars, but most wars are motivated by money, or lack of it.

A society or nation goes through a new crisis war when two things happen: a generational change, and a financial crisis. The generational change changes society's mood from "compromise and containment," and the financial crisis makes people seek justice and retribution.

Example: In America during the 1850s, there was a market bubble as people competed with each other to bid up stock prices on railroads and on the public lands that the railroads used. The bubble burst, leading to the Panic of 1857, putting many companies out of business, and leading people in the North and South to blame each other. The Civil War began shortly thereafter.

Although we frequently use the phrase "crisis war," it's more accurate to refer to a "crisis period" which includes both the crisis war and the financial crisis. The crisis period begins with the earlier of the financial crisis and the crisis war, and ends when everything is settled.

Example: The American Revolutionary War crisis period begins with the English banking crisis of 1772, and continues through the election George Washington in 1790; the Civil War crisis begins with the Panic of 1857, and ends with the end of the Reconstruction period in 1877; the World War II crisis begins with the stock market crash in 1929, and ends with Japanese surrender in 1945. The current crisis period began with the Nasdaq crash early in 2000.

Example: The first known market bubble was the Tulipomania bubble of the early 1600s, when the prices of specially bred colorful tulips were being bid up to astronomical heights. The bubble burst in 1637, just as France was entering the Thirty Years War.

Example: The French Revolution and the Napoleonic Wars began after the French Monarchy went bankrupt in 1789.

A financial crisis is a powerful motivation for war, and when combined with a generational change, energizes a population to seek justice and retribution against whomever they blame for the financial crisis.

Example: When the U.S. imposed an oil embargo on Japan in 1933, the Japanese considered it an act of war. The oil embargo was a major motivating factor in the Japanese bombing of Pearl Harbor in 1941.

> *When the U.S. imposed an oil embargo on Japan in 1933, they considered it an act of war*

The Economic Analysis part of the Generational Dynamics methodology analyzes the recent economic history of the society or nation being examined, to determine whether there is a local financial crisis, usually caused by high unemployment.

Methodology Part III: Monthly Current Attitudes Analysis

The Historical Analysis and Economic Analysis alone give you a great deal of information, but do not allow you to predict the timing of current events. After all, the 80-year cycle isn't exact, and can vary from 60 to 100 years.

Precise timing requires the Current Attitudes Analysis. This requires you to "take the temperature" of a society on a regular basis to detect the telltale signs that a generational change has taken place. It's possible to use generational changes to forecast changes in consumer behavior, but that discussion is beyond the scope of this book, where we're primarily focused on readiness for war. The telltale signs of readiness for war include such things as hardening of public opinion, desire for justice and retribution, identification of people to blame (this includes selection of identity group when there are several choices), and willingness to play brinksmanship rather than back off from confrontation. This information can be used to provide medium to long-range forecasts of major attitude changes in a society. These forecasts can be useful to international investors and policy makers.

The Current Attitudes Analysis is based on regular intelligence. Since the changes in attitudes that signal a generation change are massive, there's no need to be too finely tuned. It's possible that enough information can be obtained from a variety of sources, such as public sources like local newspapers and magazines. A relatively low-cost poll can be commissioned to send someone into a marketplace select 100 people at random, and ask them the question: "Whom do you blame for the high unemployment rate, and why? What do you think should be done about it?" Collect those 100 responses, and you'll have all the information you need about the local society, and how close they are to war. Do that once a month and you'll know exactly when that country is about to go to war.

Crisis Wars versus Mid-Cycle Wars

What's the difference between a crisis war and a mid-cycle war?

When I started studying this field, it was clear that I needed a set of criteria that I could apply objectively. The criteria that I've come up with are successful in that regard. There's some subjectivity to them, but when I've applied these criteria to actual historical wars, in just about every case there really was no question what kind of war it was.

One criterion I never used was number of battle deaths. I would have liked to, since it would make things a lot simpler, but I never could see how to use it for that purpose. How many deaths make a crisis war? Is it 0.1% of the population? 1% of the population? I could never answer that question, and in fact, I don't believe that any numeric measure would work.

Another criterion that can't be used is the behavior of the country's leader, but this is a little tricky to define. Generational Dynamics depends on the beliefs, attitudes and actions of large masses of people, not a single leader or a small group of politicians. There are many wars that are enthusiastically supported by the population (such as WW II for America) and those where the population shows its disapproval (such as the Vietnam war for America).

Generational cycles depend upon the "cultural memory" of the population, and so by the Principle of Localization, I needed to find a way to measure the impact of the war on the people of a country or region with a common cultural memory.

As we discussed in chapter 1, what makes a war a crisis war is the emotions felt by the population at large: terror, anxiety, fury at the enemy, and a desire for revenge. If I were to use a single word to describe the difference between a crisis war and a mid-cycle war, the word would be "energy." How much energy did the society use to pursue the war?

This led to a list of questions designed to measure the "energy" with which the country engaged in the war, and the effect it had. Here's the list of questions. None of these questions is determinative by itself, but several of these questions taken together can provide an answer. The symbol (+) indicates that an affirmative answer indicates a crisis war, and the symbol (-) indicates that an affirmative answer indicates a mid-cycle war.

- Did the country plan and prepare for the war in advance (+), or was the war a surprise that they didn't prepare for (-)?

- Did the country start the war or respond to it energetically (+)?

- Or was there an exogenous factor pulling the country into the war — a treaty with another country under attack, or an unexpected invasion, for example (-)?

- Was the war top-down (-) or bottom-up (+) — that is, did the energy for the war come from the leaders (-) or from the people (+)?

- Was there a financial crisis that caused enough poverty to cause being a soldier to be the only way to feed his family (+)?

- Did the people blame their war opponents for their financial crisis (+)?

- Was the antiwar/pacifist movement a major part of the political landscape (-), or was it just a footnote to the history of the war (+)?

- Were civilians targeted for attack (+), or did political considerations force civilians to be protected (-)?

- Was the war particularly violent, bloody or genocidal (+)?

- Or was the war a stalemate (even if people got killed) (-)?

- Was the military strategy primarily offensive (+) or defensive (-)?

- Did the war result in a major transformation — major governmental changes, major national boundary changes, for example (+)?
- Was the country occupied and controlled by enemy forces (+)?
- Was the war so horrible that the parties were forced into unpleasant compromises just to end the war — compromises that created fault lines that led to the next crisis war 80 years later (+)?

That's a long list of questions, but my experience is that applying those criteria makes it almost always pretty obvious whether a war is a crisis war or a mid-cycle war.

Winners and Losers: The process of national transformation

When looking back through history to determine whether a particular war was a crisis war or a mid-cycle war for a particular society or nation, probably the main determinant is the intensity and profundity with which it transformed the society or nation.

How does this transformation take place?

If war is inevitable, then it's also inevitable that there'll be winners and losers. What process does each side go through when the war ends?

As Americans, we have a feel for what happens to winners. We've developed a national feeling of certainty. We beat the depression and we beat the Nazis. We obviously know what we're doing. Our greatest danger today is one of hubris. At any rate, we understand the winning transformation better than the losing transformation, because we won World War II.

Transformation of the defeated nation

But what happens to the losers? Some insights into that question are provided by Wolfgang Schivelbusch who studied the results of defeat in war*, and found that they follow a predictable pattern:
- An almost festive jubilation accompanies the declarations of war on all sides. "The passions excited in the national psyche by the onset of war show how deeply invested the masses [are] in its potential out-

come. Propaganda [reinforces the] conviction that 'everything [is] at stake,' and the threat of death and defeat [functions] like a tightly coiled spring, further heightening the tension." The jubilation is an anticipatory celebration of victory, since "nations are as incapable of imagining their own defeat as individuals are of conceiving their own death. The new desire to humiliate the enemy, [is] merely a reaction to the unprecedented posturing in which nations now [engage] when declaring war."

- The illusion, the unshaken conviction of certain victory, turns into shock when things start going wrong. In the words of historian Carl von Clausewitz, writing in the 1830s, "The effect of [defeat] outside the army — on the people and on the government — is a sudden collapse of the most anxious expectations♦, and a complete crushing of self-confidence. This leaves a vacuum that is filled by a corrosively expanding fear, which completes the paralysis. It is as if the electric charge of the main battle had sparked a shock to the whole nervous system of one of the contestants."

- As unexpected losses turn into outright defeat, the public on the losing side experiences deep and widespread depression, contrasted to the joyous public celebrations of the victors.

- The defeat usually causes an internal revolution, "the overthrow of the old regime and its subsequent scapegoating for the nation's defeat♦." We'll discuss this more below.

- The internal revolution leads to a quick reversal of the public mood to a unique type of euphoria that the public experiences as a kind of victory. "For a moment, the external enemy is no longer an adversary but something of an ally♦, with whose help the previous regime and now deposed system has been driven from power."

- This euphoria leads to a kind of dreamland: Once the internal revolution has deposed the "old regime," then the public expectation changes: nothing stands in the way of a return to the prewar status quo♦. The prevailing public attitude is, "The victor has freed us from despotism, for which we are very grateful, but now it's time for him to go."

- However, if the victorious nation "calls its defeated enemy to account — instead of treating him as an innocent victim — the mood shifts dramatically. The enmity that had been transformed into conciliation reemerges with all its former force or is even intensified by the feeling of having been doubly betrayed. In the dreamland state, memories of the real circumstances of defeat fade away, replaced by the losers' conviction that their nation laid down its arms of its own free will, in a kind of gentleman's agreement that placed trust in the chivalry of the enemy."

Schivelbusch goes on to describe other long-term effects on the defeated nation: a desire for revenge, objectifying the victor as uncultured barbarians, and finally, learning from and imitating the victor.

Recognizing the depth of transformation

We've quoted extensively from Schivelbusch's paradigm for a defeated nation's transformation because we believe it adds considerable texture to the concept that a crisis war transforms a nation.

The key to understanding this transformation would be the "internal revolution" that usually occurs. An example of this occurred after France was overrun and defeated by German forces in 1870, resulting in 80,000 French deaths. The next year, the so-called French Commune uprising occurred. This Paris-based civil war ended France's second Republic, and resulted in 30,000 additional French deaths, and the creation of the Third Republic.

Now, contrast the French Commune uprising with the "internal revolution" that occurred in America following its only lost war in history, the Vietnam War. The American "internal revolution" forced the resignation of President Richard Nixon. This resignation contrasts sharply with the French Commune rebellion because it caused NO deaths.

This difference shows how clearly mid-cycle wars differ from crisis wars. The violence that killed 30,000 people in France served exactly the same purpose as Nixon's nonviolent resignation: by means of scapegoating, the depression of defeat is turned into the euphoria of victory.

Somewhat the same situation holds for World War I - a mid-cycle war for Germany that we'll be discussing further below. There was a change in government — the old Second Reich was replaced by a new Weimar Republic, initially led by president Friedrich Ebert.

"No enemy has defeated you," said Ebert to the returning troops after they had been ordered to capitulate. "Only when the enemy's superiority in numbers and resources became suffocating did you relinquish the fight."

This example of scapegoating provides a convenient segue to a greater discussion of whether World War I was a crisis war for Germany.

Why wasn't World War I a Crisis War for Germany?

Germany's amazing capitulation in World War I is only one of the many indications that World War I wasn't a crisis war for Germany, as it wasn't for America.

This is one of the most common questions I hear: Aren't you calling World War II a crisis war, but not World War I, just to make Generational Dynamics work?

But in fact when you drill down into the actual history of what happened in America and Germany in WW I, you find that there was so little motivation on all sides to fight that war, it's a wonder that The Great War was fought at all.

First, however, the question of whether World War I was a crisis war is a meaningless question. By the Principle of Localization, it only makes sense to ask that question for a particular local region or nation.

There is no question that World War I was a crisis war for Eastern Europe (while World War II was a crisis war for Western Europe).

- World War I was a crisis war for the Balkans, leading to the creation of the Kingdom of Yugoslavia in 1918.

- World War I was a crisis war for Turkey, leading to the destruction of the Ottoman Empire.

- World War I was a crisis war for Russia, with an internal revolution in the form of a Bolshevik (Communist) Revolution and a large violent civil war.

It's worth pointing out, in passing, that all of these wars were revisited 80 years later, in the 1990s, with the collapse of the Soviet Union, wars in Bosnia and Kosovo, the civil war in Turkey, and other regional wars.

World War I did not result in any such dramatic changes in Western Europe. There was a scapegoating change of government in Germany, but nothing like the massive structural changes in Russia or Turkey.

In chapter 2 (p. 44), we discussed why World War I was not a crisis war for America. America remained neutral for many years, despite repeated German terrorist attacks on Americans, there was a powerful pacifist (anti-war) movement that included high government officials, and it resulted in no important transformations in America.

But in fact, World War I was not even a crisis war for Germany.

First, there's the issue of advance preparation. In Germany's previous crisis period, the Wars of German Unification (1860-71), as well as in World War II (1938-45) in the following crisis period, Germany prepared for war well in advance, and initiated war because of real animus towards its enemies. But in World War I, Germany did little advance preparation, and was pulled into the war because of a long-standing treaty with Austria.

Germany never really pursued the war against France with the bloodthirsty zeal it did in 1870 and 1939. The war began in 1914, and was a stalemate for years. During the Christmas season of 1914, the German high command shipped thousands of Christmas trees to the front lines, cutting into its ammunition shipments♦. This led to a widely publicized Christmas truce between the British and German troops, where soldiers and officers on both sides all got together and sang Christmas carols♦.

To put this kind of event in perspective, shortly after the attacks of 9/11/2001, American invaded Afghanistan to destroy the al-Qaeda forces. Can you imagine American soldiers and al-Qaeda forces getting together on the battlefield in December 2001, to participate in some holiday festivities?

It's this very difference in attitude and intensity that distinguishes mid-cycle wars from crisis wars.

In fact, this lack of intensity characterizes Germany's entire campaign.

In August 1914, Germany planned a quick, total victory over France, requiring only six weeks — too quick for the British troops to be deployed to stop the advance into France. The plan went fantastically well for about two weeks — but then the Germans sent two corps of soldiers to the eastern front to fight the Russians. Without those soldiers, Germany's rapid sweep was halted by the French long enough to give the British troops time to reinforce the French. Both the German and French sides dug themselves into static trenches. It was from those positions that the Christmas truce took place. The stalemate continued with millions of each side's troops killed in battle, until 1917, when America entered the war.

Much has been written about the defeat of Germany once America entered the war, but little about the extraordinary circumstances of that defeat.

When France capitulated to Germany in the Franco-Prussian war of 1870, Germany was deep into French territory. In 1945, Hitler committed suicide when the Allies were practically in Berlin. In crisis wars, when the people of a country believe that their very existence is at stake, capitulation does not come easily.

But when Germany capitulated on November 11, 1918, German troops were still deep within Belgian and French territory. Writing in 1931, Winston Churchill said that if Germany had continued to fight, they would have been capable of inflicting two million more casualties upon the enemy*. Churchill added that the Allies would not have put Germany to the test: simply by fighting on a little longer, the Allies would have negotiated a peace with no reparations, on terms far more favorable to Germany than actually occurred in the peace dictated by the Allies.

> *If Germany hadn't capitulated in 1918, the terms of surrender would have been far more favorable to them*

Actually, the seeds of capitulation had been planted three months earlier, on August 8, when the German high command realized that too much time had passed, and the absolute military triumph over France could no longer be achieved*. From that time, the Germans lost most of whatever remaining spirit they had, and completely lost momentum. They called for cease-fire on October 4, expecting the German army and people to rise up and demand victory, and planning to launch a new attack with replenished strength, once the cease-fire had expired.

However, the mood in Germany turned firmly against renewing hostilities, in both the army and the people. By the end of October, it was apparent to the high command that it was too late. Writing after the war, Prince Max von Baden of the high command concluded*, "The masses would likely have risen, but not against the enemy. Instead, they would have attacked the war itself and the 'military oppressors' and 'monarchic aristocrats,' on whose behalf, in their opinion, it had been waged."

I've written about these events at length to illustrate the difference between mid-cycle wars and crisis wars. Try to imagine Hitler losing momentum in this way in World War II, or imagine Britain, America or Japan losing momentum and capitulating unnecessarily in World War II. It's almost impossible to imagine it, since World War II was a crisis war, while World War I was not.

Indeed, there's only one major war in the lifetime of most readers where events proceeded in any way similarly to the actions of the Germans in World War I: the actions of America in Vietnam in the 1970s.

America was forced repeatedly by its own antiwar movement to accept various Christmas truces during the Vietnam War; the Vietnamese never honored such truces, since that was a crisis war for them and a mid-cycle war for us. American soldiers were court-martialed because of the unnecessary killing of civilians during the Vietnam War, and yet America purposely killed civilians in World War II by carpet bombing Dresden, and by nuclear attacks on Japan. Finally, America withdrew from Vietnam and capitulated, when it clearly had the power to win that war if it had wanted to.

A different view of World War I

There's another way of looking at the two World Wars that may be a better explanation. The Thirty Years War (1618-48) lasted thirty years because it was actually a series of wars involving countries on different timelines, particularly Germany and France. The Thirty Years war and subsequent War of Spanish Succession (1701-14) put Germany and France on the same timeline.

Similarly, the two World Wars could be referred to as a single 31-year war (1914-45) involving two regions (West and East Europe) on different timelines. That war, and the subsequent "clash of civilizations" will put these regions on the same timeline.

Chapter 5 — Tolstoy's *War and Peace*

> *In historic events, the so-called great men are labels giving names to events, and like labels they have but the smallest connection with the event itself.*
>
> — Lev Tolstoy, in *War and Peace*

Years ago, when I first read Lev Tolstoy's *War and Peace*, Napoleon's invasion of Russia made no sense to me whatsoever. It was the most bizarre war description I had ever seen. The French under Napoleon invaded Russia, and headed for Moscow. Instead of defending Moscow, the Russians fled, made no attempt to defend the city, and just allowed the French to walk in and take it. Nothing about this seemed credible to me when I read it.

It's only now, after developing Generational Dynamics, that the war is explained, and explained fully: It was a crisis war for Napoleon's France, but a mid-cycle war for Russia.

> *Napoleon's invasion of Russia was the most bizarre war description I had ever seen*

If you didn't carefully read the material in chapter 4 (p. 86) about Germany's weak prosecution of World War I, then go back and reread it now, and get a feeling for what happened.

Now, read the excerpts in this chapter of Tolstoy's account of France's 1812 attack on Russia, and get a feeling for that war. Not only is Tolstoy's description fascinating, but it also provides tremendous additional insight and understanding into the theoretical aspects of Generational Dynamics, since it's a narrative description of the difference between a crisis war and a mid-cycle war.

Although the French fought energetically, the Russians did not. It was remarkable though that capturing Moscow proved to be Napoleon's undoing, however, since his army gorged itself on the city, and lost all discipline. Napoleon had to retreat, thus proving that it's possible for a low-energy strategy to beat a high-energy strategy.

The main purpose of this chapter is to further illustrate the generational methodology by analyzing this invasion through Lev Tolstoy's novel, *War and Peace*.

The quotation at the beginning of this chapter encapsulates one of the most important points of this book: That major events, like wars, are consequences of history, not consequences of actions by individual politicians. The Napoleonic wars that engulfed Europe at that time would have occurred with or without Napoleon.

Lev Tolstoy's 1868 epic historical novel *War and Peace* is considered by many to be the greatest novel of all time. There are hundreds of named characters, and Tolstoy shows their interrelations and how wartime affects and interferes with their lives. Characters who start out as carefree youth grow in responsibility and maturity as they suffer the horrors of war. In the end, love and marriage seem to represent man's redemption.

By the time of France's 1812 invasion of Russia, Napoleon had already conquered most of Europe and made it part of France's empire, and now he wanted to annex Russia. Tolstoy tells how he succeeded in conquering Moscow, but his conquest led to the destruction of his own army, and eventually his defeat at Waterloo.

But that's not all. Tolstoy's philosophy of history and war and peace is scattered throughout the book. Furthermore, unlike many historians, Tolstoy understood mathematics and science, and used that understanding to show how great events in history by momentum rather than by politicians or generals, even a general as powerful as Napoleon.

Tolstoy's brilliant study of Napoleon's campaign gives us a sounding board to elucidate further aspects of the generational methodology for analyzing history.

Figure 18 Napoleon Bonaparte

In particular, where Tolstoy identifies the momentum that drove the campaign, he doesn't address the question of where the momentum comes from. We'll show that it comes from a war that was a crisis war for one side (Napoleon's) and a mid-cycle war for the other side.

In doing so, we'll address the issue of the difference between generationally driven events and chaotically driven events.

Why did Napoleon invade Russia?

The particular question of why Napoleon invaded Russia at all is subsumed under the more general question of why any nation has to invade *any* other nation. It's clear that Tolstoy is confused about both the particular and the general questions, and despairs at trying to find answers.

Tolstoy was born in 1825, and fought in the Crimean War in the 1850s, so he well knew the horrors of war. Look at how he describes Napoleon's buildup of forces on the Russian border, in anticipation of the war that began on June 12, 1812. This is clearly an anti-war statement:

> From the close of the year 1811 intensified arming and concentrating of the forces of Western Europe began, and in 1812 these forces - millions of men, reckoning those transporting and feeding the army - moved from the west eastwards to the Russian frontier, toward which since 1811 Russian forces had been similarly drawn. On the twelfth of June, 1812, the forces of Western Europe crossed the Russian frontier and war began, that is, an event took place opposed to human reason and to human nature. Millions of men perpetrated against one another such innumerable crimes, frauds, treacheries, thefts, forgeries, issues of false money, burglaries, incendiarisms, and murders as in whole centuries are not recorded in the annals of all the law courts of the world, but which those who committed them did not at the time regard as being crimes.

Like many people, Tolstoy felt that war was senseless, and he could not understand why Napoleon would even want to invade.

Many people consider a war to be an almost accidental thing — someone gets pissed off at someone and decides to start a war. The book you're reading refutes that idea, but Tolstoy seemed to believe it thoroughly.

In the following paragraph, Tolstoy makes the point that different parties see completely different causes for Napoleon's invasion. You don't have to understand the meaning of each of the causes mentioned by Tolstoy to get the thrust of his point. Read his description of the various causes of the war without worrying about the specific names and events, and just feel his frustration in describing the causes:

> It naturally seemed to Napoleon that the war was caused by England's intrigues (as in fact he said on the island of St. Helena). It naturally seemed to members of the English Parliament

that the cause of the war was Napoleon's ambition; to the Duke of Oldenburg, that the cause of the war was the violence done to him; to businessmen that the cause of the war was the Continental System which was ruining Europe; to the generals and old soldiers that the chief reason for the war was the necessity of giving them employment; to the legitimists of that day that it was the need of re-establishing *les bons principes*, and to the diplomatists of that time that it all resulted from the fact that the alliance between Russia and Austria in 1809 had not been sufficiently well concealed from Napoleon, and from the awkward wording of Memorandum No. 178.

It is natural that these and a countless and infinite quantity of other reasons, the number depending on the endless diversity of points of view, presented themselves to the men of that day; but to us, to posterity who view the thing that happened in all its magnitude and perceive its plain and terrible meaning, these causes seem insufficient.

To us it is incomprehensible that millions of Christian men killed and tortured each other either because Napoleon was ambitious or Alexander was firm, or because England's policy was astute or the Duke of Oldenburg wronged. We cannot grasp what connection such circumstances have with the actual fact of slaughter and violence: why because the Duke was wronged, thousands of men from the other side of Europe killed and ruined the people of Smolensk and Moscow and were killed by them.

Was Napoleon's attack really "incomprehensible," as Tolstoy claims?

A war does not occur because of a few random provocations. Various attacks, assassinations, and so forth occur all the time. Usually these provocations are contained. But a "pressure cooker" atmosphere builds up over decades, and finally the pressure cooker explodes into war — in roughly 80-year cycles.

Writing the epic historical novel *War and Peace*, you would think that it would have occurred to Tolstoy to relate Napoleon's campaigns to historical campaigns of the past, but he evidently didn't.

France and England had been at war almost continuously for centuries. Many of these were distant wars over colonies, especially in America and India, but the most recent crisis war was the War of Spanish Succession that took place in 1701-1714, as described in chapter 8 (p. 172). That war, which engulfed all of Europe, ended with a treaty that the statesmen of the time signed because they wanted to avoid for as long as possible another conflict such as the one that had just ended.

The borders established by that treaty held until the French Revolution began in 1789, and that previous war was re-fought with a vengeance when Napoleon came to power in 1799.

Now, understanding that background, let's go back to Tolstoy's list of causes given above, and see why the invasion of Russia *had* to occur:

- **To members of the English Parliament that the cause of the war was Napoleon's ambition.** This is the first of Tolstoy's causes, and it raises a question similar to whether Hitler "caused" World War II: Did Napoleon "cause" the Napoleonic wars?

    Actually, the answer to that is quite easy. Napoleon took power in 1799, but the French Revolution was engulfing all of Europe by 1792, when a coalition of Austria, Prussia, Great Britain, Spain, Russia, Germany and other countries was already forming to lead a counter-revolution.

    > *To the generals and old soldiers the chief reason for the war was the necessity of giving them employment*

    So, a major war would have engulfed Europe at that time even if there had been no Napoleon. The name "Napoleonic Wars" wouldn't have been used, of course (duh!), but the war would have been just as devastating.

- **To businessmen that the cause of the war was the Continental System which was ruining Europe.** The Continental System was a blockade of England that Napoleon imposed on Europe in 1806. In return, England imposed a blockade of its own. (Incidentally, it's the latter blockade that caused America to declare war on England, leading to the American War of 1812.)

    Major financial crises are almost always related to crisis wars; indeed, the French Revolution was triggered by the bankruptcy of the French monarchy. Financial crises cause people to look for people to blame; they cause people to seek justice and retribution.

Napoleon's invasion was a mid-cycle war for Russia (as we'll see), and they wanted no war. Russia's response to the blockade was to ignore it, and to continue trading with England. That was an act of war to the French.

However, the Continental System blockade was not the cause of the invasion of Russia. It was part of the fabric of the financial crisis surrounding the war.

- **To the generals and old soldiers that the chief reason for the war was the necessity of giving them employment.** This is another way that a financial crisis is related to a crisis war. When men have no jobs and no way to feed themselves and their families, then they'll go to war to earn money for their families, and their wives will send them rather than see the children starve.

Tolstoy treats all these and other causes as independent random occurrences, as he explains in the following paragraph:

> The people of the west moved eastwards to slay their fellow men, and by the law of coincidence thousands of minute causes fitted in and coordinated to produce that movement and war: reproaches for the nonobservance of the Continental System, ... the French Emperor's love and habit of war coinciding with his people's inclinations, allurement by the grandeur of the preparations, and the expenditure on those preparations and the need of obtaining advantages to compensate for that expenditure, the intoxicating honors he received in Dresden, the diplomatic negotiations which, in the opinion of contemporaries, were carried on with a sincere desire to attain peace, but which only wounded the self-love of both sides, and millions and millions of other causes that adapted themselves to the event that was happening or coincided with it.

It's remarkable that Tolstoy presents these events as if they are all independent occurrences, with no mutual causality except, we would assume, only in ways so obvious that they don't need to be acknowledged.

However, let's focus on one particular phrase in the above paragraph:

> *the French Emperor's love and habit of war coinciding with his people's inclinations*

What does Tolstoy mean by this extraordinary statement? He seems to say that Napoleon wanted the war, and the people wanted the war. But why?

He explains this further in the next paragraph, which also refers to Tsar Alexander of Russia:

> The actions of Napoleon and Alexander, on whose words the event seemed to hang, were as little voluntary as the actions of any soldier who was drawn into the campaign by lot or by conscription. This could not be otherwise, for in order that the will of Napoleon and Alexander (on whom the event seemed to depend) should be carried out, the concurrence of innumerable circumstances was needed without any one of which the event could not have taken place. It was necessary that millions of men in whose hands lay the real power - the soldiers who fired, or transported provisions and guns - should consent to carry out the will of these weak individuals, and should have been induced to do so by an infinite number of diverse and complex causes.
>
> We are forced to fall back on fatalism as an explanation of irrational events (that is to say, events the reasonableness of which we do not understand). The more we try to explain such events in history reasonably, the more unreasonable and incomprehensible do they become to us.

This is really a remarkable conclusion. He argues that these great events do not occur because Napoleon or Alexander made them happen; he says that they occur because millions of people want them to occur. But then he throws up his hands in despair, because he can't understand why those millions of people suddenly, with one voice, say that they want to have a war.

Well, maybe it isn't so remarkable. Tolstoy is just stating his version of today's observation: "Everything changed on 9/11." Just as American society changed almost as one on 9/11, Tolstoy is noticing that everything changed after the French Revolution.

What Tolstoy didn't understand was the connection to the War of Spanish Succession, and how a generational change had occurred in 1789, causing those millions of soldier to be willing to take up weapons and go to war.

The Russian Background

Russia was on a different timeline than France. Russia's last crisis war occurred with the massive internal Pugachev Rebellion and wars with the Ottoman Empire in the 1770s, under Tsar Catherine the Great.

So by 1812, Russians were tired of war, and were enjoying life. They were actually in an "awakening" period, during which arts and spiritual matters typically flourish. Ironically, the elite Russian classes, including the families described by Tolstoy, loved French culture, and the French language was widely spoken.

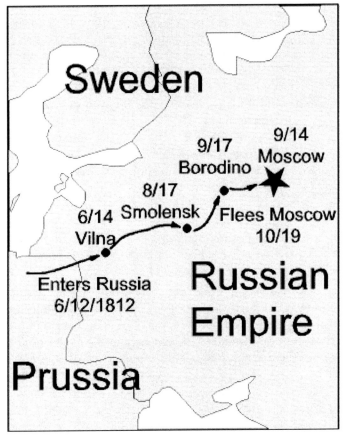

Figure 19 Stages in Napoleon's invasion of Russia in 1812*.

They watched Napoleon's march across Europe with alarm, but even as hundreds of thousands of Napoleon's troops massed on the Russian border, they did nothing about it. Here's how Alexander passed the time before the June 12 invasion:

> The Emperor of Russia had, meanwhile, been in Vilna for more than a month, reviewing troops and holding maneuvers. Nothing was ready for the war that everyone expected and to prepare for which the Emperor had come from Petersburg. There was no general plan of action. The vacillation between the various plans that were proposed had even increased after the Emperor had been at headquarters for a month. Each of the three armies had its own commander in chief, but there was no supreme commander of all the forces, and the Emperor did not assume that responsibility himself.
>
> The longer the Emperor remained in Vilna the less did everybody - tired of waiting - prepare for the war. All the efforts of those who surrounded the sovereign seemed directed merely to making him spend his time pleasantly and forget that war was impending.

The preceding paragraphs well illustrate the "no energy" concept of a mid-cycle war.

How could Alexander, knowing that an army of hundreds of thousands of men was heading in his direction, not make preparations for war? The answer is that he lived through the previous crisis war, and he knew that whatever would happen would happen. He knew that some French soldiers would be killed, and some Russian soldiers would be killed. He probably felt that no amount of preparation would, in the end, make much difference. This is an attitude that one can come by only through experiencing a crisis war, and that's why a new crisis war doesn't occur until the generation that experienced the last crisis war leaves the scene.

As Tolstoy pointed out, this indecision was not just on Alexander's part. Alexander was reflecting the feeling of all his soldiers and advisers, most of whom had some personal memory of the last crisis wars. They knew that something was coming; they didn't know exactly what it was, but they knew they would have to endure it no matter what they did, and eventually it would be over.

When Napoleon's attack began, Alexander tried a fairly typical mid-cycle stratagem to compromise and contain the situation. He sent a courier to Napoleon with the following letter. As before, read this letter to get an emotional sense of it, without worrying about the specific names and incidents it refers to:

> Sir, my brother,

> Yesterday I learned that, despite the loyalty which I have kept my engagements with Your Majesty, your troops have crossed the Russian frontier, and I have this moment received from Petersburg a note, in which Count Lauriston informs me, as a reason for this aggression, that Your Majesty has considered yourself to be in a state of war with me from the time Prince Kuragin asked for his passports. The reasons on which the Duc de Bassano based his refusal to deliver them to him would never have led me to suppose that that could serve as a pretext for aggression. In fact, the ambassador, as he himself has declared, was never authorized to make that demand, and as soon as I was informed of it I let him know how much I disapproved of it and ordered him to remain at his post. If Your Majesty does not intend to shed the blood of our peoples for such a misunderstanding, and consents to withdraw your troops from Russian territory, I will regard what has passed as not having occurred and an understanding between us will be possible. In the contrary case, Your Majesty, I shall see myself forced to repel an attack that nothing on my part has provoked. It still depends on Your Majesty to preserve humanity from the calamity of another war. I am, etc.,
>
> (signed) Alexander

Sounds a little desperate, doesn't it? Actually, it conveys a great deal of sadness. Alexander wants no war. He's seen enough war in his lifetime.

Napoleon's advance to Moscow

Napoleon angrily rejected Alexander's plea, and blamed Alexander for starting the war. The reasons that Napoleon gave to blame Alexander are unimportant: if you're determined to go to war, then you can always find a reason to do so.

It was about 550 miles from the Russian border to Moscow. The French crossed the Russian border on June 12, and traveled rapidly towards Moscow, receiving no resistance for a long time.

It was not until mid-August that Alexander was able to pull his army together enough to make a stand at Smolensk. Even there, the Russians kept arguing with one another and retreating as the French advanced.

Tolstoy makes the battle at Smolensk almost to be an accident — the French stumbled into a Russian division that hadn't retreated quickly enough. Read the following paragraphs, and notice that Tolstoy is now referring to the Russians as "we":

> While disputes and intrigues were going on about the future field of battle, and while we were looking for the French - having lost touch with them - the French stumbled upon Neverovski's division and reached the walls of Smolensk.
>
> It was necessary to fight an unexpected battle at Smolensk to save our lines of communication. The battle was fought and thousands were killed on both sides.
>
> Smolensk was abandoned contrary to the wishes of the Emperor and of the whole people. But Smolensk was burned by its own inhabitants — who had been misled by their governor. And these ruined inhabitants, setting an example to other Russians, went to Moscow thinking only of their own losses but kindling hatred of the foe. Napoleon advanced farther and we retired, thus arriving at the very result that caused his destruction.

What is it that would make the inhabitants of a city burn down the city and flee? Tolstoy doesn't answer that question, but he says that that act brought about the destruction of the French army.

The shocking loss of Smolensk brought bitter recriminations within the Russian army, and for the first time the Russians gathered enough energy to make a stand. They defeated the French, who were getting complacent after their easy victory at Borodino.

Momentum Wars: The French reach Moscow

The battle at Borodino destroyed a huge part of the French army, and in retrospect, it's clear that the French should have realized at that point that the conquest of Russia was impossible, and that they should have retreated.

Russia might have gone on to finish off Napoleon's army at that point, as Tolstoy describes:

> On the evening of the twenty-sixth of August, Kutuzov and the whole Russian army were convinced that the battle of Borodino was a victory. Kutuzov reported so to the Emperor. He gave orders to prepare for a fresh conflict to finish the enemy

and did this not to deceive anyone, but because he knew that the enemy was beaten, as everyone who had taken part in the battle knew it.

But all that evening and next day reports came in one after another of unheard-of losses, of the loss of half the army, and a fresh battle proved physically impossible.

And so, the Russians had to retreat again, leaving the road from Borodino to Moscow free for the French to travel unchallenged.

Tolstoy is now at his best as he describes how the French invasion was now almost an elemental force of nature, incapable of stopping itself. In the following description, keep in mind that the French army contained conscripts from several European nations which Napoleon had previous conquered. Now, read Tolstoy's explanation of why the attack on Moscow was inevitable:

> The forces of a dozen European nations burst into Russia. The Russian army and people avoided a collision till Smolensk was reached, and again from Smolensk to Borodino. The French army pushed on to Moscow, its goal and its impetus ever increasing as it neared its aim, just as the velocity of a falling body increases as it approaches the earth. Behind it were seven hundred miles of hunger-stricken, hostile country; ahead were a few dozen miles separating it from its goal. Every soldier in Napoleon's army felt this and the invasion moved on by its own momentum.
>
> The more the Russian army retreated the more fiercely a spirit of hatred of the enemy flared up, and while it retreated the army increased and consolidated. At Borodino, a collision took place. Neither army was broken up, but the Russian army retreated immediately after the collision as inevitably as a ball recoils after colliding with another having a greater momentum, and with equal inevitability the ball of invasion that had advanced with such momentum rolled on for some distance, though the collision had deprived it of all its force.
>
> It was impossible to give battle before information had been collected, the wounded gathered in, the supplies of ammunition

What is it that would make the inhabitants of a city burn down the city and flee?

replenished, the slain reckoned up, new officers appointed to replace those who had been killed, and before the men had had food and sleep. And meanwhile, the very next morning after the battle, the French army advanced of itself upon the Russians, carried forward by the force of its own momentum now seemingly increased in inverse proportion to the square of the distance from its aim. [Russian General] Kutuzov's wish was to attack next day, and the whole army desired to do so. But to make an attack the wish to do so is not sufficient, there must also be a possibility of doing it, and that possibility did not exist. It was impossible not to retreat a day's march, and then in the same way it was impossible not to retreat another and a third day's march, and at last, on the first of September when the army drew near Moscow - despite the strength of the feeling that had arisen in all ranks - the force of circumstances compelled it to retire beyond Moscow. And the troops retired one more, last, day's march, and abandoned Moscow to the enemy.

In this remarkable description, Tolstoy describes how both the French and Russian armies were traveling along a preordained path that neither side was any longer able to stop.

It's this description of the French army as a "ball of invasion" with so much momentum that it can't stop itself that has led me to identify certain types of battles or mid-cycle wars as "momentum battles" or "momentum wars."

In mid-cycle, societies are averse to war, and usually only go to war because of an attack on them or on allies.

However, as described in chapter 2, certain wars, such as our own Korean and Vietnam wars, are pursued even after the crisis war has ended, and for the same reasons that the crisis war was fought in the first place.

In Napoleon's case, following Tolstoy's description, the French should have retreated after their defeat at Borodino, but didn't because of their momentum as a "ball of invasion."

Tolstoy builds on this idea in explaining what happened at the battle at Borodino. He ridicules historians who claim that Napoleon might have won that battle and changed the course of history if he hadn't had a cold that day. Tolstoy rejects any such concept, believing as I do that many of these battles and wars go on because of their own unstoppable momentum. Read Tolstoy's stark description of how the French army, driven by cries of "Long

Live the Emperor [Napoleon]," move forward to their own destruction, much like the popular perception of lemmings following one another off a cliff:

> Many historians say that the French did not win the battle of Borodino because Napoleon had a cold, and that if he had not had a cold the orders he gave before and during the battle would have been still more full of genius and Russia would have been lost and the face of the world have been changed. To historians who believe that Russia was shaped by the will of one man - Peter the Great - and that France from a republic became an empire and French armies went to Russia at the will of one man - Napoleon - to say that Russia remained a power because Napoleon had a bad cold on the twenty-fourth of August may seem logical and convincing.
>
> If it had depended on Napoleon's will to fight or not to fight the battle of Borodino, and if this or that other arrangement depended on his will, then evidently a cold affecting the manifestation of his will might have saved Russia, and consequently the valet who omitted to bring Napoleon his waterproof boots on the twenty-fourth would have been the savior of Russia. Along that line of thought such a deduction is indubitable, as indubitable as the deduction Voltaire made in jest (without knowing what he was jesting at) when he saw that the Massacre of St. Bartholomew was due to Charles IX's stomach being deranged. But to men who do not admit that Russia was formed by the will of one man, Peter I, or that the French Empire was formed and the war with Russia begun by the will of one man, Napoleon, that argument seems not merely untrue and irrational, but contrary to all human reality. To the question of what causes historic events another answer presents itself, namely, that the course of human events is predetermined from on high - depends on the coincidence of the wills of all who take part in the events, and that a Napoleon's influence on the course of these events is purely external and fictitious.
>
> Strange as at first glance it may seem to suppose that the Massacre of St. Bartholomew was not due to Charles IX's will, though he gave the order for it and thought it was done as a result of that order; and strange as it may seem to suppose that the slaughter of eighty thousand men at Borodino was not due to Napoleon's will, though he ordered the commencement and conduct of the battle and thought it was done because he or-

dered it; strange as these suppositions appear, yet human dignity - which tells me that each of us is, if not more at least not less a man than the great Napoleon - demands the acceptance of that solution of the question, and historic investigation abundantly confirms it.

At the battle of Borodino, Napoleon shot at no one and killed no one. That was all done by the soldiers. Therefore, it was not he who killed people.

The French soldiers went to kill and be killed at the battle of Borodino, not because of Napoleon's orders but by their own volition. The whole army - French, Italian, German, Polish, and Dutch - hungry, ragged, and weary of the campaign, felt at the sight of an army blocking their road to Moscow that the wine was drawn and must be drunk. Had Napoleon then forbidden them to fight the Russians, they would have killed him and have proceeded to fight the Russians because it was inevitable.

> *Both the French and Russian armies were on a preordained path that neither side was able to stop*

When they heard Napoleon's proclamation offering them, as compensation for mutilation and death, the words of posterity about their having been in the battle before Moscow, they cried "*Vive l'Empereur!*" just as they had cried "*Vive l'Empereur!*" at the sight of the portrait of the boy piercing the terrestrial globe with a toy stick, and just as they would have cried "*Vive l'Empereur!*" at any nonsense that might be told them. There was nothing left for them to do but cry "*Vive l'Empereur!*" and go to fight, in order to get food and rest as conquerors in Moscow. So it was not because of Napoleon's commands that they killed their fellow men.

And it was not Napoleon who directed the course of the battle, for none of his orders was executed and during the battle, he did not know what was going on before him. So the way in which these people killed one another was not decided by Napoleon's will but occurred independently of him, in accord with the will of hundreds of thousands of people who took part in the common action. It only seemed to Napoleon that it all took place by his will. And so the question whether he had or had not a cold has no more historic interest than the cold of the least of the transport soldiers.

Moreover, the assertion made by various writers that his cold was the cause of his dispositions not being as well planned as on former occasions, and of his orders during the battle not being as good as previously, is quite baseless, which again shows that Napoleon's cold on the twenty-sixth of August was unimportant.

The dispositions cited above are not at all worse, but are even better, than previous dispositions by which he had won victories. His pseudo-orders during the battle were also no worse than formerly, but much the same as usual. These dispositions and orders only seem worse than previous ones because the battle of Borodino was the first Napoleon did not win. The profoundest and most excellent dispositions and orders seem very bad, and every learned militarist criticizes them with looks of importance, when they relate to a battle that has been lost, and the very worst dispositions and orders seem very good, and serious people fill whole volumes to demonstrate their merits, when they relate to a battle that has been won.

The dispositions drawn up by Weyrother for the battle of Austerlitz were a model of perfection for that kind of composition, but still they were criticized - criticized for their very perfection, for their excessive minuteness.

Napoleon at the battle of Borodino fulfilled his office as representative of authority as well as, and even better than, at other battles. He did nothing harmful to the progress of the battle; he inclined to the most reasonable opinions, he made no confusion, did not contradict himself, did not get frightened or run away from the field of battle, but with his great tact and military experience carried out his role of appearing to command, calmly and with dignity.

(Incidentally, St. Bartholomew's Massacre, mentioned in the previous paragraphs, is discussed in this book in chapter 8, page 168.)

CHAPTER 5 — TOLSTOY'S WAR AND PEACE

The Council of War

At what point was the destruction of the French army in Moscow preordained?

We might identify two other participants from Tolstoy's work: The Russian army that didn't want to fight the French army, but did; and the ordinary Russian citizens that didn't want to burn down their cities and desert them, but did. All of their actions were driven by the French invasion.

It's pretty clear, as Tolstoy explains in detail, that the Moscow destruction was preordained as early as the battle of Smolensk. Was it preordained as early as 1789, when the French Revolution led to a war engulfing all of Europe that could not have ended without a French invasion of Russia? That's an interesting question for historians.

But let's now move on to the Napoleon's invasion of Moscow.

After the Russians inflicted enormous damage on the French at Borodino, and still had to retreat, leaving the way open to Moscow, the Russians convened a Council of War:

> The Council of War began to assemble at two in the afternoon in the better and roomier part of Andrew Savostyanov's hut. The men, women, and children of the large peasant family crowded into the back room across the passage. ... Round the peasant's deal table, on which lay maps, plans, pencils, and papers, so many people gathered that the orderlies brought in another bench and put it beside the table. ...
>
> They were all waiting for Bennigsen, who on the pretext of inspecting the position was finishing his savory dinner. They waited for him from four till six o'clock and did not begin their deliberations all that time talked in low tones of other matters.
>
> Only when Bennigsen had entered the hut did Kutuzov leave his corner and draw toward the table, but not near enough for the candles that had been placed there to light up his face.
>
> Bennigsen opened the council with the question: "Are we to abandon Russia's ancient and sacred capital without a struggle, or are we to defend it?" A prolonged and general silence followed. There was a frown on every face and only Kutuzov's angry grunts and occasional cough broke the silence. All eyes were gazing at him. ...

> "Russia's ancient and sacred capital!" he suddenly said, repeating Bennigsen's words in an angry voice and thereby drawing attention to the false note in them. "Allow me to tell you, your Excellency, that that question has no meaning for a Russian." (He lurched his heavy body forward.) "Such a question cannot be put; it is senseless! The question I have asked these gentlemen to meet to discuss is a military one. The question is that of saving Russia. Is it better to give up Moscow without a battle, or by accepting battle to risk losing the army as well as Moscow? That is the question on which I want your opinion," and he sank back in his chair.

After much discussion, including a proposal by Count Bennigsen, Kutuzov announces his decision to abandon Moscow:

> "Gentlemen," said Kutuzov, "I cannot approve of the count's plan. Moving troops in close proximity to an enemy is always dangerous, and military history supports that view...."
>
> Kutuzov heaved a deep sigh as if preparing to speak. They all looked at him.
>
> "Well, gentlemen, I see that it is I who will have to pay for the broken crockery," said he, and rising slowly, he moved to the table. "Gentlemen, I have heard your views. Some of you will not agree with me. But I," he paused, "by the authority entrusted to me by my Sovereign and country, order a retreat."

Later, after everyone leaves him alone in the meeting room:

> When he had dismissed the generals Kutuzov sat a long time with his elbows on the table, thinking always of the same terrible question: "When, when did the abandonment of Moscow become inevitable? When was that done which settled the matter? And who was to blame for it?"
>
> "I did not expect this," said he to his adjutant Schneider when the latter came in late that night. "I did not expect this! I did not think this would happen."
>
> "You should take some rest, your Serene Highness," replied Schneider.

His question, "When, when did the abandonment of Moscow become inevitable?" is still relevant today. In the war to come, there is certain to be some retreat or some humiliating defeat, and we'll be asking ourselves, "When, when did that become inevitable?"

Moscow and the Destruction of Napoleon's Army

When the French entered Moscow, they found that the city had been deserted. Napoleon's officers immediately recognized the potential disaster, and tried to stop it:

> Order after order was issued by the French commanders that day forbidding the men to disperse about the town, sternly forbidding any violence to the inhabitants or any looting, and announcing a roll call for that very evening. But despite all these measures the men, who had till then constituted an army, flowed all over the wealthy, deserted city with its comforts and plentiful supplies. As a hungry herd of cattle keeps well together when crossing a barren field, but gets out of hand and at once disperses uncontrollably as soon as it reaches rich pastures, so did the army disperse all over the wealthy city.

The orders did no good:

> No residents were left in Moscow, and the soldiers - like water percolating through sand - spread irresistibly through the city in all directions from the Kremlin into which they had first marched. The cavalry, on entering a merchant's house that had been abandoned and finding there stabling more than sufficient for their horses, went on, all the same, to the next house which seemed to them better. Many of them appropriated several houses, chalked their names on them, and quarreled and even fought with other companies for them. Before they had had time to secure quarters the soldiers ran out into the streets to see the city and, hearing that everything had been abandoned, rushed to places where valuables were to be had for the taking. The officers followed to check the soldiers and were involuntarily drawn into doing the same. In Carriage Row, carriages had been left in the shops, and generals flocked there to select caleches and coaches for themselves. The few inhabitants who had remained invited commanding officers to their houses, hoping thereby to secure themselves from being plundered. There were masses of wealth and there seemed no end to it. All around the quarters occupied by the French were other regions still unexplored and unoccupied where, they thought, yet greater riches might be found. And Moscow engulfed the army ever deeper and deeper. When water is spilled on dry ground both the dry ground and

the water disappear and mud results; and in the same way the entry of the famished army into the rich and deserted city resulted in fires and looting and the destruction of both the army and the wealthy city.

Why did Moscow burn? The French and the Russians blamed each other, but Tolstoy says it was unavoidable:

Figure 20 Moscow is burning

> In reality, however, it was not, and could not be, possible to explain the burning of Moscow by making any individual, or any group of people, responsible for it. Moscow was burned because it found itself in a position in which any town built of wood was bound to burn, quite apart from whether it had, or had not, a hundred and thirty inferior fire engines. Deserted Moscow had to burn as inevitably as a heap of shavings has to burn on which sparks continually fall for several days. A town built of wood, where scarcely a day passes without conflagrations when the house owners are in residence and a police force is present, cannot help burning when its inhabitants have left it and it is occupied by soldiers who smoke pipes, make campfires of the Senate chairs in the Senate Square, and cook themselves meals twice a day. In peacetime, it is only necessary to billet troops in the villages of any district and the number of fires in that district immediately increases. How much then must the probability of fire be increased in an abandoned, wooden town where foreign troops are quartered. "*Le patriotisme feroce de Rostopchine*" and the barbarity of the French were not to blame in the matter. Moscow was set on fire by the soldiers' pipes, kitchens, and campfires, and by the carelessness of enemy soldiers occupying houses they did not own. Even if there was any arson (which is very doubtful, for no one had any reason to burn the houses - in any case a troublesome and dangerous thing to do), arson cannot be regarded as the cause, for the same thing would have happened without any incendiarism.

However tempting it might be for the French to blame [Moscow Mayor] Rostopchin's ferocity and for Russians to blame the scoundrel Bonaparte, or later on to place an heroic torch in the hands of their own people, it is impossible not to see that there could be no such direct cause of the fire, for Moscow had to burn as every village, factory, or house must burn which is left by its owners and in which strangers are allowed to live and cook their porridge. Moscow was burned by its inhabitants, it is true, but by those who had abandoned it and not by those who remained in it. Moscow when occupied by the enemy did not remain intact like Berlin, Vienna, and other towns, simply because its inhabitants abandoned it and did not welcome the French with bread and salt, nor bring them the keys of the city.

The Russians remained in Moscow for five weeks, and were destroyed as a fighting force:

Though tattered, hungry, worn out, and reduced to a third of their original number, the French entered Moscow in good marching order. It was a weary and famished, but still a fighting and menacing army. But it remained an army only until its soldiers had dispersed into their different lodgings. As soon as the men of the various regiments began to disperse among the wealthy and deserted houses, the army was lost forever and there came into being something nondescript, neither citizens nor soldiers but what are known as marauders. When five weeks later these same men left Moscow, they no longer formed an army. They were a mob of marauders, each carrying a quantity of articles that seemed to him valuable or useful. The aim of each man when he left Moscow was no longer, as it had been, to conquer, but merely to keep what he had acquired. Like a monkey which puts its paw into the narrow neck of a jug, and having seized a handful of nuts will not open its fist for fear of losing what it holds, and therefore perishes, the French when they left Moscow had inevitably to perish because they carried their loot with them, yet to abandon what they had stolen was as impossible for them as it is for the monkey to open its paw and let go of its nuts. Ten minutes after each regiment had entered a Moscow district, not a soldier or officer was left. Men in military uniforms and Hessian boots could be seen through the windows, laughing and walking through the rooms. In cellars and storerooms similar men were busy among the provisions, and in the yards unlocking or breaking open coach house and stable doors, lighting fires in kitchens and kneading and baking bread with rolled-up sleeves, and cooking; or frightening, amusing, or caressing women and children. There were many such men in both the shops and houses - but there was no army.

During that five-week period, Napoleon twice sent messages to Russian command Kutuzov suggesting peace talks, and twice Kutuzov refused.

During the month that the French troops were pillaging in Moscow and the Russian troops were quietly encamped at Tarutino, a change had taken place in the relative strength of the two armies - both in spirit and in number - as a result of which the superiority had passed to the Russian side.

Kutuzov's strategy was simply to wait it out. Finally, the French tried to flee back in the direction they originally came from, but Kutuzov was prepared.

> *Why did Moscow burn? The French and the Russians blamed each other, but Tolstoy says it was unavoidable*

He adopted a strategy of "guerrilla warfare," where small groups of Russian soldiers attacked larger French groups. Tolstoy explains how this works mathematically:

In military affairs, the strength of an army is the product of its mass and some unknown x.

Military science, seeing in history innumerable instances of the fact that the size of any army does not coincide with its strength and that small detachments defeat larger ones, obscurely admits the existence of this unknown factor and tries to discover it - now in a geometric formation, now in the equipment employed, now, and most usually, in the genius of the commanders. But the assignment of these various meanings to the factor does not yield results which accord with the historic facts.

Yet, it is only necessary to abandon the false view (adopted to gratify the "heroes") of the efficacy of the directions issued in wartime by commanders, in order to find this unknown quantity.

> That unknown quantity is the spirit of the army, that is to say, the greater or lesser readiness to fight and face danger felt by all the men composing an army, quite independently of whether they are, or are not, fighting under the command of a genius, in two - or three-line formation, with cudgels or with rifles that repeat thirty times a minute. Men who want to fight will always put themselves in the most advantageous conditions for fighting. ... Ten men, battalions, or divisions, fighting fifteen men, battalions, or divisions, conquer - that is, kill or take captive - all the others, while themselves losing four, so that on the one side four and on the other fifteen were lost.

Tolstoy's "spirit of the army" bears a similarity to what I call "energy," and Tolstoy's point is that now the Russians had most of the energy, while the French had less.

> The French, retreating in 1812 - though according to tactics they should have separated into detachments to defend themselves - congregated into a mass because the spirit of the army had so fallen that only the mass held the army together. The Russians, on the contrary, ought according to tactics to have attacked in mass, but in fact, they split up into small units, because their spirit had so risen that separate individuals, without orders, dealt blows at the French without needing any compulsion to induce them to expose themselves to hardships and dangers.

The Russian guerrillas were merciless and destroyed the French army piece by piece. Before long, Napoleon abandoned the army and fled back to France to raise more troops. In 1815, Napoleon was defeated by the first Duke of Wellington, British General Arthur Wellesley, in the famous battle of Waterloo.

Napoleon and Hitler

I am not an expert on tragedy as an art form, but as a Greek, I know that a sense of tragedy is in my bones. Tragedy as an art form was invented in ancient Greece, and three of four great tragic artists of all time were Aeschylus, Sophocles and Euripides of ancient Greece, with the fourth being Shakespeare.

Many people misunderstand the deepest meanings of tragedy. If a child is killed in a random traffic accident, then it's a terrible event but it's not a tragedy in the classical sense, because of that randomness.

The essence of classical tragedy is that the tragic event is not random. The tragic event is inevitable: it *must* occur, and the reason it must occur is because of the nature, the personality, the very *character* of the protagonists. A true tragedy cannot be prevented, even by those who foresee it, because the forces bringing about the tragedy are too powerful for anyone to stop.

Tolstoy's description of Napoleon's invasion on Russia is stunning for the way it describes how the invasion proceeded like a Greek tragedy, with inevitable consequences that were preordained by the character of the protagonists.

However, there's one piece from Tolstoy's tragedy that needs to be addressed: How did the protagonists develop the character that preordained the result? Tolstoy admits almost total despair in trying to answer that question when he writes, "To us it is incomprehensible that millions of Christian men killed and tortured each other."

The missing piece is supplied by Generational Dynamics. The reason that these protagonists, millions of Christian men, killed and tortured each other to produce a preordained result is because the protagonists were in certain generations. The French protagonists were in the fourth generation following the War of Spanish Succession, and the Russian protagonists were in the second genera-tion following the Pugachev Rebellion in the reign of Catherine the Great.

There are just two more footnotes to the story.

The first footnote is to answer the question: How did Tolstoy have such a deep understanding of the emotions and feelings of the French and Russian soldiers? He wrote *War and Peace* in the 1860s, almost 50 years after the events he was describing. What was there in his personal experience that helped him to understand what happened?

The answer is that Tolstoy fought in another crisis war. He fought in the Russian army in Crimean War in the early 1850s (p. 206). He was part of a Russian "ball of invasion" that was humiliated in the Crimean War, just like the soldiers he described in the Napoleon's invasion of Russia.

The second footnote is a remarkable triple coincidence involving the events of 1812 occurring in two other wars, one earlier and one later.

In 1700, Russia under Peter the Great and Sweden fought the Great Northern War (page 205). Russia would have lost the war, but Sweden was distracted by its crisis war in Western Europe - the War of Spanish Succession (page 172). When Sweden came back to defeat the Russians, the Swedish army was swallowed up by Russia.

Incredibly, the same sort of thing happened in Russia's Great Patriotic War (World War II), when Hitler invaded Russia in 1942. World War II was crisis war for the Germans, but it was a mid-cycle war for the Russians — World War I had been their crisis war. Just like Napoleon, Hitler was swallowed by Russia.

So there were three wars: the Great Northern War, the Napoleonic War, and the Great Patriotic War. In each case, the war was a mid-cycle war for Russia, but was a crisis war for the other belligerent — Sweden, France, and Germany, respectively. And in each case, the army that invaded Russia was simply swallowed up by Russia.

Chapter 6 — Another Great Depression?

Once I built a railroad, made it run, made it race against time.
Once I built a railroad, now it's done. Brother can you spare a dime?
Once I built a tower way up to the sun, with bricks and mortar and lime.
Once I built a tower, now it's done. Brother can you spare a dime?
Once in khaki suits, gee we looked swell,
Full of that Yankee Doodley Dum
Half a million boots went slogging through hell,
I was the kid with the drum
Oh say don't you remember, you called me Al, It was Al all the time,
Say don't you remember, I'm your pal, Brother, can you spare a dime?
— 1930s Song, written by Edgar "Yip" Harburg

It shouldn't be surprising that a crisis period also goes along with some sort of financial crisis: after all, any society going through a major war is bound to suffer economic dislocation.

What *is* a surprise is that it seems to be that the prototypical case is like the Great Depression of the 1930s — a general business collapse resulting from the end of a credit bubble like the one in the 1920s.

Most surprising of all is that the evidence indicates that the Nasdaq crash in Spring 2000 is like the October, 1929, stock market crash, and was the beginning of a new 1930s-style Great Depression, to last throughout the decade of the 2000s.

Since I first made this prediction in spring 2002, the amount of skepticism I've heard was universal. Later, as this is being written early in 2003, there are many analysts concerned about America entering a new depression, but the analysts overwhelmingly believe that the Federal Reserve can prevent such a result by rapidly expanding the money supply. Unfortunately, the evidence I'm presenting here and in Chapter 11 shows that the prediction of a new Great Depression will not be affected by anything the Fed will do.

I'm presenting two different kinds of evidence. This chapter contains generational evidence, and Chapter 11 contains analytical evidence.

CHAPTER 6 — ANOTHER GREAT DEPRESSION?

Irrational Exuberance in the 1990s

Let's begin by using the Generational Dynamics methodology to explain why a new financial crisis is occurring about 80 years after the last one.

Ask any financial counselor who worked during the 60s, 70s, 80s or 90s, and he'll agree with the following: Anyone who grew up or lived through the Great Depression is "risk aversive." People who lived through the Depression were extremely cautious about spending money or making risky investments.

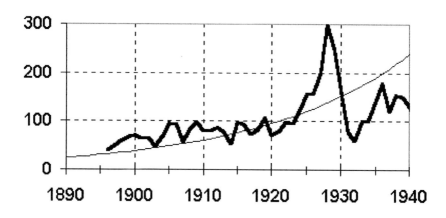

Figure 21 Dow Jones Industrial Average — 1896 to 1940

They had good reason to feel that way. Kids who grew up in the 1930s saw homelessness and starvation all around them. My own mother often told me how her father's business had gone bankrupt, and how she talked her way into a job to keep her family from starving — the job paid $8.00 per week!

Money had been flowing freely in the "roaring 20s." Everyone was rich, and everyone spent money freely. In the 30s, surrounded by starvation and homelessness, people were bitter not only at the government and businessmen, but also at themselves: they would be living comfortably if they had only saved the smallest amount of the money they had throwing around so freely a few years earlier.

So they learned to save money, never knowing when the next depression would come. My mother lived in fear of another depression in the years I

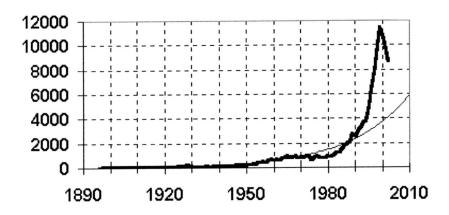

Figure 22 Dow Jones Industrial Average — 1896 to 2002

was growing, and when I started going to college, any bad financial news she heard on television would prompt her to ask me if this was a new depression.

People like my mother were so cautious that they were often mocked by younger people (perhaps including myself) and caricatured.

And yet, people in my mother's generation also worked in financial institutions, and carried the same caution and risk aversion in making institutional investments.

Those people, more than anyone, understood the significance of this graph. The heavy black line shows the ups and downs of the Dow Jones Industrial Average from 1896 to 1940. Something crazy happened, starting around 1922. People started borrowing money from one another and using it to leverage stock purchases, and then used those stock purchases as collateral to get more loans, and purchase more stocks.

The graph above shows how the value of stocks skyrocketed throughout the 1920s. The stock market bubble burst in 1929 when the interlocking credit structure collapsed. Over the next 4 years, stocks lost about 80% of their peak value.

The people who lived through those times advanced in their jobs over the years. By the 1980s, they were the senior people in banks, investment houses and other financial institutions. They brought an atmosphere of caution to the entire financial industry.

But in the 1990s, things started to change. Then, people who had grown up in the 1930s began to retire or die. Their senior positions in financial institutions were taken over by younger people with no personal memory of the depression, and no self-blame for not having saved a few bucks during the 20s.

Now look at the graph above to see what happened: a bubble very similar to the one that occurred in the 1920s.

Alan Greenspan, head of the Federal Reserve, recognized the situation very early. In 1995, Greenspan tried to warn the financial community by coining the phrase "irrational exuberance" to describe the new stock market bubble that was growing dangerously. No wonder he recognized the danger: Greenspan was born in 1926, and well remembered the last time it happened!

If we compare the 1990s in this graph to the 1920s in the preceding graph, we can see that if history repeats itself, then the DJIA will fall to about 3,000.

Investor hysteria

The above argument uses Generational Dynamics concepts to explain why there was a big stock market bubble in the 1990s, and why it's leading to a major stock market fall in the 2000s decade.

In order to make this understandable, this section attempts to provide an ordinary explanation in words why this is happening.

Take another look at the DJIA graph above. This graph shows very dramatically how huge the bubble was in the last half of the 1990s. Starting in 1995, stock values took off like a rocket. The bubble in the last half of the 1990s decade was so huge by historical standards that it'll take an enormous additional drop in stock prices to compensate for it.

First, it's worth pointing out that the DJIA surge between 1982 and 1994 was quite justified, based on what was happening in the American workplace. Personal computers started becoming popular in the early 1980s, and they enormously improved the productivity of the workforce.

Huge numbers of repetitive jobs were eliminated in the office and the factory. Huge masses of paper, that formerly had to be distributed and filed by administrative employees, now are handled with e-mail. Many factories have become a lot more automated and efficient using automation. Even many professional jobs, especially in various financial areas such as budgeting and financial planning, could be cut back because these jobs could be done much more quickly with the help of computerized spreadsheets and other tools. Even management jobs were eliminated, and corporate organization charts flattened, as the tedious repetitive and paperwork management tasks became computerized.

The productivity gains through 1994 or so were enormous, and explains the spurt in the DJIA up to that time. There were additional productivity gains after that time, but not the enormous ones we'd previously seen. If stock prices had leveled off at that time, then we'd be fine today. Instead, something went wrong.

It was perfectly obvious what was going on. Alan Greenspan called it "irrational exuberance," but other less diplomatic commentators called it "hysteria."

Craziness at this level had not occurred in decades — not since the 1920s, when a similar technology bubble occurred —

> *The DJIA surge between 1982-95 made sense; after that, something went terribly wrong*

but then the technology was the automobile, not computer software. Since then, financial executives remembered the Great Depression and the bubble that caused it, and held enough influence to keep it from happening again. However, most of those executives retired or died in the early 90s, and all the financial decision makers by 1995 were men and women with no personal memory of what happened the last time.

When the personal computer became available in 1981, there were some spectacular moneymaking successes in the 1980s, from such companies as Compaq Computer Corp. and Lotus Development Corp. When new World Wide Web technology became widely available around 1993, every investor in the world wanted to replicate the Compaq and Lotus experience with some internet-based product.

Investors poured every available investment dollar into venture capital for these companies, or into stocks for these companies. This continued even though almost none of these companies made money, unlike Compaq and

Lotus, which had made money almost immediately when they were launched.

This is an important point to remember when judging how insane this level of investment was. It was pretty well known by 1997 or so that the only internet-based companies making money were online services providing real-time financial data (like stock quotes) or online services providing pornography. Thousands of these companies were being funded by anxious investors, but not one single e-commerce company made money before the year 2000 Nasdaq crash.

How could this possibly happen? Well, consider the following reasoning.

The investing atmosphere of the 1990s led people to be overly optimistic, to the point of making both ordinary citizens and sophisticated investors make irrationally optimistic investments.

Now everyone, to my knowledge, agrees with the above paragraph. Well, what about the next paragraph:

Both ordinary people and sophisticated investors have learned their lessons, and are now becoming increasingly risk aversive (as people did in the 30s). As a result, they will be irrationally pessimistic about making investments.

If you believe, as most people do, that investors were irrationally optimistic in the 90s, why isn't it likely that they would react by becoming irrationally pessimistic today?

So if you're trying to understand the Generational Dynamics explanation in the preceding sections, then this section gives you two reasons to support it: (1) millions of businesses that haven't fully adopted computer technology are too inefficient; and (2) investors are likely to become irrationally pessimistic, just as they were irrationally optimistic in the 1990s.

Bubbles in American history

Now let's look at the issue of financial crisis in another. We're going to show that each of America's crisis war occurred after a bubble burst to create a financial crisis.

This is material that's hard to find in any history book. You'll find the stuff about the wars in American history books, and you'll find the stuff about the financial crises in financial history books. This is the only presentation I've seen that brings these two together.

First, a little background information. For those who are not familiar with finance, let's take a look at what a bubble is.

It's easy to understand what a "bubble" is when you look at a simple example. Suppose I have $1,000, and I put it in the bank. Suppose you borrow the $1,000 from the bank. Then I "have" $1,000 (in the bank), and you "have" $1,000 (in cash). So $1,000 has become $2,000. That's a simple example of a bubble, and there's no crisis unless I go to the bank and demand to withdraw my $1,000. Then either the bank gets the money back from you, or else goes bankrupt. If you've spent the money, then you might go bankrupt as well.

Even worse, you might have deposited the $1,000 in another bank, which then loaned that money to a third person. At that point, there are three people who each "have" $1,000, so $1,000 has become $3,000. This can continue for a long time, with a financial crisis occurring as soon as someone wants to make a withdrawal.

That's the essence of a bubble: People lending money to other people, who in turn lend it to other people, with those transactions occurring millions or billions of times. It's almost like a pyramid investment scheme, and it has to run out eventually. At some point, someone wants his money back. If something causes many people to want their money back at the same time, then there's a "panic," a financial crisis that causes many people to lose a lot of money.

The exact mechanism by which the money is loaned over and over again has varied with each American crisis, but there is always a big bubble that bursts before each crisis.

Tulipomania

By way of example, let's start with one of the most famous bubbles in history. However, it occurred in Europe, not in America. It's the first reasonably well-documented bubble in history, and it was called "Tulip Mania" or "Tulipomania" — because it had to do with the pricing of Dutch tulips in the early 1600s. This bubble grew for decades, but it only burst completely in 1637, just as France was entering a major "world war" of that time, the Thirty Years' War.

CHAPTER 6 — ANOTHER GREAT DEPRESSION?

It's almost hilarious to compare the Internet products of the 1990s with tulips of the 1630s, but in fact, tulips were the high-tech product in the Netherlands at that time.

Those were heady days in the Dutch Republic. Amsterdam was the major gateway between London and Paris, and the city had benefited hugely from having established Europe's first central bank in 1609, giving Dutch merchants a big competitive advantage around the world. It was still the biggest bank in Europe in the 1630s, and the whole of the Netherlands was prosperous, not having yet been affected by the Thirty Years War.

Figure 23 Tulips

Tulips did not originate with the Dutch. The first bulbs had arrived from Turkey only a few years earlier, in the late 1500s. By means of breeding experiments, Dutch botanists were able to produce tulips with spectacular colors. These tulips were sought by wealthy people, and by 1624, one particularly spectacular bulb sold for the cost of a small house*.

Prices remained elevated for over another decade, and soon investors from all over Europe began purchasing a kind of "Tulip future," a certificate purchased in the fall which can be traded for a specific actual tulip to be grown the following spring. In some ways, these certificates were similar to "stock options" in the 1990s.

In 1636, speculation in tulip futures went through the roof, and on February 3, 1637, the tulip market suddenly crashed, causing the loss of enormous sums of money, even by ordinary people, including many ordinary people in France and other countries.

A mood of retribution began immediately, and even the tulips themselves suffered. Evrard Forstius, a professor of botany, became so reviled by the mere sight of tulips that he attacked them with sticks whenever he saw them*! At this point, the Thirty Years War enveloped all of Europe, as we'll discuss in chapter 8.

American bubbles

Let's look at the bubbles associated with each of the crisis wars in American history.

Revolutionary War. In pre-Revolutionary days, the bubble was caused by the issuance of too much paper currency by banks.

In those days, paper currency was issued by individual banks rather than by governments. A bank would distribute banknotes that could only be redeemed at that particular bank. In effect, receiving a bank note was like receiving a loan from that bank. If a bank issues too much currency, then the bank could fail if too many people at once tried to redeem the currency.

In an effort to impose control over the colonies, England imposed the Currency Act of 1864 on the colonies. This act forbade the colonial banks from issuing their own paper currency. This was resented as much as any tax, and it also created financial problems due to the lack of currency. As a result, banks ignored the edict and not only issued paper currency but issued a lot of it. This transfer of paper currency from business to business created a bubble that burst in 1772 when the Bank of Rhode Island failed.

The same sorts of activities were going on in Europe. In particular, the Ayr Bank in Scotland had issued paper currency freely to aid speculators in housing and toll roads. A bad crop harvest on the Continent triggered the failure of a speculative investment by London banker Alexander Fordyce, which triggered the failure of the Ayr Bank, leading to the Panic of 1772. This triggered the failure of the Bank of England, and the collapse of numerous colonial businesses, as previously described in this chapter. How easy it is for a simple problem like a crop failure to trigger the collapse of a bubble, leading to widespread financial calamity!

Civil War. In the 1850s, before the Civil War crisis, the bubble was caused by something called "call loans♦." A bank would loan money to brokers who would use it to loan money to clients to buy stocks. However, the phrase "call loan" comes from the fact that a bank could call the loan at any time, requiring the broker and its clients to sell stock immediately to get the money to repay the loan.

The "call loan" system was terribly abused in the 1850s, with financiers using the same money over and over again to bid up the price of stocks. The railroads were the high tech items of the day, as people competed with each other to bid up stock prices on railroads and on the public lands that the railroads used.

On August 24, 1857, a cashier in the New York office of the Ohio Life Insurance and Trust Company was found to have embezzled many of the firm's assets, triggering a series of failures reverberating to Liverpool, London, Paris, Hamburg, and Stockholm, leading to the Panic of 1857♦.

World War II. The high-tech item of the 1920s was the automobile, and it was a variant of the call loan, called a "margin sale," that caused the bubble. It was the same idea — brokers lending money to clients to buy stocks — but lenders were required to pay a certain margin or percentage (often as little of 10%) of the cost of the stocks in cash.

Today. In the 1990s, where the Internet was the high-tech item *du jour*, the bubble was caused by a brand new mechanism — the stock option. A financier (venture capital company) would lend money to a group of entrepreneurs to form a company and develop a product. The entrepreneurs would pay its workers a lower than market wage, augmented by stock options — a promise to allow the employee to purchase cheap stock at a later date, and resell it at a much higher price. In essence, the stock options became similar to the paper currency issued by banks in the 1760s. (There really is nothing new under the sun.) When the stock options were finally called, the entire bubble collapsed, resulting in the Nasdaq crash in 2000, and subsequent large drops in stock values on the New York Stock Exchange.

What these examples show is that financial crises are very closely tied to war crises. In fact, they feed on each other, and energize each other.

A war crisis makes people extremely risk aversive, reluctant to make purchases or investments, for fear of being left with nothing, leading to a worse financial crisis.

A financial crisis makes people restless and desperate, looking for justice and retribution against the people whom they blame for causing the financial crisis. In many cases, the result is war.

Can Federal agencies protect us from a new depression?

Ask almost anyone about a depression in the 2000s decade, and they'll give you an answer like this: "It can't happen. In the 1930s, the Roosevelt administration put in new agencies and regulations to prevent another depression from every occurring."

People don't realize it, but the agencies and regulations that were created in the 1930s to prevent another depression have *already* failed.

Take the Securities and Exchange Commission. When I was high school in the 50s, my teachers all told me how the SEC was going to prevent a future depression. The 1930s depression was caused by the huge stock market bubble of the 1920s, where millions of investors drove up the prices of stocks by borrowing money from each other, a situation that led to a huge stock market correction in the 1930s. The SEC would prevent that from ever happening again by regulating margin rates, which would reduce buying stocks on credit, and prevent another huge stock market bubble. My 1950s high school teachers knew that because they lived through the 1930s, and understood that piece of wisdom.

Well, today all the people who remember that wisdom from personal experience are gone. And guess what? The SEC failed to prevent the huge 1990s stock market bubble. The SEC has completely failed to perform the principal function that it was originally set up for.

Today, there's only one agency left to protect us from a new depression: the Federal Reserve Bank. Among its many duties, it uses "monetary policy" to control the total amount of money in circulation.

The idea is that the more money there is in the economy, then the more money each person and family will have to spend. Therefore, people will buy more products, providing money to businesses to hire employees, preventing another depression.

So far at least, this kind of monetary policy has not been working. The Fed has lowered the prime interest rate to the 1% range — a move which would have caused massive inflation in an earlier decade — is not preventing near-zero inflation or even deflation in 2003.

The analysis in this chapter indicates that monetary policy will not forestall a new depression for the following reason: The current economic problems are occurring because firms are producing goods that people don't need or want, and that they won't purchase even if they have the money to do so. In the meantime, the low interest rates keep inefficient businesses going, and only postpone the inevitable.

The "Crusty Old Bureaucracy" Theory

Let's take a look at one more explanation of why the 2000s decade will be a decade of depression. This is meant to be an intuitive explanation, not a rigorous argument.

As we mentioned above, the 1930s agencies and regulations designed to prevent another depression didn't work because they didn't change human nature. Now we're going to explain why human nature is such that we *must always* have a financial crisis like the Great Depression every 80 years or so, and that there's nothing we do to prevent it.

I got the idea for this when I heard a television business news story that described some company as having financial troubles because the "crusty old bureaucracy" that was running the company was moving too slowly keep the company competitive with newer upstarts.

The problem with any organization that lasts a long time is that it gets set in its ways; it gets departments and divisions that are slow to change; employees lose their energy and don't want to rock the boat.

Ordinarily, such an organization will go out of business because it's not competitive enough, and its business will be taken over by more up to date and aggressive competitors.

The problem is that a society (or country) can be thought of in exactly the same way. Looking at a country as a whole — its entire government, all its businesses, labor unions, educational institutions, and non-profit institutions taken together — a certain, ever-increasing percentage of these organizations viewed as a whole are going to become inefficient. The crusty old bureaucracy will grow with time.

It's the word "ever-increasing" in the preceding paragraph that is the crux of this argument. Some readers may not agree that the amount of inefficiency constantly increases with time; that businesses, government agencies, educational institutions, and so forth, constantly renew and improve themselves, so that they're always just as efficient as ever. If you believe that a society as a whole stays just as efficient as ever over time, then you won't agree that we have to have a Great Depression every now and then.

But if you believe, as I do, that the buildup of bureaucracies, politicians and layers of control, and the tendency of people and organizations to do their job without rocking the boat with changes means that society as a whole becomes inefficient as time goes on, then the conclusion that Great Depressions are always necessary is inevitable.

In my many years of experience as a computer industry consultant, I've seen what happens with my own eyes. There are many businesses that have computerized, eliminating layers of management, streamlining accounting, manufacturing, order processing and other departments, eliminating large groups of employees doing work that can just as easily be done by a computer that doesn't require a salary.

But I've also seen many, many other businesses that haven't done that: doctors' offices with racks of patient records in paper folders; business offices which use computers for no more than word processing and an occasional budget; rooms full of pencil-pushing employees that perform repetitive tasks all day long - tasks that could better be done by computers. These are the businesses that will be wiped out by a new Great Depression.

Elsewhere in this book, I discussed the concept that "war is senseless" to many people. It's true that war is senseless to the individual, but from the point of view of survival of the human species, war — including genocide and mass rape — is extremely sensible, because it guarantees that the strongest races, civilizations and nations will survive, and the weaker ones will die off.

A Great Depression is, like war, another of "nature's ways" of renewing a society. When poverty is rampant and the unemployment rate is above 25%,

> *A Great Depression is, like war, another of nature's ways of renewing a society*

as it was in the 1930s, then not rocking the boat is impossible. Thousands of businesses will shut down, eventually to be replaced by new businesses that are more efficient. Governments at all levels will be forced to shut down and cut back on all its agencies, because the level of tax collections will be way down. Similar observations will be true for educational institutions, labor unions, non-profit institutions, and so forth.

Organizations in all sectors will disappear, as they did in the 1930s. The ones that survive are able to do so only by completely reinventing themselves, and accepting inevitable cutbacks in all but the most essential jobs, and letting employees in non-essential jobs go to fend for themselves. That's how society renews itself.

When I talk about things like this, people criticize me for being too negative. Heck, even I get depressed reading the paragraphs that I've just written. But being warm and fuzzy is for another book on another day, or by a different author. This book was not written to make people feel good; it was written to describe what I, as a mathematician and researcher, consider is likely to happen.

What does a "depression" mean for our lives?

Since the word "depression" means different things to different people, it's worthwhile to point out that in this book it refers to one specific thing: A big drop in stock market value, similar to the big stock market fall in the 1930s.

But what does that mean in terms of people's lives? In the 1930s, it meant massive unemployment, bankruptcies and homelessness. Are we facing the same fate today?

The forecasting tools that I've used to forecast the massive drop in stock prices do not tell us what ups and downs stocks will take before reaching bottom, and do not answer the questions about bankruptcies and homelessness, so we can only guess.

In the 1930s, money was very tight. People and businesses that owed money were forced to pay their debts or go bankrupt. Businesses that went bankrupt laid off employees, causing more unemployment and more personal bankruptcies. People who went bankrupt often lost their homes, becoming homeless.

Today, the Fed is acting to prevent these massive results by flooding the economy with money — by keeping the federal funds interest rate close to 0%, and possibly by repurchasing long-term bonds. Businesses that are close to bankruptcy can often borrow cheap money and keep going. People who are close to bankruptcy can often borrow against credit cards, which pass along the low interest rates to their customers.

So we're seeing a different effect on people's lives of the massive stock price drop than we saw in the 1930s. In the 1930s, people went bankrupt and homeless. Today, people and businesses are going massively into low interest rate debt.

It's not known what effect this will have in the long run. In the optimistic scenario, it will give businesses time to change to produce 21st century products, instead of the old 20th century products. In the pessimistic scenario, it will keep the "crusty old bureaucracy" in place a few years longer, thus causing an even harder fall when the fall finally comes.

Chapter 7 — Great Awakenings in World History

This book is about the major crises in world history, especially those involving great crisis wars.

But there's a special delight in studying the awakenings — those spectacular times of new ideas and new revolutions that appear midway between two crisis wars.

Some awakenings produce little, perhaps a few ideas that fizzle out to nothing. Other awakenings produce ideas and movements that change history. Those are the awakenings that excite us and teach us what moves men.

The 80-year cyclical view of history is also a methodology — that sometimes allows us to fill in the blanks in history, to let us make reasonable inferences about things that happened years ago, and have been lost in history.

In this chapter, we look at some of the most interesting, delightful and important awakenings in world history: The golden age of ancient Greece, the ministry of Jesus Christ, and the birth of Islam.

Understanding Awakenings

Before beginning, let's remember what an awakening is. The word "awakening" comes from a particular historical event known as the "Great Awakening." It occurred in colonial America in the 1730s-40s. For the first time in history, multiple religious denominations were born, as evangelists moved around the colonies.

Let's summarize two recent awakenings, to make it clear what kinds of things happen during an awakening.

- **America's "Vietnam War" Awakening.** During the 1960s and 1970s, there were massive student demonstrations and social unrest, giving rise to the antiwar movement, women's lib movement, environmental movement, racial pride movement, and so forth. The social unrest was completely defused by the resignation of President Nixon, allowing the demonstrators to claim a major victory.

- **China's "Tiananmen Square" Awakening.** Anyone watching the news in 1989 will remember the amazing student demonstrations in Tiananmen Square in Beijing. Some three million Chinese students came from all over the country for peaceful demonstrations against the government. The government brutally and violently repressed the demonstrators, which means that China's next crisis rebellion, expected around 2020, will be particularly brutal and violent.

What both of these awakenings have in common — as do all awakenings — is a "generation gap" between the youngsters who were born after the last crisis, and their elders, who lived through the last crisis and do not want to see it repeated.

The Golden Age of Ancient Greece

It lasted only about 30 or 40 years, but it influenced the art and culture of the entire world for centuries.

During the fifth century BC in Athens, there was an explosion of architecture, playwriting, statesmanship, governance, and philosophy. The names are still familiar: the Acropolis, the Parthenon, Pericles, Thucydides, Socrates, Aristophanes, Aeschylus, Sophocles and Euripides — spectacularly great works and the people who produced them, works that are still admired throughout the world today, all at the same time in this brief period.

Historians often notice that this period happened to occur between two major wars, but rarely make any attempt to relate the three events (the two wars and the Golden Age). Using the methodology of Generational Dynamics, we can show how they're all related, and how the first of the wars led to both of the other two events — as inevitably as the events in one of Euripides' plays leads to a preordained tragic conclusion that occurred 2,500 years ago.

In using Generational Dynamics to analyze this period, the timeline isn't entirely clean, because there are so many parties involved, and they all come to the period with their individual timelines. As a result, the two crisis periods are each 30 years long, and the mid-cycle period is just under 50 years long, and includes several mid-cycle wars. Nonetheless, the awakening that occurred during this mid-cycle period is quite real.

Today, we think of the world consisting of about 250 nations, or "nation-states."

However, no one ever heard of nation-states in fifth-century BC Greece. Nor did ancient Greece consist any longer of mobile warring tribes. Instead, ancient Greece was made up of "city-states," small societies tied down to fixed geographical locations. Each city-state had its own form of government, and many of them were democracies. The two most well known city-states were Athens and Sparta.

Persian Wars, 510-478 BC

There were three major parties to the crisis period that began in 510 BC: Athens, Sparta and Persia. All three were historical enemies of each other, but in the beginning of this period, Sparta encouraged the Persians to attack Athens. By the end, Athens and Sparta were allies.

Figure 24 Ancient Greece and Persia, and city-states Athens and Sparta

In the final major battle, in 480 BC, Persia had 5 million men, according to the historian Herodotus, considered the first true historian of the western world. However, modern estimates range up to 500,000 men*. In addition, Persia had 600-1200 ships. During the ensuing battles, Persia attacked and occupied Athens, and destroyed the city.

At a time like today, when the world may be headed for a major war, it's time to remember that some hostilities last seemingly forever. The Persians lived on what is Turkey today, and today, 2,500 years later, there is still a great deal of hostility between Greece and Turkey, and the island of Cyprus is a major fault line in that war. It's possible that Greece versus Turkey will play a major part in a future war.

As usual, the period immediately following a war is very austere, as steps are taken to make sure that "nothing like this ever happens again." Very often, there's some great compromise imposed on one side or the other that unravels years later.

In this case, the great compromise occurred in 478 BC, when Sparta proposed to Athens that they form a Delian League (named after the island Delos) of all the city-states: Each ally would contribute to the league, which would use the money to drive away all Persians*. The League was supposed to be controlled jointly by the allies, but Athens was the most powerful, and soon completely dominated the league.

The Awakening Period

The kids who were born after the Persian war would have a different point of view. They would see Persia as a distant, weak enemy, and any money saved for a possible future war against Persia to be wasted. Their attitudes would be quite different from those of their parents, the people who had actually fought in the war and seen their friends die. As usual, this created a generation gap.

Beyond that, the kids from Athens would have quite a different view from the kids from Sparta and the other city-states. The kids from Sparta would want to end the Delian League and stop paying taxes to Athens for a defense they wouldn't believe was necessary.

The kids from Athens wouldn't want to end the League, but they would want to see fewer "defense expenditures," and would want to see the money spent instead on program for "social good." These are the typical views heard during awakenings, whether today or in ancient times.

This is a good example of how a compromise that ends a war can lead to the next war between future generations. The young generations of Athens and Sparta both felt "entitled," because their elders had all contributed to the great heroic victory over Persia. But they interpreted their entitlement differently, and in conflicting ways.

The result was that the Delian League turned into an Athenian empire. Athens could exert control over the other city-states because it had control of the vast taxes and resources collected for the common defense. Whenever any city-state tried to withdraw from the League, Athens would use its power and resources to force it to return. At its peak, there were about 140 city-states in the Delian League.

Pericles, the great statesman of Athens at this time, played a major role. He had been born at the beginning of the Persian War, and grew up during it. Kids who grow up during a crisis war have a unique attitude toward life. They personally experience the horror of the crisis war, and want any future wars to be prevented; but they're too young to actually participate in the war, as their older hero brothers did. And when their younger brothers are born, to become the post-war generation, they end up being mediators between these two hardheaded generations.

Pericles rose to power by juggling the demands of both of these generations. For the older generation, he maintained Athens' defenses, and even extended Athens' hegemony to other nearby regions.

> *The kids from Athens would have a different view from the kids from Sparta*

For the younger generation, he instituted a modest welfare program for the poor, sponsored artists like Aeschylus, and initiated public works projects that both provided jobs and beautified the city.

In the period between two crisis wars, an "unraveling" typically occurs in the last couple of decades before the next crisis war in the cycle. At this time, mediators like Pericles are no longer caught between two hardheaded generations, because the older generation of heroes has retired or died. They're at the height of their power and influence, but they're only being pushed in one direction.

Under Pericles' influence, Athens commissioned the Parthenon and other buildings of the Acropolis, some of the greatest and most beautiful buildings of all time. The reason given was to replace the buildings that had been leveled by the Persians during the war. But nothing was too good for the Acropolis. The Persians had leveled buildings constructed with porous stone, available near Athens, but the buildings of the Acropolis were constructed from the finest hard white marble, quarried from miles away.

Peloponnesian War, 431-404 BC

This was great fun for the Athenians, but not much fun for the other city-states, since the others were footing the bill for Athens' beautiful buildings. The result was the next crisis war: the Peloponnesian war between Athens and Sparta that started in 431 BC, 59 years after the beginning of the Persian War. That civil lasted 27 years, leaving the entire region exhausted and weak.

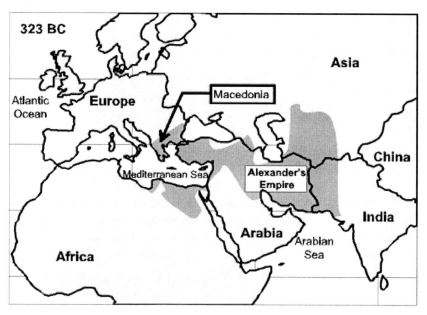

Figure 25 Alexander the Great's empire at his death in 323 BC. Alexander spread Greek culture throughout the entire region, affecting the direction of history for centuries.

The spread of Greek Culture

The weakened Greeks were unable to withstand the next major war. King Philip, king of Macedonia and father of Alexander the Great, invaded and conquered the Greeks in 359 BC, and uniting all the Greek city-states as part of the Macedonian empire. But that's not all.

King Philip's son, Alexander the Great, formed an army of Macedonians and the conquered Greeks, and went on to capture Egypt, the Persian Empire, and parts of India and central Asia, as shown in the accompanying map.

In doing so, Alexander the Great spread Greek culture, including the Greek language and the accomplishments of the golden age of Greek culture, throughout the entire region. Three centuries later, when Jesus Christ was born and Christianity was founded, the New Testament of the Bible was written in Greek, the *lingua franca* of most of the known world.

The generational analysis

At this point, it's appropriate to ask: What has this analysis of the Golden Age given us that we didn't already know? For example, the fact that Athens used Sparta's tax money to build the Parthenon, and that this triggered a new war between the parties, has already been well established by historians. So why bother?

What the generational methodology adds is a lot of context and relevance to the bare facts. We can understand that the Delian League was supported immediately after the Persian War for the same reasons that our own FBI and CIA were supported. We can understand how the existence of Delian League was questioned by activists very similar to our own anti-war activists in the 1960s and 70s. We can see that the Parthenon was built at a time of craziness or unraveling, like our own 1990s, when there are no social rules and no financial controls.

Finally, as we look at example after example, and see the same patterns repeated over and over again, we can really begin to understand our own futures — how in 2003 America is at a point just before a major crisis war, how the war will last ten years, more or less, how it will lead to a great period of austerity, followed once again by a generation gap will lead to new challenges to authority in the 2030s.

Judaism and the Spread of Christianity

Great ideas are born during awakenings, and frequently they're spread (or extinguished) during crisis wars. Now we're going to look at another great idea, born during an awakening, and spread throughout the world for millennia to come — the ministry of Jesus Christ and the spread of Christianity.

It's impossible to understand Jesus Christ without first understanding the history of Judaism, as well as the unique qualities of Jews that have caused them to excel at whatever they did — the same qualities that have led them to be the targets of attack by other civilizations throughout the centuries.

Judaism and Diaspora

The seminal crisis war that set the pattern for Hebrew life for millennia to come occurred somewhere around 1200 BC (give or take a century), when Moses liberated the Hebrew people from Egyptian slavery by means of two miracles: the crossing of the Red Sea and survival in the desert. That legendary story, told in the book of Exodus in the Bible, has influenced major world events ever since, to an extent that must not be underestimated. If that event hadn't occurred, the Hebrews might have been just another cult that eventually disappeared, and Jerusalem might have been just another ordinary city, rather than a location that has been the epicenter of one major historical event after another.

> *The seminal crisis that set the pattern for Hebrew life for millennia was the crossing of the Red Sea*

Just as the heroic victory of Athens over the Persians started a chain of events that spread Greek culture throughout the world, the heroic victory of Moses and his people over the Egyptians started a chain of events that sustained Jews and Judaism to this day.

For, in the eyes of the Hebrews, this event made them the "chosen people." The two miracles caused them to renew their covenant with God that Abraham had made several centuries, and confirmed their faith that God would protect them.

In the austere days following the exodus, Moses took steps to make sure that "nothing like that must ever happen again." He imposed the Ten Commandments on the people, and then developed an entire moral and religious code, a code of political and social organization*. The covenant with God, made centuries earlier by Abraham, presumably during an awakening period, was now confirmed and established by a crisis war.

This time, the awakening that followed went in a different direction, to the worshippers of the Golden Calf. There must have been many struggles and crisis wars in the centuries that followed, creating a historical fault line between the followers of Moses' law and the others - the heathens.

The view of Jews as the "chosen people" was sealed several centuries later when the Jews were conquered, exiled into Babylon, and eventually allowed to return to their homeland. This was once again interpreted through Jewish law: God had punished the chosen people for their heathen practices, but then had shown mercy by ending their exile[*].

The point of all of this history is the set of ideas surrounding the word "Diaspora." This word was originally coined to describe groups of Jewish people scattered around many countries, but now the word "diaspora," without capitalizing, is used to describe any group of people of common religion or ethnicity who are living in a community not in the native country of their religion or ethnicity.

But while diaspora is a general word, it's the Jewish Diaspora that have influenced world events the most. Why is that? Mainly because Judaism has not had a homeland for the overwhelming portion of its history, and so it's always been mainly a Diaspora religion.

No religion could possibly survive without a base, a homeland, and certainly not a religion whose adherents have been exiled, moved or slaughtered so many times in history. Yet, Judaism *has* survived.

It survived because the Jewish law, starting with the laws of Moses, was designed so that God's chosen people could survive as Diaspora.

As a "chosen people," the Jews could live in any country and still maintain their Jewish identity. Whether in Jerusalem, Egypt, Italy or later in other countries throughout the world, the Jews had a collection of scriptures and laws to live by, and they could reestablish their identity simply by gathering together in a group of two or more and reading and discussing those scriptures. This ability of Jewish Diaspora to live anywhere, anytime, and still maintain a Jewish identity, without merging into the local society, makes the Jews almost unique among major civilizations of world history.

And that's the uniqueness that creates the irrational xenophobia among other people toward the Jews. Jewish people had their own laws that took precedence of the laws of the society around them. (They viewed their laws as coming from a "higher power," a concept that the Christians later inherited, as did the Muslims even later.) Even in earliest times, Jewish communities were insulated, and even had their own courts of law. Some societies tolerated Jewish disobedience of local laws better than others, and the ones that didn't tolerate it often responded by moving the local Jewish community elsewhere, passing the problem on to someone else. This common solution to the local "Jewish problem" meant that Jewish history has almost always been of Jews in other countries, rather than of Jews in their own country.

Historian Henri Daniel-Rops puts it as follows:

> Everything, then was related to the Chosen People's certainty that they were unique, different from all others and superior to them*: everything, their monotheistic faith, love of their country, submission to moral laws, desire to order their social and political lives according to given principles, and their feeling for the highest kind of mystical experience. It was, therefore, theology rather than ethnology that determined their racial characteristics.

It's important to understand that most of this description — a monotheistic faith and submission to moral laws — is common to Christianity and Islam (and, in fact, was inherited by them). The distinctive difference is the form those laws took resulting from the fact that there was no Jewish homeland.

> *As a Chosen People, the Jews could live in any country and still maintain their Jewish identity*

A Jewish Homeland

Following the Golden Age of Greece, Alexander the Great had spread Greek culture and Greek language throughout the Mediterranean area, and into points further east. Whether in Jerusalem or elsewhere in the region, the ordinary people spoke the local language, but the educated elite spoke Greek, enjoyed Greek art, and lived in expensive homes with a Greek architecture. To use modern day terminology, "Hellenization" was associated with the rich, making it a resented symbol of the class struggle between the rich and the poor.

However, the Greeks were not the rulers of this Greek-based culture. These were the days of the Roman Empire, and the Romans were the rulers.

The Roman rulers had to deal with large Jewish populations of Jewish Diaspora in Babylon and Rome, and mostly got along well with them (with some painful exceptions) because they granted Jews the right to violate Roman law when it conflicted with traditional Jewish law.

Nonetheless, Judea, the region containing Jerusalem, was a special problem. The Jews actually took control of Judea in 142 BC, and it became a Jewish homeland, an independent Jewish state. In 63 BC, the Romans took over, and there was no Jewish homeland again in 1948.

King Herod

In 42 BC, Rome appointed Herod to rule Judea. It's hard to imagine any ruler with the ability to cause more dissension and despair among the people. Consider these factors:

- Herod was given the title "King of the Jews" by the Romans.

- Herod was half-Jewish, half-Arab, a combination that caused many people to consider him impure, and hold him in contempt.

- Herod ruled by cruelty and terror, killing anyone who stood in his way, even members of his own family. (According to one anecdote, when Herod had his own son executed, a Roman master quipped, "I would rather be Herod's pig than Herod's son.")

- Herod enforced his terror by using Roman forces, hated by the people.

- Herod collected enormous amounts in taxes, and used them to build lush palaces in the hated Hellenized style. One building that might have helped with the people was his rebuilding of the ancient Jewish temple of Jerusalem. But he spoiled it by adorning it prominently with the hated golden Roman eagle.

Added to all that, there was a natural disaster. In 31 BC, an earthquake killed 30,000 people and leveled thousands of buildings.

Herod ended his reign with especially cruel forms of terror. When some students tried to remove the golden Roman eagle from the temple, some 40 students were burned alive. And the Matthew 2 tells a (possibly exaggerated) story of the "Massacre of the Innocents": When Herod learned of a ruler that the real "King of the Jews" had been born, he ordered the murder of all babies younger than 2 years. Christ was born in 6 BC, and Herod died in 4 BC. The kingdom was divided among three of his sons.

Aftermath of Herod: Jesus Christ and Christianity

The long reign of terror ended with Herod's death. A crisis period is always followed by a period of austerity, where people who lived through the crisis set rules for society so that nothing like that will ever happen again. For the Jews, this meant that they would not provoke the Romans, and for the Romans, this meant that any minor revolt had to be put down quickly, in order to avoid a larger revolt. There was an extended period of peace between 7 and 26 AD.

Jesus Christ was born too late to have any personal memory of Herod's reign of terror. There's always a "generation gap" between the generation of children born after a crisis period and the people who lived through the crisis period. That's why so may great new ideas, like a new religion, almost always occur 20-40 years after a crisis period ends — that's when there's a new awakening.

As a member of that young rebellious generation, we can well imagine that Jesus Christ would have wanted to rebel against not only the Romans but also against the elders in his own community, people who would be telling him to keep quiet, lest he cause trouble for himself and themselves.

Although this is a secular presentation of Jesus' life using Generational Dynamics, it may seem strange, especially to Christians, to be talking about these kinds of generational issues with regard to Jesus, but doing so is no disrespect to the Christian religion, according to Professor Gene Chase of Messiah College in Grantham, Penn.

"Of course Jesus was a man of His time," says Chase. "The very essence of the doctrine of His incarnation is that He is fully man, not just physically but also socially, intellectually, and emotionally. Jesus was a man of his culture, and hence a man of the culture of his time. He studied the Torah as a boy; He enjoyed parties as a young man; His parables are agrarian to connect with the culture of His time; He taught peripatetically. These are the sorts of things that one would have expected of a good Jewish boy who became a rabbi. In fact, the Bible even says explicitly that Jesus came at just the right time."

So, for Christian and non-Christian readers alike, there is nothing unreasonable to say that his rebellion got many people angry. He got the Romans angry because of his popularity. He got many of the Jews angry because of his attitude toward the Jewish laws. (According to Matthew 5:17-20, he said, "Do not think I have come to set aside the Law and the prophets; I have not come to set them aside, but to bring them to perfection." So he "perfected" the laws by ignoring the unnecessary parts, including the dietary laws which were considered extremely important.) So he was a very charismatic rabble-rouser, and he was considered "dangerous" by both the Romans and the Jews.

Why didn't Jesus flee? This is a question that demands an answer from both a secular and a Christian point of view. Jesus knew that the Romans were coming to arrest him and execute him. Why didn't he flee the region (as Mohammed did in a similar situation six centuries later)?

The answer, according to Chase, is that Jesus saw himself as the Messiah as described in Isaiah 53:7, which was written 600 years before Jesus: "He was oppressed and afflicted, yet he did not open his mouth; he was led like a lamb to the slaughter, and as a sheep before her shearers is silent, so he did not open his mouth."

According to Chase, "Jesus saw himself as the person described there, not as molded by his time. Jesus knew Isaiah's writings well and lived in the light of them."

So Jesus was executed / crucified.

During the next 30 years, there were many uprisings among the Jews, resulting in many skirmishes with the Romans. Such skirmishes are typical of the years immediately preceding the next crisis. The hostilities end quickly because, as we've seen, the opinion makers are people who lived through the last crisis, and happily resort to containment and compromise.

By 66 AD, the generation that had personal memory of Herod's reign of terror were gone, replaced as leaders by the post-Herod generation, and the most conservative Jewish extremists had taken over the temple. The entire region was in rebellion against Romans, and the Romans had to "solve the problem once and for all." The Romans massacred tens of thousands of Jews. The city of Jerusalem was destroyed, especially the Herod's new Temple.

This was the end of the Jews in Jerusalem for centuries, but it was the beginning of the spread of Christianity.

Converting to a new religion

How does one convert to a new religion? It depends on the religion, of course.

We're getting a little ahead of ourselves by discussing religions we haven't come to yet, but let's look at how you convert to various religions:

- **Judaism.** Perform a long course of study in Jewish law, customs and life.

- **Christianity.** Agree to be baptized. A baptism is usually given by Christian clergy, but it can be performed by anyone with the proper intent. The person performing the baptism pours water on the head of the person to be baptized, and says, while pouring the water, "I baptize thee in the name of the Father, and of the Son, and of the Holy Ghost."

- **Islam.** Recite the words, "There is no God except Allah, and Mohammed is the Messenger of Allah."

- **Hinduism.** It's practically impossible to convert to Hinduism, because of the caste system.

- **Buddhism.** Agree to accept the precepts of Buddhism.

Of these religions, Judaism and Hinduism are "hard" to convert to, while Christianity, Islam and Buddhism are "easy" to convert to.

When I write the last paragraph, I mean no disrespect to any religion. Any Christian, Muslim or Buddhist will tell you that you haven't really converted to that religion just by reciting a few words; you have to study and accept an entire way of life. Nonetheless, you *can* convert to these religions in a matter of a few minutes, just by reciting a few words or performing a simple rite.

Proselytizing and Non-Proselytizing Religions

Consider the following: There are Catholic missionaries in China whose purpose is to convert people to the Catholic religion, but there are no Jewish missionaries in China to convert people to the Jewish religion. What's the difference?

The Jewish concept of a "chosen people" is contrary to the idea of proselytizing. That's not to say that proselytizing has never occurred, especially in the old days, but no one would ever expect Judaism to become a universal religion. No one would expect a Chinese Buddhist to convert to Judaism except in very unusual circumstances.

Christianity is the universal version of Judaism. (Incidentally, Buddhism is the universal form of Hinduism.) Any person can become a Christian by becoming baptized. That's why Christianity could spread while Judaism couldn't. And that's why, eventually, someone would have to come along and provide a universal version of Judaism, if Jesus Christ and his followers hadn't done so.

Top-Down and Bottom-Up Religions

Just as there's no Jewish missionary in China doing proselytizing, you're not too likely to see a Greek Orthodox missionary in China to convert Chinese to the Greek Orthodox religion, or a Russian Orthodox missionary converting Chinese to the Russian Orthodox religion. Once again, what's the difference?

The religion that grew out of Jesus' ministry became the Orthodox religion. It was adopted by the Romans, and then moved east, became centered in Constantinople (Istanbul), and later spread northward to the Slav peoples. Today, the two main branches are Greek Orthodox and Russian Orthodox, although there are dozens of other minor branches.

Orthodox Christianity differs from Catholic (and Protestant) Christianity because the former is a "top-down" religion, adopted first by rulers and then spread to the people, while the latter is a "bottom-up" religion, spreading among the people, and then adopted by the state during fault line wars.

The Orthodox religion moved east to Constantinople (now Istanbul, Turkey) because Rome was being attacked and pillaged from the west and north, especially by the Teutonic tribes from the North. The Teutonic (German) tribes adopted Christianity, but not in the Orthodox form. Instead a new form, Catholicism, was born. This was a "bottom-up" religion because, as we said, any individual could become a Catholic by being baptized. The same was true of the Protestant religions that split off from the Catholic religions in the 1500s in Germany (then known as the Holy Roman Empire, even though, to use the words of Voltaire, it wasn't holy, it wasn't Roman, and it wasn't an empire).

These are some of the many reasons why Orthodox Christianity is different from Western Christianity.

The Teachings of Mohammed

Let's now do a similar generational analysis on the life of Mohammed, the founder of Islam, and compare his life to Jesus'.

In the case of Jesus' life, there were contemporary Roman and Jewish historians who chronicled the reign of Herod and its aftermath, so that the Biblical accounts are supplemented by a lot of third party information about the environment in which Jesus was born and raised.

By contrast, there is relatively little third party information on the environment in which Mohammed was born and raised. Almost everything we know about Mohammed comes from religious sources. In fact, there are three sources of information about Mohammed's life*:

- The Quran, the holy book of Islam. This book consists of the religious teachings of Mohammed, but few details about the life of Mohammed himself. The teachings of Mohammed were written down during his lifetime, and then compiled in the Quran after his death.

- Biographies and histories, written 100 to 200 years after Mohammed's death. The writers lived in luxurious and sophisticated societies, and often weren't Arabs.

- The *Hadeeth* or The Traditions — the stories and anecdotes about Mohammed that were passed from person to person, and retold from generation to generation. These were compiled more than 200 years after Mohammed's death.

Except for Mohammed's religious teachings that were written down during his lifetime, most of these sources were not in written form prior to Mohammed's death, so much of what we know about Mohammed's life depends on the memories of the writers. A good summary of all of these sources is Sir John Glubb's book*, *The Life and Times of Muhammad*.

Let's start with what we do know about Mohammed.

The early life of Mohammed

He was born around 570 AD in Mecca, and became an orphan during his childhood.

None of the writings seems to indicate exactly how his father and mother died, or whether the death of his parents should be blamed on any particular tribes or events; we're simply told that his father died while on a business trip to Medina. We're also told that there were violent wars, beginning in the 580s, involving Jews, Christians and pagans, going on around Mohammed while he was growing up, and that as a teen, Mohammed helped out with some of the battles♦.

Around his fortieth birthday, while he was wandering and meditating, he had an experience that he and his believers say was a visit from an angel of God, telling him to become the messenger of God♦. The angel told him to recite certain verses that he would receive from God regularly. These verses were eventually collected and organized into Islam's holy book, The Quran.

His wife, Khadija, and her family were his first supporters, and in time a small group of believers from Mecca began to gather around him. However, his converts included another group as well: traders from the city of Medina (named Yathrib at that time) who visited Mecca regularly. He developed close relationships with these traders, and got to know many of them personally.

> *Both Jesus and Mohammed spread their ideas and gained their adherents during an awakening period, midway between two crisis wars*

Mohammed's life took a dramatic turn in 622, at age 52, when he became so popular that Mecca's ruling Quraish tribe was threatening his life♦. As a result, he and his followers were forced to flee to Medina, about 200 miles from Mecca.

This is a major difference in the lives of Jesus and Mohammed.

Both Jesus and Mohammed spread their ideas and gained their adherents during an awakening period, midway between two crisis wars. Both of them became extremely popular, enough so that the local authorities became concerned about fomenting a rebellion, and threatened each of their lives.

Today, many critics of Islam claim that Mohammed was a "man of war," while Jesus was a "man of peace." Is that a fair criticism of Mohammed?

From a generational point of view, Mohammed was more inclined to be a warrior, simply because he was in the generation that fought in the preceding crisis war, a generation of people that are typically identified as heroes. This distinguishes him from Jesus, who was born *after* the last crisis war. Some scholars question whether Jesus was totally a man of peace, pointing to the fact that the Bible indicates that Jesus' disciples carried swords.

However, the most dramatic difference between Jesus and Mohammed is how they reacted to these death threats from local authorities. Mohammed's reaction was to flee to Medina, and from there to build an army of adherents. In the case of Jesus, he felt constrained by the writings of Isaiah, as we've already described; in addition, the local authorities were the Romans, who controlled the entire region, so Jesus may have had no opportunity to take his adherents and flee. If things had been different and Jesus had fled, perhaps he might have ended up leading an army of his adherents back to Jerusalem, as Mohammed did to Mecca, but we'll never know the answer to that question.

So there's no way to compare Jesus and Mohammed as warriors, since Jesus never had the opportunity to become a warrior, as Mohammed had.

So, probably a more relevant question is: What kind of warrior was Mohammed?

The Years in Medina (Yathrib)

Both Westerners and Islamic fundamentalists make statements about Mohammed and Islam that frequently aren't justified by the Quran. Let's take a look at the life that Mohammed led in Medina.

It's most important to understand that war was a way of life in the Arabian Desert at the time of Mohammed — and continued to be so until the early 20th century. The Bedouin tribes regarded perpetual war to be a desirable, or at least inevitable, result of human existence. The Quraish, by contrast, were merchants who considered war to be inimical to commerce.

Some of population lived in fixed homes in one place, such as Mecca or Medina. Others, like the nomadic Bedouin tribes, were constantly on the move. The danger of starvation — for oneself or for one's animals — was never far from people's minds.

The tribes formed alliances for mutual protection. Moving around the desert meant moving from oasis to oasis, and if two unallied tribes ran into each other on the desert, it's quite possible that one of them would raid the other. However, such a raid would not necessarily be a fight to the death, and indeed there was no honor in simply killing your enemies; the purpose of the fight was to gain resources, such as food, water, gold, silver and weapons*.

This way of life was not some sort of peculiar cultural phenomenon, dictated by any of the local religions (Judaism, Christianity, paganism), but rather an adaptation to the desert. The desert produced only enough food and water to support a certain population, and after thousands of years, the local tribes had adapted by developing a pattern of life that selected who will live and who will die — either from battle or from starvation.

Medina itself was not what we think of as a bustling city; actually, it was little more than a large oasis in the desert supporting several thousand people in settlements of a mix of populations — Arabs and outsiders of the various religions, including Jews, Christians and pagans.

So this is the way of life of the entire region as Mohammed and his followers fled to Medina. In Medina, Mohammed actually had two different roles: His religious role was as the leader of the Muslims, but he also had a secular administrative role as the leader of the multi-cultural city of Medina. Many people, especially those who had followed him from Mecca and had no homes in Medina, were facing starvation. Mohammed was soon leading raids by Muslims against Quraish caravans*.

Mohammed's actions as a warrior were not out unusual for most of the people at this time.

Far from being a violent, genocidal killer, and some people say, Mohammed is more accurately described as an indecisive warrior and killer.

He was frequently uncertain what to do. Should we attack that caravan or not? He would equivocate, vacillate, sometimes changing his mind or giving in to pure emotion*, often postponing a final decision until he had absolutely no choice.

Mohammed was of an older and wiser generation than his young followers, and he often had trouble restraining them — not surprising, since these men were born after the last crisis war. Many of his young followers were sons of the Quraish elders*, and following Mohammed was an act of rebellion against their parents.

Indeed, Mohammed's experience, and the rapid growth of Islam, is almost a textbook example of an awakening in the generational methodology.

Awakening wars are rarely especially bloody or genocidal, since the elders on both sides are unwilling to replay the genocides of the last crisis war.

Both Mohammed and the Quraish elders in Mecca that he was fighting against would have been the heroes who had fought and survived the last violent crisis war, and their passionate desire was to avoid another such war. Their children, born after the war, would have found adherence to Mohammed's new faith an appealing way to rebel against their parents. The resulting "generation gap" fueled the emotional fires that allowed Mohammed to return to Mecca as ruler.

Today, in the highly politicized atmosphere following the 9/11 attacks, many Westerners have been making exotic charges about Islam in general and Mohammed in particular.

As we've discussed, Mohammed was a person of his times, not given to unnecessary killing.

Still, the histories and traditions do report some occasions when Mohammed used excessive violence. These are sometimes hard to explain, given the fact that most often he spared the lives of his enemies, or used diplomacy rather than war to achieve a goal.

On those occasions, Mohammed was most violent with people who attempted to prevent him from establishing his new religion*. Thus, people who actively opposed him would almost always be killed or massacred. He was also merciless with people who defamed Islam, either by becoming hypocrites (false converts who pretended to convert without really doing so) or even just by mocking him or his religion. An example of the latter was two singing girls who were executed because their act satirized Islam.

According to the histories, on some occasions, he massacred Jews or Christians, and this has been used by non-Muslims to criticize Mohammed, and by Islamic fundamentalists to justify murder of Jews, even though the histories indicate that such massacres occurred for these other reasons, not because the people were Jews or Christians.

However, these stories of excessive violence by Mohammed should be discounted as untrue, according to Edip Yuksel, an Islamic scholar who promotes reformation in Islam.

"The Quran says that you cannot force people, even hypocrites, to change their beliefs," says Yuksel. "The Quran treats hypocrites worse than nonbelievers, because they have no moral basis for their actions. But there's nothing specified as a punishment. That book says that you cannot hurt people, so Mohammed could not have sent people to hurt people who were hypocrites."

Yuksel says that the stories of excessive violence should not be believed, since they're not in the Quran. "Those stories come from other sources, and there are big lies in those books," he asserts. "Islamic histories written centuries later by other historians created a portrait of Mohammed according to what was going on at the time the histories were written."

According to Yuksel, "Mohammed stood for his rights and for his freedom - for his beliefs, and he defended himself very powerfully. But I disagree with anyone who says that he killed people because they criticized him or his faith*."

With regard to Mohammed's attitudes towards the Jews, he had what would appear to be a love-hate relationship with Jews. At first, Mohammed had hoped to be accepted by the Jews, and even to be recognized as the Savior*. He adopted the Jewish rules and rites, and declared Jerusalem to be the holy city toward which prayer should be made. However, many of the Jews in Medina ridiculed him and opposed him, and became his enemy. After that, he changed some of his religious rules and rites so that they differed from those of the Jews. Furthermore, Mecca, rather than Jerusalem, became the holy city toward which prayer should be made.

> *Arabs and Jews got along fine for the most part in Jerusalem and the surrounding region until the 20th century*

Actually, Mohammed held Jews and Christians in higher esteem than those who followed pagan beliefs. Although he insisted that pagans be converted to Islam, he didn't make that requirement for Jews and Christians, and endeavored to live in peace with them.

Even more important, in the wars of conquest following the death of Mohammed, Jews and Christians were not required to convert to Islam*. Muslim conquerors exercised enormous religious tolerance toward Jews and Christians, even to letting them follow their own laws and customs in conquered lands.

This is a very important point in today's political climate, because it shows that Islamic fundamentalists are simply lying when they say that Mohammed called for the extermination of Jews and Christians. Quite the opposite, Mohammed tolerated them and even honored them.

As we've already discussed, Arabs and Jews got along fine for the most part in Jerusalem and the surrounding region until the 20th century. After World War I, Jews and Arabs formed nationalist-type identity groups that opposed each other. The real crisis began in the 1930s, when hundreds of thousands of European Jews began fleeing to Jerusalem because of persecution by Germans. Wars between the Jews and Arabs in Palestine began in 1936, and reached a climax in 1948-49, after the creation of the Israel. This has led to the situation in the Mideast today, with the Palestinian Arabs and Jews replaying the events of 1936-49, with a new, major war almost certain.

However, it's important to make the point that this situation is not caused by any reasonable reading of Mohammed's life or the history of Islam. Most wars are fought simply for money, and resources, and then rationalized later with great, noble ideas. What they Jews and Arabs are fighting over today is land and resources, not any great religious beliefs. In the end, it's only about money, and all the stuff about religion is mostly bloviation and rationalization.

Finally, although this point is not directly related to the current Mideast situation, we hear about it so much that it's worth discussing: The charge that Mohammed was indecent because he had many wives, and that a Muslim man is permitted to have several wives.

In today's politically correct society, it's easy to forget that polygamy serves a valuable social purpose at times in history when war had killed off many men, leaving many women without partners. In those situations, the only way for most women to receive protection is through polygamous marriages.

This is exactly the situation that obtained in the Arabian peninsula for centuries, where war was a way of life. Many of Mohammed's wives were widows*, and there is evidence that many of the marriages were specifically for the protection of the women.

The Conquest of Mecca

During his ten years in Medina, Mohammed continued to gain adherents. He gained the loyalties of many tribes, and built up his army.

Finally, in 630, he led his army back to conquer the Quraish in Mecca. The Quraish, seeing that they would lose, simply accepted Mohammed as the new ruler, allowing his return to Mecca in triumph.

There's no doubt that Mohammed achieved this victory through his remarkable skill as a diplomat and politician, as well as his military skills.

But it's also worthwhile to point out that this was a mid-cycle war. Mohammed did not want to see a repeat of the bloodbath he had lived through as a teen and young adult, and neither did the elder Quraish.

Aftermath of Mohammed's death

The next bloodbath was saved for the next crisis war, a civil war in 656 among three community groups who were competing to inherit the mantle of Mohammed's leadership*. This serves to illustrate the point that Muslims have killed other Muslims far more than they've killed others.

After that, thanks to the aggressiveness of Mohammed's followers, Islam spread like wildfire throughout northern Africa, into parts of Eastern and Western Europe, and farther West into India.

The spread of Islam will be discussed more fully in chapter 9.

Hinduism and the Life of The Buddha

Even less is known about the life of the Buddha, the founder of Buddhism, than about Mohammed, and what little we do know of his words and actions has been enhanced by legend. But by using Generational Dynamics techniques, we can try to make some inferences.

Buddhism was born out of Hinduism, the ancient religion of India. The basic culture of Hinduism evolved over millennia, and to Westerners, the most remarkable feature of Hindu culture is the caste system.

It began around 2000-1500 BC, when the existing Indian population assimilated the Indo-European invaders. The invaders created the caste system as a means of enforcing racial purity, separating the conquerors from the conquered*. The priestly "Brahmins" were the highest caste. Other castes were for the warrior-aristocracy, the ordinary peasant-farmers, and the conquered "unclean."

Into this milieu, the Buddha was born around 563 BC into the wealthy warrior caste. His story is a fascinating one, because of its remarkable similarity to a 1960s peace activist. I mean no disrespect but in fact admiration, when I say that the Buddha's story resembles what we Americans might call a well-to-do youth who turned into a disillusioned hippie.

The Buddha became disenchanted with his life of luxury. "I lived in refinement, utmost refinement, total refinement. My father even had lotus ponds made in our palace: one where red-lotuses bloomed, one where white lotuses bloomed, one where blue lotuses bloomed, all for my sake" At age 29, he left his life of luxury and became homeless. His father was appalled. "You are young, ... endowed with the stature and coloring of a noble-warrior. You would look glorious in the vanguard of an army, arrayed with an elephant squadron. I offer you wealth; enjoy it."

He lived a very austere life, fighting temptations and evil. Eventually he reconciled with his father, and found a "Middle Way" of living, between luxury and austerity. During this period, he developed this philosophy of enlightenment, until he had his Awakening. (Fortuitously, the word "Awakening" is used in translations of the Sanskrit text, and corresponds in this case to the word "awakening" used in this book.)

After his Awakening, he spent the rest of long life teaching, and had thousands of followers. His teaching targeted the caste system, because he showed how everyone, even the untouchables and outcasts, could achieve enlightenment. He died in 483 BC at age 80, still teaching on his deathbed.

What additional information about the Buddha can we infer from his life using Generational Dynamics tools? Not a great deal, but a little.

Unlike Mohammed, who evidently spent a portion of his earliest childhood in a crisis war where he lost both his parents, both Jesus and the Buddha were born after the end of a crisis war. But unlike Jesus, whose family was on the "losing side" of the crisis war, the Buddha's family was evidently on the "winning side."

The Buddha's warrior father would have fought in that war. He might have come close to losing his own life, would have seen many of his friends die in battle, and might even have participated in what today we'd call genocide of groups of outcasts. When the rebellion was put down, he and his contemporaries would have renewed strict controls on the activities of people in the lower castes to keep them from rebelling again and endangering his life, as well as their own lives.

The Buddha himself would have been a participant in an "awakening" — not only his own spiritual Awakening, but also a societal awakening which began to remove some of those restrictions on the lower castes. Eventually, many of the controls and compromises implemented by his father would have unraveled, and there would be a new crisis war or rebellion.

One thing that seems to be missing from the story of the Buddha is another crisis war towards the end of his 80-year lifetime. There are several possibilities. One is that the next crisis war was delayed for some reason, as sometimes happens (see our discussion of the American Revolutionary War, for example). A second possibility is that he didn't want to talk about a new rebellion, since he had personally overseen the unraveling of controls that made that rebellion possible. And a third possibility is that the Buddha's death was the generational change that led to the next rebellion.

A lot of this is speculative, of course, but it provides some interesting inferences that historians can test with further research.

Chapter 8 — History of Western Europe

Before 1500, Europe consisted of many small regions. One division into 50 regions is shown by the adjoining map that we reproduce from chapter 3.

By the Principle of Localization, each of these regions would have to be analyzed separately, showing how all their timelines eventually merged together, and that's

Figure 26 Map of Europe divided into 50 separate cultural regions

way too much work for this book. That's a project for some history graduate student.

However, we can get our feet wet without immersing ourselves completely in the ocean. Because England is separated from the European continent by the English Channel, we can present a fairly clear timeline throughout its medieval period, starting from the Norman Conquest in 1066.

Likewise, Spain is in a corner of Europe all its own, and so it's fairly insulated as well, and we present a timeline for Spain starting from the 1300s.

These two examples serve as responses to the claims from some that Generational Dynamics does not apply before the 1500s. In fact it does, provided that the Principle of Localization is observed.

From there, we can see how timelines merge throughout Europe, especially in the Thirty Years' War (1618-48) and the War of Spanish Succession (1701-14). After that, wars involving France, Germany and England recur every cycle with painful regularity, through World War II.

And as we've discussed in previous chapters, and will continue in chapter 9, Eastern Europe is on a different timeline, with World War I on its timeline, as well as more recent wars in the Balkans, Iran, Iraq and Turkey. The next war, which will involve all of Western Europe, Russia, and the Mideast, will serve to merge the West and East European timelines.

So let's begin with medieval Spain and England, and then move on to the major wars that merged the Western European timelines.

Medieval Spain

Spain provides a good, clear example of generational timelines during the medieval period, and it's an interesting example at that.

Spain is a good example for another reason: The Golden Age of Spain provides some interesting lessons for America today.

Spain's Anti-Jewish Pogroms of the 1390s

In many cases, a crisis war is a violent civil war (like America's Civil War, the bloodiest war in America's history).

The 1390s civil war in Spain was marked by especially violent anti-Jewish pogroms that were triggered by a serious financial crisis for which the wealthy Jews were blamed. Almost every crisis war ends with some sort of imposed compromise that unravels 80 years later, leading to the next crisis war.

The compromise that ended the 1390s civil war was an interesting one: The Jews would convert to Catholicism, or else would be expelled. During the next few decades, over half of the 200,000 Jews on the peninsula formally converted to Catholicism[*].

Compromises of this sort only work for so long, but the failure of this compromise was especially ironic. The Conversos, as the converted Jews were called, were now officially Christian, bringing them further wealth and status. A large part of the Castilian upper class consisted of Jews and Conversos, naturally generating a great deal of class jealousy among the lower classes. It's typical for riots and demonstrations to occur during an "awakening" period, midway between two crisis wars, and that's what happened here. The riots against the Conversos began in 1449, and became increasingly worse as the old compromise began to unravel. Thus, an old fault line between the Catholics and the Jews was replaced by a new fault line between the old line Catholics and the Converso Catholics.

Those who remember America's most recent "awakening" period in the 1960s and 70s will remember the fiery rhetoric that demonstrators used in the antiwar movement at that time. Johns Hopkins University professor David Nirenberg found that the "anti-Converso movement" rhetoric of 1449 and beyond was just as heated: "The converts and their descendants were now seen as insincere Christians, as clandestine Jews, or even as hybrid monsters, neither Jew nor Christian. They had converted merely to gain power over Christians. Their secret desire was to degrade, even poison, Christian men and to have sex with Christian women: daughters, wives, even nuns♦."

This is exactly what Generational Dynamics is all about. The generation of kids who grew up during the 1390s pogroms became risk-averse adults who were willing to look for compromises to avoid new bloody violence. Thus, there were anti-Converso riots during the 1450s and after, but that risk aversive generation that grew up in the 1390s were still around to contain the problem, and look for compromises, to keep things from getting too far out of hand, despite the heated rhetoric. When that generation died, no one was left to look for compromises, and new pogroms began in the 1480s.

The Spanish Inquisition and the Reconquest — 1480s-1490s

As the old compromise unraveled completely, the riots against the Conversos got worse, and a common charge against the Conversos was that they were "false Christians♦." The most common charge against Conversos was that of "Judaizing," that is, of falsely pretending conversion and secretly practicing Jewish rites.

This is what gave rise to the Spanish Inquisition. The idea was to have an official body empowered to determine whether those who had claimed to convert to Catholicism had really converted. As new pogroms began in the 1470s and 1480s, the Inquisition was particularly targeted to find the "Judaizers." At first, the Inquisition was directed specifically at Conversos, but later was extended to unconverted Jews. Thousands of Conversos and Jews were executed under the Inquisition, and entire Jewish communities were eliminated.

The new crisis war reached its climax in the year 1492, when three different things happened that affected Spain for the entire next 80-year cycle:
- A final decree was issued, expelling all Jews who refused to convert. Hundreds of thousands of Jews were forced to leave the country.
- Christopher Columbus left Spain and discovered the New World.
- The Reconquest of Spain from the Muslims was completed, with the expulsion of the Muslims from Grenada.

With regard to the last point, Muslims had crossed over to southern Spain from Africa as early as the 700s, and had conquered almost all of Spain. The Catholics had dreamed of reconquering Spain from the Muslims for centuries. The Reconquest was finally completed in 1492.

The Golden Age of Spain and Manifest Destiny

We now need to step back and look at the reasons why Spain became the most powerful nation in Europe during the 1500s.

For two very important reasons, Spain is unique among the West European countries:
- It's somewhat geographically isolated from the rest of Europe, on the Iberian Peninsula. Geographic isolation affected Spain almost as much as it affected Britain.
- It was occupied by Muslims for eight centuries, from the 700s to the 1400s.

Throughout history, some invasions are acceptable to the people being invaded and some are not. When the Romans conquered Spain in the second century BC, the Spanish initially resisted, but later adopted the Romans' cultural characteristics of family, language, religion, law and municipal government.

However, things were not so easy for the Muslims, when they conquered Spain in the early 700s. By that time, Spain was a clearly Christian society, and had no desire to convert to Islam.

Islam began in the Mideast in the early 600s. The Muslims spread rapidly all across Northern Africa, jumped the Strait of Gibraltar in 711, and soon conquered almost all of Spain.

Chapter 8 – History of Western Europe

Spain flourished under the Muslims, who built schools and libraries, cultivated mathematics and science, and developed commerce and industry.

But the desire for "Reconquest" by the Christians was always foremost in the minds of the Spanish people. The Christians reconquered bits and pieces of Muslim-occupied territory over the centuries.

In 1469, Spain was united by the marriage of Isabella and Ferdinand, the Catholic Monarchs of two Spanish kingdoms, Castile and Aragon, respectively. Thus, the crisis war we described above, triggered by rioting against upper class Conversos and unconverted Jews, also had another component: there was to fierce infighting among other royal relatives of the two Monarchs. But Spanish unity prevailed, and in 1478, the Spanish Inquisition was authorized, with the purpose of investigating the sincerity of Muslims and Jews who claimed conversion to Christianity. In 1492, the Catholics were able to complete the Christian Reconquest of Spain from the Muslims.

As we've pointed out, a bloody, violent crisis war changes the character of a nation, and the nation retains that character throughout the next 80-year cycle. That's what happened with the 1480s civil war. Spain saw itself as the home of true Catholicism, and saw itself as having the duty to spread Catholicism throughout Europe. Thus, the crisis war that climaxed with the Reconquest and the expulsion of the Jews in 1492 resulted in a new Catholic Spain. "It was at this moment that the concept of manifest destiny - so easy to take hold in any country at the height of its power - sank deep into the Spanish conscience[*]," says Manuel Fernandez Alvarez of the University of Salamanca. "The Spaniard felt he had a godly mission to carry out, and this was to make it possible for him to withstand bitter defeats in later years."

> *It was at this moment that the concept of manifest destiny sank deep into the Spanish conscience*

During the 1500s, there were three factors that fed into this sense of manifest destiny:

- The Muslims had recently (in 1453) captured Constantinople, destroying what was left of the original Roman Empire (see chapter 9). Spain actively defended against further Muslim incursions into Europe.

- Beginning with Martin Luther's challenge to the Catholic Church in 1517, the Protestant Reformation was challenging the Catholic

Church throughout Europe. The Spanish Monarchs felt they could play a key role in stopping the Protestants.

- There were other worlds to explore, particularly the New World. The Spaniards initiated active development of the New World, with the intention of colonizing and spreading Christianity.

Immediately after the Reconquest, Spain sent Columbus to find a new route to East Asia, and Columbus discovered America in 1492.

New discoveries and conquests came in quick succession. Vasco Nunez de Balboa reached the Pacific in 1513, and the survivors of Ferdinand Magellan's expedition completed the circumnavigation of the globe in 1522. In 1519, the conquistador Hernando Cortes subdued the Aztecs in Mexico with a handful of followers, and between 1531 and 1533, Francisco Pizzaro overthrew the empire of the Incas and established Spanish dominion over Peru.

These were heady discoveries in the days following the Reconquest, and yet Spain's "manifest destiny" plans might have led to nothing except for something that Spain itself considered to be a gift from God to help them achieve that destiny: The Spaniards were able to bring thousands of tons of silver and gold from the New World back to Europe.

This was Spain's Golden Age. Spain became wealthy, and led Europe in music, art, literature, theater, dress, and manners in the 1500s. It exercised military strength throughout Europe, and led the fight against the Protestant Reformation.

However, problems arose. Spain's imported wealth was wasted on consumption, with nothing saved or invested. The precious metals created price inflation throughout Europe. Once again, as usually happens in any society's generational cycle, the controls and restrictions that are imposed just after a crisis war become unraveled late in the cycle. Money was used to paper over Spain's own internal divisions, and to fund more military adventures.

In 1568, with the Inquisition becoming ever more intrusive, serious rebellions broke out among the Muslims who had remained in Spain after the Reconquest. This led to mass expulsions throughout Spain of Muslims, leading to exodus of hundreds of thousands of Muslims, even those who had become devout Christians.

In the midst of the increased turmoil, Spain attempted to continue to serve God with its military might.

Disaster came in 1588 when Spain decided to invade England, which had succumbed to the Reformation in 1533. The plan was to overthrow the Protestant Queen Elizabeth and install a Catholic King. Spain's huge Invincible

Armada sailed up the English Channel and waited to be joined by transports with invasion soldiers. The soldiers never arrived. The English fleet trapped the Armada and scattered it. The Armada fled into the open sea, where a storm drove the ships into the rocks on the shores of Scotland.

The crisis war ending in England's defeat of the Spanish Armada was an enormous victory that signaled the decline of Spain as the leading military power in Europe.

This provides an important lesson for America today. Since World War II, this has been the Golden Age of America, and just as Spain felt obligated to spread Catholicism around Europe, we feel obligated to spread democracy around the world. Spain was too ambitious, and came to disaster; America may do so as well.

Medieval England

Because of its insularity, England has followed a fairly clean line of generational cycles that we trace here back to the Norman Conquest in 1066.

England wasn't *entirely* insular: England shared borders with at least two other regions, Wales and Scotland. However, it appears that it was England (rather than either Wales or Scotland) that initiated the crisis wars that forced the two regions to merge timelines with England and to merge physically with England, and so it's the English timeline that dominated the medieval period.

This insularity has also made it possible for Britain to advance ahead of other countries in other ways. Later in this chapter, as we discuss the transition of European governments from monarchy to parliamentary democracy, it's worth remembering that England had a parliamentary form of government as early as the 1200s. True, the Crown still had most of the power, and Parliament had to submit to the Crown's will almost always, but the fact is that because of the Parliament and Common Law, England has had internal peace for most of the time for centuries.

Let's briefly summarize the history of England during the medieval period.

The Norman Conquest in 1066

England and France have probably been at war with each other for millennia. We take up the battle from 1066, when the Normans of northern France (Normandy), led by William the Conqueror, completed their conquest of England from the Saxons*.

With that, England and France were united, with Norman kings running both regions. This brought peace between the two regions for decades.

Naturally, a fault line developed among the kids born in England and the kids born in Normandy after the conquest. Their parents knew each other from before and during the war, but the kids had no personal connection with each other. As these kids reached their 20s, a generation gap would have resulted in an awakening.

The exact nature of the disagreements between the younger and older generations at that time is lost in history, but we can be pretty sure it had to do with taxes. In fact, William the Conqueror completed a national census called the *Domesday Book* in 1086, so that he could raise income and property taxes. The kids would have been unhappy about that, and might well have blamed not only William, but also his old friends back in Normandy.

Eventually, William died, as did the kids who grew up during the Norman invasion, leaving in charge the people born after the Norman Conquest.

Civil War, 1135-54

William was followed as King by William II and then by Henry I. At the death of Henry I in 1135, a succession dispute arose because Henry left no male heir*.

A civil war broke out between, on one side, those who wanted the original Norman conquerors and their descendants in England to retain control, and on the other side, those who wanted Normandy to retain direct control. (This was not unlike the context of America's Revolutionary War, which was really a civil war fought between descendants of the original English settlers versus those who wished England to retain direct control.)

The civil war was not resolved until 1154, when Henry II, a new Norman king from Anjou in Normandy, took the English throne. The adjective corresponding to the word "Anjou" is "Angevin," and so the new line of kings was called the Angevin line.

During the awakening period of Henry II's reign, there were dramatic changes to make the law fairer*. The Common Law required courts to make rulings based on precedent, thus limiting its power to make arbitrary rulings; and the jury system required a citizen's guilt or innocence to be decided by his peers, not by a court official.

Two different fault lines were exacerbated by these developments. First, there was the ancient fault line between England and Normandy (France); and second, there was the fault line within England itself, between partisans of the new Angevin kings and the Barons of the old order. The next crisis brought war across both of these fault lines.

War with Normandy and Magna Carta, 1204-15

> *The Civil war among the Normans was not unlike the context of America's Revolutionary War*

Back at the end of the last civil war, it made sense that a king who had just been imported from Normandy should remain in control of Normandy as well. However, that made less and less sense as years went by and generations passed.

Starting in 1204, King John suffered a crisis of confidence when he lost battles in Normandy, forcing him to cede control of most regions of Normandy*. This precipitated a renewed civil war with the English Barons who had been paying high taxes to support that losing war in Normandy.

The crisis was resolved in 1815, when King John was forced to sign the Magna Carta, the great charter of liberties, which restrained the king's power.

Civil war and war with Wales, 1264-1282

An ambitious attempt to conquer Sicily in 1254 left the Crown bankrupt. In 1264, a new civil war broke out between the Barons and partisans of the king*.

The problem was resolved in 1275, when the king was forced to accept a national assembly of king, lords and commons — the first parliament.

However, the civil war moved westward to another region - Wales. By 1282, the king had conquered all of Wales, and imposed harsh conditions.

However, a mid-cycle war with Scotland failed, and in 1327, the Treaty of Northampton gave Scotland its independence.

During the awakening period, the English parliament was given increased powers.

Hundred Years' War begins, 1337-47

The perennial war between England and France resumed in 1337, with the commencement of the Hundred Years' War, which was fought intermittently until 1453.

The first phase of that war was a major victory for the English, thanks to technology. A 14,000 man English army wiped out a 50,000 man French army in 1347, thanks to advanced weaponry*.

In centuries to come, wars of this type would be settled by some sort of international meeting that would set boundaries and assign spoils of war in such a way as to prevent war for another few decades. (See examples in this chapter of the Peace (treaty) at Westphalia, Treaty at Utrecht, Congress at Vienna, and so forth.)

No such mechanisms were available in 1347, however, so the war continued through a series of mid-cycle wars.

However, we can't ignore another major development: The Black Death reached the continent in 1348*.

Nature provides one method — sex — to keep population growing rapidly, and three methods to keep population from growing too rapidly: war, famine and disease.

The effect of disease on population is shown dramatically by this graph. The Black Death (bubonic plague) struck the entire world at various times in 1334-49 and killed enormous numbers of people.

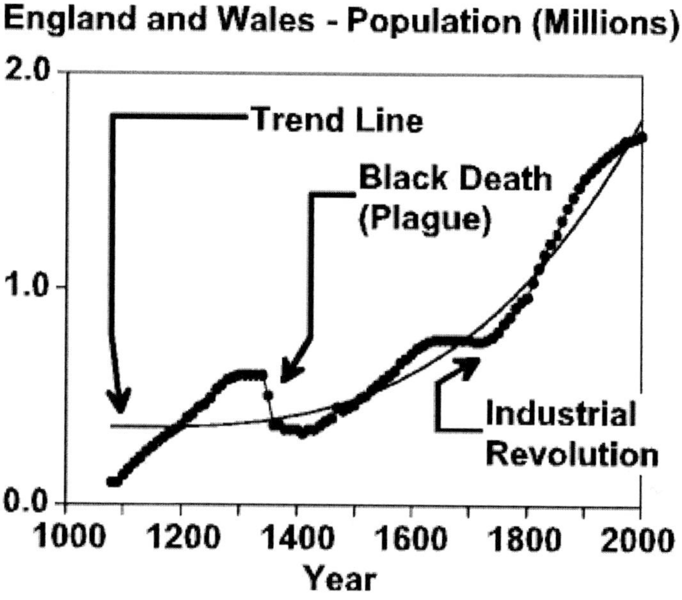

The Black Death turned out to have a major social effect, inasmuch as it killed commoners and royalty without any apparent distinction.

During the next awakening, numerous peasant rebellions took place all around Europe, including the Peasants' Revolt in England in 1381. This was a sign of things to come in the religious wars of the 1500s.

Figure 27 Population (millions) of England and Wales*, years 1000-2000.

Civil war and Welsh Revolt, 1386-1409

While the Hundred Years' war battles were being fought in France in the background, new wars were breaking out on English soil.

Tensions between king and parliament led to a new civil war in 1386*. It was resolved in 1400, but at that point, the war shifted to Wales, which was taking steps to declare its independence. Full-scale war took place between 1404 and 1409, at which time harsh restrictions were placed on the Welsh people.

The Hundred Years' war continued as a series of mid-cycle battles. The last English victory over the French was at Agincourt, France, in 1415. After that, the English became less energetic in fighting the war. By contrast, France rallied in 1429, supposedly because of the spirit of the peasant girl, Joan of Arc. By the end of the Hundred Years' war in 1453, France had almost completely expelled England.

Wars of the Roses, 1455-85

This civil war was fought over a new succession crisis, where members of both the ruling Lancaster family and the York family wanted to be the next king. The name "Wars of the Roses" is based on the badges used by the two sides, the red rose for the Lancastrians and the white rose for the Yorkists*. Incidentally, the Yorkists won.

The awakening period that followed was dominated, as it was throughout Europe, by the Protestant Reformation, and the resulting religious wars.

However, the religious wars in England were postponed because the new Protestant religion was adopted by the king. King Henry wanted to dump his current wife and marry Anne Boleyn, but the Pope wouldn't grant the divorce. So King Henry, with the acquiescence of parliament, declared himself to be head of the Catholic Church in England, and granted himself a divorce. He married Anne Boleyn and later beheaded her - but that's a story for another time.

In addition, a 1536 Act of Union changed the status of Wales from a dependent territory to an equal partner in a union with England. Welsh citizens were represented in parliament, and had full rights as English citizens.

War with Spain, 1559-88

When Queen Elizabeth was crowned in 1558, she immediately moved to consolidate the position of the Church of England. This raised tensions with Spain that, as we've seen, was trying to fulfill its "manifest destiny" to spread Catholicism. Attitudes in Spain were pretty hostile to England anyway, because that woman whom Henry had divorced to marry Anne Boleyn had been a Spanish princess.

Spain had a plan: They'd get rid of Queen Elizabeth (somehow), and then the next in the line of succession would be Mary Tudor, Queen of Scots — a Catholic.

Queen Elizabeth had a plan: Stall, stall, stall. Keep the Catholic Mary Tudor under control, but make sure she's OK. Hold off the inevitable Spanish invasion until England could build up its weak navy.

But destiny played a hand in 1568, when Queen Mary of Scotland was forced to flee for her life from her enemies in Scotland, and ended up safe and sound in Queen Elizabeth's prison.

Mary was imprisoned, but not helpless. When it was proved in 1587 that Mary was part of a plot to assassinate Elizabeth, Elizabeth was forced to execute Mary, and Spain was forced to launch the Invincible Armada to invade England in 1588. Elizabeth's plan had worked: she had stalled and used the time well to build a powerful navy which was able to defeat the overconfident Spain.

Britain's Great Civil War, 1638-60

Britain's great civil war began with the Scottish rebellion in 1638*. By 1642, the war was engulfing all of England, with parliament and the king serving as the main protagonists, battling each other for power, and control of the army. The British Monarchy was destroyed when the King was beheaded in 1649, and was restored in 1660 when a new king was crowned.

Aftermath of the Civil War: The Glorious Revolution

Once the monarchy was restored in 1660, the tensions between the Crown and parliament came back as well, since nothing had changed in terms of the balance of power.

By 1688, tensions had grown so great that there might have been another civil war, but now you can see once again the flow of history through generational analysis: There were too many people around who remembered the horrors of the last civil war, and didn't want to see another one.

Great things often happen in an awakening period — the period midway between two crisis wars, and that's what happened in England. Just as President Nixon was forced to resign during America's awakening period in

1974, King James was forced to resign in 1688. Here's how it happened (complete with a sex angle):

James II was a Catholic King, not working well with a Protestant Parliament. The Parliament had allowed him to become King in 1685 because he was old, soon to die, and had no children except for Mary, who was Protestant and married to the Dutch Prince William. Thus, as soon as James died, the Protestant Mary would become Queen.

Well suddenly, late in 1687, word spread that James' wife was pregnant, which would have created a new Catholic heir to the throne if the child turned out to be a boy. Well, it was a boy, born in June 1688, and the Parliament had already put steps into motion to get rid of James: They invited James' Dutch son-in-law William (Mary's husband) to invade England. When the Dutch army landed, late in 1688, James fled, headed to France, hoping that France's Catholic King would help him drive the Dutch army back. In something that the English at the time considered to be a miracle, James was captured by fishermen. He escaped, but by then it was too late. William and Mary were named King and Queen of England.

> *The Dutch invaded and conquered England in 1688, in England's Glorious Revolution.*

In fact, the English considered James' capture by fishermen to be only one of many miracles that year. They referred to the events of 1688 as the "Glorious Revolution." It was glorious because there was no war, no bloodshed, and because it settled the question of power sharing between the Crown and the Parliament.

There's a bit of real irony to the Glorious Revolution. The English like to point out that England was never invaded by a foreign power after the Norman Conquest until the German bombings in the two World Wars, but when they make that claim, they conveniently forget the Dutch invasion by Prince William. The fact that no shots were fired does not change the fact that the Dutch invaded and conquered England in 1688, in England's Glorious Revolution.

One more note: In 1693, the King and Queen established William and Mary College in America. The college broke its ties with England in 1776, but still retains the same name today.

CHAPTER 8 — HISTORY OF WESTERN EUROPE

The Protestant Reformation in France and Germany

In the 1500s, wars were still regional, rather than engulfing the entire continent, and crisis wars still occurred on different timelines. The religious wars were the context in which the different timelines were merged.

Corruption was widespread in the Catholic Church, and it's natural that any people suffering financial setbacks would blame the Catholic Church, and would adopt the Protestant religion as a means of protest. As a result, the Protestant religion spread rapidly in some regions, not in others, and religious fault lines began to develop.

Religious wars in Germany

In the region around Germany and Austria (the Habsburg Empire), there was a series of bitter wars in the 1540s between Protestants and Catholics. These wars were settled in 1555 with the Peace at Augsburg.

Crisis wars are often settled with a major compromise, typically by forcing people to accept fixed national or regional boundaries. Frequently, these compromises unravel over an 80-year period, resulting in the next crisis war.

As we'll see, that's what happened with the Peace at Augsburg. The great compromise was a regional one — that each region of the Habsburg Empire would be ruled by someone of the prevailing religion in that region (Catholic or Protestant). An interesting observation is that the Peace at Augsburg recognized religious pluralism for the first time in Europe*, and was thus a first step to recognizing full-fledged freedom of religion in America's Bill of Rights, 240 years later.

Religious wars in France

Turning now to France, the crisis war occurred 20 years later and was punctuated by the St. Bartholomew's Night Massacre, an atrocity that is remembered today.

Like Germany, France was also a Catholic country when Protestantism started spreading in the early 1500s. Various clashes broke out frequently over the decades, and the major civil war between the Catholics and the Hu-

167

guenots (the name adopted by French Protestants) began in 1562. Both sides were extremely violent, especially targeting each other's churches and clergymen and even lay people. (Attacks on civilians are a typical sign of a violent crisis war.)

The crisis climaxed on August 24, 1572, when Catholics massacred some 1,000 to 2,000 Huguenot civilians in Paris in a single night, known as the St. Bartholomew's Night Massacre. During the next two months, some 10,000 to 100,000 civilian Huguenots were slaughtered throughout the country, often in their own homes.

In the years that followed, some half million of the country's two million Huguenots fled to other countries. Many others renounced their Protestant religion, not being able to understand how God had deserted them.

The feelings generated by the massacre were greatly inflamed when the Catholics in Rome, led by the Pope, celebrated the deaths of so many "heretics" as a miracle, to be remembered as a holy event.

Figure 28 Contemporary rendering of St. Bartholomew's Night Massacre

The massacre haunts France to this day, though some tensions were relieved when Pope John Paul made a plea for forgiveness and reconciliation in a visit to France in 1997.

Thirty Years' War

With England, France, Germany and Spain on different timelines in the 1500s, it took the entire 1600s to merge the timelines of these countries, converging (as we'll see) on the War of Spanish Succession that began in 1701.

Germany's crisis war in the 1500s climaxed in 1555, and France's climaxed in 1572. This is a classic "merger of timelines" situation, and it's not surprising that the Thirty Years' War began in Germany in 1618, and France entered the war much later, in 1635.

German Civil War begins, 1618

The Thirty Years' War first began as a civil war in the Habsburg Empire (Germany and Austria), following the unraveling of the 1555 Peace at Augsburg.

We can identify a big financial crisis component to the Thirty Years' War, caused by the debasing of coins, and leading to the great "Tulipomania" bubble, as we'll see.

The financial crisis had, at its base, the price inflation caused by the precious metals that Spain imported from the New World during the Golden Age of Spain in the 1500s. After the disastrous destruction of the Invincible Armada by England, Spain rebuilt its Armada, but was forced to pull back many of its military adventures, especially as sources of precious metals in the New World began to peter out.

This led to financial hardship, but it doesn't take long for clever people to devise sneaky new methods for making money.

The habit of debasing coins had begun around 1600. The value of a coin was determined by the value of the precious metal in it. Princes and clergymen started to debase the coins by substituting cheap metal for good metal, or by reducing their weight. Trading in these coins became increasingly speculative during the "unraveling" period, since one could never be sure whether a coin was debased, or how much it was worth. By 1618, debasement was widespread throughout the Habsburg Empire, causing widespread financial hardship.

So by 1618, we had the two factors needed to forecast a new crisis war — a financial crisis and a generational change, the latter coming from the death or retirement of people who were around during the Peace at Augsburg.

The German civil war began.

The war expands

The reason that the Thirty Years' War lasted 30 years is that it comprised several different wars, because of the merger of timelines. It's as if we described World War I and World War II as a single war running from 1914 to 1945.

The Thirty Years' War was extremely destructive. It laid waste large parts of central Europe. Population declined from 21 million in 1618 to 18 million in 1648*. It started in Eastern Europe in the early 1620s; then it spread to the north and enveloped Denmark and Sweden in the late 1620s and 1630s.

Recall that France's timeline was about

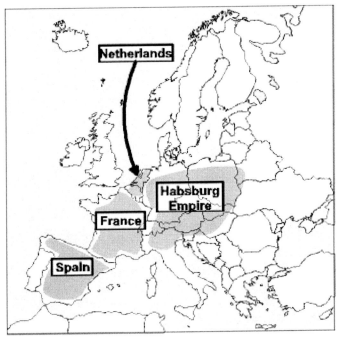

Figure 29 Rough map of Europe showing main participants in last decade of the Thirty Years' War

20 years behind Germany's timeline in the religious wars of the 1500s, and so it's not surprising that France entered the Thirty Years' War 20 years later than Germany did.

By the 1630s, Spain and Germany were closely linked by religion and marriage. A Habsburg cousin was ruling Spain through marriage.

More important, the two empires shared a common religious vision of serving God by spreading Catholicism and defeating the Protestants.

Furthermore, the Netherlands was also controlled by the Habsburg Empire.

So, if you take a look at the adjoining map, you can see that France was pretty nervous, being surrounded on all sides by the Habsburgs.

Furthermore, the financial health of Europe continued to decline. Spain was becoming increasingly in debt, as the supply of precious metals from the New World continued to decline, and the debasement of coinage around Europe was unabated.

This was the time of one of the most remarkable financial crises in recorded history, the "Tulipomania" bubble. Tulips were the "high tech" products of the day, and people were buying and selling tulips at increasingly high prices, just as people bought and sold high tech stocks at increasingly high prices in the 1990s. The Tulip Mania bubble is described in detail in chapter 6.

France's religious wars occurred in the 1550s-60s, with the brutal St. Bartholomew's Massacre occurring in 1572, and so the generational change in France occurred in the 1530s.

> *This was the time of one of the most remarkable financial crises in recorded history, the "Tulipomania" bubble*

France declared war on Spain in 1634 and on Germany in 1635. This extremely brutal war, which also involved Denmark and Sweden as allies of France, lasted until 1648.

Aftermath of the Thirty Years' War

The war ended with the Peace of Westphalia, agreed in 1648. It was called the "Peace of Exhaustion" by its contemporaries.

What was the great compromise that settled this war? Mainly, it settled by treaty the boundaries between France and its ally Sweden on the one hand and the Habsburg possessions on the other hand. About 250 separate German states were recognized as sovereign•.

Unfortunately, setting a boundary by treaty does not mean that the boundary is going to be observed "on the ground." Populations swell or move around, and these demographic changes can make old boundaries subject to renewed conflict.

A particular provision made the Netherlands an independent country. This became a particular issue half a century later, in the War of Spanish Succession.

The War of Spanish Succession, 1701-1714

The War of Spanish Succession broke out 87 years after the start of the Thirty Years' War, and 52 years after the treaty at Westphalia was signed. This war merged the timelines of the major West European countries, and put them onto the same timeline.

The war was triggered by the death of the King of Spain in 1700. Since he was childless, the person who would inherit Spain was not known until his will became known at his death. Today, it would be considered a peculiar thing to have one person inherit an entire country from another person, but that in fact is what happened in those days.

> *Today, it would be considered a peculiar thing to have one person inherit an entire country from another person*

Even more bizarre by today's standards is this: Because of numerous marriage alliances, the country might have gone to either French or German royalty, or split between them. It would not be known until the will was read. In addition, since France and Germany were long-term enemies, the will could have an enormous effect on the balance of power in Europe. How's that for a situation?

Well, when the will was read, it turns out that Spain was bequeathed to the grandson of the King of France, who then became King of Spain, and so Spain became allied with France, where previously it had been allied with Germany. It was previously Spain's alliance with Germany that triggered France's entry into the Thirty Years' War, and prompted the final settlement with the Peace at Westphalia.

Bequeathing Spain to French royalty completely unraveled the Westphalia Treaty, and the War of Spanish Succession began.

Like the Thirty Years' War, this war was filled with genocide and atrocities. It ended in 1714 with the Treaty at Utrecht, which the statesmen of the time signed because they wanted to avoid for as long as possible another violent conflict such as the one that had just ended*.

Aftermath of the War of Spanish Succession

England and France remained enemies for centuries, until World War I, and were at war somewhere in the world almost constantly.

England and France ceased active direct warfare on the European continent until the 1790s, but they were still virulent enemies, and fought on other battlefields, especially in America and India, in the meantime.

The largest of these wars in America occurred when the French formed an alliance with the American Indians, with the purpose of driving the English out of North America. The French had formed outposts in Canada, and south along the Mississippi River. The Seven Years' War ensued (known in America as the French and Indian War), from 1756 to 1763. France was decisively defeated not only in America but also in India, leaving England as the preeminent power in the world, by the time the two countries signed the Treaty of Paris in 1763. France later retaliated by supporting the colonists fighting England in America, but the next full-fledged war between England and France didn't occur until the French Revolution.

Tensions remain between England and France to this very day.

The French Revolution and Napoleonic Wars, 1789-1815

Now let's move on to the next crisis war between France and Germany.

Many historians say that the American Revolution *inspired* the French Revolution, and some even imply that it *caused* the French Revolution. The reasoning is that, in supporting the Americans against the British, the French became acutely aware of the Declaration of Independence and the ideals it represented, and wanted to implement those ideals in France as well.

We'll discuss America as a cause of the French Revolution below, but as you might expect, this book is going to present an entirely different analysis of the causes of the French Revolution.

Most of all, the French Revolution occurred because of a generational change. The last great war had been so violent that the statesmen who had signed the treaty ending it did so specifically saying that they never wanted to see another war like that again. Well, those people were dead, or at least gone. New people were in place, people who were tired of what was happening at that time.

And what was happening at that time?

Prelude

In the 1780s, France was in the midst of a major financial crisis. France had developed an enormous national debt — money it owed to other monarchies, to the Church, to wealthy individuals, and so forth. Just like a person who uses his MasterCard to pay off his Visa bill, France was running out of time. The debt had been increasing for decades, and was reaching a critical point by the 1780s.

Even worse, there was a shortage of food. Taxes were high to pay off the debt, causing sharp inflation in the price of food, with starvation among the working classes.

In the end, the country was put into the hands of a sort of bankruptcy court. And this was done not because of some great moral or ethical epiphany, but because the country was bankrupt. The French Revolution was thus a financial decision more than anything else.

From Bankruptcy to Waterloo

The "bankruptcy court" was called the Estates-General, and it consisted of three groups of "estates": The First Estate was the clergy; the Second Estate was the nobility; and the Third Estate comprised the common people. (Today, we use the phrase "fourth estate" to refer to the newspapers.) Within a few months, this turned into a National Assembly and Legislative Assembly which fulfilled its bankruptcy court responsibilities by wresting power from the monarchy and passing numerous reform laws — many of which *were* inspired by the experience in America where, just a few brief weeks earlier, the new Constitution had been adopted.

We will not attempt here to list all the fun facts of the French Revolution, such as how the National Assembly got locked out of its usual meeting place and, fearing a conspiracy, met in an abandoned tennis court and passed new laws targeting the supposed conspirators.

Instead, we'll focus here on the issues that make this crisis like the other crises that we've considered in this book — a financial crisis in combination with a generational passing, giving rise to desire for retribution, resulting in a series of shocks and surprises leading to war.

When Enron Corp. in 2001 became America's largest bankruptcy, Americans demanded retribution — in the form of sending Corporate CEOs to jail.

Within 1790s Paris, the principal tool for retribution was not jail, but the guillotine. The word "terror" was coined during this time, and during the Reign of Terror, 1793-94, some 200,000 people were executed by guillotine. And it's worth remembering that while "terror" is a negative term today, it was considered a positive thing during the Reign of Terror, because the people being terrorized were considered to be "bad" people.

> *Terror was considered a positive thing during the Reign of Terror because the people being terrorized were considered to be bad people*

To understand the feelings of rage and retribution, imagine if today we started executing people in Washington D.C. with public beheadings that everyone could see. Now imagine this happening 200,000 times in two years — the number people executed by guillotine in France during the Reign of Terror.

I mention this to remind you, again, that this is how genocide occurs. Whether we like to admit it or not, it's part of the natural human condition. In modern times, we've had huge acts of genocide in Cambodia in the 1970s and in Bosnia in the 1990s, and genocidal acts are going on today in Africa.

When money is at stake, the feelings of retribution spread quickly. All of Europe was controlled by monarchies, locked together through intermarriage and through promissory notes. Much of Europe had a lot at stake in restoring France's monarchy, and with the War of Spanish Succession now 70 years past, the statesmen who vowed never to have another such war were dead and gone. War felt right again.

Marie Antoinette, Queen of France and wife of France's King Louis XIV, was the brother of the Emperor of Austria, so it's not surprising that, after deposing the King and Queen, France's new Legislative Assembly declared war against Austria in 1792, especially since the Emperor of Austria declared his intention to sponsor a counter-revolution to restore the monarchy in France. A French invasion of Austrian land was quickly beaten back by Austrian forces, and Austria threatened to burn Paris to the ground if the French Royal family were hurt.

By the end of 1792, a new coalition formed by the European Monarchs, including Austria, Prussia, Great Britain, Spain, Russia, Sardinia, Tuscany, the Netherlands Republic and the states of the Holy Roman Empire (Germany) had formed to sponsor the counter-revolution.

The violent Reign of Terror, then, was fomented to punish counter-revolutionaries. The King was among the first to be guillotined (in Jan, 1793), and his wife was felled several months later (in October).

By 1797, the war had mostly settled down, but it couldn't end there. Unlike mid-cycle wars, crisis wars do not end until there is someone has forced a resolution — agreement that painful compromises must be accepted so that the fighting can stop.

However, this crisis was not settled. Before 1789, Western Europe consisted of a chain of over 300 political units with different principles of organization*, locked together by numerous treaties, marriages, and financial arrangements. France was the biggest and most important link in that chain, and when it disappeared through bankruptcy, the entire chain had to fall apart. So war was really a foregone conclusion.

The agent of this war was Napoleon Bonaparte, a brilliant soldier and general in the French army, who staged a *coup d'état* in 1799 to become military dictator.

Through a series of brilliant military campaigns, France's army under Napoleon overran almost all of Western Europe, effectively ending the interlocking chain of monarchies, and consolidating the French Revolution throughout Europe. He only came to grief when he invaded Russia to capture Moscow — a campaign we discussed in detail in chapter 5. By 1815, the 300 political units had been reduced to 38 states.

Could the French Revolution have been predicted?

A skeptical friend asked me sarcastically, "So you're saying that you could have predicted the French Revolution in 1750?"

The answer is "No," but this question provides a convenient launching pad to discuss the issue of exactly what we can and cannot predict using the Generational Dynamics methodology that we've been applying.

Suppose an alien from a distant galaxy had landed in Europe in 1750. Let's suppose that he was a mathematician who knew the mathematics that we know today, as well as the generational methodology for analyzing history on his own faraway planet, and wanted to apply what he knew to Earth in the year 1750. What could he have predicted?

First, he could have predicted that the age of monarchies would have to come to an end at some point in the not too distant future. That is, he could not have specifically predicted the French Revolution, but he could have predicted that its principal effect would have to come about one way or another.

Why is that? The answer has to do with complexity, a quantity that can be measured mathematically. The interlocking fabric of monarchies was becoming too complex to match realities "on the ground." As populations grew and moved around, the "ownership" of these populations would have to change to match the populations themselves, but that could not happen when inheritance determined "ownership," which then depended on who married whom, who had children with whom, and who owed money to whom.

In chapter 11, we'll show how the mathematics of complexity theory can predict the end of any form of centralized control over an entire economy, whether by dictatorship, monarchy, socialism, or communism, and that capitalism and representative government (republicanism) are the only organizational forms that can survive forever. But for now we simply make the observation that the end of the monarchies could have been predicted in 1750.

What about time frames? Could the alien visitor in 1750 have predicted that the European monarchies would collapse in the early 1800s?

I believe so, but only if we assume that the alien had the power to fly around in his space ship and gather a great deal of demographic information about Europe over the preceding 100-200 years. By using this information, the alien could have used his spaceship's computer to forecast how quickly the complexity of the interlocking relationships would grow, and would then be able to show that within 50-75 years it would become too complex to continue.

Before ending this speculation, let's consider one more question: What happens if the alien remains on earth for 32 years, and is in France in 1782. Could he have predicted the French Revolution at that time?

Here, the job of predicting is quite a bit easier. France's financial situation was already dire, and it could have been predicted that France was going into bankruptcy: there was no other possible outcome by 1782.

What does going into bankruptcy mean for France in the 1780s?

The answer to that question would depend on the mood of France and its people. If the country had been in a mood of "deterrence, compromise and containment," then the King and Queen might have felt forced to find a way to repay its debts — spend a lot less money, force the clergy and the nobility to give up some of their lands to be used for debt repayment, and so forth.

In fact, the first moves of 1789 were to do just that — by impaneling the General Assembly, France was trying to find a peaceful means to pay its debts.

And that might have worked a few decades earlier, when the violence of the War of Spanish Succession was still in people's minds. The French people might have swallowed their pride and set up a program of fiscal austerity to put France's finances back on course.

But too much time had passed, and once the important generational change is made, then desires for compromise always become desires for retribution, and so event spiraled into a war that engulfed the entire continent. And the alien in France in 1782 could reasonably have predicted, at that time, that some such scenario was likely.

The important analogy is, of course, to today, 2003. The generational change has occurred, the Nasdaq has crashed, as have the World Trade Center towers. There is a mood of retribution today, not only in America, but in many other countries as well, and that's why we can predict that some series of as yet unknown events will lead us and the Islamic world to a major war in the next few years.

Aftermath of the Napoleonic Wars

When analyzing the aftermath of a crisis war, it's usually best to start with the painful compromises that were made so that the fighting could finally stop (like slavery in the American Revolution). Those compromises often get revisited in the next awakening, and especially in the next crisis war (like slavery in our own Civil War).

To analyze what happened in Europe during the nineteenth century, we have to understand what the great compromises were at the truce for the French Revolution and Napoleonic Wars.

What were the painful compromises that everyone accepted in order to settle the French Revolution? The complex web of interrelationships between monarchies around Europe had collapsed from the sheer weight of its complexity.

There were two major areas of painful compromises adopted by the major European powers at the Congress of Vienna in 1815:

- Many of the old monarchies were restored to their old pre-Revolution statuses, though presumably with additional human rights granted to the people.

- In going from 300 political units (before 1789) to 38 states, many boundaries were arbitrarily assigned in ways that couldn't last. For example, the kingdom of the Netherlands was formed by lumping together the Protestant Dutch in the north with the French-speaking Catholics in the south. (Within 25 years, the south had split off into a separate country, Belgium.)

Both of these compromises had to be revisited — the first in the awakenings of the 1840s, and the second in the wars of the 1860s.

The Revolutions of 1848

The words "revolutionary explosion" have been used to describe the riots, revolts and demonstrations that were widespread in Europe in that one year, 1848.

There had been numerous rumblings before that. As usual, we expect awakenings to be 15-20 years after the previous crisis war is settled, because it's at that time that the "generation gap" appears — the people who are too young to have personal memory of the war start to become adults.

And indeed, various rebellions did start in the 1830s. One of them — the 1830 rebellion of Belgium against Dutch rule — led to Belgian independence a few years later.

But the Belgian situation was unique. For the most part, as is typical of awakenings, no boundaries changed until the wars of the 1860s. What did happen is that the revolutionary awakenings forced many gradual changes throughout Europe. These changes included things like major reform laws in England, and the 1830 overthrow and replacement of Charles X, latest King of France.

In fact, the only reason that 1848 is so noteworthy is because so many rebellions occurred in that one year — in England, France, Hungary, Germany, Italy, and other locations.

What was so special about that particular year? What was the event that caused so many youngsters of the postwar generation to rebel at once?

Presumably, the commonality was triggered by the Irish potato famine, which began in 1846. The famine produced massive starvation in Ireland, and a deep recession throughout Europe in 1847. All the rebellions of 1848 would have happened sooner or later, but the potato famine, focused them all on a particular year.

Of particular interest is that Karl Marx published his *Communist Manifesto* in the same year (though under a different title at the time). Communism and socialism took hold in much the same way a religion might have taken hold in other times. In chapter 7, we examined the lives of Jesus, Mohammed and the Buddha to show how religions begin in awakening periods. The experience of Communism shows what might happen after that.

Communism and socialism started to spread among a number of disaffected groups; trade unions were particularly targeted. Communism became especially popular in Paris, where proponents associated communism with the French Revolution and its true revolutionary meaning, before the monarchy was restored in 1815. Communism's greatest victory came in Russia, where it was adopted as the Bolshevik Revolution in 1917, during World War I. This illustrates how the ancient religions might themselves have become popular: creation by a charismatic founder during an awakening; spread in popularity; adoption by a society during a crisis war. Communism of course only lasted one 80-year cycle after adoption — it effectively ended with the breakup of the Soviet Union in 1991. In another time, it might have transmuted into a religion, and lasted for years.

The Crimean War, 1853-56

The Crimean War is on the East European timeline, leading to World War I. It was a crisis war for Russia and Turkey. We'll discuss the Crimean War in chapter 9.

An interesting fact from the West European viewpoint is this: Both England and France fought in the Crimean War as a mid-cycle war, and it was the first major war where these two countries fought as allies.

Wars of German Unification — 1864-1871

The Wars of German Unification, which began 74 years after the beginning of the French Revolution, are little discussed in history books, but these wars, especially the Franco-Prussian war, were the crucial 19th century wars on the West European timeline leading to World War II.

Because of its strategic position in central Europe, Germany's borders have always been under constant pressure from all sides.

In preceding centuries, when Germany was known as the Habsburg Empire or the Holy Roman Empire, the boundaries of the empire were always in flux and were modified by many wars, both crisis wars and mid-cycle wars.

If you want to understand World War II and Hitler, forget most of what you've learned in school. You have to imagine yourself sitting in the middle of Germany as the centuries pass, and looking around in all directions. Whether it's France in the east, Russia in the west, Denmark and Sweden in the North, or the Muslims in the southeast, you always had to fight someone for land. WW II was just a continuation of that.

The 1815 Congress at Vienna, which ended the Napoleonic wars, was like many of the treaties we've been discussing — a temporary band-aid on a never-ending problem. It finalized the end of the Habsburg Empire, and left the Germanic people scattered in various different regions.

A need for the unification of all German people into one state was felt almost immediately after the treaty, but it was not until the revolutions of 1848 that the deep support for unification became undeniable. At that time, in the midst of a severe recession, popular uprisings in Berlin, Vienna and elsewhere drove some regional leaders from office and elicited promises from others for a common German constitution.

Who would lead the German unification? There were two major Germanic empires at the time, Prussia and Austria, and they competed with each other for the leadership role.

Adding to the atmosphere was a kind of ghost: Louis-Napoleon Bonaparte, nephew of Napoleon I, took power in France as Emperor Napoleon III in a coup d'état in 1852. This was a shock to the people of the British public, who feared another era of Napoleonic conquest. However, the people of the British public were incredulous when Napoleon III sought friendship with England*. This marked a dramatic change into British-French relations after centuries of warfare, and the two countries were allies in the Crimean War of 1854-56.

Into this atmosphere came Otto von Bismarck, an obscure Prussian diplomat who became Chancellor of Prussia in 1862. History records Bismarck as both master politician and brilliant military tactician, in that he seems to have snookered just about everybody, while building up and using his army to achieve his goal of German unification under Prussia.

In an 1864 war with Denmark, Prussia and Austria wrested two German territories from Denmark, and Bismarck used the opportunity to enlarge the Prussian army. Then in 1866, he provoked Austria into declaring war on Prussia, and defeated Austria with his enlarged army. Finally, in 1870, he provoked France into declaring war on Prussia. In both cases, he gained political advantages the sympathy generated when another country declared war on Prussia, and he gained territory by actually winning both wars.

This war was a disaster for France. German forces overran and occupied France for months — something that was repeated 70 years later in World War II. It was followed in 1871 by a violent civil war known as the French Commune — resulting in 30,000 killed, the end of France's Second Republic, and the beginning of the Third Republic.

In addition, France was forced to cede the regions of Alsace and Lorraine to Germany. These territories, which were adjacent to the German territories, had been made part of France by the Treaty of Utrecht 57 years earlier, but now they were made part of the new German Reich.

The future of France and Germany

World War II has been covered elsewhere in this book (pp. 50, 86 and 210), and won't be treated again here.

The history of these two countries is clear: They've been warring with each other for centuries, with crisis wars every 70-80 years or so: Thirty Years' War (1635-48), War of Spanish Succession (1701-14), Napoleonic Wars (1793-1810), Wars of German Unification (1860-71), World War II (1938-45). The only thing that's surprising is that it never occurs to anyone that things won't be different this time.

However, there's a strange historical twist in progress this time. In the past, England was allied with one of the countries and opposed to the other. There is a historical reason given for this: England always allies itself with the opponent of the country that is threatening to conquer all of Europe. Thus, England opposed Napoleon's France, and Hitler's Germany.

So what's happening today, with Germany and France appearing to line up against England in the war against Iraq? The historical twist is that the Germans and the French see England and America trying to take over the world the way the French or the Germans used to try to take over Europe. The generational change has already occurred throughout Western Europe, and there is a severe recession in progress. The attitudes of the Germans and French will continue to harden in the next few years, and they may continue to harden against England and America.

This is all very, very speculative of course. Still, it's the direction we currently appear to be headed in, and it is a possible scenario. The Generational Dynamics forecasting methodology (see page 76) with a regular current attitudes analysis will detect how this is playing out, long before any actual actions are taken.

Chapter 9 — Islam versus Orthodox Christianity

Let's face it: Most Americans know almost nothing about Eastern Europe, and if they think about it at all, they think it's pretty much the same as Western Europe.

And many Americans don't even know that Orthodox Christianity exists, and if they think about it at all, they think that it's just a simple variation of Catholic and Protestant Christianity.

Figure 30 Eastern Europe / Western Asia, showing major Orthodox/Muslim fault line regions: Balkans, Crimea, and Caucasus (mountains). Not shown: Muslim Bosnia, east of Serbia in Balkans.

Neither of these beliefs could be farther from the truth.

First, Orthodox Christians and Western Christians have never been particularly friendly ever since the Roman Empire collapsed, and later they became bitter enemies. That bitterness still exists today, and could be seen in 2000 in the anti-Catholic riots and demonstrations when the Pope visited Greece. It could be seen again in 2003, when the Pope was greeted with similar riots when visiting Serbia.

Second, Eastern Europe cannot be understood except through the centuries-old conflict between Orthodox Christianity and Islam, a struggle that's still being fought in wars today, especially in the Mideast.

In recent history, the fault line between Islam and Orthodox Christianity is being expressed through conflict in the following geographical areas:

- **The Balkans.** It was a war in the Balkans that triggered World War I in 1914, and then that war was replayed in the Bosnia war in the 1990s. This is actually the region where all three civilizations — Western Christians, Orthodox Christians and Muslims — converge for war on a regular basis.

- **The Crimea.** Although part of Ukraine today, the Crimean Peninsula was inhabited by Muslim Tatars until 1944, when Stalin forcibly relocated the entire population to central Asia. Today, descendants of relocated Crimean Tatars are demanding to return to their confiscated land.

- **The Caucasus.** These mountains are extremely valuable real estate, since many Asian trade routes are squeezed through this bottleneck between the Black and Caspian Seas. Therefore, whoever controls this region can also control much valuable trade.

Of these three regions, there is one that is even more volatile than the others are, because it's where "east meets west": In the Balkans, Western Christianity, Orthodox Christianity and Islam all meet.

Having noted that, we'd have to add one more fault line region, perhaps the most volatile of all: Jerusalem. Among Christians, there has been a historic struggle between Catholics and Orthodox over who is the primary protector of Jerusalem.

Considering Eastern Europe as a whole over the past 2000 years, the struggle between Orthodox Christianity and Islam has led to massive invasions and wars that caused the rise and fall of huge empires. There are cultural memories of those wars on both sides, and the desire on both for revenge for actions committed centuries ago has not abated. From our America-centric point of view, we have little understanding of how deep this struggle goes, and why it's far from over.

So, as you read this chapter, and see how Islam changed the map of the world, keep in mind that the map of the world is going to change again in the next 20 years. Even if the United States once again escapes massive invasion on its soil, as it always has in the past because of its isolation from the rest of the world, there will still be major changes to the map of the world in Africa, the Mideast, and the region between Pakistan and India, and probably also to the region of eastern Europe and western Asia. It doesn't take rocket science to figure this out — just look at the explosion in the population of Muslim adherents that's occurred in the last few decades. In a world where we know few things with certainly, we can be fairly certain that these country boundaries are going to change in the next 20 years.

The World prior to Mohammed

In chapter 7, we showed how the Golden Age of Greece was an awakening that led to the spread of Greek culture, and we showed how Judaism grew from ancient times, leading to the ministry of Jesus as an awakening that led to the spread of Christianity — and by that we mean what today is called Orthodox Christianity.

The life of Mohammed and the birth of Islam was yet another awakening, as we showed, creating a new empire that clashed with the existing empire based on Judaism and Orthodox Christianity.

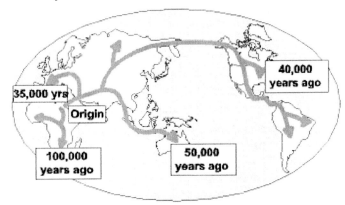

Figure 31 The spread of humans from north Africa around the world*.

Let's begin by putting all the events before the birth of Mohammed into perspective.

The spread of humans and civilizations

Because of the scope of the conflict we're describing, it's worthwhile taking just a moment to get a big picture. Let's briefly go back tens of thousands of years to the origins of our human species (Figure 31).

Anatomically modern human beings began to appear in North Africa around 100,000 years ago. From there they spread around the world — south into Africa, into Europe 35,000 years ago, south to Australia 50,000 years ago, north to Russia, and then east across what is now the Bering Strait (there used to be a land bridge there), to populate the Americas 40,000 years ago.

Figure 32 The nine major civilizations today*.

Eventually, these migrations created the thousands of civilizations that have merged into the nine civilizations we know today. The adjoining map shows today's major civilizations, and where they're located. Any region on the boundary of two of these civilizations has the potential for a major war, or at least a battle site.

The rise and fall of the Roman Empire

We begin with the history of several empires that existed before Mohammed's birth. Then we'll be able to continue by showing how Islam affected these civilizations.

Let's start with something we've seen before (chapter 7): The empire created by Alexander the Great.

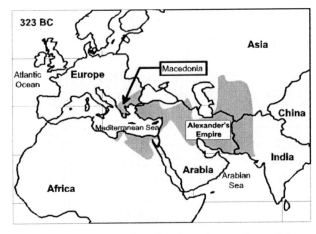

Figure 33 Alexander the Great's empire at his death in 323 BC.

The significance of Alexander's empire is that it spread Greek culture and the Greek language throughout the Mideast, northern Egypt, the Arabian Peninsula, and even further east into western Asia. This provided the region with a cultural cohesion that later resulted in one empire after another — the Roman Empire, the Byzantine Empire, and the Islamic

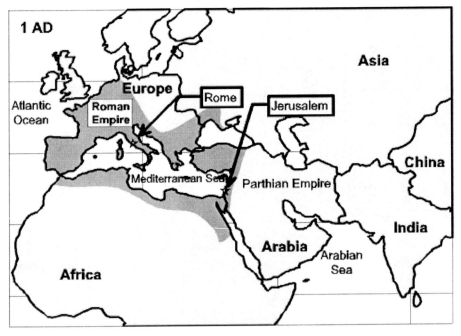

Figure 34 Roman Empire at its peak, around 120 AD

empire.

It's one thing to create an empire, it's an entirely different thing to maintain it and administer it. You have to set up a local government in each region to collect taxes and provide public services, and you have to have an army to protect each region from attack by other empire builders.

Under Alexander the Great, the Macedonians weren't too good at long-term administration, and so Alexander's empire didn't last long after his death. But when the Romans started moving in a century later, things were different. The Romans were masters at administration and in maintaining an empire.

As shown in this map, the Roman Empire was quite extended. To the east, the Romans conquered Greece and Macedonia, and from there went on to conquer much of Alexander's old empire. However, the Romans went west as well, conquering much of northern Africa, all of Western Europe, even extending into the British Isles.

However, the Germanic regions were not subjugated, and those peoples became the downfall of the Roman Empire. The Romans used the word "barbarians" to describe the uncivilized hordes with colorful names that poured in from other regions, especially Germany, starting in the 200s.

Figure 35 Byzantine Empire around 600 AD. The Roman Empire in the West had been completely destroyed by the invading barbarian hordes.

As we've already said, it's hard to administer and protect a far-flung empire, and in 285, the Roman Empire was administratively split into an eastern and western region.

The western Romans held off the hordes for a long time, but finally the Visigoths, under the leader Alaric, sacked Rome in 410. The Romans recaptured Rome, but then succumbed to the Huns, under Attila the Hun. The

Huns were driven off, but in 476, the Roman Empire collapsed under attack from the Vandals out of Germany. There were just so many "barbarians" that the Roman Empire could withstand.

The separation of Orthodox and Catholic Christianity

The split of the Roman Empire into Eastern and Western regions was not just purely administrative; it was the beginning of a fateful split in Christianity that has enormous effects in today's world.

The collapse of Rome and the Western Roman Empire was also the end of the original Orthodox Christian religion in Western Europe.

That left the Eastern Roman Empire, much of which still spoke Greek from Alexander's days.

The city that we know today as Istanbul, Turkey, had the Greek name of Byzantium in Alexander's days, and was renamed Constantinople by the Romans, after Constantine the Great, the first Christian Roman emperor. Constantinople became the center of the new Byzantine Empire, which was based on the old East Roman Empire.

By 600, there was no longer any recognizable Roman Empire, although there was still the Pope and Catholicism in the West. As the map above shows, the Byzantine Empire, centered in Constantinople, held sway in the East and northern Africa.

This period also produced doctrinal splits between the Catholic and Orthodox Christian religions. The major difference between the two was a philosophical difference, having to do with the separation of Church and State.

The Byzantine Church was based on Greek culture, and an old pagan religion where the Greek gods were immortal, but had the same weaknesses and foibles as regular human beings. The pagan Greek gods were heavily involved in human affairs and affairs of state as well. The Greek cultural view was that religion and politics are intertwined. That's why today there's a Greek Orthodox Church, closely related to the Greek government, and a Russian Orthodox Church, closely related to the Russian government.

This is related to the concepts of "top-down" and "bottom-up" religions that we discussed in chapter 7.

The Catholic Church evolved quite differently. When the barbarian hordes were sacking Rome, the view of the Catholics was that Rome was one thing, but the Church was quite another thing. Sacking Rome shouldn't mean sacking the Church. So the Catholic view, that Church and state should be completely separate, was quite different from the Byzantine view which intermingled them. That's why the Catholic religion today, and also its Protestant offshoots, are considered to be stateless religions (except insofar as Vatican City can be considered a "state").

A final note on the last map: The Byzantine Empire had spread into Africa as far south as Ethiopia. Although the Muslims soon pushed the Byzantines out of Africa, an Ethiopian Orthodox church remained, creating a fault line between Muslims and Orthodox Christians in eastern Africa. Today, there is still a war going on across that fault line.

The Rise and Fall of the Muslim empires

Following Mohammed's death in 632, his followers conquered and converted many people. The resulting empire grew, then pulled back, and then grew again under the Turks, and them pulled back again. The final Muslim empire ended with the destruction of the Turkish Ottoman Empire after World War I. The following pages describe this in more detail.

The spread of Islam

It's not too much of an exaggeration to say that Islam spread like wildfire. As early as 12 years after Mohammed's death, Islamic warriors had taken over most of the Arabian Peninsula, including some lands formerly under control of the Byzantine Empire.

The main problems faced by the early Muslims were determining who would be "caliph*," the man inheriting Mohammed's mantle of leadership. There were three groups of contenders: Those who had been with Mohammed in his early days in Mecca, those who converted when he went to Medina, and those who converted later, when he returned to Mecca.

A crisis civil war within the community occurred in 656 among different followers, resulting in the selection of Ali ibn Abi Talib, an early convert and distant relative of Mohammed, as the fourth caliph. His victory did not end the battle, however. He was assassinated in 661, giving power to another clan, the descendants of al-Abbas, an uncle of Mohammed. This resolved the civil war, but when Ali's son was killed during a rebellion in 680, a new movement within the community was formed: The "partisans of Ali" or "shi'at Ali," called "Shi'a" for short, to distinguish themselves from the Abbasids, the descendants of al-Abbas.

This was the beginning of the division of Muslims into two groups, known today as Shi'a and Sunni Muslims.

Differences between the two groups differed along geographical and philosophical lines. The geographical differences were resolved with the center of Islam was transferred to Baghdad.

Figure 36 Further spread of Islam

This quarreling does not seem to have hindered the spread of Islam at all. By 750, Islam had spread much farther than some of early partisans probably believed could even be possible. To the north, the Byzantine Empire in the Mideast was squeezed closer to its capital in Constantinople. To the west, all former Byzantine possessions in northern Africa were conquered, and in eastern Africa, Islam even jumped over to Europe and took control of much of Spain. To the east, Islam spread far into what is India today, challenging the Hindu culture, and setting the stage for the wars between Pakistan and India today.

However, the philosophical differences that grew out this family went much deeper, and have not really been resolved to this day.

The philosophical quarrels were over which theologians, besides Mohammed himself, could define Islamic doctrine. Could doctrine change with the times, or even be redefined by new theologians who came on the scene, claiming the mantle of Mohammed?

The philosophical differences were resolved by a sort of "holier than thou" argument. The Abbasids challenged the Shi'as by asserting that only the prophet Mohammed could be a source of Islamic doctrine. This meant that the only valid sources of spiritual guidance are the Quran itself, and also the "sunna," the habitual behaviors of Mohammed himself, as recorded by his contemporaries. This created a mode of thought that came to be known as Sunnism, as distinct from Shi'ism*.

This battle reverberates to today in two different ways.

First, the Sunni and Shi'ite Muslims form a sometimes violent fault line within the Islamic community itself. This fault line was exploited in the extremely violent Iran/Iraq war of the 1980s.

Second, this philosophical difference gives rise to Islamic extremism and terrorism today. The Quran is a fixed, well defined work, but how well defined are the Sunna, Mohammed's habitual behaviors? Ahhh, that's not so clear, and is subject to all sorts of interpretations.

All of these philosophical discusses were lost, of course, on the ordinary farmer or merchant trying to get through the day and feed his family. In fact, it's not likely that belief in Islam went deep at first, even in regions conquered by Muslim warriors. For example, Muslims paid lower taxes than non-Muslims did, and so anyone could save money simply by converting to Islam, whether he really believed in it or not, by simply reciting a few words ("There is no God except Allah, and Mohammed is the Messenger of Allah").

However, Islamic culture spread to the conquered areas, and became deeper with time, for two reasons.

First, because it was the official religion and people could gain political favor by public prayer and attending mosques. In the course of several generations, the Islamic culture became the common culture.

The second reason for the spread of Islamic culture was the spread of the Arabic language. Conversion to Muslim may be easy, but it carried with it the acceptance that Arabic was the language in which the revelation had been given. Since Arab rulers spoke Arabic, the easiest way to deal with the government was to do so in Arabic*, and so Arabic became the language of everyday life, as part of the general spread of Islamic culture.

The invasions of the Asians

By 1100, both Islam and Orthodox Christianity were on the ropes, threatened with extinction, or at least marginalization to a few enclaves. As we'll now see, both religions experienced resurgence based on conversions by large populations from the vast steppes of central Asia.

In the process, numerous hostile regions came into existence, regions where the two religions faced each over fault lines, and where these hostilities continue to the present day.

The map below shows four important regions in 1100 AD:

- Dark area: Controlled by Muslim Arabs

- Medium dark area: Controlled by Seljuk Turks

- Light crossed area: Remaining pieces of Byzantine Empire, centered around Constantinople.

- Dark crossed area: Slavic area, converting to Orthodox Christianity.

These regions contained fault lines that are still hostile today.

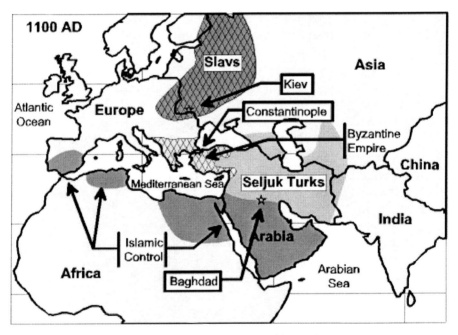

Figure 37 Arrival of Seljuk Turks

This allows us to illustrate an important fact: That the fault lines that may lead us into war today were troubled regions 900 years ago.

So let's take a look at what happened.

The Seljuk Turks

Starting from around the year 1000, the Islamic Empire was under attack from all sides*, in Europe, Africa and Asia; furthermore, the state was becoming increasingly inefficient, bureaucratic and disrespected.

The thing that confuses many people about this period is that they think that the Turks came from Turkey. Actually, the country that we call Turkey today is so called because the Turks came to occupy it. The Turks originated in central Asia, and they attacked, conquered and occupied the region now known as Turkey, which is the reason it's come to be known as Turkey.

Actually, the Turks were not new to the Arabs. The Turkish Empire had spanned much of Asia, from end to end, in the 600s, and was attacked in East Asia by the Chinese and in west Asia by the Arabs. By the 800s, the Arabs were using Turks as slaves and mercenaries, even entire armies of Turkish mercenaries.

Eventually, the Turks poured into the region in waves, and an incredible thing happened that changed the course of history: The Turks wholeheartedly adopted the religion of Islam, becoming Sunni Muslims, and in some ways were more Muslim than the Arabs*.

> *The thing that confuses many people about this period is that they think that the Turks came from Turkey*

The most important of the invading waves was known as the Seljuks, after the name of the family that led them. Under their leadership, the entire Islamic Empire was brought under control, and the empire itself was expanded.

On the eastern end of the Islamic Empire, there were created two religious fault lines that are of importance today: On the border with India, the Kashmir region has remained an area of major contention, today between Islamic Pakistan and Hindu India. And on the northern border, the region of Chechnya is a fault line within today's Russia between the Muslims and (as we'll see below) the Orthodox Christians.

The Kingdom of Jerusalem

Speaking of fault lines, the champion fault line of them all, that perennial, enduring, never ending region of hostility is the line separating Jerusalem from the Arab community around it. Time after time after time, throughout history, every major war in western civilization, going back thousands of years, seems to involve Jerusalem in one way or another.

The arrival of the Turks created a ping-pong effect of attacks and counter-attacks between Christians and Muslims, and bitter feelings between Roman Christians and Orthodox Christians. As we'll see, the bitter feelings among these three populations continue to the present day, resulting in World War I in the 1910s, and the genocidal war in the Balkans in the 1990s.

The Christians in Europe became increasingly aware and nervous about the Muslim Turks pouring into East Asia, pushing back the Byzantine Empire, especially when the Turks won a major victory against the Byzantines in 1075.

The Pope called for European Catholics to form an army to recapture Jerusalem. The first Crusade left in 1095, and by 1099, the Kingdom of Jerusalem had been established.

The Kingdom of Jerusalem was under constant attack by the Muslim Turks, and finally collapsed in 1187. Subsequent Crusades were all disastrous, and Jerusalem has remained in Muslim hands ever since — until the 1967 war following Israel's creation in 1948.

Catholics vs. Orthodox: The Great Schism

The split between the Catholic and Orthodox Christians is called a "schism" because it was basically a political split, not a major difference over religious doctrine; such doctrinal differences as there were were minor, or not fundamental to the Church. The schism is contrasted to the later split between the Catholics and the Protestants, called a "heresy" because religious doctrine was fundamentally changed by the Protestants.

Many scholars claim that the schism was nothing more than a kind of lovers' quarrel that could have been avoided if the two parties had simply been a little more sensitive to each other needs, but in my opinion a break could never have been avoided, for reasons given earlier in this chapter.

The Romans had captured Greece centuries earlier, but now the Roman Empire was gone and the Byzantine Empire still survived. The sacking of Rome had made Catholicism an intentionally stateless religion, with a religious leader, the Pope, having dominion over all Christians everywhere. By contrast, the Byzantine Emperor was both a head of the Church and a head of state. There was no way that they wouldn't clash, or that either would give in to the other when their spheres of influence overlapped.

Political differences created bitter hostilities between the Pope and the Emperor. In 1054, the Emperor closed all the Catholic churches in Constantinople, which provoked the Great Schism, when the Pope excommunicated the Emperor, and the other Byzantine bishops supported the Emperor against the Pope. The two Churches were officially separate.

> *The split between the Catholic and Orthodox Christians is called a "schism" because it was basically a political split, not a major difference over religious doctrine*

The Crusades were not welcomed by the Byzantines, who feared that crusading armies, traveling on their way to capture Jerusalem, would try to subdue Constantinople along the way.

That didn't happen in the first Crusade, but it did later, after the Kingdom of Jerusalem had come and gone. In 1204, a new Crusade was heading back to recapture Jerusalem back again from the Muslim Turks. Along the way, the Christian army sacked Constantinople, starving and murdering its citizens, and plundering the Church's treasures accumulated over the centuries. The deed was capped by placing a prostitute on the Emperor's throne at the church of St. Sophia, at that time the most beautiful church in Christendom.

There's a commonly used English phrase, "forgive and forget," and I've found that many people seem to have a romantic notion that the human psyche embraces this phrase, despite the enormous body of human experience to the contrary.

Acts of savagery that occur when two people divorce can cause hatred that lasts for decades, and atrocities that occur when two Churches divorce can cause desires for vengeance and retribution that last for century. Even though the Church was restored to the Byzantines a few decades later, "forgive and forget" never really happened throughout the following centuries.

Orthodox Russia and Catholic/Protestant Germany were bitter enemies in both World War I and World War II. And in the Balkans in the 1990s when the Orthodox Serbs attempted ethnic cleansing against the Catholic and Protestant Croats and Muslim Bosnians, there's little doubt that they were at least partially motivated by the Catholic sacking of Constantinople in 1204 and the Muslim conquest of Constantinople in 1453 (see p. 199).

It's worth remembering this if, as this book predicts, we find ourselves in the midst of a major world war in the next few years, the fault lines over which that war will be fought were created centuries ago. If the world is a train hurtling towards world war, then that train left the station long ago and nothing can be done to stop it today.

One more note about the atrocities of 1204: Tensions between the Catholic and Orthodox communities were reduced when the Pope finally apologized for the first time — in 2001! Pope John Paul's visit to Athens in May, 2001, generated vocal anti-Catholic demonstrations among the Greek priests and citizens, until finally the Pope said, "For occasions past and present, when the sons and daughters of the Catholic Church have sinned by actions and omission against their Orthodox brothers and sisters, may the Lord grant us the forgiveness we beg of him."

The Slavs: Russian Orthodox

This is a story of one of those events of history that would be simply cute or amusing if it weren't for the fact that it changed the world.

In 980, a pagan named Vladimir became ruling prince of the Slavs, headquartered in Kiev (see previous map). And Vladimir went religion shopping.

According to legend, he rejected Islam, because it forbade alcoholic drink. He sent commissions to visit the Christian Churches. The Bulgarians, they reported, smelt. The Germans had nothing to offer. But Constantinople had won their hearts. There, they said in words often to be quoted, "we knew not whether we were in heaven or earth, for on earth there is no such vision nor beauty, and we do not know how to describe it; we know only that there God dwells among men." Around 986-8, Vladimir accepted Orthodox Christianity for himself and his people*.

In the centuries to come, the Slav culture moved east and formed the Russian Empire.

Vladimir might have chosen Catholicism, and thus would one man have changed the history and the map of the world. Then the Orthodox religion might have disappeared completely. It wouldn't have prevented religious wars, however, as the later wars between the Catholics and the Protestants showed.

As things stood, two major separate Christian civilizations have come about. The Western civilization, combining the Catholic, Protestant and Jewish religions; and the Orthodox civilization, comprising mainly Russia and Greece, but with numerous other smaller ethnic Orthodox churches.

Even more important, Russia became separate from Western Europe, and thus did not usually become involved in the west European war timeline. Russia, along with Muslim Turks and later the Ottoman Empire, formed their own timelines which included World War I.

The Ottoman Empire and the fall of Constantinople

Around 1300, a Muslim Turkish tribe led by its chieftain, Osman, started to expand beyond its original border*. It became the Ottoman Empire, and was ruled by Osman's descendants in unbroken succession through the 1600s, when it became the greatest empire in the world, and continuing until it was destroyed shortly after World War I.

Even the early days were not without defeats. In 1402, the central Asian conqueror Timur defeated the Ottomans, and almost destroyed them completely*. After Timur died in 1405, the Ottomans recovered, and went on to more conquests. However, Timur's victory over the Ottomans had one major unintentional effect: It delayed for several decades the final destruction of the Byzantine Empire*.

If someone were to compile a list of the major events of the last millennium, the fall of Constantinople to the Muslim Turks in 1453 would have to be right near the top.

The Byzantine Empire had been getting weaker and smaller anyway, but this was its final destruction. It was the destruction of a Hellenistic culture dating back to antiquity, and it was also the final destruction of the remains of the Roman Empire. Nothing quite like it had happened for a long time.

The Ottomans and Islam were definitely on a roll. Islam had spread around the known world, and even countries that were not controlled by Islamic governments had substantial Muslim populations. This visibility extended from Western Europe to eastern Asia, and south to Indonesia.

By 1600, the world had changed enormously. The heart of Islam was now the Ottoman Empire, headquartered at Istanbul, the new name for Constantinople. St. Sophia's Church was now a mosque. In a long line of great empires — Alexander's empire, the Roman Empire, the Byzantine Empire — the Ottoman Empire was now the greatest empire in the world.

We'll come back to the Ottomans later, but first we'll shift our point of view to the north — to Russia.

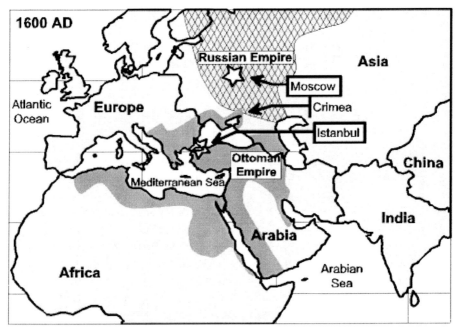

Figure 38 Eastern Europe in 1600 AD

CHAPTER 9 — ISLAM VERSUS ORTHODOX CHRISTIANITY

Russia's Generational Timeline

Much of Russia's history falls out of the cataclysmic fall of Constantinople to the Ottomans in 1453, destroying the Byzantine Empire.

The Orthodox Church would have been completely extinguished, had it not been for the Slavs whose Prince Vladimir, as previously described, had selected the Orthodox religion for himself and his people.

When the Roman Empire was destroyed, Constantinople believed that it had inherited the mantle of being the true (or "orthodox") Christian Church, the Church that could be traced back to the original teachings of Jesus. Now that the Byzantine Empire was destroyed, it fell to Moscow to take the mantle for itself.

The Catholic Pope had a different idea. In 1472, he arranged for Grand Prince Ivan III ("Ivan the Great") to marry Sophia, the orphan niece of the last Greek Emperor of Constantinople, in the hope of bringing the Russians back into the Roman Church*. Undoubtedly the two Churches were so far apart by then that they never could have merged anyway. In fact, submission to the pope was for most Greeks a renegade act, denying the true Church, whose tradition Orthodoxy had conserved*. In the end, the Pope's gesture backfired.

Ivan immediately took the title of Tsar, and thus became the first Tsar of the new Tsarist Russia. ("Tsar," or "Czar," was derived from the name of the Roman Emperor Caesar, as is the German word "Kaiser.") Thus, Ivan would be not only the head of Russia, he would also be head of the Orthodox Church — and never part of the Roman Church.

Russia made great territorial expansions under Ivan the Great, especially the huge territory of Novgorod after a series of wars ending in 1485.

Livonian War, 1557-82

Ivan the Great's grandson, Ivan IV assumed power as Tsar in 1547. In generational terms, this was an "unraveling" period, where problems are typically handled using compromise and containment. The problem was the power struggle between the tsar and boyars, the wealthy landowners who owned most of the land (as well as the peasants living on the land).

He really began living up to his nickname, Ivan the Terrible, when the crisis period began around 1557, and he began a war to annex Livonia, a region north of Poland on the shores of the Baltic Sea. This conflict drew in Poland, Sweden and Denmark. Russia ended up with a portion of Livonia.

By 1564, he was at war with the boyars (landowners), and executed a reign of terror that took the lives of many boyars. He would have violent rages (during one of which he killed his own son), alternating with deep repentances. In 1570, he ravaged Novgorod, and massacred many of the inhabitants, whom he suspected of sympathy for the Poles*.

This was the first time we see the Crimea playing an important role in Russian history.

The Tatars were a tribe of Mongols with a glorious history: Under the leadership of Genghis Kahn, probably the greatest conqueror in the history of the world, they had defeated China in 1215, and then turned westward and conquered much of southern Russia by 1227*.

The Crimean Tatars had intermingled with the central Asian Turks, and spoke a Turkish language. By the 1400s, they adopted Islam as their religion.

Russia drove the Tatars back, and by the time of Ivan the Terrible, they occupied only three remaining regions. Two of those regions (Kazan, Astrakhan) were conquered by Ivan in 1552-56, thus uniting all of southern Russia. But one region remained under Tatar control: the Crimea.

It was in 1571 that the Crimean Tatars attacked and sacked Moscow. Ivan's adventures in Livonia received a response from the Swedes, who defeated Ivan in 1578. In 1581, Poland invaded western Russia. In 1582, Ivan was forced to sign a peace treaty with Sweden and Poland, giving up all the territory he had gained*.

Almost 20 years of war had been for nothing, but that's not atypical of crisis war periods; as this book shows over and over, war is like sex: societies go to war regularly, whether the wars make sense or not.

Russian Conflict Fault Lines

When looking at Russian conflicts over the last few centuries, several fault line themes thread through them:

- **Internal power**: The main power centers are: The Tsar; the Russian Orthodox Church; the large, wealthy landowners (boyars); and the peasants. Each of the transformations that accompanied all the crisis wars included a component that substantially changed the relationships between two or more of these power centers.

- **Looking west**: Relations with Europe. Russia had numerous wars with Sweden, Poland and various West European powers, but they almost always turn out to be mid-cycle wars.

- **Looking south**: Relations with Turkey and the Ottomans. These wars tended to be crisis wars. The reason that these wars were relatively more important to Russia's survival is because they affected Russia's access to the Mediterranean Sea, and important trading routes. There may also be a long-term visceral enmity, since the same Turkic people who created Turkey also once captured much of Russia.

- **A special case**: The Crimean peninsula is a special case of note to Russia's south, for the reasons already explained: The Crimean Tatars were geographically located in the Ukraine, but they were Muslims and remained emotionally connected to Turkey and the Ottomans.

All of these fault lines came into play during the Livonian War period of Ivan the Terrible.

Because of Russia's huge size, the Principle of Localization indicates that different regions of Russia will have different timelines until the timelines merge. We have a simplified Moscow-centric view in this discussion, but cycle lengths are affected by the merging of timelines.

Peasant Rebellions and Church Schism, 1649-71

In 1642, an enemy (the Cossacks) of the Crimean Tatars offered to Moscow a fortress that they had captured from the Tatars — and Moscow refused it, to avoid conflict with the Ottoman Turks*. This is interesting to us because it's a typical conflict-avoidance strategy during an unraveling period.

However, the mood changed to "let's solve this problem once and for all" by 1649 in a different arena — the control of peasants.

During Ivan the Terrible's 1564 reign of terror against the landowners, many large estates had been destroyed, and the peasants who had formerly worked on those lands had fled to other regions, especially Siberia. The Moscow region lost half its peasants♦. As a result, Moscow imposed stronger and stronger laws restricting freedom of movement of the peasants.

In 1649, a new law (Ulozhenie) essentially turned all peasants into ordinary slaves, who were bound to their masters and could be bought or sold. This triggered a series of peasant rebellions, starting in the central regions in 1655, and reaching Moscow by 1662, where 7,000 peasants were executed♦. In 1669, an army of 200,000 rebels led by Stephen Razin overran large regions of the South, killing landowners and middle class people as they went. The rebels were finally defeated in 1671.

During this same crisis period, there was a major battle for supremacy between the Russian Orthodox Church and the state, and between their respective heads, Patriarch Nikon and Tsar Alexis. That issue was resolved in 1666 when Nikon was deposed, but then the Church went to war with itself, creating a schism with a secessionist group called the Old Believers which has never been entirely healed. By 1691, some 20,000 of the faithful had burned themselves in huge fires♦. Church was forever weakened in relation to the Tsar.

The Great Northern War, 1700-1720

Is Russia an Asian country or a European country? Obviously, the answer is both, but Russia's relationship with Asia is more intimate, more familial, while Russia's attitude towards Europe is more as a celebrity to be admired in the distance.

This attitude toward Europe translated into a fascinating result with regard to Western Europe's crisis wars: In most cases, a crisis war in Western Europe resulted in a significant mid-cycle war for Russia. We see this, for example, in the Napoleonic Wars and World War II, where France and Germany, respectively, invaded Russia in (and were defeated) in crisis wars for them, but mid-cycle wars for Russia.

At Russia's end of Europe, the great power in the 1500s and 1600s was Sweden. The wars over Livonia were fought on Sweden's timeline, not on Russia's timeline, and Sweden's timeline was Western Europe's timeline.

The Livonian War (1557-82), which gave Russia a piece of Livonia, took place while the major religious wars were going on in Europe. Sweden entered the Thirty Years' War along with France in 1635 (till the Treaties of Westphalia in 1648), and won back all of Livonia.

So Western Europe's next crisis war was the War of Spanish Succession (1701-14), and again Russia fought a major mid-cycle war with a European country — Sweden.

It was Tsar Peter the Great who led Russia through this "awakening" period that included the Great Northern War against Sweden.

Peter's vision was to expand to become a great world power, modeled on the great European powers.

Peter had always been aware of Europe. He had been educated by foreigners in a German suburb of Moscow, and became acquainted with western techniques*.

Peter felt that a connection with Europe required sea routes for trade. For the south, in 1695, he launched an attack against the Ottomans, hoping to get a trading route through the Black Sea to the Mediterranean, but failed after an initial success*. (Mid-cycle wars are seldom fought with much energy.)

Separately, he sought a northern trade route through the Baltic Sea, resulting in the Great Northern War. He was initially defeated by Sweden, and might have lost the war completely, but Sweden became preoccupied fighting with Poland in the War of Spanish Succession*. Peter won after many years, and established his seaport on the Baltic Sea: St. Petersburg.

During this "awakening" period, Peter instituted many other reforms. simplified both the alphabet and the calendar. He consolidated the changes made in the last crisis, strengthening the power of the Tsar, by demanding service to the government for life*. These demands were made of serfs and nobility alike, and even extended to the Church, made possible by the diminished power of the Church following its wrenching internal struggles. From Peter's time until the Bolshevik Revolution of 1917, the Church was an arm of the state.

War with Ottomans and Pugachev's Rebellion, 1762-83

The next crisis period began in 1762 when a military revolution deposed and killed Peter the Great's grandson, Peter III, and replaced him with his wife, Catherine the Great.

A war with the Ottomans ensued, starting in 1768. Russia captured the whole northern shore of the Black Sea, and annexed the Crimea in 1783.

The peace treaty (at Kuchuk Kaynarja) that Catherine signed with the Ottomans was one of the most important of the whole century*. Russia gained the right to build an Orthodox church in Istanbul and protect the Orthodox in Istanbul. This right to protect "the church to be built in Constantinople and those who service it" was used by the Russians to become the protector of all Orthodox Christians living under Ottoman control. This proved to be a blank check for Russian interference in Ottoman affairs.

However, the most notorious episodes of Catherine's reign were the dozens of bloody rebellions of the 1760s, culminating in the savage Pugachev's Rebellion of 1773-75*. 30,000 rebel peasants plundered southern Russia, until they were brutally put down by Catherine's army, with many of the rebels beheaded, dismembered and burned.

France's invasion of Russia, 1812

Just as the Great Northern War was a mid-cycle war for Russia but a crisis war for Sweden during the War of Spanish Succession, Napoleon's invasion of Russia was a mid-cycle war for Russia but a crisis war for France. It's been described in chapter 5.

Tsar Alexander I, on the throne from 1801-25, instituted many reforms during this "awakening" period, by granting amnesty to political prisoners and exiles, abolishing torture, and passing the first laws leading (during the next crisis period) to the abolition of serfdom*.

Crimean War and Emancipation Edict, 1853-61

The Crimean War is little known today, but was like World War I in that it brought big changes to Russia, not to mention nearly a million deaths from battle and disease. It also had a big cultural effect on Western Europe, with some effects still felt today:

- Florence Nightingale treated the wounded, and went on to invent the nursing profession.

- "Into the valley of Death rode the six hundred" is the well-known line from Lord Alfred Tennyson's poem, *The Charge of the Light Brigade*, describing the results of one particularly gruesome battle of the war, where 600 English soldiers were massacred.

As is often the case, this crisis war grew out of the compromises enforced by the previous crisis war — specifically, the agreement that Russia was the protector of Orthodox Christians living under Ottoman control.

Under this agreement, Russia sent troops into an Ottoman region (now Romania) in 1853. In response, the Ottomans declared war on Russia, and England and France joined on the Ottomans' side*.

None of the participants exhibited any exemplary skill, but the war was a disaster for Russia, which had to admit a humiliating defeat, losing territories on the Black Sea, and was exposed for all to see as an increasingly weak power, having been a military powerhouse at the beginning of the century*.

Losing a war is a traumatic experience for any country and, as we discussed in chapter 4, it often leads to an internal revolution and scapegoating. In the case of Russia, the internal revolution was simplified by the fact that Tsar Nicholas I died in 1855 and was replaced by Alexander II.

The loss of the Crimean War ended up being blamed on Nicholas' support of serfdom, or at least his reluctance to end it*. The previous years had been marked by increasingly frequent rebellions, including attacks on landlords, crop-burning and cattle-maiming. Slavery had become almost completely eliminated in the West (and was just about to be eliminated in America), and Alexander decided that the time had come to end it in Russia. The Emancipation Edict, issued in 1861, ended serfdom.

Aftermath of the Crimean War and Emancipation Edict

The United States freed its own slaves at almost the same time the Russians did, but it was a smaller proportion of the population, and in a single geographic region. America already had an industrialized North with institutions to support the poor.

Russia was much larger, and the overwhelming majority of its citizens had been slaves (serfs). It's not surprising that the transition was difficult.

Occasional rebellions continued, but as Russia entered the "awakening" period, the rebellions increased and became radicalized. The weaknesses exposed by the Crimean War caused the country to industrialize, and the rebellions extended to an industrial proletariat working for the railroads, the coal mines, and the iron fields*.

The awakening period was intensified by a mid-cycle war against the Ottomans in 1875-78. The indecisive results of the war led to an antiwar movement that caused increasing opposition to the tsarist regime*.

Karl Marx had written the *Communist Manifesto* in 1848, and it had taken the intellectuals by storm, and the strikes, riots and demonstrations became tied to socialism and communism. In 1904, Russia lost a war it had initiated against the Japanese, and this triggered a massive series of strikes, demands and demonstrations.

Bolshevik Revolution, 1905-1927

Russia's next crisis period began for real on Bloody Sunday, January 22, 1905, when troops fired on workers demonstrating workers making demands in St. Petersburg, resulting in hundreds of casualties*. This was followed by a general strike of workers across the country. Riots increased, and spread to external

> *Stalin, Hitler and Mao Zedong are the three most violent murderers of the 20th century, each responsible for massacring tens of millions of people.*

war as Russia played a major part in the Balkan wars of 1912-13. World War I began in 1914, and Germany and Austria declared war on Russia.

The government's management of the war was disastrously wild and frenzied, and led to one defeat after another. To all this was added a grave economic problem: shortage of labor, due to repeated mobilizations; disorganization of railroad transport; and failure of food and fuel supplies in the cities*.

The 500-year-old tsarist government collapsed, leading to the Bolshevik (Communist) revolution of 1917, and to a new government headed by Nicolai Lenin, and further civil war.

The Russian Orthodox Church was reduced to near wreckage. Since Peter the Great's reforms centuries earlier, the Church had lost its independence, and was under the control of the Tsar, and so had no support when the

Tsarist government ended. Lenin's militant atheism destroyed thousands of churches and monasteries, and massacred thousands of monks and priests.

Lenin's strategy has only recently been confirmed by the release of previously secret Russian document archives from the Lenin era. In a letter to the Politburo, Lenin wrote:

> We must pursue the removal of church property by any means necessary in order to secure for ourselves a fund of several hundred million gold rubles (do not forget the immense wealth of some monasteries and lauras). Without this fund any government work in general, any economic build-up in particular, and any upholding of soviet principles in Genoa especially is completely unthinkable. In order to get our hands on this fund of several hundred million gold rubles (and perhaps even several hundred billion), we must do whatever is necessary. But to do this successfully is possible only now. All considerations indicate that later on we will fail to do this, for no other time, besides that of desperate famine, will give us such a mood among the general mass of peasants that would ensure us the sympathy of this group, or, at least, would ensure us the neutralization of this group in the sense that victory in the struggle for the removal of church property unquestionably and completely will be on our side.

Lenin's rejection of the Church had an important symbolic consequence: Russia was also abandoning its role as the successor to the Roman Empire, the protector of the Orthodox Religion.

Lenin suffered a stroke in 1922, and died in 1924. A power struggle ensued between Leon Trotsky and Josef Stalin. The crisis era was resolved in 1927 when Stalin defeated Trotsky.

Aftermath of the Bolshevik Revolution

Stalin, Hitler and Mao Zedong are the three most violent murderers of the 20th century, each responsible for massacring tens of millions of people.

Russia had been humiliated in World War I, as it had been humiliated in the Crimean War, and Josef Stalin was determined to improve the country's industrial and military capabilities through socialism. In 1928, Stalin implemented a five-year plan: All farms were collectivized, and any peasants who refused would be executed: five million peasants were killed. To resist collectivization, crops were burned and livestock were slaughtered, resulting in 10-15 million peasants dying of starvation*. The "gulag" death camps that Stalin and his successors used were described years later in *The Gulag Archipelago* by the famous dissident, Alexander Solzhenitsyn.

Special mention should be made of Ukraine*: First, 7 million peasants died in Stalin's collectivization campaign in the 1930s. Next, when World War II began, Hitler invaded and occupied Ukraine, killing 5 million more people. Hitler withdrew from Ukraine in 1944, but then Stalin deported 200,000 Crimean Tatars to Siberia. Today, descendants of the deported Crimeans are demanding the right to reclaim their grandparents' land in Crimea, making the Crimea a possible future battlefield.

The Great Patriotic War (known as World War II to the rest of us) was a mid-cycle war for the Russians. Stalin tried to stay neutral, but was forced into the war when Hitler invaded Russia. The people of Russia had never really given up their religion, and even attended religious services in secret. During the "awakening" period whose beginning coincided with WW II, Stalin was forced to reconcile with the Church and reinstate many of its rights. This reconciliation with religion even extended to the point that Russia was the second country (after America) to officially recognize the new state of Israel in 1948.

Russia's Future

Communism in Russia lasted one and only one 80-year cycle, ending in 1991.

However, there's been no major war, no peasant rebellion. One possible scenario is that Russia's crisis period will pass with no violence.

History tells us that there will be a new war for Russia, during the current crisis period. It's impossible to predict the exact timing, but we note that there are repeated terrorist attacks from Chechnyan based terrorists in Moscow and other parts of Russia.

Any American who remembers the impact of our own 9/11/2001 terrorist attacks knows the impact that one attack had on America, and how ready we were to go to war in Afghanistan, once President Bush suggested it.

The most likely scenario for Russia is that at some point the Russians will demand to "solve the terrorism problem once and for all," and that will lead to the next war.

With regard to religion, in 1990 the Russian Duma passed a law granting freedom of religion to all citizens and all religions. However, the 1990 law was rescinded in 1997 by a new law, "On Freedom of Conscience and Religious Associations," that re-established a special relationship between the state and the Russian Orthodox Church. It's fairly safe to predict that there will continue to be further changes in the relationship between Church and state in Russia.

The Ottoman Empire's Generational Timeline

For centuries after the time of Mohammed, Islamic empires had their ups and downs, but they generally coexisted with the Christians and the Jews. There were many wars, of course, but these were regional wars, without identity group expansion (see chapter 3).

However, by the 1600s, Islam had identified itself as a religious identity group, and Christianity (both Western and Orthodox) as a major opposing identity group. Furthermore, Christianity was unique in this regard, since the civilizations of India and China had never seriously threatened Islam to anything like the extent Christianity did, for Christianity was a world faith, with a sense of mission much like their own, and a duty to proselytize*.

From 1300 to 1600, the Ottomans' history was one of almost unbroken successes and expansion against Christianity. By that time, the empire had grown so large that it had become hard to manage and hard to defend. Its large size became a weakness, and gave the opportunity the Western and Eastern Christians to consolidate their gains and nibble away at the edges of the Ottoman Empire.

War with the Holy League, 1683-99

At what point in history did the balance of power shift from Islam to Christianity? There are several candidates for the crucial moment, but the best choice is the defeat of the Muslims by the Habsburgs (Germans) in 1683*. In a siege of Vienna, the Habsburg capital, a large Ottoman army was assaulting the city walls in a renewed attempt to spread the forces of Islam deeper into Europe.

The Ottomans had had to withdraw from sieges before, but this one was different. Their army was almost destroyed when Polish reinforcements arrived to help the Habsburgs, forcing the Ottoman army to retreat in disarray*.

This led immediately to the War with the Holy League, where an alliance of the Habsburgs, Venice, Poland and Russia attacked the Ottomans on several fronts and inflicted unprecedented territorial losses.

In 1699, the Ottomans and the Habsburgs signed the Treaty at Karlowitz that clearly signaled a change between Europe and the Ottomans, and also a change between Islam and Christendom*. Whereas the Ottomans had dictated the terms of peace treaties in the past, in this case the Ottomans were forced to accept peace terms dictated by the Habsburgs. "This was a calamitous defeat of such magnitude that there has never been its like since the first appearance of the Ottoman state*," according to a contemporary Turkish writer.

War with Russia, 1768-74

> *At what point in history did the balance of power shift from Islam to Christianity?*

This reversal in 1699 stunned the Muslim world in much the same way that the fall of Constantinople to the Ottomans had stunned the Christian world two centuries earlier. After having sustained victory after victory for centuries, Muslim writers were now asking why the miserable infidels were suddenly winning over the formerly victorious armies of Islam*. However, the worst was yet to come.

A series of mid-cycle clashes throughout the 1700s between the Russians and Ottomans didn't have much effect on the *status quo,* until the next crisis war, a major rout occurred starting in 1768, 85 years after the start of the War with the Holy League. The Russians began a new offensive against the Ottomans, this time with overwhelming superiority and success.

The resulting treaty at Kuchuk Kaynarja was a huge humiliation for the Ottomans, and not just because of the additional territory ceded to the Russians*.

The Ottomans were forced to withdraw their forces from the Crimean peninsula, still inhabited by Muslim Tatars, permitting Russia to annex the Crimea in 1783. The Ottomans had been forced to withdraw before, but only from recently captured Christian lands; but this was the first time that they had to withdraw from a Muslim land*.

Capping the humiliation, the treaty permitted the Russians to build an Orthodox church in Istanbul, and granted Russia the right to "protect" those of the Orthodox faith throughout the Ottoman Empire.

Crimean War, 1853-56 and Aftermath

A new major invasion by Russia against the Ottomans occurred in 1853, when the Crimean War began. The Ottomans pushed the Russians back, but only with the help of the English and French.

This was very significant because it was the first time that a significant number of European forces were present on Ottoman soil*. This resulted in enormous changes in the decades to come, for it led to the way European forces encroaching on Ottoman lands throughout the empire.

Following their stunning defeat with the Treaty at Karlowitz in 1699, the Ottomans began more and more to imitate the victors*. At first the imitation was primarily in the area of military technique and weaponry, but by the 1800s began to include some cultural imitation.

However, the Wars of German Unification and Italian Unification that occurred in the 1860s and 1870s also had a significant effect on the Ottomans in the awakening period following the Crimean War: A "pan-Islamic" movement began among the Muslims to unify all Muslims along a common front*, and Istanbul would be center of this worldwide identity group.

Instead of becoming larger and more unified, however, the Ottoman Empire continued to lose large parts of their former empire. By 1914, Egypt, Cyprus, Aden and all of North Africa were being occupied by European powers. Furthermore, the Europeans were exerting influence in the Balkans, and Russia was exerting control in Iran and Afghanistan.

These losses caused increasing discontent among the Ottoman people. The most significant development occurred in 1889, when students of the military medical school in Istanbul formed a secret society to fight the government*. Similar secret societies sprang up in other colleges and among junior officers in the army, despite crackdowns by the authorities. The best-known group was the Ottoman Freedom Society, founded in 1906. It united with other groups and became the Committee of Union and Progress in 1907.

The Committee of Union and Progress was the leading faction in the Young Turk Revolution.

Young Turk Revolution to Destruction of Empire, 1908-1922

In 1908, the Young Turks launched a rebellion in the Balkans that soon engulfed the entire empire. In 1914, the Ottomans entered World War I on the side of Germany, resulting in enormous dislocations. Of the three million men drafted for the army, half of them deserted*. Inflation was enormous, resulting in a 2500 percent increase in cost of living between 1914 and 1918. A famine in Syria and Lebanon (still part of the empire) in 1915-16 claimed 100,000 lives.

In the late 1800s, a Turkish identity movement had begun to form, promoting Turkish (as opposed to Ottoman) literature and culture*. However, the Turkish nationalism movement didn't gain much traction with the public at that time, mainly because for 1,400 years the great strength of the Ottoman Empire, and indeed all of the Islamic empires, was that they were all multi-ethnic and the Muslim rulers were really very good at preserving the rights and meeting the needs of their various ethnic minorities.

Turkish nationalism began to grow during World War I because it was becoming clear that only the Turkish people would remain from the Ottoman Empire, and furthermore, some Europeans wanted to even break off even pieces of Turkey. By 1919, there were so many Allied forces in Istanbul that the Ottomans feared that the Allies intended to keep Istanbul for themselves*.

Actually, there were three separate Muslim identities within the Ottoman Empire that formed in the Mideast around this time: The Turkish identity (in what is now Turkey), the Arab identity (Saudi Arabia), and the Persian identity (Iran).

With the encouragement of the English, the Arab nationalists turned against the Ottomans.

Another group that turned against the Ottomans must be mentioned: The Armenians. This Orthodox Christian population lives in the midst of the Muslim population of what was the eastern portion of the Ottoman Empire. An Armenian uprising that occurred in Istanbul in 1894-96 was brutally put down, with a large-scale massacre of Armenians in Istanbul*.

In 1914, Russia organized four large Armenian volunteer guerrilla units to support the war effort against the Ottomans*. In reaction, the Ottomans began deporting the entire Armenian population — millions of people — resulting in deaths of over a million Armenians in what amounted to a death march*.

Finally, in October, 1922, the Turkish Republic was declared, putting an official end to the Ottoman Empire after 600 years. The president of the new nation was Mustafa Kemal, an activist who had led the fight to keep Turkey from being split up among the Europeans.

Mustafa Kemal, who later took the name Attaturk (father of the Turks), led the new country in a distinctly Turkish direction*. He did everything he could to sweep away the Ottoman past. He abandoned the Ottoman policy of territorial expansion, required Turks to wear Western-style clothing, abolished polygamy, adopted the Christian Gregorian calendar, and adopted the Latin alphabet for writing in the Turkish language, which had previously been done in Arabic script. He even sought to purge Arabic and Persian words from the Turkish language*.

Perhaps most important is that he sought to secularize Turkish society. The caliphate, the office of the supreme spiritual leader for Sunni Muslims worldwide, was abolished*. Religious schools were closed, and Islamic law courts were dismantled. A new constitution separated religion from the state, and gave all male Turkish citizens over 21 the right to vote,

As for the other pieces of the Ottoman Empire, they were turned into independent nations: Iraq in 1924, Saudi Arabia in 1932, Syria in 1945, Lebanon and Jordan in 1946.

Zionism and the state of Israel

Because of Russian persecution, Russian Jews began migrating to the Palestine area in the late 1800s. Perhaps also inspired by the Wars of Unification in Germany and Italy, the first Zionist Congress met in 1897 to advocate a Jewish homeland in Palestine*. By 1917, the British issued the Balfour Declaration, which called for a Jewish state in Palestine.

Historically, Jews and Arabs had always been peaceful and friendly with one another, but this changed with the call for a separate Jewish state in Palestine.

In 1917, there were ten times as many Arabs as Jews in Palestine: 700,000 Arabs, and 70,000 Jews*.

The Zionists encouraged Jewish migration to Palestine, and the migration of European Jews became a flood in the 1930s, thanks to Nazi persecution of Jews. By 1939, Arabs outnumbered Jews by only two to one*.

Rioting between Jews and Arabs began in 1936, and continued through the 1940s. In May 1948, Palestine was partitioned, creating an independent state of Israel. Following statehood, there was a full-scale war between Israel and the neighboring Arab states. In 1949, an armistice was declared.

The Future of the Mideast

Ever since the 1989 intifada began, the Mideast appears to be replaying the Mideast wars of 1936-1949. If history is any guide (and it is), then the next generational change will bring a new major war between Israel and its Arab neighbors. This generational change can only be predicted approximately, but it's expected that it will be signaled by the disappearance of Yasser Arafat from the scene.

Chapter 10 — History of Asia

Although the American heritage is mostly European, Asia has recently played an enormous role in the lives of ordinary Americans — the Japanese attack on the United states that led us into World War II, the war in Vietnam, and the American-Japan economic relationship of the last few decades have all assumed major importance recently.

The generational methodology provides some unique insights into both Japan and Vietnam — insights that are not mentioned in standard histories of these countries.

And in the case of China, we'll apply some trend forecasting and mathematical complexity techniques, recognizing that with 1.4 billion people, the mathematics of infinity really begins to apply.

China

We present a history of China since roughly 1800.

There have been two crisis wars since that time, both of them civil wars:

- The Taiping Rebellion, 1851-64

- The Nationalist Revolution and Communist takeover, 1927-49

In addition, we'll discuss some mid-cycle wars with England and Japan.

China is a very interesting example of the methodologies being described in this book because of its size and its relative isolation. When mathematicians talk about the "complexity" of doing something, there's always a background concept that can be stated as: how complex is it to do something as the number of objects you're handling approaches infinity?

Well, guess what? For most practical purposes, the number of people in China is about as close to infinity as we're going to get.

When you're talking about smaller societies, a government can avoid the complexities of governing by numerous *ad hoc* measures, such as building larger bureaucracies to handle problems.

But when you have 1.4 billion people, as China does today, there are no *ad hoc* methods to speak of. Almost every governance technique that might be used with that many people can be modeled mathematically and shown to be inadequate.

Analyzing China's history

It's natural to analyze China's history in the usual way — struggles between brilliant and stupid leaders, wars triggered by bad weather or aggressive outsiders, and so forth.

Out treatment will be quite different. We're going to use our new tools — trend extrapolation and complexity analysis — to sort which of China's problems in the last two centuries were man-made, and which of them would have to have happened one way or another.

Here is the basic outline:

- The Manchus (the warriors from Manchuria who ruled China starting in 1644) chose the only style of government that would have worked, because it's the only style that managed complexity: namely, the Manchus protected their position by keeping China isolated from the rest of the world.

- Inevitably, thanks to technology trends driven by the Industrial Revolution in England, China had to open up to foreign trade and internal technology development. Even worse, the centuries-old Manchu bureaucracy was becoming victim of the "crusty old bureaucracy" syndrome (see page 125).

- The combination of foreign trade, internal technology development, population growth, and bureaucratic inefficiency made the country more and more unmanageable, and eventually brought down the Manchus.

- However, in spite of several changes in government in the 20th century, the formula for governing China has not yet been found, and China appears once again to be on the verge of an explosive civil war within a decade or two.

That's the outline of what *had* to happen, one way or another, to China since 1800. Now let's see how these events actually played out.

CHAPTER 10 – HISTORY OF ASIA

China's past

While European nations are at most a few hundred years old, China has been identifiable as a nation for over 2,000 years. How could such a vast, populous territory be managed and governed? What is the paste that held this nation together all this time?

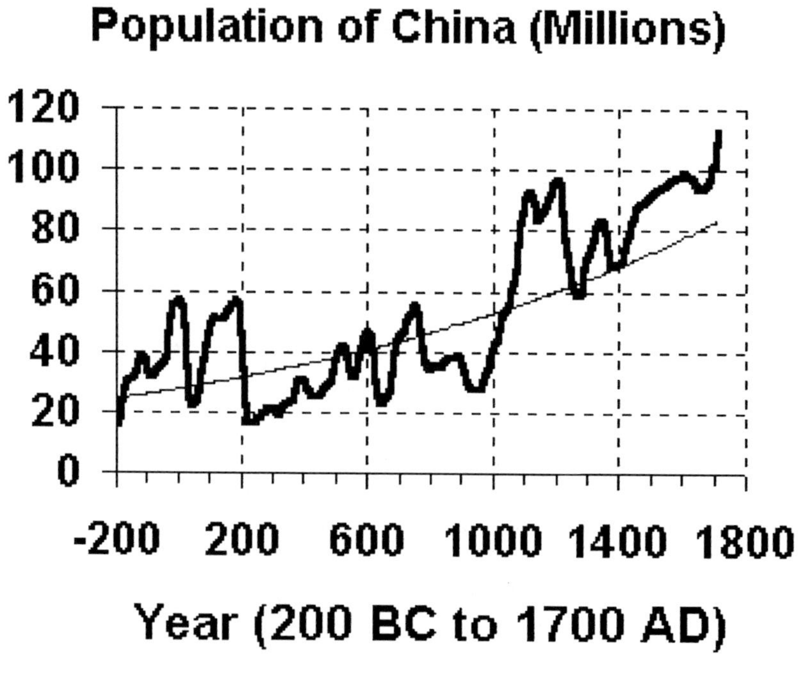

Population of China (Millions)

[Graph showing population from -200 to 1800, Y-axis 0 to 120]

Year (200 BC to 1700 AD)

Figure 39 Population of China in millions of people* from 200 BC to 1710 AD

The answer would have to be a relatively homogeneous population (that is, no major fault lines along religious or ethnic lines), and Confucianism, an ingenious religion, philosophy, and set of social rules. It gave each person a specific place in society, and defined specific duties and modes of conduct. For example, it defined Five Relationships of superiors over inferiors: prince over subject; father over son; husband over wife; elder brother over younger brother; and friend over friend. As long as each individual knew his place, and knew how to act, it would not be necessary for someone else to direct his activities, thus simplifying government.

As China was ruled alternately by warriors of different regions, or dynasties, all were tied together by the rules devised by Confucius in the fifth century BC. In the last thousand years, for example, China was ruled by warriors from Mongolia (1271-1368) in the north, from the south of China (1368-1644), and then from the north again by warriors from Manchuria (1644-1912).

However, as Figure 39 shows, the population of China has had wild swings throughout its history. It's hard for contemporary Americans to even imagine this, but wars, famine and disease have, at various times, killed tens of millions of Chinese people in a relatively short period of time.

The complexity of managing China's huge population is inescapable. China is geographically slightly smaller than the US, but has almost five times the population — 1.3 billion people. When you're dealing with numbers that large then, like it or not, the full force of mathematical complexity theory must be applied in order to make sense of what's going on and what happens to be done.

Even in 1800, China had about 400 million people — 300 million farmers, plus 80-100 million city folk: artisans, merchants, landlords, scholars and government officials*.

That's why, even as late as the year 1800, a typical Chinese village pretty much took care of itself* — handling contracts, real estate transfers, boundary disputes, and organizing collective actions such as irrigation projects or business enterprises — without reference to any government officials*.

This is the heart of low-complexity government: Keep all decision making, as much as possible, at the village level. As soon as you try to centralize any activities to a higher government level, whether regional or national, then the complexity of governing (which can be measured mathematically) becomes greater. And when you're dealing with millions of people, even a small change in governing policy can have truly enormous consequences at the national level.

The Manchus (people from Manchuria) had invaded and conquered China in 1644, and had a unique, low-complexity method for managing the empire. The army was entirely Manchu, and was used to put down any rebellions. They used ethnic Chinese in all administrative positions, but had a separate secret administrative force consisting entirely of ethnic Manchu for intelligence gathering and extorting additional taxes.

By the year 1800, China under Manchu rule was coming apart at the seams. With population growth, prostitution and slavery were increasing, and there were numerous gangs of unemployed laborers looking for work.

Even worse, centuries of bureaucratic buildup had taken its toll. An example is the Grand Canal, the canal system that was used to deliver rice from the south to feed Beijing*. A huge bureaucracy had been built up over centuries to manage it. Engineers would build canal locks with "built-in obsolescence" that guarantee that they'd need replacement every few years, guaranteeing huge imperial expenditures to keep them in repair. The barges themselves were operated by thousands of bargemen who had their jobs through heredity, but who hired gangs of workers to do the actual work. China in 1800 was a poster child for the "crusty old bureaucracy" that we discussed in chapter 6 (see page 125).

The White Lotus Rebellion - 1796-1805

There have been numerous regional crisis wars and massacres throughout China's history, as in the rest of the world. Presumably, most of those were fought over land and resources as usual. Because these crisis wars were all regional, and happened at different times, it was possible for the Manchus' ethnic army to suppress each rebellion in turn, as it occurred, and to maintain control in this way. In fact, the legacy of Emperor Ch'ien-lung, who ruled for sixty years until 1799, describes "Ten Great Campaigns" to suppress rebels on the frontiers*. One rebellion, for example, occurred in Taiwan in 1786-87*. Presumably, the "great compromise" that ended each of these regional wars and rebellions was that the Manchu army would leave people alone if they'd stop fighting and just pay their taxes.

The first rebellion that forced a major compromise in the Manchu government itself was the White Lotus Rebellion in central China (see adjoining map). It broke out in 1796, over the issues of poor public service in return for high taxes*.

As often happens, the rebel leaders used religion as the face of the rebellion. The White Lotus religious sect was based on Buddhism, and had faced previous attempts by the Manchus to suppress it, presumably because the sect was a menace to social order. The pattern by which the rebellion took place has happened many times before and since and many places in the world: the religious sect appeals to unhappy people by making various promises, the leaders of the sect mobilize them into a military force with political goals, and then the military force either achieves its political goals or it's suppressed.

Figure 40 China and adjoining countries* (modern names and boundaries). Note the regions of the White Lotus Rebellion and the Taiping Rebellion.

Although the White Lotus rebellion was a regional rebellion, it played out over a larger region than previous rebellions had done. As a result, the ethnic Manchu army was not enough to contain it.

By 1800, it was pretty clear that the corrupt, bureaucracy-ridden Manchu army would not be able to suppress the rebellion. The Manchus were forced to take an unprecedented step: They employed Chinese militia under Manchu control to quell the rebellion. This proved to be the first major step in the downfall of the Manchus, but just one of many steps to come.

In fact, the White Lotus rebellion was a kind of prototype for what was to come. Within 50 years, a much larger rebellion was to bring about massive violence.

First Opium War, 1840-1842

First though, the Opium Wars of 1840-42 are portrayed as a shameful incident in British history, and indeed, they were shameful because of the trade in opium. But as usual, the situation is far more complex, and much of its outcome would have had to occur anyway, even if opium hadn't been involved.

From Britain's point of view, the issue was open and free trade. The Industrial Revolution had made England had become the world's greatest industrial power. Ever since Adam Smith had published *Wealth of Nations* in 1776, many policy makers believed that free trade was best for everyone, and so forcing free trade on a backward China was a natural extension of the expansionist policies of the day.

It should first be pointed out that China was not entirely isolated from international commerce in the early 1800s. It's just that all commerce was controlled as tightly as possible by the national and regional governing entities*, especially by the imposition of stiff import tariffs. On the export side, tea, silk and porcelain was getting very popular in Europe, and all this resulted in a fairly substantial balance of trade deficit, which favored China's rulers. With the Industrial Revolution proceeding in England, Europe and America, it was only a matter of time before someone found some product or products that would be irresistible to the Chinese, and would reverse the balance of trade deficits.

Unfortunately, that product turned out to be the addictive drug opium, which not only became very popular, but also was not subject to import tariffs, since it entered the country via pirates in violation of Chinese laws. Opium was already illegal in England, so it's hard for the English to claim innocence in selling opium to the Chinese. But complicating the issue were the attitude of the Chinese rulers, who treated outsiders as inferiors, and who did not always live up to the terms of previous treaties.

The war was triggered in 1840 when the government confiscated tons of opium and blockaded the ports, not just to opium but also to all outside trade. That was too much for the English, who declared war. The First Opium War lasted until 1842, when Beijing was forced to capitulate and sign a treaty. The treaty forced all ports open to foreign trade and gave Hong Kong to the British. (It was not returned until 1997.)

China's easy defeat was an enormous blow to the Manchu leaders. In the long run, it led to a program of "Self Strengthening" which was implemented throughout the last half of the 1800s. Its purpose was to develop technology, factories and military capabilities to prevent another such defeat.

Returning now to our earlier point, China would eventually have had to open up its trade to outsiders, and would eventually have had to develop its own technology. The fact that these changes increase the complexity of the national government is beside the point. These trends must occur because they always occur. The government regimes must figure out how to deal with these changes, since nothing can stop the changes.

The Taiping Rebellion, 1851-64

As we use our study of China's history to focus on how the trends that every society goes through, we have to understand that we've been describing two different kinds of trends that go on at the same time in every society:

- A growth (technology / financial / population) trend that generally grows all the time. (Growth trend forecasting is described in detail in chapter 11.)

- A cyclic trend, the generational cycle, that drives generally societies to major crisis wars every 80 years or so; each new crisis war begins after all the people with personal memory of the previous crisis war are retired or dead.

These two kinds of trends go on at the same time, and they interact with one another. If a crisis war occurs, a historian will search for causes of the war among the growth trends, and he will always find them, because any growth is going to strain a society somewhere, causing some dissatisfaction. The thing to keep in mind is that there are *always* growth strains going on, but they don't lead to a crisis war except as the result of a generational cycle.

Presumably, the previous regional crisis war in the southeast of China began in the 1760s or so, and was violently suppressed by the Manchu army. By the 1840s, society would have been unraveling: men were becoming addicted to opium in violation of Manchu laws, and opium was pouring in, first because of pirates, and later legally, after the Opium War agreements had been signed. The effect would have been greatest in the southeast, where all the ports were, and where the opium was pouring in. The money to pay for the opium would have created a fiscal crisis, which would only have been exacerbated by a famine that occurred in the southwest in 1846-48.

As usual in China, the rebellion was first voiced through a religious sect. In this case, the sect was a version of Christianity, created by taking the teachings of the missionaries, mixing in a little Buddhism and politics, and coming up with the God-Worshipper's Society, which appealed to large numbers of disaffected citizens✦.

The rebellion exploded to the north to Beijing, and then into the heartland of central China. Armies of tens of thousands of men would live off the land, gaining new recruits as it went along.

The rebellion was not put down until 1864, and then not by the Manchu army but by an army of Chinese recruits. Modern estimates are that China's population had been about 410 million in 1850 and 350 million in 1873 — after the end of the Taiping rebellion and several other rebellions that occurred in the west✦.

This indicates a loss of about 15% of China's entire population; compare this to the most devastating of America's wars, the Civil war, where we lost less than 1% of the entire population.

Aftermath of the Taiping Rebellion

The Taiping Rebellion forced some changes on the government structure, but remarkably, the Manchus were left in place, as were most of the centuries old Manchu bureaucracies. The major changes that did occur were in the militias, which were no longer composed just of ethnic Manchus, but became majority Chinese.

The next few decades saw China struggle vehemently to catch up to the rest of the world in technology, finance and trade. The aforementioned "Self Strengthening" was the government program that was to accomplish this, but events crowded the Chinese faster than they could make changes.

- The Second Opium War, 1858-60, forced the Manchus to open China up to even more trade concessions.
- The war with Japan in 1894-95 was another great shock to the Chinese, who had considered the Japanese to be an inferior race. The

war was an enormous victory for Japan, and led to Japan's annexation of the Korean peninsula by 1910.

- The Boxer Rebellion of 1900 was directed against foreign influences in and around Beijing.

- The Chinese Revolution of 1911 finally brought down the Manchu government that had been in place since 1644. A parliamentary republic replaced it briefly, but by 1913, the parliament was dissolved, and the result was a military dictatorship.

- The Treaty of Versailles, which ended World War I in 1919, granted additional disputed territories to Japan.

Many people view these events in a purely political light: The imperialist Eurocentric Western society imposed its values on the workers of China and took advantage of them repeatedly.

Here's a more politically neutral interpretation:

China and the West were both on the same technology growth curve, but by pure historical happenstance, Europe was about 200 years ahead of China. This could have happened simply because the first humans to populate China came 15,000 years after they populated the Mediterranean basin, and China did not completely catch up by 1800.

Since 1845 and the "Self Strengthening," China has been marshalling its resources to develop the technology to make up for that 200 year difference.

The problem is that with over a billion people, China is almost impossible to govern at all, let alone to govern and transform all at once.

Nonetheless, China is moving as fast as it can, and hopes to catch to the West and be at a technological parity within a few decades.

Why wasn't the Chinese Rebellion a crisis war?

The Chinese Rebellion of 1911 removed the Manchu control of China for the first time in hundreds of years. Why isn't so major a change counted as a crisis war?

The answer is that the Chinese Rebellion didn't really change Chinese society. While the ruling families at the top changed, the basic structure of Chinese society didn't really change.

It's important to remind ourselves again what the basic premise of this book tells us. The Taiping Rebellion was a horror greater than we can even imagine today, even for those who remember World War II. Tens of millions of people were massacred over an almost 20 year period, and no one who had lived through it would ever want to see anything like it happen again. In 1911, there were still plenty of people around who had lived through the Taiping Rebellion, and there was little energy for the kind of explosion that had occurred only a few decades earlier.

Although there was some fighting associated with the Chinese Rebellion, it probably makes sense to compare it to England's Glorious Revolution, in that a major change of Chinese government occurred with little blood spilled, as a result of a traumatic civil war that occurred only a few decades earlier.

> *Exactly 82 years after the Taiping Rebellion moved north from the southern provinces, Mao Zedong began his Long March from the same region*

The Nationalist / Communist war, 1934-49

During the 1920s, the Chinese government split into two major factions: A Nationalist faction, led by Chiang Kai-shek, which began to ally itself with Germany, and a Communist faction, led by Mao Zedong (Mao tse Tung), which allied itself with Russia after the latter's Bolshevik Revolution.

The two worked together until 1927, but split openly at that time, with the Nationalist faction taking over and forcing the Communist faction into the countryside.

The Nationalist government still had not solved the problem of governing the vast Chinese population, and had developed an insufficient technique for dealing with the problem. Chiang followed the example of his German ally by installing a secret police to closely control the large cities and collect taxes. This might have been a good strategy in urban Germany, but with China's huge agrarian population, the army was left to manage the provinces and collect land taxes. This dual strategy permitted modernization of government at the highest regional levels, but it allowed for a great deal of corruption in the countryside, where the army officers became wealthy landowners*. (We won't dwell on this here, but this situation is similar to the situation faced by Mao in the Great Leap Forward discussed below; in both case, you can use the mathematics of Complexity Theory to prove that it's impossible to manage a huge population in this way.)

At another time, the Nationalists may simply have been able to abolish the Communists completely, but the time of the generational cycle was approaching: the people who had personal memory of the Taiping Rebellion were almost gone. The generational anxiety was exacerbated by a financial development: hard money reserves were being drained, forcing Chiang to abandon the gold standard in 1934.

Exactly 82 years after the Taiping Rebellion moved north from the southern provinces, Mao Zedong began his Long March from the same region. To the Chinese, Communism was not unlike a religious sect; and just as Buddhism and Christianity had both been heavily modified to inspire the White Lotus and Taiping rebellions, respectively, Mao heavily modified Stalin's Communism to adapt to the Chinese ways. Nonetheless, one thing remained: the hostility to wealthy landowners, and to the rents that they collected, and this factor highly motivated the peasants to follow Mao.

Of the 100,000 followers who began the 6,000-mile Long March, only 20,000 or so survived. But along the way, Mao became the unquestioned leader of the Communist movement, and the Communists were established as a credible alternative to the Nationalists.

Undoubtedly a massive civil war would have begun immediately, but for the fact that World War II had already begun for China. The Japanese, who had annexed Korea in 1910, used it as a base to invade and conquer Manchuria (northeastern China) in 1932. In 1937, Japan and China were in full-scale war, with Japan headed for Beijing, and Mao Zedong and Chiang Kai-shek had come to an agreement to cooperate to defeat the Japanese.

All in all, the Japanese invasion proved an advantage for Mao. Chiang was allied with Germany, but Germany withdrew much of its help in deference to its other ally, Japan. Russia's Stalin was not so encumbered, and was fully engaged in seeing another country implement a Communist government.

When Japan surrendered to America in 1945, the civil war broke out for real. By 1949, the Nationalist government had surrendered to the Communists, and Chiang Kai-shek had fled to the island of Taiwan. The continued separation of Taiwan from China remains a fault line to this day, a fault line which may well play a part in the next world war.

The Great Leap Forward, 1958-60

Mao was certainly a very charismatic figure who captured the admiration of his country and of the world, but his period as China's leader cannot be considered anything but a disaster.

Millions of people died from execution even in the "good times" of Mao's leadership, but no period was worse than the Great Leap Forward, during which some 20 to 30 million people died of starvation in a man-made famine*.

It's really very hard to explain what happened in the Great Leap Forward in any rational way. That the Great Leap Forward could never have achieved its goals is obvious today, and perhaps Mao could be forgiven for not knowing that at the time, but he can't be forgiven for putting the lives of some billion peasants at risk without implementing even the elementary management controls and an unwillingness to stop his experiment earlier.

> *It's really very hard to explain what happened in the Great Leap Forward in any rational way*

As we describe in Chapter 11 (page 246), the problems of governing a huge population can be modeled using the mathematics of Complexity Theory. In a nutshell, the problem is this: If you have a small population, say a feudal region of 300 people, then the leader and one or two aides can monitor all the transactions that go on between people: Buying and selling, employee-employer, loaning money, and so forth. But as the population grows, then the number of transactions to be monitored grows much faster than the population, meaning that a greater and greater percentage of the population has the job of monitoring transactions. If this continues, then eventually the whole population would do nothing but monitor each other's transactions, but the system breaks down long before that happens. That's why, as the population gets larger and larger, the only economic system which is mathematically possible is a free market system, where the government monitors almost no transactions, and things like product pricing are determined by competition in the marketplace.

What does this have to do with the Great Leap Forward?

Mao tried to devise a set of ideological rules that would defeat the mathematical realities just described. When it started to become evident, within a few months, that the system was breaking down (which the mathematical theory says must happen), then Mao purposely allowed ideology to override reality, with the resulting tens of millions of death from starvation.

Mao's plan to implement "true" communism in China began in 1958 with the Great Leap Forward. Here's a summary of how the program worked*:

1. 500,000,000 million peasants were taken out of their individual homes and put into communes, creating a massive human work force. The workers were organized along military lines of companies, battalions, and brigades. Each person's activities were rigidly supervised.

2. The family unit was dismantled. Communes were completely segregated, with children, wives and husbands all living in separate barracks and working in separate battalions. Communal living was emphasized by eating, sleeping, and working in teams. Husbands and wives were allowed to be alone only at certain times of the month and only for brief periods. (This was also a birth control technique.)

3. All workers took part in ideological training sessions, to provide for ideological training of the Chinese masses.

Mao's stipulated purpose was to mobilize the entire population to transform China into a socialist powerhouse — producing both food and industrial goods — much faster than might otherwise be possible. This would be both a national triumph and an ideological triumph, proving to the world that socialism could triumph over capitalism.

First, Mao dismantled the Central Statistical Bureau, the organization responsible for keeping track of all the economic activity going on in the country*. As a result, China's leadership had no real idea whether the Great Leap Forward was meeting its objectives or not.

Early in 1959, and again in July 1959, officials in Mao's government had begun to see that the program was failing. Their objections were rewarded with punishment. Mao was determined to follow his ideological course, no matter what else happened.

The program failed because of the complexity of closely governing a large population, as described above.

The individual peasants and managers were required to report the size of the crop harvests up the line to the central government, but there was no way to guarantee that the reports were accurate.

On the one hand, there was no economic incentive for the farmers and managers to provide accurate reports, since everyone in a socialist society is paid the same ("according to his need").

On the other hand, there was no independent check of the crop harvest estimates. If the population had been much smaller, then the central government might have been able to send out enough bureaucrats to check the reports, or at least do spot checks. But with about a billion peasants, no such meaningful checks were possible.

For the farmers and managers themselves, there was plenty of political incentive to overreport the crop harvest results.

> *Mao dismantled the Central Statistical Bureau, and so had no real idea whether the Great Leap Forward was meeting its objectives or not.*

As a result, even though actual crop yield in 1959 was a little smaller than it had been in 1958, the crop reports added up to an enormous increase in production, more than a doubling of output*.

By the time that Chairman Mao was finally ready to accept the situation, it was too late. There was too little food to feed everyone, and tens of millions died of starvation.

Chairman Mao was disgraced by the disastrous failure of the Great Leap Forward, and his critics proliferated*. By 1966, Mao had devised the Great Cultural Revolution to repair the situation, and formed the Red Guards to implement the assault on dissidents:

> The Red Guards, mostly younger students, soon brought the country to the verge of chaos*; they fought pitched battles, carried out summary executions, drove thousands to suicide, and forced tens of thousands into labor camps, usually far from home. Intellectuals were sent to the countryside to learn the virtues of peasant life. Countless art and cultural treasures as well as books were destroyed, and universities were shut down. Insulting posters and other per-

sonal attacks, often motivated by blind revenge, were mounted against educators, experts in all fields, and other alleged proponents of "old thought" or "old culture," namely, anything pre-Maoist.

Hundreds of thousands more deaths occurred under the Red Guards.

Tiananmen Square (1989) and Beyond

Probably the most dramatic "awakening" event ever televised occurred in 1989, over a million Chinese colleges students from all of the country crowded into Tiananmen Square in Beijing for a peaceful demonstration. Government troops entered Tiananmen Square at night and fired at the sleeping student. In the end, several thousand were killed.

This violent reaction indicates that China has not yet figured out how to govern its population, and that another violent rebellion will envelope the country within the next 20 years.

Figure 41 College student blocks path of a row of tanks in Tiananmen Square in China, 1989

Japan

Civilization came rather late to Japan — after 500 AD. As an island, it had relatively little contact with outsiders until the 1800s. As a result, the Japanese developed a remarkably homogeneous appearance and a homogeneous culture — a sense of conformity, acceptance of hereditary authority, devotion to the soldier, ideal of self-discipline, and its sense of nationalism and superiority of the political unit over the family*.

Commodore Perry and the Meiji Restoration, 1853-68

This 15-year crisis, culminating in a civil war and the first structural change in government in centuries, was the event that exploded Japan into the rest of the world, and set the stage for Japan's entry into World War II, and its attack on Pearl Harbor in 1941.

The Tokugawa family had been ruling Japan since 1603, after a coup at that time which overthrew the existing rules. This era is called the "Edo Era" because the Tokugawas were able to unify Japan under rule from the city of Edo, which was renamed Tokyo in 1868.

The pattern in Japan after 1853 was similar to what happened in China after the Opium Wars. Like the Manchus in China, the Tokugawas in Japan had built up an enormous bureaucracy, crusted with inefficiency. To protect this bureaucracy, and to reduce the complexity of governing, they had strictly forbidden trade with other nations. Foreign travel was forbidden, and Christianity was banned.

The crisis began in 1853, when US Commander Matthew Perry brought four warships to Edo (Tokyo). There was a brief naval battle that the Americans won easily. In 1854, Japan signed a treaty with the US that opened up several Japanese ports in a limited way. In the next two years, Japan signed similar treaties with Great Britain, Russia and the Netherlands.

This alone would have caused turmoil by shaking up the bureaucracy, but a disaster occurred: an earthquake that killed thousands of people in Edo.

A series of wars ensued — mostly civil wars, but also a brief war with England in 1862. By 1868, the Tokugawas were overthrown, and rule by the Emperor was restored. It was called the Meiji Restoration, where the word

Meiji means, "governing clearly," hinting at simplicity rather than complexity.

Japan's defeat by America was as much a shock to them as the China's defeat in the Opium Wars was to them. And Japan instituted some reforms like China's "Self Strengthening," whose purpose was to catch up the world in technology, industry and military capability.

In fact, along with its industrialization initiative, Japan instituted numerous other reforms following the Meiji Restoration, including nine years of compulsory education for everybody. It's possible that this reform is what made the difference between Japan succeeding where China failed.

Japan's Imperialist Period — 1894-1945

In this book, we've discussed a wide variety of types of awakenings — great art in the "golden age of Greece," new religions in the lives of Jesus, Mohammed, and the Buddha, and the anti-war movement in our own awakening of the 1960s.

> *Writing in 2003, there's a startling parallel between Korea today and Japan in the 1930s*

However, an awakening can take many forms, and Japan's awakening took the form of becoming militaristic and imperialistic. The Japanese were well aware of the successes in empire building by the Europeans, and they felt that if the Europeans could do it, then the Japanese could also do it.

From 1894-1910, Japan engaged in a series of wars against China and Russia, resulting in one victory after another. In the treaties resulting from these wars, Japan was given Taiwan, Korea, and southern Manchuria, along with other territories.

We should make clear that Japan was not considered to be an enemy of the West at this time. In fact, Japan was considered to be an advanced, "westernized" nation. Japan mostly sat out World War I, but at the Treaty of Versailles ending that war, Japan was granted additional territorial awards.

Never having been an imperialistic nation, Japan was becoming giddy with its successes. An awakening period is followed by an unraveling period, and in the unraveling period of the 1920s, Japan became a completely militaristic state. There was censorship of the press, complete state control by the military, and open plans for military expansion into China and Russia.

The stock market crash in America didn't affect Japan until America enacted the Smoot-Hawley Tariff Act (see page 48), which caused a collapse in international trade, and started Japan's own financial decline. Japan already felt insulted by America's 1924 decision to limit immigration into the US — citizens of all non-North American nations were restricted, but immigration by Japanese was singled out as being totally excluded.

Exactly 63 years after the Meiji Restoration (78 years after Commander Perry's visit), Japan went to war in Manchuria in 1931. This was the first major military action of World War II.

Japan was then at war until America's nuclear weapons fell on Hiroshima and Nagasaki on August 6 and 9, 1945. Japan surrendered on September 2.

Almost overnight, the Japanese people reverted to the old non-imperialistic selves they used to be before Commodore Perry's visit. The country became strongly pacifist and disbanded its armed forces.

However, Japan's change does not dissolve the ethnic fault line between Korea and Japan, resulting from Japan's colonization of Korea from 1910 to 1945. We're likely to see a war of Korean unification during the next few years, and it's likely that Japan will be drawn into that war.

Writing in 2003, there's a startling parallel between Korea today and Japan in the 1930s. North Korea's Kim Jong-il has been making extremely belligerent statements, quite evidently imitating the behavior of the Japanese during the 1930s that led to the bombing of Pearl Harbor, as we described in chapter 2. Because of Japan's colonization of Korea during that time, Koreans still have a vivid memory of that period.

Vietnam

In order to understand what happened in America's Vietnam war in the 1960s and 1970s, it's necessary to go back in time 80-90 years.

France developed a close relationship with Southeast Asia throughout the 1800s, largely through Catholic missionaries. French activity in the area increased, with France attempting to annex various regions as French protectorates. Full-scale war broke out in 1882, leading to war against China in the region. By 1893, France had consolidated its hold on the entire region known as French Indochina (see adjoining map). Japan held the region until 1940, when they were forced to relinquish it to a Japanese invasion. French control was reestablished in 1946, but the French were defeated and driven out by Ho Chi Minh in 1954.

America, fresh from defeating Nazism, was determined that "nothing like that must ever happen again." It was (and is) widely believed that if Hitler had only been stopped in 1935, then World War II could have been avoided completely — a belief that this book claims to refute.

But the fact that it was believed led the Americans to try to prevent the Communist Chinese, operating through Ho Chi Minh, to gain control of the entire country, believing that if Communism could be stopped early, then World War III could be avoided. American entered the war in the 1960s on the side of South Vietnam, to prevent the Chinese to gain control over the whole country.

Between 1965 and 1980, about 80-90 years after the French Indochina wars in the late 1800s, the entire region was in a genocidal civil war.

The Vietnam War was a crisis war for the Vietnamese, but a mid-cycle war for America, which was still exhausted from World War II, and suffered substantial anti-war resistance at home.

Figure 42 French Indochina in the 1880s and 1890s consisted roughly of today's Vietnam, Cambodia and Laos.

Starting with the Tet offensive of 1967, the North Vietnamese fought with enormous energy, while the Americans fought half-heartedly. American was defeated by 1974.

Cambodia and Laos

Many commentators have offered the view that huge genocide that occurred in Cambodia and Laos in the 1970s was caused by the Vietnam War, but there seems to be no more than the slightest connection.

Many Americans believe that the entire population of Southeast Asia is fairly homogeneous, but in fact, the opposite is true. As can be seen from the map shown above, Vietnam's population belongs to the Sinic (Chinese) civilization, having been infiltrated by the Chinese as early as the second century AD.

But Cambodia and Laos were from an entirely different civilization — Buddhist cultures that grew out of settlers from India coming through Thailand.

Vietnamese attempts to control Cambodia date back centuries, with a major genocidal war involving Cambodia, Vietnam and Thailand occurring in 1840. According to the 80-year cycle view of history, this war would have recurred in the 1920s, if France hadn't intervened in the late 1880s.

In the 1970s, 80-90 years after the French intervention, both Cambodia and Laos exploded into civil war. In both cases, the civil wars followed the disastrous examples of Mao Zedong in China two decades earlier, with the same results — massive genocide and starvation.

The Future of Southeast Asia

The line separating Vietnam from Laos and Cambodia is more than just a boundary — it's a major fault line between two civilizations, one coming out of India and one coming out of China. These countries are "scheduled" to have another crisis war around 2030-40, about 20 years later than China itself is "scheduled" for another massive nationwide rebellion. It's possible that these two crisis periods will coalesce into a single larger crisis period.

Chapter 11 — Trend Forecasting

This chapter is unlike the rest of the book, but is included here for one principal reason: To provide the analytical evidence that we're currently entering a new 1930s style Great Depression. This book presents two different types of evidence, both of which point to the same conclusion: The generational evidence is presented in chapter 6 (page 114), and the analytical evidence is presented at the end of this chapter (page 263), once the foundations have been laid. Since this chapter is a bit more mathematical than other chapters, most readers should feel free to skip it.

However, once this chapter is included, it serves other purposes as well. This whole book is about trend forecasting, mostly generational trend forecasting. This chapter describes other types of trend forecasting, including the very mysterious technological trend forecasting.

This chapter provides emotional support for the rest of the book in the following way: Some people believe that it's impossible to forecast *anything whatsoever* about human behavior, and reject Generational Dynamics for that reason alone. This chapter shows that in fact some kinds of forecasting do indeed work, and so total non-believers will have to rethink their beliefs.

There are many different kinds of trends. Some trends can be forecast or predicted in the short term, some in the long term, and some not at all.

This chapter summarizes the different kinds of trends, and provides information on what kinds of forecasts and predictions can be made.

Types of trends

Let's start with a summary of the different kinds of trends.

Cyclic Trends

The most obvious example of a cyclic trend is the seasons — spring, summer, fall, winter. The same seasons keep repeating over and over again.

Furthermore, they're completely predictable: you can always be certain the next Spring will start exactly one year after the last Spring began.

Here are some other examples of cyclic trends:

- **Fashion trends** tend be short-term, usually lasting one or two seasons. Fashion trends may be one-shot (such as the Nehru jacket), or may be cyclic (such as skirt length). Generally, they're completely unpredictable.

- **Political trends** are usually cyclic, with varying cycle lengths. You frequently hear the phrase "the political pendulum" to capture the cyclic nature of political trends. Some political trends are roughly predictable: e.g., the American President cycles between Republican and Democrat every 2-4 elections.

- **Economic trends** can often be cyclic. For example, there's an economic recession every ten years or so. A more complex example are the Kondratieff Cycles, which have been studied most recently by author Mike Alexander, which measure the inflation rate and have a cycle length of 40-50 years.

- **Generational trends** are what this book is about. They tend to have a cycle length of around 80 years, the length of a human lifetime.

The above are all examples of cyclic trends. An interesting distinction can be made between global and local cyclic trends, which I won't discuss further here.

Growth Trends

Cyclic trends usually apply to values that remain relatively the same over long periods of time. Any increases or decreases are only temporary.

Growth trends apply to values that grow over long periods of time. In particular, when some value in nature grows, it almost always grows at an exponential growth rate, and so we'll restrict our discussion to exponential growth trends.

- **Population growth.** Generally speaking, for any population of humans or animals, a certain percentage of the population will have offspring each year, and a certain percentage will die. These percentages tend to be roughly the same each year. The result is that the population tends to grow by the same fixed percentage each year, which is the formula for exponential growth.

However, it's a little more complicated: Most populations (including humans) will tend to grow faster than the amount of food available to feed that population. When the population grows to the point where not enough food is available, then a segment of the population is killed — by famine, by a disease epidemic, or by war. This is the "Malthusian problem" that we'll discuss more below.

- **Population-based trends.** Many growth trends are directly related to the size of the population, and exhibit exponential growth simply because the population exhibits exponential growth.

For example, how many shoes are manufactured each year? I don't have the figures, but I assume that it's one or two pairs per person around the world, and that's probably been true for centuries. Thus, the number of shoes manufactured each year grows exponentially because the population grows exponentially.

Here's a crucial fact: If there's a temporary perturbation in the size of the population, it will affect the shoe trend. For example, if a world war or an epidemic temporarily causes a 20% drop in the population, then the number of shoes manufactured will probably drop about 20% as well.

- **"Doubly exponential" population trends.** Other growth trends might be described as "doubly exponential," because they depend on the population and in addition, they grow exponentially PER PERSON.

How much energy is used each year? Once again, I don't have the figures, but I would expect the amount of energy used per person worldwide to be growing exponentially. So the total amount of energy used by the entire population grows at a faster exponential rate than the population itself.

- **Technological growth trends.** This is the most fascinating — and mysterious — kind of exponential growth trend. It's completely independent of population.

An example is the power of calculating machines and computers, which has been growing at an exponential rate for over a century, but with no relationship to the population size.

Technological growth is not affected by perturbations in the size of the population. For example, if a world war or epidemic killed 20% of the population, the power of desktop computers would NOT drop 20%. It would stay the same. So the power of desktop computers is unrelated to population.

Actually, it wouldn't stay the same: It would continue growing at exactly the same rate. This is the fascinating thing about technological growth — that it's on a growth path entirely its own, completely independent of population, wars, politics or skirt lengths.

The mysterious thing about technological growth is the steadfastness with which exponential grow trends are maintained for decades or centuries, across wildly varying technologies. We'll discuss several examples of this later.

- **Technology-related growth trends.** There are many social trends that are exponential because they're technology related. Some of these are very surprising. For example, we'll discuss the divorce rate, which is technology related because laborsaving devices allow women to leave the home and hold an outside job.

Combined Growth / Cyclic Trends

It's worth mentioning briefly that sometimes a trend value can combine both cyclical and growth elements. Graphically, this is shown when the overall trend grows exponentially over time, but the actual value oscillates up and down, above and below the exponential trend line, as it follows the trend line. We'll give an example of this with stock prices.

Population Growth

As we've said, generally speaking, for any population of humans or animals, a certain percentage of the population will have offspring each year, and a certain percentage will die. These percentages tend to be roughly the same each year. The result is that the population tends to grow by the same fixed percentage each year, which is the formula for exponential growth.

To understand what exponential growth means, think about some of the statements you see commonly in newspaper and magazine articles all the time. You might read "the number of AIDS cases increases by X% per year" or "the number of people owning cell phones increases by Y% per year."

Sometimes these statements are made in a different way, but one that is mathematically equivalent. You might hear, "Such and such doubles every 18 months," or "triples every 5 years."

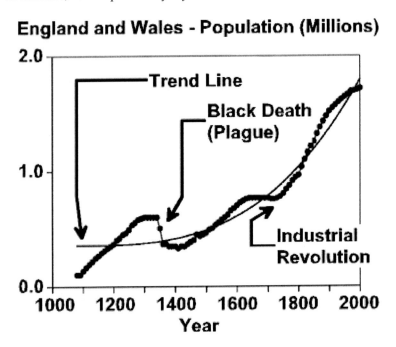

Figure 43 Population (millions) of England and Wales*, years 1000-2000, with an exponential trend line.

Statements like this are extremely common in the news. What the statements all have in common is that a population (or quantity) changes by a fixed constant ("increase by X%" or "doubles") every fixed time period ("per year" or "every five years").

Exponential growth

Any population or quantity that exhibits such constant change is said to change exponentially, or exhibit exponential growth.

CHAPTER 11 – TREND FORECASTING

For example, if some quantity X doubles every year, then in successive years, the quantity will have the values 2X, 4X, 8X, 16X, 32X, 64X, 128X. Exponential growth can be very rapid.

Take a look at the Figure 43. It shows the population of England and Wales from 1000 to 2000. The black dots on the graph are the actual population values for the years shown.

Notice that the population took a sharp drop in the 1300s because of the Bubonic Plague (Black Death) that killed huge numbers of people around the world. Later, there was a sharp increase in the rate of population growth around 1750, evidently because prosperity from the Industrial Revolution made mothers want to have more children.

What these incidents show is that population doesn't grow steadily. Sometimes it speeds up; sometimes it slows down or even drops. But in the long run, it always follows an exponential growth trend line.

That trend line is also shown on the graph as a thin curved line. Notice

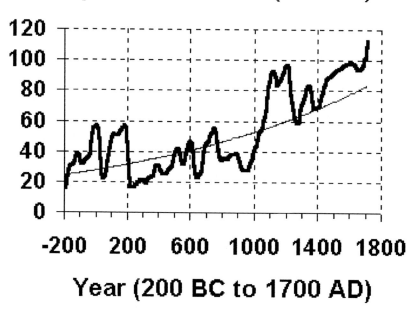

Figure 44 Population of China in millions of people* from 200 BC to 1710 AD

how the actual population oscillates above and below the trend line, but never strays far away.

What does the trend line represent? For simplicity, think of the trend line as representing the amount of food being grown in England and Wales (or, more precisely, the number of people who can be fed by the food being grown). When the actual population falls below the trend line, then food is plentiful and women have more children, pushing the population curve up. When the population curve gets above the trend line, then there's not enough food, and people begin starving to death — unless they're killed by war or disease.

Figure 44 represents an even more dramatic example of population growth. It shows the ups and downs of the population of China over a 1500-year period. As you can see, China's population has undergone wild oscillations, alternating periods of growth with periods where tens of millions of people were killed by massive rebellions, disease, or famine. Even so, the population growth still follows an exponential growth trend line, over long

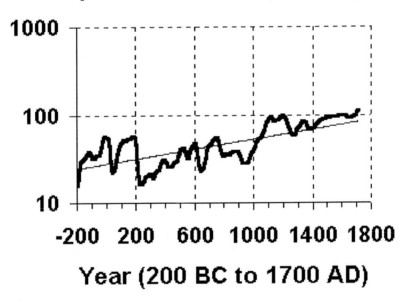

Figure 45 Population of China in millions of people* from 200 BC to 1710 AD, shown with logarithmic scale

periods of time.

Figure 45 shows this more clearly. This graph displays exactly the same data as the preceding graph, except that the y-axis is measured using a logarithmic scale, instead of an evenly spaced linear scale. This means that the evenly spaced y-axis values are 1, 10, 100, and so forth, with each value being ten times the previous one.

When this is done, exponential curves turn into straight lines. This makes it very easy to visually verify that the data values are, in fact, exhibiting exponential growth.

Thomas Roberts Malthus

The reason that economics is called "the dismal science" is largely because of a book, *Essay on Population*, by Thomas Roberts Malthus, published in 1798.

This book shocked the British populace because it was the first to lay out the awful truth: That since population would always grow faster than the available food supply, there would always be starvation.

He even made some social recommendations. However, his recommendations would be considered bizarre by today's standards:

> It is an evident truth that, whatever may be the rate of increase in the means of subsistence, the increase in population must be limited by it, at least after the food has been divided into the smallest shares that will support life. All the children born, beyond what would be required to keep up the population to this level, must necessarily perish, unless room be made for them by the deaths of grown persons. ... To act consistently, therefore, we should facilitate, instead of foolishly and vainly endeavouring to impede, the operation of nature in producing this mortality, and if we dread the too frequent visitation of the horrid form of famine, we should sedulously encourage the other forms of destruction, which we compel nature to use.
>
> Instead of recommending cleanliness to the poor, we should encourage contrary habits. In our towns, we should make the streets narrower, crowd more people into the houses, and court the return of the plague. In the country, we should build our villages near stagnant pools, and particularly encourage settle-

ments in all marshy and unwholesome situations. But above all, we should reprobate specific remedies for ravaging diseases: and those benevolent, but much mistaken men, who have thought they were doing a service to mankind by projecting schemes for the total extirpation of particular disorders. If by these and similar means the annual mortality were increased ... we might probably every one of us marry at the age of puberty and yet few be absolutely starved.

It's hard to read these two paragraphs without laughing. His recommendations were never adopted, but I guess that they made sense to him: since millions of people are going to die anyway, why not help it along? Fortunately, today's societies could never tolerate any policy that would allow politicians to decide who lives and who dies.

Nonetheless, Malthus' basic conclusion is true. Nature has provided us with a powerful sex drive to cause us to have too many children for the available food supply to support, and nature has provided us with famine, disease and a built-in desire for genocidal war as ways to make sure that enough people die off, and to select the people who survive to the be the tribes, societies and nations that are the best equipped and most able to survive.

Generational Dynamics adds to our understanding of Malthus' predictions by providing insight into one of the mechanisms that nature (or God) provided us with to get rid of excess people.

The most bloody, violent and genocidal wars occur in 80-year cycles, the length of a human lifetime. Whether we like it or not, wars are not senseless, at least not to nature's (or God's) overall purpose in regulating population size on earth.

Complexity Theory: Why Communism and Socialism must fail

This is an aside to the main point of this chapter, but it's interesting because it shows how simple mathematical arguments can be applied to the problem of governing large populations.

In 1991, I visited CeBit, the huge computer show in Hanover, Germany. It was a special occasion because the Berlin Wall had just fallen, and East Germans were visiting the show for the first time. "They're in a state of shock," I was told. "They're still using punched card equipment from the 1950s." Why had Communist East Germany gotten stuck in the 1950s?

Cuba's another example: They're still using 1950s automobiles. Why?

Why do Communist countries become frozen in time? It turns out there's a good reason, and it can be proven mathematically.

The branch of mathematics is called Complexity Theory. This branch was developed for computers to answer the questions about how long it will take a computer to solve certain types of problems. For example, suppose it takes a certain computer program one hour to process 1,000 data values. How long will it take the program to process 2,000 data values or 3,000 data values?

It depends on what the computer program does with the data. It some cases it will take 2 hours or 3 hours, respectively, but in other cases it will take 4 hours or 9 hours, respectively. Complexity Theory sorts all that out.

Malthus' argument, described in the last section, was essentially a Complexity Theory argument.

Now, if we apply the same concepts to governing the population of a Communist state, we see why Communism has to fail.

In order to provide a worker's paradise, Communism requires that every financial transaction be price-controlled, so that no entrepreneur can make an unfair profit. The state determines how much any store manager can charge for a product, so that poor people are not taken advantage.

As a practical matter, that means that each time a new service is offered, or a new kind of product is developed, or is manufactured in a new way, or is distributed in a new way, or is sold with different kinds of customizations, some bureaucrat has to make a decision on how much may be charged for that product or service.

Now, how many how many government bureaucrats does it take to do all this? That's the problem. Let's do a little computation.

The population of the country grows exponentially with time, so let's assume that the population is $P = A\ e^{pt}$ (A times e to the power p times t) as a function of time t. The number of products and services grows at least proportionately to the number of people, so let's make a conservative estimate that the number of products and services uses the formula $P = B\ e^{pt}$. Assuming that each transaction involves two people, the number of transactions will be $T = C\ e^{3pt}$, so the number of transactions grows at a much faster rate than the population grows. In order to enforce the economic controls, a fixed percentage (at least 1%) of these transactions will have to be monitored. So, as the population grows, it requires a greater and greater proportion of the population to enforce the economic controls, and so Communism falls apart.

That's why Communist countries like North Korea, East Germany and Cuba were stuck in the 50s. They had to freeze the introduction of new products, because their bureaucrats could never keep up with the economic controls on an exponentially growing product set.

That's why, once the population becomes large enough, larger than a few million people, a free market is the only form of economic management that's mathematically possible.

Using similar Complexity Theory arguments, it's possible show mathematically why feudal government had to give way to monarchies, and why monarchies had to give way to republics. (We already discussed this in conjunction with the French Revolution in chapter 8, p. 176.) The argument is similar in all cases: As the population grows, the number of transactions between people grows much faster, and so the only forms of government that work are those that do not require the government to monitor individual transactions.

One more point: Some historians have claimed that Western civilizations invented representative government and forced third world countries to adopt it. These complexity theory arguments show that representative governments (republics) are in fact the only ones that are mathematically possible.

Technology Growth Trends

Technology growth is very mysterious because it also grows exponentially, just like population, but has nothing to do with population.

Let's repeat the example given previously: The number of shoes manufactured each year depends on the size of the population, and so it grows exponentially as the population grows; and if a plague kills 20% of the population, then the number of shoes manufactured in the next year will be 20% smaller, because the population is smaller.

But the processing power of calculating machines and computers also grows exponentially, but has nothing to do with population. If a plague kills 20% of the population, then the power of computers will not only NOT go down, it will actually continue to grow steadfastly at the same exponential rate as before.

The best way to understand this is to look at several different kinds of examples.

Artificial Light Sources

Let's return to an example briefly considered earlier — Thomas Edison's invention of the incandescent light bulb.

You know that Thomas Edison invented the light bulb in 1879. Well, suppose Thomas Edison had never been born, and so could never have invented the light bulb. Does that mean we would we still be using candles instead of light bulbs?

The answer is no: If Edison hadn't invented the incandescent bulb, then someone else would have invented it shortly thereafter. There were several other inventors working on the same problem at the same time, and one of the others would have gotten the patent if Edison hadn't. One of the others, Joseph Swan, actually invented an improved light bulb, with the result that Edison and Swan went into partnership together.

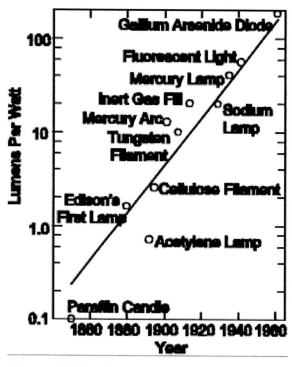

Figure 46 This diagram shows how numerous different technologies for artificial light have always been invented at almost exactly the right time*.

That's the point: that technological advances come at exactly the right time.

Edison's light bulb is only one of many very different technologies that have been used to produce artificial light.

The adjoining graph shows various inventions of artificial light sources, using wildly different technologies. The "efficiency" of a light source is a measure of how little energy is wasted in heat: If a light bulb gets hot, then it wastes a lot of energy in heat; if it stays cool, then it's using energy much more efficiently.

Notice in the adjoining graph how new inventions have been improving the efficiency of artificial light sources over time, and how the efficiency has been growing exponentially. Also, notice how each new invention comes at exactly the right time to maintain the steadfast exponential growth.

This graph illustrates how mysterious technological growth is. Why should all these wildly different technologies produce light sources that increase efficiency according to a well-defined predictable growth curve?

Notice also that these technological advances have absolutely nothing to do with population.

Speed of combat aircraft

This is a very interesting example because it refutes a commonly held misconception about the history of aircraft: That the jet plane was invented *because of World War II.*

The graph below shows the top speed of combat aircraft

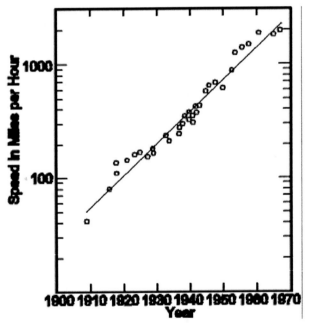

Figure 47 Top speeds of combat aircraft (bombers and fighters)[*].

since 1909. There were numerous technological innovations, including the closed cockpit, the monoplane, the all-metal airframe, and the jet engine.

When the jet engine was introduced in 1944, many people thought that it was invented *because of* World War II, and that it brought about a sizable jump in the speed of combat aircraft.

However, that's not true. The jet engine was introduced at just the right time to keep the previous trend going, and it did not bring about a significant jump in speed, indicating that it would have been introduced at this time even if it had been a time of peace.

What the jet engine did do was to supply a brand new technology that allowed combat aircraft to stay on the same exponential trend line, at a time when the speed of propeller-driven aircraft was topping out.

All of these examples illustrate the same thing: the relentlessness of technological improvements when following exponential growth curves.

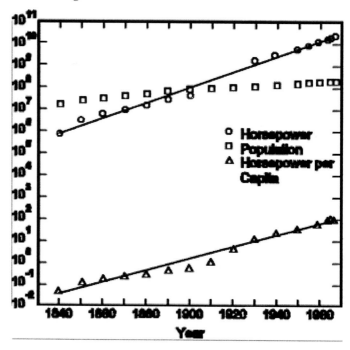

Figure 48 Installed Technological Horsepower in the United States, Population of the United States, and Installed Technological Horsepower per Capita*.

Installed Technological Horsepower

This final example is included to illustrate an interesting point.

We've been distinguishing between exponential growth based on population and exponential growth based on technology. Can you have both kinds of growth at the same time?

Figure 48 displays the growth in installed technological horsepower in the U.S. As we'll see, it indicates that the *total* installed horsepower is growing exponentially — and that's related to the growth in population — but also, the installed horsepower *per person* is growing exponentially, and that's probably mostly due to technological improvements.

But let's start at the beginning. What do we mean by "installed technological horsepower"? We're talking about such things as electrical generators or any motors that generate electrical or other power. To keep it simple, we're saying that we're generating more electricity and other forms of power, and the growth is exponential. Of course, this is sometimes a controversial political issue, since Americans use more power per capita than most other people in the world, raising environmental issues.

Notice the following:

- The trend line near the top of the graph, following the data points represented by circles, shows that the total amount of power used by the entire country has been growing exponentially.

- However, a suspicious person might object that the amount of power being used on a per person basis is staying roughly the same, but the total amount of power is growing exponentially, since the population is growing exponentially.

- The population is shown on the graph using squares as data points. Note that the population growth data points also follow a rough straight line (line not drawn), but that line is much less steep than the trend line for total horsepower. This indicates that total horsepower and population are both growing at an exponential rate, but that the horsepower is growing at a much greater exponential rate.

- Finally, by dividing the total horsepower by the population, you get the total horsepower per person, graphed on the bottom using triangles as data points. The trend line shows that the total horsepower per person is growing at an exponential rate.

This example shows how different exponential growth effects can be combined into a single growth trend.

Growth of Computing Power

We'll look at one final example of technologic growth, the computing power of computers.

Back in 1964, I had a summer job computer programming for Honeywell Corporation, and I well remember a conversation I had with the engineer sitting at a nearby desk. He said, "Computers can't get much faster. The circuits in today's computers require signals to travel at almost the speed of light, and there is no way to get around that. Thus, computers may get a little faster, but not much faster than they are today."

He was making the point that for computers to get any faster, the signals that move around within the computer would have to move faster and faster. But since nothing can move faster than the speed of light, the speed of computers is limited.

Of course, computers have gotten a lot faster since 1964. The fascinating thing is that if a large powerful supercomputer fills most of a room, then ten years later a desktop computer will be more powerful than that old supercomputer was. And this keeps happening — the end is not in sight. (See http://www.top500.org)

How do you measure the rate at which computer power has been increasing? One answer is provided by Moore's Law, the most well-known exponential growth prediction, and this prediction was made in the early 1960s, right around the time that my friend was telling me that computers would not get much faster because signals could not travel faster than the speed of light.

Moore's Law predicted in the early 1960s that the number of transistors on a computer chip would grow at an exponential rate. History has shown that the number of transistors on a computer chip has been doubling every 18 months or so since then, and so the power of computers has been doubling every 18 months. (The prediction was made by Gordon Moore of Intel Corp. For more information, including a link to his original paper, see http://www.intel.com/research/silicon/mooreslaw.htm — however it's interesting to note historically that Moore's original prediction was that the number of transistors would double every year, rather than every 18 months.)

How does Moore's Law get around the speed of light problem?

When my friend told me in 1964 that the speed of computers was limited by how fast signals could move around the various computer components, he overlooked the fact that the distances between the computer components could be reduced substantially.

When transistors are packed more densely on a computer chip, it naturally means that the transistors are closer to one another. Therefore, signals traveling from one transistor to another have to travel shorter distances, and so they can move from transistor to transistor much faster, without violating the principle that they can't travel faster than the speed of light.

When Moore's Law predicts that the number of transistors on a chip will double every 18 months, that's an example of exponential growth. The real power of forecasting exponential growth becomes most evident when you draw a graph of such values.

The adjacent graph shows the number of transistors per chip for various Intel Corp. chips that have become available over the years, starting from an experimental 1965 chip with 50 transistors, the Intel 4004 chip from 1971 with 2,250 transistors, all the way up to the Pentium 4 processor from the year 2000 with 42 million transistors.

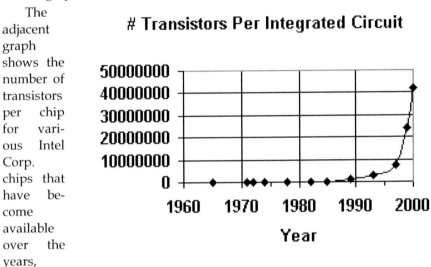

Figure 49 The number of transistors per chip for new chips produced by Intel[*].

As you can see, the graph seems fairly flat until around 1985, and then it really takes off very quickly. Since all the values before 1985 are fairly small, it's hard to read them individually.

That's why it's common practice to graph exponential values using a logarithmic scale, as shown on the graph below. Notice that the y-axis values are 1, 10, 100, and so forth, with each value equal to ten times the preceding value.

When this is done, exponential curves turn into straight lines. This makes it very easy to visually verify that the data values are, in fact, exhibiting exponential growth.

What's remarkable about Moore's Law is that it was formulated in the early 1960s, even though there was absolutely no way, at that time, to predict what new technologies would be needed to make the prediction come true. And yet, the prediction *has* come true, with steadfast reliability.

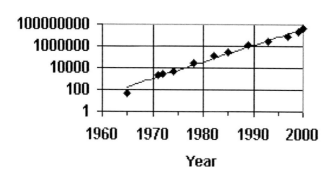

Figure 50 The number of transistors per chip for new chips produced by Intel. This graph is like the preceding one, except that the y-axis has a logarithmic scale.

However, the number of transistors can't keep doubling forever. Experts estimate that the natural limit on the density of transistors will be reached around 2015, after which further doubling would violate the laws of physics.

But that doesn't mean that computer power will level off in 2015. That's because new technologies will be coming along to replace transistors and integrated circuits.

To see that, let's step back for a moment. Ray Kurzweil has gone back as far as the late 1800s to show that computing speed started increasing exponentially long before integrated circuits were invented. Just like the previous examples we've seen — artificial light sources, speed of combat aircraft, and so forth — the speed of computers has been growing according to a predictable exponential rate through may wildly different technologies.

Here's the list of technologies identified by Ray Kurzweil[*]:

1. Punched card electromechanical calculators, used in 1890 and 1900 census
2. Relay-based machine used during World War II to crack the Nazi Enigma machine's encryption code.
3. The CBS vacuum tube computer that predicted the election of President Eisenhower in 1952.
4. Transistor-based machines used in the first space launches
5. Integrated circuits - multiple transistors on a chip (Moore's Law)

Kurzweil has shown that all of these technologies cause computing speed to increase according to a steadfast, predictable exponential growth curve.

We've already said that computing power due to improvements in integrated circuits will level off around 2015. What technology will replace them?

We can't be absolutely certain, of course, but there are two different candidates today:

- "Protein folding" DNA technology which will be used to develop computers that work something like the human brain. (See IBM's Blue Gene project, http://researchweb.watson.ibm.com/bluegene.)

- Nanotechnology, particle physics technology that will, essentially, use special "molecules" consisting of the tiniest physical particles to act as computers.

One of these technologies, or a combination, will cause an explosion in computer power in the 2010s and 2020s. As computers become increasingly powerful, they'll also become increasingly intelligent, and by 2030 or so, computers will actually become more intelligent than human beings.

Sociological changes related to technology

It may seem surprising, but many sociological changes can be related to technology. We'll present here a sampling.

Divorce Rate

Why would the divorce rate be related to technology?

In past centuries, there were many structural factors preventing women from either getting divorced or working outside the home: Taking care of kids really was a full time job. It took all day for a woman to cook a meal from scratch, using vegetables from the garden, along with meat that her husband had obtained by hunting and killing an animals. Making clothes for the family was another major factor.

However, technology has been providing many labor saving devices, reducing the amount of time that a mother has to stay home, unless she chooses to do so. Vegetables and cuts of meat are purchased already pre-

Figure 51 The number of divorces in each year per 1,000 marriages from 1860 to 1988[♦].

pared in the supermarket, modern ranges and microwave ovens speed up cooking, dishwashers reduce cleanup time, washers and dryers reduce laundry time, and vacuum cleaners reduce house cleaning time.

As technology provided more labor saving devices for the home, women became freer to work outside the home and earn incomes independently, also giving them the freedom to divorce at will.

With that background, let's see how the divorce rate has been increasing exponentially. We'll look at two different measures of the divorce rate, because this will give us an opportunity to examine how different measurements can give slightly different results.

The first method for computing the divorce rate is to measure the number of divorces in a given year as a fraction of the number of marriages in that year. This method shows, for each year, how likely a divorce is to occur

Figure 52 Same as preceding graph, but with logarithmic scale.

CHAPTER 11 — TREND FORECASTING

in that year.

Figure 51 shows the number of divorces as percentages of the number of marriages in the same year. This is the way that the Census Bureau normally presents divorces, although it causes confusion because it measures the number of divorces, but not the proportion of marriages likely to end in divorce (which we'll present later).

This is a good example of exponential growth because it illustrates how a value can grow exponentially as an overall trend, but still oscillates above and below the trend line.

Figure 52 shows that many divorces occurred *during* World War II, but the number of divorces dropped significantly *after* the war. Still, on an over-

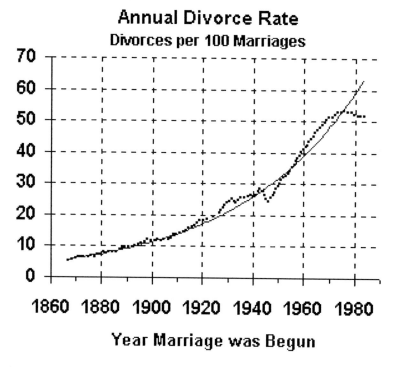

Figure 53 The number of marriages ending in divorce, 1867 to 1985, based on year marriage was begun*.

all basis, the divorce rate has been growing exponentially.

Figure 52 uses the same data as the preceding one, but this graph has a logarithmic scale, so that the exponential trend becomes a straight line.

259

When using a linear scale (as in the first graph), recent values become exaggerated, and historical values become diminished in importance. However, when a logarithmic scale is used, then recent and historical values receive equal treatment and emphasis.

Now let's look at the divorce rate based on year of marriage.

Figure 53 measures the rate of divorce in a different way, as the number of marriages ending in divorce. While the previous graphs showed the divorce rate in the *year of divorce*, this graph shows the divorce rate by the *year of marriage*.

These are the divorce figures that are most often quoted in the press, and they indicate that about 50% of all marriages end in divorce. However, unlike the previous set of figures, these figures are based on Census Bureau

Figure 54 Same as preceding graph, but with logarithmic scale.

estimates. Why? Because the Census Bureau can get data on how many divorces occur in a current year, but they have no way of collecting data on how many of this year's marriages will eventually end in divorce; those figures have to be estimated.

The next graph, with a logarithmic scale, shows clearly how these data values have been closely hugging the exponential trend line, much more closely than the divorces per 1,000 marriages figures do.

Why is that? Both sets of figures — based on year marriage ended in divorce and on year marriage was begun — follow an exponential growth curve, but why do the first figures oscillate wildly at times, while the second figures show very little oscillation?

The answer is simply that people time their divorces based on current political and economic conditions. Thus, people postponed divorce during the depression, because money was scarce, but then got those postponed divorces during the war, when economic times were better.

The leveling off of the divorce rate

The two sets of divorce figures we've just used were published by researcher Andrew J. Cherlin in 1992. At that time, there was a big puzzle in the research community: The divorce rate had begun to level off in 1975. Would it continue to stay level, or would it start to increase again?

Everyone knew that the divorce rate had to level off some time; after all, the divorce rate could never exceed 100%, and so it had level off sometime before reaching 100%. But had that leveling off in fact occurred at 50%?

Census figures since 1990 now show that in fact the divorce rate has leveled off at 50%, and so the puzzle seems to have been solved.

This illustrates a standard phenomenon in exponential trend forecasting: That exponential trends start to level off when they reach some physical barrier.

However, in the case of technological trend forecasting, we've seen that when a particular technology begins to level off, a new technology replaces it, as in the examples we've already seen:

- The growth of computer power and the improvement in efficiency of artificial light sources encompass numerous technologies, each of which leveled off individually, but when maintained the exponential growth when taken as a group.

- The growth in speed of combat aircraft maintained an exponential growth through various improvements to propeller-driven aircraft, and continued this growth when jet engines, a brand new technology, were introduced.

Now that the divorce rate has leveled off, the question arises: Have we been measuring the wrong thing? In the case of computers, if we measure

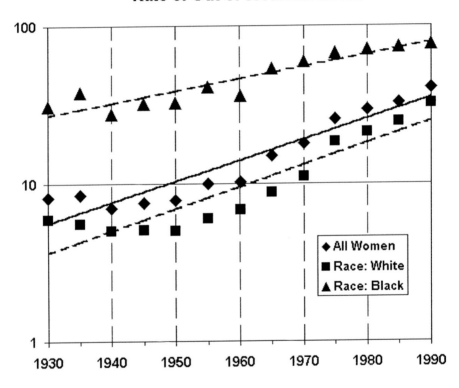

Figure 55 Rate of out of wedlock births for all women, and for black and white women

the number of transistors on a chip, then we know that that will level off before 2015, but if we measure instead the power of "calculating machines," then we get an exponential trend line that continues through numerous technologies.

Out of Wedlock Births

The question is: Is there something else we can measure that will continue the exponential growth of the leveled off divorce curve?

There appear to be other candidates, a likely one being "number of children born out of wedlock." Figure 55 shows that these values exhibit exponential growth for all women, and for black and white races. The values for black mothers are nearing 100% and so should be topping out, while the figures for white mothers still have a while to go before they catch up.

Future biotechnology developments, such as cloned human beings and modified DNA, may provide the technological means to keep this exponential growth trend on track. Work in this field by researchers can identify the precise measure to be used.

Forecasting Stock Trends

In chapter 6, we described how generational trends lead us to conclude that we're entering a new 1930s-style Great Depression.

The same conclusion is also supported by standard trend forecasting techniques of the kind that we've been describing. In this section, we summarize those results.

Should stock prices grow exponentially?

In the long run, the value of a company is represented by its stock price. Good news may push a stock price up temporarily, and bad news may push a stock price down temporarily, but in the long run, the stock price will return to the value of the company. More precisely, over a long period of time, the value of the company will be accurately represented by its market capitalization, which equals its stock price times the number of outstanding shares.

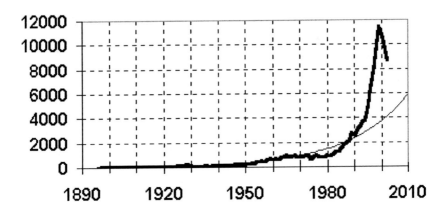

Figure 56 Dow Jones Industrial Average — 1896 to Present, with best-fit exponential growth line.

The value of a single company may go up or down, but the value of all companies together should increase exponentially for two reasons: (1) As the population increases exponentially, the number of customers increases exponentially, and so does the company value; (2) As technology improves, companies' productivity and efficiency will grow exponentially, and so will the companies' value.

So, standard stock market index values represent the aggregate values of stocks, and the values of stocks represent the values of the corresponding companies. Thus, we expect the values of standard market indexes, such as the Dow Jones Industrial Average and the S&P 500 Index to increase exponentially.

Dow Jones Industrial Average

The above graph shows the value of the Dow Jones Industrial Average (DJIA) since 1896. This graph shows how spectacular the bubble of the late 1990s was. The thin line is the exponential growth trend line, and you can see how the DJIA far exceeds the trend line.

In early 2003, the DJIA index was in the 8000s. This graph shows that the trend value in 2010 is just below 6000 — it's actually about 5800.

To see more clearly what's going to happen, take a look at the same graph, but with a logarithmic scale.

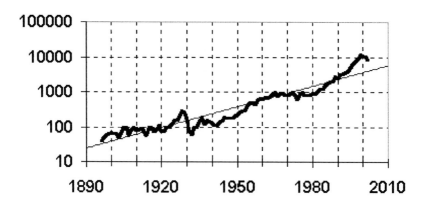

Figure 57 Dow Jones Industrial Average — 1896 to Present (log scale).

This graph makes it clearer how the 1990s bubble was similar to the 1920s bubble, and it shows how today's stock market fall is roughly following the 1930s path.

We expect today's stock market to follow roughly the same path as in the 1930s. This means that the DJIA will fall well below the trend line, to the 3,000 to 4,000 range, and won't return to the trend value, or exceed 6000, until well into the 2010s decade.

S&P 500 Stock Index

Some people consider the S&P 500 Stock Index to be more reliable than the DJIA. However, the results are the same.

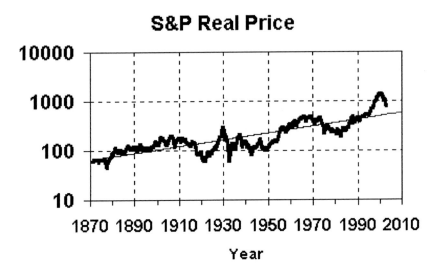

Figure 58 S&P 500 Real Price Index — 1870 to Present (log scale), with best fit exponential growth line.

Figure 58 shows the S&P 500 Stock index, adjusted for inflation, since 1870. The value in early 2003 is around 800. The graph shows a 2010 trend value of 589. These results are comparable to those obtained with the DJIA.

The S&P Price Earnings Ratio

Let's now do a different kind of historical analysis, using a cyclic trend value rather than an exponential trend value.

The "price earnings ratio" (P/E ration) of a stock has historically indicated whether a stock is overpriced or underpriced. It's computed by dividing the price of each share of stock by the company's annual earnings per share of stock. (This can also be computed by dividing the total value of all outstanding shares of stock by the company's total annual earnings.)

This is not an exponential growth value, so we can't use exponential growth trend forecasting to analyze it. But we can use a historical comparison technique — comparing the 1920s and beyond to the 1990s and beyond.

CHAPTER 11 – TREND FORECASTING

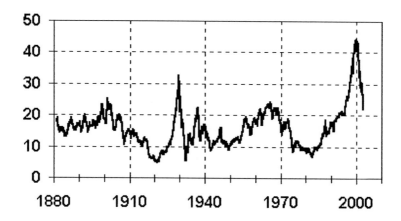

Figure 59 Historical price/earnings ratio for S&P 500, 1881 to 2002.

Figure 59 shows the P/E ratio for the S&P 500 stocks from 1881 to 2002.

As you can see, P/E ratios are typically between 10 and 20. (That is, stocks generally are priced between 10 and 20 times the company's annual earnings per share.) The value oscillates over time, and rarely goes below 5 or above 25.

There are only two times since 1881 when the average P/E ratio went above 30: in the 1920s and the 1990s. If we compare the 1930s values to today, we can see that we can expect the average P/E ratio to drop to about 6 or 7 in the 2005 or so time frame. This is consistent with the other findings we've presented.

The average P/E ratio is a very interesting value because it shows the level of confidence of investors. If an investor is willing to pay a price exceeding 20 times the earnings per share for a share of stock (P/E ratio greater than 20), then the investor would have to be very confident that the company was going to succeed and grow much faster than current earnings indicate.

Conversely, if an investor isn't willing to pay even 10 times earnings for a share of stock, then the investor is pessimistic about the company, and may believe that the company is going to lose market share, or even go bankrupt.

Using this measure, you can see that investor confidence spiked irrationally high in the 1920s, but then dropped very low as investors became increasingly risk aversive. Investor confidence grew steadily starting around 1950. As I've previously mentioned from my personal experience, my mother (and probably a lot of other people) were still very afraid of another depression and had little confidence that the stock market was safe. But confidence grew at that time, because we'd beaten the depression and we'd beaten the Nazis.

The P/E ratio grew until around 1967, when the country started to experience substantial unrest with demonstrations and riots protesting the Vietnam War. The P/E ratio fell fairly steadily until the personal computer started revolutionizing business in the early 1980s.

The P/E ratio spiked sharply upward starting around 1992, the time when investors who had any personal memory of the last P/E ratio spike (from the 1920s and 1930s) were retiring or dying off.

Since 2000, the P/E ratio has been falling steadily. Note that this crash was *not* caused by the 9/11/2001 attacks — the crash began over 1 1/2 years before the 9/11 attacks.

Today, there's very little reason for any investor to regain anything like the confidence he had in the 1990s. Everyone has sobered up, and everyone now realizes that the 1990s bubble was a mistake that should not be repeated. That's why we should expect investor confidence to keep falling, and the P/E ratio to keep falling, and with it, the stock market.

Comparison to 1980s Japanese Nikkei Stock Market Index

It's fairly common these days for analysts to compare America's economic situation to Japan's situation.

Japan is ten years ahead of America, in the sense that The Tokyo Stock Exchange (TSE) had its big stock market bubble in the 1980s, rather than the 1990s. The TSE's bubble burst in 1990, while America's burst in 2000.

It's instructive therefore to look at what's happened to Japan since 1990, since the same thing may happen to America.

The graph below shows the value of Japan's Nikkei Stock Market Index since 1973. As you can see, the Nikkei stock market index was at around 40,000 in 1989, following a large bubble throughout the 1980s. The Japanese stock market crash began in January 1990, and *has not ended to this very day*, 13 years later.

CHAPTER 11 – TREND FORECASTING

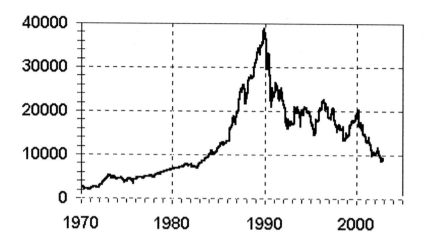

Figure 60 Japan's Nikkei Stock Market Index, 1973 to 2002

The Nikkei's value has dropped by 80%. This is a little more than the amount that the forecasting techniques we've used predict will happen in America.

For those who believe that the 1930s experience have taught us how to avoid a major stock market crash, the Japanese experience provides an answer. If we'd figured that out, then the Japanese would have applied that knowledge.

There *is* something remarkable about Japan's experience however: Although Japan's stock market has suffered an 80% loss, much greater than the American stock market loss in the 1930s, Japan has suffered a major financial crisis, but without massive business closings and homelessness. Why isn't there massive starvation and homelessness in Japan?

A new analysis of the Japanese economy provides the answer[*]. By examining data from thousands of companies, the researchers uncovered a consistent pattern of Japanese banks loaning massive amounts of money throughout the 1990s to firms that would otherwise have gone out of business.

"The glue holding stock prices together in Japan has been copious lending by banks at ultralow rates, allowing even nearly insolvent companies to survive for years," according to the findings.

These loans have been possible because of the nature of the Japanese banking system, which essentially guarantees that the government will prop up any bank that otherwise would fail. The loans have permitted very weak companies from failing, and have also put many banks themselves into near insolvency. In fact, several major banks did fail in November 1997 and early 1998, and they were nationalized and saved. Since that time, stock prices on the TSE have been showing a remarkable volatility, very similar to the volatility of the New York Stock Exchange in the Great Depression of 1930s, but unlike anything seen since then.

The report indicates that time is quickly running out. More banks are approaching insolvency, and cash reserves are running out. This indicates that a major business collapse may be in the offing for Japan.

Sub-cycles in economic growth

It's worth mentioning briefly that sometimes a trend value can combine both cyclical and growth elements. Graphically, this is shown when the overall trend grows exponentially over time, but the actual value oscillates

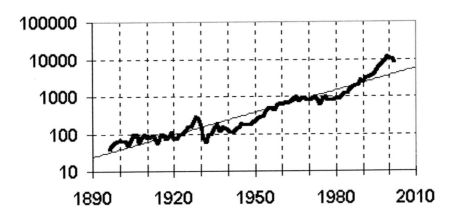

Figure 61 Dow Jones Industrial Average — 1896 to Present (log scale).

up and down, above and below the exponential trend line, as it follows the trend line.

Take a look at the DJIA graph (Figure 61), which appears previously in this chapter. This represents economic growth, which grows exponentially but has cyclic elements.

Economic growth appears to grow according to the following rules:

1. **Exponential growth:** Economic growth oscillates around an exponential growth trend line.
2. **Generational cycle:** The main oscillation is an 80-year generational cycle.
3. **Technological cycle:** There appears to be secondary cycle, about 40-50 years in length, based on technological developments. The technological improvements in the last century include the following: Electricity at the end of the 1800s; mass factory automation starting around 1935; and person computers starting around 1980.
4. **Daily cycle:** In terms of stock prices, there's a day-to-day oscillation that is chaotic (random). For example, a weather report or a rumor can affect day-to-day stock prices.

The three oscillations in the last three paragraphs are completely independent and asynchronous. Sometimes they add to each other, sometimes they cancel each other out. But they have to be considered separately if one is to understand the cyclical nature of economic growth.

In the long run (time periods decades long), the oscillations are generally meaningless, and only the exponential growth is important. In the short run, it's the exponential growth that's generally meaningless, and the shorter cycles are more important.

Reflating the Money Supply

The graph below is predicting a deflationary period after 2003, and in fact, as of early 2003, the economy has been getting increasingly deflationary. The Federal Reserve Open Market Committee, under Alan Greenspan, has adopted a reflationary policy by setting the overnight bank lending rate to historic lows, around 1%.

The purpose of this policy is to pump money into the economy. With more money in the economy, people will have more money and spend more money, creating a demand for products, causing businesses to expand to meet that demand. This concept has been the basis of theoretical economics for fifty years, whether in the form of "liberal" fiscal policy as developed by Maynard Keynes or "conservative" monetary policy, as developed by Milton Friedman.

However, the current economic problems are being caused by a very different problem, as described in chapter 6. The analysis in that chapter implies that deflation is being caused by very different problems: Because of generational changes, businesses have become increasingly inefficient, producing products that are of little interest to new generations.

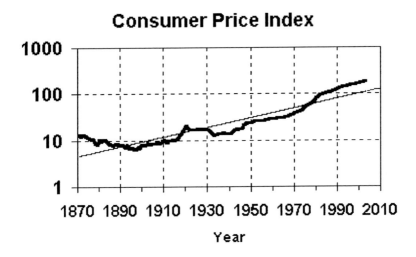

Figure 62 Consumer price index (CPI) from 1870 to present, with an exponential growth trend line. The CPI is 185 in 2003, and 2010 has a trend value of 129.

Under this analysis, deflation is occurring because people simply don't want the products being produced, and money has nothing to do with it. For example, teens aren't interested in buying CDs at any price; they want their music available over the Internet.

Furthermore, under this analysis, the Fed's reflation policy will have the same effect it's had in Japan since 1990: It permits companies that otherwise would have disappeared to stay in business by borrowing more and more cheap money, thus only postponing the problem, not repairing it.

CHAPTER 11 — TREND FORECASTING

As the nation heads for war, this will all be resolved. As the nation becomes militarily overextended and the draft is reactivated, weak businesses will go under and will be replaced by businesses producing products for the war effort. These businesses will be using the latest technologies and will be extremely efficient (as always happens in a crisis war, when the nation's survival is at stake), and will quickly adapt to become successful producers of commercial products when the war ends. The 2020s will be one of the most affluent, thriving decades in America's history.

Chapter 12 — The Next Century

After reading this book you're probably convinced that we're going to have wars forever, with major new world wars every 80 years or so. By the year 3000, we'll have had about a dozen more world wars. Right?

Well, no, not exactly.

If you didn't read the last chapter carefully, then you might have missed the following sentence:

> One of these technologies, or a combination, will cause an explosion in computer power in the 2010s and 2020s. As computers become increasingly powerful, they'll also become increasingly intelligent, and by 2030 or so, computers will actually become more intelligent than human beings.

This is not science fiction. It's as mathematically certain to happen as anything involving human behavior can be. Today, this technology is under active development at MIT, IBM, Dow Chemical, Dupont, Bayer, and numerous other colleges and corporations, along with startups with names like Chemat and Nanoslayers. And this technology is being funded by the American, European Union, Japanese and other governments. Researchers around the world are competing to be the first to create the technology to make super-intelligent computers a reality.

Is this really credible? I know that it is. As a technologist and software developer, I can tell you what algorithms to implement in computer software so that the result is a computer that is "self-aware," invents things, makes decisions, sets goals, achieves goals, talks and listens to people and understands them, designs marketable products, creates works of art, writes the "great American novel," does windows, and so forth — pretty much anything that a human being can do. In addition, I can tell you how to design the computer so that it can improve itself and make itself more intelligent — something that human beings cannot do. If I know how to do this today, then why don't I do it? I can't, because computers aren't yet powerful enough to implement these brute force algorithms. However, computers *will* be powerful enough by the 2020s.

The Singularity

The point where computers become more intelligent than human beings is being called "the Singularity" by many writers. As we've said, the Singularity is expected to occur in the 2030 time frame.

Once computers are more intelligent than human beings are, then things will change rapidly. For one thing, computers will then rapidly become far more intelligent than human beings, because they'll be able to research and invent better versions of themselves. Within a few decades, computers will be as much more intelligent than human beings as human beings are more intelligent than dogs and cats.

On a personal level, many parents who are considering whether to have children should factor this development into their decision.

On a public policy level, many public policy areas have to be reevaluated. A good example is environmental policy. Intelligent computers can perform environmental cleanups that human beings can't do.

> *Once computers are more intelligent than human beings are, then things will change rapidly*

The need for philosophers and theologians

There are many unanswered questions. Computers will be intelligent, will be able to do research, will be able to fight wars, will be able to kill human beings and each other, and will be able to make more intelligent versions of themselves. But will they have "feelings"? Will they be "alive"? Will they have "a soul"? Can they be found guilty of murder if they kill someone?

There are real questions as to whether the human race can survive the arrival of intelligent computers much past the year 2030 or so. If humans do survive, it will be because intelligent computers have decided to keep us around — as pets or as scientific experiments or whatever. Who knows?

The issues surrounding the Singularity are well known to people in the technical community, and science fiction authors have been writing about it for years.

The Singularity is still "below the radar" for the public. I think this will change within the next few years, when something happens to bring the subject into the news. And since this is a "problem" that will not go away, but is as inevitable as sunrise, there's even a possibility of public panic and riots and demonstrations in some parts of the world, reminiscent of the Luddites in England in the early 1800s, who expressed their anger at the Industrial Revolution by going around destroying "high tech" wool and cotton mills.

Once the Singularity occurs and intelligent computers are able to improve themselves, humans will no longer have any role in their development. All we can do is have a role in the development of the *first* intelligent computers, and hope that our influence will last through future generations. That's why we should be thinking about this now.

Chapter 13 — America's Manifest Destiny and You

War is God's way of teaching Americans geography.
-- Satirist Ambrose Bierce (1842-1913)

How the nation and the world have changed since 2001!

Since World War II, America has acted as "Policeman of the World," defending freedom and democracy wherever it could. However, in the space of a few years, that's changed from a defensive role to a preemptive role. This is how the people of the idealistic Baby Boomer generation think of America, and how they want us, as a country, to act.

As the world's only remaining superpower, America is viewed not only by Americans but also by people around the world as the country that protects freedom and democracy around the world.

> *America is viewed not only by Americans but also by people around the world as the country that protects freedom and democracy around the world*

We use the phrase "manifest destiny" to describe what America's role has become. We chose that phrase to relate America today to Spain during the 1500s.

The 1500s were the Golden Age of Spain. The country was rich and powerful, and had just "discovered America," and had just completed the reconquest of Spain from the Muslims (see page 156). It became, in the minds of the Spanish people, the manifest destiny of Spain to be the power that would spread true Christianity throughout Europe and the New World.

The period since World War II has been the Golden Age of America. Today it's our manifest destiny to defeat terrorism and lead the world to Democracy and Freedom.

This is an awesome responsibility. All Americans will be tested.

What you should do — as an individual

Ever since I discovered, in 2002, that the Generational Dynamics methodology implies that we were already in a 1930s-style depression, I've been telling my friends the following: Even if you don't believe this conclusion, you should still protect yourself and your family by saving money and making only necessary purchases. I've been gratified to see several of my friends save themselves by exercising great care that they might not otherwise have exercised.

Unfortunately, it's human nature that human lives become cheap in times of war and financial crisis. So each person has to fill a dual role: Look for ways to serve your community and your country, but also make sure that you protect yourself and your family.

- **Manage money wisely.** During the 1990s, there were plenty of jobs and plenty of money. As we enter a time of worsening financial crisis, many people will become bankrupt and homeless. Take measures to make sure that this doesn't happen to you.

- **Stay close to your family and community.** When survival (financial or physical) is in question, then people need to gather together to protect each other.

- **Develop 21st job skills.** Computers and the Internet have changed the world and every job drastically in the last 20 years. It's not enough any more just to learn word processing and other basic computer skills. You have to develop new skills in music, writing, trade, management, and everything else. People who try to get along with 20th century skills will find that they no longer have jobs.

- **Be kind and decent to people.** Many people will be in distress, and a little kindness and decency can go a long way.

- **Pay attention to current events, especially international events.** If you've read this book carefully, then you have an idea what direction the world is going in. And remember, Generational Dynamics is a long-range forecasting tool; it tells you where we're going, but not you get there. This is a historic time, and you owe it to yourself to see how the world gets to wherever it's going.

- **Consider joining the armed forces or taking a defense-related job.** Patriotism isn't the only reason. An increasingly large portion of the nation's jobs will be defense-related, and this may be the best way to find a job. Eventually, some people may have no choice: it's hard to see how we'll get through a crisis war without reinstituting the armed forces draft.

What you should do — as a community leader

If you're a political leader of a town, if you're the head of a school, business, labor union, church, youth group, or other organization, then you're in a position to help people, or to help people help each other.

- **Encourage people to start community projects.** With many unemployed people around, there are plenty of opportunities to organize people to do some good. These could be civic projects, such as repairing abandoned homes to give shelter to homeless people.

- **Provide educational opportunities for people to learn new skills.** Similarly, when there are many unemployed people around, there are opportunities for those with special knowledge or skills to give courses to the others. Everything from home repair to computer skills can be taught in this way.

- **Keep businesses afloat by borrowing money.** Interest rates are expected to remain near zero, making it possible for shaky businesses to stay afloat by borrowing money.

- **Make your business a 21st century business.** 20th century businesses will not survive. Transform your business into a 21st century business by taking advantage of high tech and the Internet.

- **Promote community civil defense efforts.** The last major war on American soil was the Civil War. America has been insulated from world wars in the past because the Atlantic and Pacific oceans have provided insulation. However, the spread of terrorism and weapons of mass destruction (including disease and chemical weapons) may bring war to American soil again. Local community preparation can save a lot of lives in such a case.

- **Change your business to support the defense effort.** It's legendary that when World War II began, General Motors changed overnight from a manufacturer of cars to a manufacturer of tanks. Look for ways for your business to do the same.

What you should do — as a national politician

- **Mute political differences.** During a crisis period, when there's so much at stake, the public does not want to hear political bickering.
- **Don't be too America-centric.** It always amazes me how politicians and journalists blame or credit almost everything that happens in the world on America, sometimes even crediting something as trivial as a speech by a politician. This is particularly true of events in the Mideast region, where much that happens is because of the Orthodox Christian / Muslim fault line, or various ethnic fault lines — things that few Americans even know anything about, let alone control. If you've read this book carefully, then you know that actually very little that happens in the world happens because of America.

> *America's greatest danger is the belief that it can do everything*

- **Avoid hubris.** America's greatest danger is the belief that it can do everything. Remember the mythical story of Icarus, who escaped with his father from a prison island by wearing fabricated wings made out of feathers and wax and flying away. His father warned him that if he flew too near the sun, the sun would melt the wax in the wings. However, filled with hubris, Icarus thought he could fly to the heavens and become a god. When he tried, the sun melted his wings and he fell into the ocean and died.
- **Prepare for the worst.** There's a tendency in Washington to "shoot the messenger" who brings bad news about the economy or the world situation. The result is that the nation can't properly prepare for the future.
- **Choose your battles carefully.** Be especially careful to save firepower in the early battles, since things will get much worse before they get better.

History also tells us that we can win over terrorism during this crisis period. By proceeding with caution, America can fulfill its manifest destiny, can defeat terrorism, and can remain the greatest country the world has ever known by bringing freedom and democracy to the rest of the world!

Appendix — List of Crisis Periods

Distinguishing between crisis wars and mid-cycle wars is crucial to the theory underlying Generational Dynamics. This list of criteria is given in chapter 4 (page 80) and illustrated by detailed examples in chapters 4 and 5.

The following list summarizes all the generational timelines described in this book, focusing on the crisis periods. In some cases, dates can't be identified with absolute precision, but this is not important to Generational Dynamics, as long as the crisis period is identified to within a few years. In some cases, the dates given below identify only the crisis war; in other cases, the dates include the preceding financial crisis period. This represents an annoying lack of precision that can be corrected with more detailed study of the historical period in question, but is not crucial to the success of Generational Dynamics.

> Chapter 2 - American History
>   America from Plymouth Rock, 1620
>   King Philip's War, 1675-1678
>   Revolutionary War, 1772-1790
>   Civil War, 1857-1870
>   Great Depression + World War II, 1929-1945

> Chapter 7 - Great Awakenings in History
>   Golden Age of Greece, 5th century BC
>   Persian Wars, 510-478 BC
>   Peloponnesian War, 431-404 BC
>   Macedonian conquest, 359-338 BC
>   Life of Jesus, 1st century AD
>   King Herod's Reign of Terror, 40-4 BC
>   Roman massacre of Jerusalem, 66-71
>   Life of Mohammed, 7th century AD
>   War involving Jews, Christians, pagans, 580s
>   Muslim civil war, 656-660s

APPENDIX — LIST OF CRISIS PERIODS

- > Chapter 8 - History of Western Europe
- > Medieval Spain from 1300s
- > Spain's Anti-Jewish Pogroms of the 1390s
- > The Spanish Inquisition and the Reconquest — 1480s-1490s
- > Destruction of Spanish Armada, 1588
- > Medieval England from Norman Conquest, 1066
- > The Norman Conquest, 1066
- > Civil War, 1135-54
- > War with Normandy and Magna Carta, 1204-15
- > Civil war and war with Wales, 1264-1282
- > Hundred Years' War begins, 1337-47
- > Civil war and Welsh Revolt, 1386-1409
- > Wars of the Roses, 1455-85
- > War with Spain, 1559-88
- > Britain's Great Civil War, 1638-60
- > Western Europe from 1500s
- > Regional religious wars, 1500s
- > Thirty Years' War, 1618-48
- > War of Spanish Succession, 1701-14
- > French Revolution and Napoleonic Wars, 1789-1815
- > Wars of German Reunification, 1860-1871
- > World War II, 1937-1945

- > Chapter 9 - Islam versus Orthodox Christianity
- > Russia, from fall of Constantinople, 1453
- > Livonian War, 1557-82
- > Peasant Rebellions and Church Schism, 1649-70
- > War with Ottomans and Pugachev's Rebellion, 1762-83
- > Crimean War and Emancipation Edict, 1853-61
- > Bolshevik Revolution, 1905-1927
- > Ottoman Empire, from conquest of Istanbul, 1453
- > War with the Holy League, 1683-99
- > War with Russia, 1768-74
- > Crimean War, 1853-56
- > Young Turk Revolution to Destruction of Empire, 1908-22

> Chapter 10 - History of Asia
>   China, from White Lotus Rebellion, 1796
>   The White Lotus Rebellion - 1796-1805
>   The Taiping Rebellion, 1851-64
>   Mao's Long March to Great Leap Forward, 1932-1960
>   Japan from Commodore Perry and the Meiji Restoration, 1853-68
>   Commodore Perry and the Meiji Restoration, 1853-68
>   World War II, 1931-1945
>   Southeast Asia, from French Indochina, 1880s-90s
>   French Indochina - France versus China, 1880s-90s
>   War with America, Cambodian genocide, 1960-1976

Bibliography

The following is a list of the books used in the preparation of this book.

[Braudel] Fernand Braudel, *A History of Civilizations*, 1963, translated by Richard Mayne, Penguin Books, 1993.

[Chancellor] Edward Chancellor, *Devil Take the Hindmost, a History of Financial Speculation*, Plume (Penguin Group), 1999

[Cherlin] Andrew J. Cherlin, *Marriage, Divorce, Remarriage*, Harvard University Press, 1992

[Cook] Jean Cook, Anne Kramer and Theodore Rowland-Entwistle, *History's Timeline*, Kingfisher Publications Plc, 2002

[Daniel-Rops] Henri Daniel-Rops, *Daily Life in Palestine at the Time of Christ*, Phoenix Press, 2002, originally published as *La Vie quotidienne en Palestine au temps de Jésus*, 1962.

[DK] Jeremy Black, general editor, *DK Atlas of World History*, Dorling Kindersley Publishing Inc., 2001

[Fairbank] John King Fairbank, *The Great Chinese Revolution 1800-1985*, Harper & Row, 1986

[Fukuyama] Francis Fukuyama, *The End of History and the Last Man*, The Free Press (Simon & Schuster Inc.), 1992

[Glubb] Sir John Bagot Glubb (Glubb Pasha), *The Life and Times of Muhammad*, Cooper Square Press, 1998. Originally published: Stein & Day, 1970.

[Gould] Stephen Jay Gould, *The Structure of Evolutionary Theory*, Harvard University Press, 2002

[Hourani] Albert Hourani, *A History of the Arab Peoples*, MJF Books, 1991

[Huntington] Samuel P. Huntington, *The Clash of Civilizations and the Remaking of World Order*, Touchstone, 1996

[Kindleberger] Charles P. Kindleberger, *Manias, Panics, and Crashes, a History of Financial Crises*, Fourth Edition, John Wiley & Sons Inc., 2000

[Lewis] Bernard Lewis, *The Middle East, a Brief History of the Last 2,000 Years*, Touchstone, 1995

[Martino] Joseph Paul Martino, *Technological Forecasting for Decision Making*, American Elsevier Pub. Co., 1975

[Parker] Geoffrey Parker, editor, *Compact History of the World: A history of the world from the Stone Age to the Space Age*, Barnes & Noble Books, Times Books, London, 2002.

[Payne] Stanley G. Payne, *A History of Spain and Portugal, Volume One*, University of Wisconsin Press, 1973, online at http://libro.uca.edu/payne1/spainport1.htm.

[Phillips] Kevin Phillips, *The Cousins' War: Religion, Politics, & the Triumph of Anglo-America*, 1999

[Power] Samantha Power, *"A Problem from Hell" - America and the Age of Genocide*, New Republic, 2002

[Roberts] J. M. Roberts, *The Penguin History of the World*, Penguin Books, 1995

[Schivelbusch] Wolfgang Schivelbusch, *The Culture of Defeat: On National Trauma, Mourning, and Recovery*, 2000, translated by Jefferson Chase, Metropolitan Books, Henry Holt and Company LLC, 2001

[Schlesinger] Arthur M. Schlesinger Jr., general editor, *The Almanac of American History, Revised and Updated Edition*, Barnes & Noble Books, 1993

[Schultz] Eric B. Schultz, Michael J. Tougias, *King Philip's War: The History and Legacy of America's Forgotten Conflict*, Countryman Press, 1999

[Smith & Smith] Jean Reeder Smith and Lacey Baldwin Smith, *Essentials of World History*, Barron's Education Series Inc., 1980

[Stearns] Peter N. Stearns (Editor), *The Encyclopedia of World History, 6th edition*, Houghton Mifflin Co., 2001

[Stewart] Robert Stewart, *The Illustrated Encyclopedia of Historical Facts, from the Dawn of the Christian Era to the Present Day*, Marshall Editions, 2002

[Strauss & Howe] William Strauss and Neil Howe, *The Fourth Turning, an American Prophecy*, Broadway Books, 1997

[Toynbee-1] Arnold J. Toynbee, *A Study of History, Abridgement of Volumes I-VI by D. C. Somervell*, Oxford University Press, 1946

[Toynbee-2] Arnold J. Toynbee, *A Study of History, Abridgement of Volumes VII-X by D. C. Somervell*, Oxford University Press, 1957

[Trevelyan] George Macaulay Trevelyan, *A Shortened History of England*, Penguin Books, 1942

[Turchin 1] Peter Turchin, *Complex Population Dynamics: A Theoretical/Empirical Synthesis (Monographs in Population Biology)*, Princeton University Press, 2003

[Turchin 2] Peter Turchin, *Historical Dynamics*, Princeton University Press, 2003

End Notes

Note: In some cases, a page reference actually refers to the bottom of the preceding page or the top of the next page.

Pg	Reference
10	"Strauss and Howe call this a "high" period": William Strauss and Neil Howe, *The Fourth Turning, an American Prophecy*, Broadway Books, 1997, p. 145
24	"Today, there are about 250 nations, comprising about 9 major civilizations": Samuel P. Huntington, *The Clash of Civilizations and the Remaking of World Order*, Touchstone, 1996, p.26-27
26	"In the year 1600, throughout what is now the United States, there were some 2 million Indians within 600 tribes speaking 500 languages.": Arthur M. Schlesinger Jr., general editor, *The Almanac of American History*, Revised and Updated Edition, Barnes & Noble Books, 1993, p.23
26	"There is some historical evidence that a major war among these tribes had occurred in the years preceding the colonists' arrival": Eric B. Schultz, Michael J. Tougias, *King Philip's War: The History and Legacy of America's Forgotten Conflict*, Countryman Press, 1999, pp. 12ff
26	"The Wampanoag Indians taught the colonists how to hunt and fish": Robert Stewart, *The Illustrated Encyclopedia of Historical Facts, from the Dawn of the Christian Era to the Present Day*, Marshall Editions, 2002, p. 137
27	"The relationship between English and Native American had grown inordinately more complex over forty years": Eric B. Schultz, Michael J. Tougias, *King Philip's War: The History and Legacy of America's Forgotten Conflict*, Countryman Press, 1999, p. 22
34	"The financial crisis occurred in July, 1772, when the English banking system suffered a major crash.": Schlesinger, *op. cit.*, p. 111
36	"In fact, England did nothing to strengthen its forces in America that year, and even actually reduced the size of its Navy.": George Macaulay Trevelyan, A Shortened History of England, Penguin Books, 1942, pp. 404ff
36	"Once the war began, there was a strong anti-war movement of sorts in England.": Trevelyan, *op. cit.*, p. 406
39	"His intention was to spur a massive slave insurrection or even a civil war which would end slavery.": Schlesinger, *op. cit.*, p. 275
49	"Japan's exports of its biggest cash crop, silk, to America were almost completely cut off by the Smoot-Hawley Act.": Jude Wanniski, referencing his 1977 book, *The Way the World Works*, in "Remember Pearl Harbor?" appearing in *WorldNetDaily*, May 16, 2001, http://www.worldnetdaily.com/news/article.asp?ARTICLE%5fID=22850
57	"Some 10 million of California's 35 million people — almost 1/3 — are Mexican immigrants, 70% of them illegal": Steve Brown, "Illegal Immigration Turning Calif. Into 'Apartheid State,' Expert Warns," Cybercase News Service, August 20, 2003, http://www.cnsnews.com/ViewNation.asp?Page=%5CNation%5Carchive%5C200308%5CNAT20030820a.html
60	"he found it necessary to divide Europe into 50 separate geographical units, taking into account both terrain features (mountains, coastlines) and ethnic divisions (language, religion)": Peter Turchin, *Historical Dynamics*, Princeton University Press, 2003, pp. 82-83
61	"Consider a member of the Ibo ethnic group": Donald L. Horowitz, "Ethnic Conflict Man-

Pg	Reference
	agement for Policy-Makers," in Joseph V. Montville and Hans Binnendijk, eds., *Conflict and Peacemaking in Multiethnic Societies*, Lexington Books, 1990, p. 121, quoted by Samuel P. Huntington, *The Clash of Civilizations and the Remaking of World Order*, Touchstone, 1996, p. 68
62	"Khaldun's concept, *asabiya*, measures the cohesiveness or solidarity of a group": Peter Turchin, *Historical Dynamics*, Princeton University Press, 2003, pp. 40-41, referring to Ibn Khaldun, *The Muqaddimah: An Introduction to History* (written in 14th century), translated and edited by Franz Rosenthal Khaldun and N. J. Dowood, Princeton University Press, 1969
62	"The nine major civilizations today": Samuel P. Huntington, *The Clash of Civilizations and the Remaking of World Order*, Touchstone, 1996, p.26-27
62	"Samuel P. Huntington in his book, *The Clash of Civilizations*": Samuel P. Huntington, *The Clash of Civilizations and the Remaking of World Order*, Touchstone, 1996, p.26-27
63	"Fault line wars go through processes of intensification, expansion, containment, interruption, and, rarely, resolution.": Samuel P. Huntington, *The Clash of Civilizations and the Remaking of World Order*, Touchstone, 1996, p.267
65	"Slobodan Milosevic was appealing to Serbian nationalism.": Huntington, *op cit.*, p. 261
65	"Huntington shows how identity groups rallied in the most predictable ways in the Bosnian wars:": Huntington, *op cit.*, p. 281
67	"Huntington analyzes the cause of the Bosnian war in the context of wars worldwide between Muslims and non-Muslims,": Huntington, *op cit.*, p. 262-65
82	"Wolfgang Schivelbusch who studied the results of defeat in war": Wolfgang Schivelbusch, *The Culture of Defeat: On National Trauma, Mourning, and Recovery*, 2000, translated by Jefferson Chase, Metropolitan Books, Henry Holt and Company LLC, 2001, pp. 3-35
83	"The effect of [defeat] outside the army — on the people and on the government — is a sudden collapse of the most anxious expectations": Carl von Clausewitz, *On War*, 1832 edition, translated and edited by Michael Howard and Peter Paret (Princeton, 1976), p. 231, quoted by Schivelbusch, *op. cit.*, pp. 6-7
83	"the overthrow of the old regime and its subsequent scapegoating for the nation's defeat": Schivelbusch, *op. cit.*, pp. 10-11
83	"For a moment, the external enemy is no longer an adversary but something of an ally": Schivelbusch, *op. cit.*, p 11
83	"nothing stands in the way of a return to the prewar status quo": Schivelbusch, *op. cit.*, p 14
86	"the German high command shipped thousands of Christmas trees to the front lines, cutting into its ammunition shipments": H.D.S. Greenway, "The forbidden friendship," *Boston Globe*, December 20, 2002, p. A31
86	"soldiers and officers on both sides all got together and sang Christmas carols": Malcolm Brown and Shirley Seaton, *Christmas Truce: The Western Front December 1914 (Pan Grand Strategy Series)*, Trans-Atlantic Publications, Inc., 1999, adapted by "The Christmas truce," BBC News online, November 3, 1998, http://news.bbc.co.uk/hi/english/special%5freport/1998/10/98/world%5fwar%5fi/newsid%5f197000/197627.stm
86	"Germany planned a quick, total victory over France, requiring only six weeks — too quick for the British troops to be deployed to stop the advance.": Robert Stewart, *The Illustrated Encyclopedia of Historical Facts, from the Dawn of the Christian Era to the Present Day*, Marshall Editions, 2002, p. 214

END NOTES

Pg	Reference
87	"Writing in 1931, Winston Churchill wrote that if Germany had continued to fight, they would have been capable of inflicting two million more casualties upon the enemy": Winston S. Churchill, *The World in Crisis*, London, 1931, p. 800, quoted by Schivelbusch, *op. cit.*, pp. 189-90
87	"the German high command realized that too much time had passed and the absolute military triumph over France could no longer be achieved": Schivelbusch, *op. cit.*, pp. 190-200
87	"Prince Max von Baden of the high command concluded": Prince Max von Baden, *Erinnerungen und Dokumente*, Berlin, 1927, p. 344, quoted by Schivelbusch, *op. cit.*, pp. 189-90
96	"Stages in Napoleon's invasion of Russia in 1812 (graphic)": Jeremy Black, general editor, *DK Atlas of World History*, Dorling Kindersley Publishing Inc., 2001, p. 201
121	"one particularly spectacular bulb sold for the cost of a small house.": Edward Chancellor, *Devil Take the Hindmost, a History of Financial Speculation*, Plume (Penguin Group), 1999, p. 16
121	"Evrard Forstius, a professor of botany, became so reviled by the mere sight of tulips that he attacked them with sticks whenever he saw them!": Chancellor, *op. cit.*, p. 20
122	"In the 1850s, prior to the Civil War crisis, the bubble was caused by something called 'call loans.'": Chancellor, *op. cit.*, p. 157
123	"triggering a series of failures reverberating to Liverpool, London, Paris, Hamburg, and Stockholm, leading to the Panic of 1857.": Charles P. Kindleberger, *Manias, Panics, and Crashes, a History of Financial Crises*, Fourth Edition, John Wiley & Sons Inc., 2000, p. 78
130	"In the final major battle, in 480 BC, Persia had 5 million men, according to the historian Herodotus, considered the first true historian of the western world. However, modern estimates range up to 500,000 men": Peter N. Stearns (Editor), *The Encyclopedia of World History, 6th edition*, Houghton Mifflin Co., 2001, p. 64
131	"In this case, the great compromise occurred in 478 BC, when Sparta proposed to Athens that they form a Delian League (named after the island Delos) of all the city-states: Each ally would contribute to the league, which would use the money to drive away all Persians": Stearns, *op. cit.*, p. 65
136	"He imposed the Ten Commandments on the people, and then developed an entire moral and religious code, a code of political and social organization.": Henri Daniel-Rops, *Daily Life in Palestine at the Time of Christ*, Phoenix Press, 2002, originally published as *La Vie quotidienne en Palestine au temps de Jésus*, 1962, pp. 31-32
136	"God had punished the chosen people for their heathen practices, but then had shown mercy by ending their exile.": Daniel-Rops, *op. cit.*, p. 32
137	"Everything, then was related to the Chosen People's certainty that they were unique, different from all others and superior to them": Henri Daniel-Rops, *op. cit.*, pp. 32-33
143	"In fact, there are three sources of information about Mohammed's life": Sir John Bagot Glubb (Glubb Pasha), *The Life and Times of Muhammad*, Cooper Square Press, 1998. Originally published: Stein & Day, 1970, pp. 17, 312
143	"Sir John Glubb's book": Glubb, *op. cit.*
144	"Mohammed helped out with some of the battles": Glubb, *op. cit.*, pp. 69-72
144	"telling him to become the messenger of God.": Albert Hourani, *A History of the Arab Peoples*, MJF Books, 1991, p. 16
144	"Mohammed's life took a dramatic turn in 622, at age 52, when he became so popular that

Pg	Reference
	Mecca's ruling Quraish tribe was threatening his life.": Glubb, *op. cit.*, p. 118
146	"the purpose of the fight was to gain resources, such as food, water, gold, silver and weapons.": Glubb, *op. cit.*, pp. 173, 200, 243, 247, 266
146	"Many people, especially those who had followed him from Mecca and had no homes in Medina, were facing starvation. Mohammed was soon leading raids by Muslims against Quraish caravans": Glubb, *op. cit.*, pp. 163, 184
146	"He would equivocate, vacillate, sometimes changing his mind or giving in to pure emotion": Glubb, *op. cit.*, p. 204-5
146	"Many of his young followers were sons of the Quraish elders": Glubb, *op. cit.*, pp. 194, 270
147	"Mohammed was most violent with people who attempted to prevent him from establishing his new religion.": Glubb, *op. cit.*, pp. 308-9
148	"But I disagree with anyone who says that he killed people because they criticized him or his faith": Dr. Yuksel provides the following Quranic references for his statements: "The Quran states frequently that there is no compulsion in religion (2:256; 10:99; 88:21,22). The Quran advocates perfect freedom of belief and expression (18:29). The basic law regulating relations with unbelievers is stated in 60:8,9. Apostates can not be killed unless they fight against the believers (4:90). However, according to *hadith* and *sunnah*, teachings fabricated and attributed to Muhammad centuries after his death, a person who leaves Islam should be killed. ... The vicious laws that exist in hadith books altered Islam into a tyrannical religion. According to *hadith* and *sunnah* if a Muslim does not practice daily contact prayers (*salat*), he or she should be warned and if they still do not pray, they should be put in prison or killed. The perfect, complete, clear and fully detailed Quran (6:19,38,114,115,116; 11:1; 12:111; 54:17), nowhere tells us to punish those who do not obey this commandment. A careful study will show that all punishments decreed by God involve social and individual relations, not religious belief and practices. However, scholars who were puppets of corrupt theocratic kingdoms produced a myriad of vicious laws and attributed them to God (6:21; 42:21). According to the Quran, violence and belligerence are signs of disbelief (22:72)."
148	"At first, Mohammed had hoped to be accepted by the Jews, and even to be recognized as the Savior.": Glubb, *op. cit.*, pp. 221, 295
148	"Jews and Christians were not required to convert to Islam": Glubb, *op. cit.*, p. 388
149	"Many of Mohammed's wives were widows": Glubb, *op. cit.*, pp. 237-38
150	"among three community groups who were competing to inherit the mantle of Mohammed's leadership": Albert Hourani, *A History of the Arab Peoples*, MJF Books, 1991, p. 22
150	"The invaders created the caste system as a means of enforcing racial purity, separating the conquerors from the conquered.": J. M. Roberts, *The Penguin History of the World*, Penguin Books, 1995, pp. 119ff
154	"During the next few decades, over half of the 200,000 Jews on the peninsula formally converted to Catholicism.": Stanley G. Payne, *A History of Spain and Portugal, Volume One*, University of Wisconsin Press, 1973, chapter 11, online at http://libro.uca.edu/payne1/payne11.htm, pp. 208-9
155	"Their secret desire was to degrade, even poison, Christian men and to have sex with Christian women: daughters, wives, even nuns": David Nirenberg, "Conversion, Sex and Segregation: Iberian Jews and Christians after 1391," http://www.history.umd.edu/Faculty/BCooperman/Medieval/DNirenbergConvsexsegr.html

END NOTES

Pg	Reference
155	"a common charge against them was that they were 'false Christians.'": Payne, *op. cit.*, p. 208
156	"Hundreds of thousands of Jews were forced to leave the country.": Payne, *op. cit.*, p. 211
157	"It was at this moment that the concept of manifest destiny ... sank deep into the Spanish conscience": Manuel Fernandez Alvarez, University of Salamanca, *A Short History of Spain*, http://www.conquistador.com/spanhistory.html
158	"New discoveries and conquests came in quick succession": Library of Congress Studies, *History of Spain*, http://lcweb2.loc.gov/frd/cs/estoc.html
160	"the Normans of northern France (Normandy), led by William the Conqueror, completed their conquest of England from the Saxons": Robert Stewart, *The Illustrated Encyclopedia of Historical Facts, from the Dawn of the Christian Era to the Present Day*, Marshall Editions, 2002, p. 67
160	"a succession dispute arose because Henry left no male heir.": Stewart, *op. cit.*, p. 75
161	"During the awakening period of Henry II's reign, there were dramatic changes to make the law fairer": George Macaulay Trevelyan, *A Shortened History of England*, Penguin Books, 1942, pp. 135, 138
161	"King John suffered a crisis of confidence when he lost battles in Normandy, forcing him to cede control of most regions of Normandy": Stewart, *op. cit.*, p. 81
162	"In 1264, a new civil war broke out between the Barons and partisans of the king": Stewart, *op. cit.*, p. 87, 88
162	"A 14,000 man English army wiped out a 50,000 man French army in 1347, thanks to advanced weaponry": Stewart, *op. cit.*, p. 94
162	"The Black Death reached the continent in 1348": Stewart, *op. cit.*, p. 93
162	"Population of England and Wales (graphic)": Peter Turchin, *Historical Dynamics*, Princeton University Press, 2003, p. 163
163	"Tensions between king and parliament led to a new civil war in 1386": Stewart, *op. cit.*, p. 98-99
164	"The name Wars of the Roses is based on the badges used by the two sides, the red rose for the Lancastrians and the white rose for the Yorkists": http://www.warsoftheroses.com/
165	"Spain had a plan: They'd get rid of Queen Elizabeth": Trevelyan, *op. cit.*, pp. 242-257
165	"Britain's great civil war began with the Scottish rebellion in 1638": Trevelyan, *op. cit.*, p. 295
167	"the Peace at Augsburg recognized religious pluralism for the first time in Europe": J. M. Roberts, *The Penguin History of the World*, Penguin Books, 1995, p. 556
169	"The habit of debasing coins had begun around 1600": Charles P. Kindleberger, *Manias, Panics, and Crashes, a History of Financial Crises*, Fourth Edition, John Wiley & Sons Inc., 2000, p. 121
170	"Population declined from 21 million in 1618 to 18 million in 1648": Jeremy Black, general editor, *DK Atlas of World History*, Dorling Kindersley Publishing Inc., 2001, p. 196
171	"About 250 separate German states were recognized as sovereign": Peter N. Stearns (Editor), *The Encyclopedia of World History*, 6th edition, Houghton Mifflin Co., 2001, p. 304
173	"the statesmen of the time signed because they wanted to avoid for as long as possible another violent conflict such as the one that had just ended.": Roberts, *op. cit.*, p. 586
176	"Prior to 1789, Western Europe consisted of a chain of over 300 political units with different principles of organization": Roberts, *op. cit.*, p. 714
182	"However, the people of the British public were incredulous when Napoleon III sought

Pg	Reference
	friendship with England.": George Macaulay Trevelyan, *A Shortened History of England*, Penguin Books, 1942, p.486
187	"The spread of humans from north Africa around the world (graphic)": Geoffrey Parker, editor, *Compact History of the World: A history of the world from the Stone Age to the Space Age*, Barnes & Noble Books, Times Books, London, 2002, p. 14
187	"The nine major civilizations today": Samuel P. Huntington, *The Clash of Civilizations and the Remaking of World Order*, Touchstone, 1996, p.26-27
191	"The main problems faced by the early Muslims were determining who would be 'caliph'": Albert Hourani, *A History of the Arab Peoples*, MJF Books, 1991, p. 22
193	"This created a mode of thought that came to be known as Sunnism, as distinct from Shi'ism": Hourani, *op. cit.*, p. 37
193	"Since Arab rulers spoke Arabic, the easiest way to deal with the government was to do so in Arabic": Hourani, *op. cit.*, p. 29
195	"Starting from around the year 1000, the Islamic Empire was under attack from all sides": Bernard Lewis, *The Middle East, a Brief History of the Last 2,000 Years*, Touchstone, 1995, pp. 86-87
195	"The Turks wholeheartedly adopted the religion of Islam, becoming Sunni Muslims, and in some ways were more Muslim than the Arabs.": Lewis, *op. cit.*, p. 88
199	"Around 986-8, Vladimir accepted Orthodox Christianity for himself and his people.": J. M. Roberts, *The Penguin History of the World*, Penguin Books, 1995, p. 355
199	"Around 1300, a Muslim Turkish tribe led by its chieftain, Osman, started to expand beyond its original border": Peter N. Stearns (Editor), *The Encyclopedia of World History*, 6th edition, Houghton Mifflin Co., 2001, p. 123
199	"In 1402, the central Asian conqueror Timur defeated the Ottomans, and almost destroyed them completely": Stearns, *op. cit.*, p. 125
199	"However, Timur's victory over the Ottomans had one major unintentional effect: It delayed for several decades the final destruction of the Byzantine Empire": J. M. Roberts, *The Penguin History of the World*, Penguin Books, 1995, p. 370
201	"He arranged for [Ivan] to marry Sophia, the orphan niece of the last Greek Emperor of Constantinople, in the hope of bringing the Russians back into the Roman Church": Stearns, *op. cit.*, p. 271
201	"In fact, submission to the pope was for most Greeks a renegade act, denying the true Church, whose tradition Orthodoxy had conserved": Roberts, *op. cit.*, p. 372
201	"The problem was the power struggle between the tsar and boyars, the wealthy landowners who owned most of the land (as well as the peasants living on the land)": Stearns, *op. cit.*, p. 306
202	"In 1570, he ravaged Novgorod, and massacred many of the inhabitants, whom he suspected of sympathy for the Poles": Stearns, *op. cit.*, p. 306
202	"Under the leadership of Genghis Kahn, probably the greatest conqueror in the history of the world, they had defeated China in 1215, and then turned westward and conquered much of southern Russia by 1227": Stearns, *op. cit.*, p. 81
202	"In 1582, Ivan was forced to sign a peace treaty with Sweden and Poland, giving up all the territory he had gained": Stearns, *op. cit.*, p. 308
203	"In 1642, an enemy (the Cossacks) of the Crimean Tatars offered to Moscow a fortress that they had captured from the Tatars — and Moscow refused it, to avoid conflict with the

END NOTES

Pg	Reference
	Ottoman Turks": Stearns, *op. cit.*, p. 308
204	"The Moscow region lost half its peasants": Fernand Braudel, *A History of Civilizations*, 1963, translated by Richard Mayne, Penguin Books, 1993, p. 544
204	"This triggered a series of peasant rebellions, starting in the central regions in 1655, and reaching Moscow by 1662, where 7,000 peasants were executed": Jean Reeder Smith and Lacey Baldwin Smith, *Essentials of World History*, Barron's Education Series Inc., 1980, p. 160
204	"By 1691, some 20,000 of the faithful had burned themselves in huge fires": Stearns, *op. cit.*, p. 346
205	"He had been educated by foreigners in a German suburb of Moscow, and became acquainted with western techniques": Smith & Smith, *op. cit.*, p. 162
205	"he launched an attack against the Ottomans, hoping to get a trading route through the Black Sea to the Mediterranean, but failed after an initial success": Stearns, *op. cit.*, pp. 346, 357
205	"He was initially defeated by Sweden, and might have lost the war completely, but Sweden became preoccupied fighting with Poland in the War of Spanish Succession": Smith & Smith, *op. cit.*, p. 172
205	"He consolidated the changes made in the last crisis, strengthening the power of the Tsar, by demanding service to the government for life": Smith & Smith, *op. cit.*, pp. 164-65
206	"The peace treaty (at Kuchuk Kaynarja) that Catherine signed with the Ottomans was one of the most important of the whole century": Roberts, *op. cit.*, p. 604
206	"However, the most notorious episodes of Catherine's reign were the dozens of bloody rebellions of the 1760s, culminating in the savage Pugachev's Rebellion of 1773-75": Robert Stewart, *The Illustrated Encyclopedia of Historical Facts, from the Dawn of the Christian Era to the Present Day*, Marshall Editions, 2002, p. 159
206	"by granting amnesty to political prisoners and exiles, abolishing torture, and passing the first laws leading (during the next crisis period) to the abolition of serfdom": Stearns, *op. cit.*, p. 509
207	"In response, the Ottomans declared war on Russia, and England and France joined on the Ottomans' side": Stewart, *op. cit.*, p. 188
207	"and was exposed for all to see as an increasingly weak power, having been a military powerhouse at the beginning of the century": Roberts, *op. cit.*, p. 737
207	"The loss of the Crimean War ended up being blamed on Nicholas' support of serfdom, or at least his reluctance to end it": Roberts, *op. cit.*, pp. 737-38
208	"The weaknesses exposed by the Crimean War caused the country to industrialize, and the rebellions extended to an industrial proletariat working for the railroads, the coal mines, and the iron fields": Stearns, *op. cit.*, p. 511
208	"The indecisive results of the war led to an antiwar movement that caused increasing opposition to the tsarist regime": Stearns, *op. cit.*, p. 510
208	"Russia's next crisis period began for real on Bloody Sunday, January 22, 1905, when troops fired on workers demonstrating workers making demands in St. Petersburg, resulting in hundreds of casualties": Stearns, *op. cit.*, pp. 511-12
208	"To all this was added a grave economic problem: shortage of labor, due to repeated mobilizations; disorganization of railroad transport; and failure of food and fuel supplies in the cities": Stearns, *op. cit.*, p. 711
210	"To resist collectivization, crops were burned and livestock were slaughtered, resulting in

Pg	Reference
	10-15 million peasants dying of starvation": Stewart, *op. cit.*, p. 229
210	"Special mention should be made of Ukraine": BBC Online, *Timeline: Ukraine*, http://news.bbc.co.uk/hi/english/world/europe/newsid%4f1107000/1107869.stm
211	"Furthermore, Christianity was unique in this regard, since the civilizations of India and China had never seriously threatened Islam to anything like the extent Christianity did, for Christianity was a world faith, with a sense of mission much like their own, and a duty to proselytize": Bernard Lewis, *The Middle East, a Brief History of the Last 2,000 Years*, Touchstone, 1995, pp. 273-74
211	"There are several candidates for the crucial moment, but the best choice is the defeat of the Muslims by the Habsburgs (Germans) in 1683": Lewis, *op. cit.*, p. 276
212	"Their army was almost destroyed when Polish reinforcements arrived to help the Habsburgs, forcing the Ottoman army to retreat in disarray": Stearns, *op. cit.*, p. 356
212	"In 1699, the Ottomans and the Habsburgs signed the Treaty at Karlowitz that clearly signaled a change between Europe and the Ottomans, and also a change between Islam and Christendom": Lewis, *op. cit.*, p. 276-77
212	"This was a calamitous defeat of such magnitude that there has never been its like since the first appearance of the Ottoman state": *Silihdar Tarihi* (Istanbul, 1928), vol II, p. 87, quoted by Lewis, *op. cit.*, p. 277
212	"After having sustained victory after victory for centuries, Muslim writers were now asking why the miserable infidels were suddenly winning over the formerly victorious armies of Islam": Lewis, *op. cit.*, p. 277
212	"The resulting treaty at Kuchuk Kaynarja was a huge humiliation for the Ottomans, and not just because of the additional territory ceded to the Russians": Lewis, *op. cit.*, p. 279
213	"The Ottomans had been forced to withdraw before, but only from recently captured Christian lands; but this was the first time that they had to withdraw from a Muslim land": Lewis, *op. cit.*, p. 280
213	"This was very significant because it was the first time that a significant number of European forces were present on Ottoman soil": Lewis, *op. cit.*, p. 284
213	"Following their stunning defeat with the Treaty at Karlowitz in 1699, the Ottomans began more and more to imitate the victors": Lewis, *op. cit.*, pp. 306-07
213	"A "pan-Islamic" movement began among the Muslims to unify all Muslims along a common front": Lewis, *op. cit.*, pp. 313-14
213	"These losses caused increasing discontent among the Ottoman people. The most significant development occurred in 1889, when students of the military medical school in Istanbul formed a secret society to fight the government": Stearns, *op. cit.*, p. 532
214	"In 1914, the Ottomans entered World War I on the side of Germany, resulting in enormous dislocations. Of the three million men drafted for the army, half of them deserted": Stearns, *op. cit.*, p. 752
214	"In the late 1800s, a Turkish identity movement had begun to form, promoting Turkish (as opposed to Ottoman) literature and culture": Stearns, *op. cit.*, p. 533
214	"By 1919, there were so many Allied forces in Istanbul, that the Ottomans feared that the Allies intended to keep Istanbul for themselves": Stearns, *op. cit.*, p. 752
214	"An Armenian uprising that occurred in Istanbul in 1894-96 was brutally put down, with a large-scale massacre of Armenians in Istanbul": Stearns, *op. cit.*, p. 532
215	"In 1914, Russia organized four large Armenian volunteer guerrilla units to support the

END NOTES

Pg	Reference
	war effort against the Ottomans": Lewis, *op. cit.*, p. 339
215	"In reaction, the Ottomans began deporting the entire Armenian population — millions of people — resulting in deaths of over a million Armenians in what amounted to a death march": Stearns, *op. cit.*, p. 752
215	"Mustafa Kemal, who later took the name Attaturk (father of the Turks), led the new country in a distinctly Turkish direction": Stearns, *op. cit.*, p. 753
215	"He even sought to purge Arabic and Persian words from the Turkish language": Stearns, *op. cit.*, p. 754
215	"Perhaps most important is that he sought to secularize Turkish society. The caliphate, the office of the supreme spiritual leader for Sunni Muslims worldwide, was abolished": Stearns, *op. cit.*, p. 753
215	"Perhaps also inspired by the Wars of Unification in Germany and Italy, the first Zionist Congress met in 1897 to advocate a Jewish homeland in Palestine": Roberts, *op. cit.*, p. 903
215	"In 1917, there were ten times as many Arabs as Jews in Palestine: 700,000 Arabs, and 70,000 Jews": Smith & Smith, *op. cit.*, p. 34
216	"By 1939, Arabs outnumbered Jews by only two to one": Smith & Smith, *op. cit.*, p. 34
219	"Population of China in millions of people (graphic)": Peter Turchin, *op. cit.*, p. 169
220	"Even in 1800, China had about 400 million people — 300 million farmers, plus 80-100 million city folk: artisans, merchants, landlords, scholars and government officials": John King Fairbank, *The Great Chinese Revolution 1800-1985*, Harper & Row, 1986, p. 23
220	"That's why, even as late as the year 1800, a typical Chinese village pretty much took care of itself": Fairbank, *op. cit.*, p. 51
221	"Even worse, centuries of bureaucratic buildup had taken its toll. An example is the Grand Canal, the canal system that was used to deliver rice from the south to feed Beijing": Fairbank, *op. cit.*, p. 65
221	"In fact, the legacy of Emperor Ch'ien-lung, who ruled for sixty years until 1799, describes 'Ten Great Campaigns' to suppress rebels on the frontiers": Fairbank, *op. cit.*, p. 38
221	"One rebellion, for example, occurred in Taiwan in 1786-87": Peter N. Stearns (Editor), *The Encyclopedia of World History, 6th edition*, Houghton Mifflin Co., 2001, p. 379
222	"China and adjoining countries (graphic)": Fairbank, *op. cit.*, pp. 64, 73
221	"It broke out in 1796, over the issues of poor public service in return for high taxes": Fairbank, *op. cit.*, pp. 64-65
223	"It's just that all commerce was controlled as tightly as possible by the national and regional governing entities": Fairbank, *op. cit.*, pp. 97-99
225	"coming up with the God-Worshipper's Society, which appealed to large numbers of disaffected citizens": Fairbank, *op. cit.*, pp. 73-79
225	"Modern estimates are that China's population had been about 410 million in 1850 and 350 million in 1873 — after the end of the Taiping rebellion and several other rebellions that occurred in the west": Fairbank, *op. cit.*, p. 77
228	"This dual strategy permitted modernization of government at the highest regional levels, but it allowed for a great deal of corruption in the countryside, where the army officers became wealthy landowners": Fairbank, *op. cit.*, p. 219
229	"during which some 20 to 30 million people died of starvation in a man-made famine": Fairbank, *op. cit.*, p. 296
230	"Mao implemented 'true' communism in China in 1958 with the Great Leap Forward.

Pg	Reference
	Here's a summary of how the program worked": Jean Reeder Smith and Lacey Baldwin Smith, *Essentials of World History*, Barron's Education Series Inc., 1980, p. 345
230	"First, Mao dismantled the Central Statistical Bureau, the organization responsible for keeping track of all the economic activity going on in the country": Fairbank, *op. cit.*, p. 300
231	"the crop reports added up to an enormous increase in production, more than a doubling of output": Fairbank, *op. cit.*, p. 302
231	"Chairman Mao was disgraced by the disastrous failure of the Great Leap Forward, and his critics proliferated": Peter N. Stearns (Editor), *The Encyclopedia of World History, 6th edition*, Houghton Mifflin Co., 2001, p. 1023
232	"The Red Guards, mostly younger students, soon brought the country to the verge of chaos": Stearns, *op. cit.*, p. 1024
233	"a sense of conformity, acceptance of hereditary authority, devotion to the soldier, ideal of self-discipline, and its sense of nationalism and superiority of the political unit over the family": Smith & Smith, *op. cit.*, p. 353
242	"Population of England and Wales (graphic)": Peter Turchin, *Historical Dynamics*, Princeton University Press, 2003, p. 163
243	"Population of China in millions of people (graphic)": Peter Turchin, *op. cit.*, p. 169
244	"Population of China in millions of people (graphic)": Peter Turchin, *op. cit.*, p. 169
249	"This diagram shows how numerous different technologies for artificial light have always been invented at almost exactly the right time (graphic)": Joseph Paul Martino, *Technological Forecasting for Decision Making*, American Elsevier Pub. Co., 1975
250	"Top speed of combat aircraft (bombers and fighters) (graphic)": Martino, *op. cit.*
251	"Installed Technological Horsepower in the United States, Population of the United States, and Installed Technological Horsepower per Capita (graphic)": Martino, *op. cit.*
254	"The number of transistors per chip for new chips produced by Intel": Source: Intel Corp. The figures for the different Intel chips are as follows: 1965: 50, 1971: (4004) 2,250, 1972: (8008) 2,500, 1974: (8080) 5,000, 1978: (8086) 29,000, 1982: (286) 120,000, 1985: (386 processor) 275,000, 1989: (486 DX processor) 1,180,000, 1993: (Pentium processor) 3,100,000, 1997: (Pentium II processor) 7,500,000, 1999: (Pentium III processor) 24,000,000, 2000: (Pentium 4 processor) 42,000,000.
255	"Here's the list of technologies identified by Ray Kurzweil": Ray Kurzweil, "The Law of Accelerating Returns," http://www.kurzweilai.net/articles/art0134.html
257	"The number of divorces in each year per 1,000 marriages from 1860 to 1988 (graphic)": Andrew J. Cherlin, *Marriage, Divorce, Remarriage*, Harvard University Press, 1992, p. 21
259	"The number of marriages ending in divorce, 1867 to 1985, based on year marriage was begun (graphic)": Cherlin, *op. cit.*, p. 22
269	"A new analysis of the Japanese economy provides the answer": Yasushi Hamao of the University of Southern California's Marshall School of Business, Jianping Mei of New York University's Stern School of Business and Yexiao Xu of the School of Management at University of Texas at Dallas, *Idiosyncratic Risk and Creative Destruction in Japan*, at http://www.stern.nyu.edu/fin/workpapers/papers2002/html/wpa02053.html. The PDF file for the study can be found at http://www.stern.nyu.edu/fin/workpapers/papers2002/pdf/wpa02053.pdf

Concept Index

The following pages contain a *Concept Index*. For example, one entry is "Bankruptcy triggers French Revolution of 1789." This phrase is indexed under all of the words it contains, and so you find it by looking up any of these words in the concept. So if you're looking for information about some concept, you can find that information if you can think of just one word in the concept.

1000
  Invasion of Seljuk Turks from Asia, 1000, 195
1204
  Catholic sacking of Constantinople, 1204, 197
1215
  Genghis Kahn and Mongols (Tatars) defeated China, 1215, and Russia, 1227, 202
1227
  Genghis Kahn and Mongols (Tatars) defeated China, 1215, and Russia, 1227, 202
1390S
  Spain's anti-Jewish pogroms of 1390s and 1480s, 154, 155
1402
  Timur defeats Ottomans, 1402, 199
1453
  Fall of Constantinople (Istanbul) ends Byzantine Empire, 1453, 199
  Muslims capture Constantinople in 1453, 157
1469
  Marriage of Isabella and Ferdinand, Spain 1469, 157
1480S
  Spain's anti-Jewish pogroms of 1390s and 1480s, 154, 155
1485
  Ivan the Great captures Novgorod territory, 1485, 201

1492
  Christopher Columbus discovers New World in 1492, 156
  Reconquest of Spain from the Muslims in 1492, 156
1500S
  Golden age of Spain in 1500s, 156
1513
  Vasco Nunez de Balboa reaches Pacific in 1513, 158
1519
  Conquistador Hernando Cortes subdues the Aztecs in Mexico in 1519, 158
1522
  Ferdinand Magellan's expedition to circumnavigate the globe in 1522, 158
1533
  Francisco Pizzaro overthrows Inca Empire in Peru in 1533, 158
1552-56
  Ivan the Terrible conquers Kazan, Astrakhan, 1552-56, 202
1555
  Civil war in Germany and Austria (Habsburg Empire), Peace at Augsburg in 1555, 167

1557
  Russia, Poland, Sweden, Denmark fight Livonian War on Baltic, 1557, 201
1564
  Ivan the Terrible versus wealthy landowners (boyars), 1564, 202
1568
  Mass expulsions of Muslims from Spain, 1568, 158
1570
  Ivan the Terrible massacre in Novgorod, 1570, 202
1572
  St. Bartholomew's Night Massacre by Catholics of Protestant Huguenots, France, 1572, 168
1588
  England defeats Spain's Invincible Armada in 1588, 159
1600S
  Debasing of coins in Germany in early 1600s, 169
1618-48
  Merger of timelines in Thirty Years' War, 1618-48, 168
1637
  Tulipomania market bubble panic in 1637, 79, 120, 171
1638-60
  Scottish rebellion and English civil war, 1638-60, 165

1642
  Cossacks offer Moscow Crimean Tatar fortress, 1642, 203
1648
  Peace of Westphalia ends Thirty Years' War in 1648, 171
1649
  Ulozhenie, Russian law makes peasants into slaves, 1649, 204
1663-80
  Mohawk war, 1663-80, 28
1666
  Russian Orthodox Church Great Schism - Nikon and Old Believers, 1666, 204
1669-71
  Stephen Razin, Russia peasant revolt, 1669-71, 204
1675-78
  King Philip's War: Colonists versus Indians 1675-78, 25
1683
  Ottoman siege of Vienna, Habsburg capital, 1683, 211
1688
  Dutch (Holland, Netherlands) invasion of England, 1688, 166
  William and Mary named King and Queen of England, 1688, 166
1692
  Salem Witch Trials 1692, 29
1699
  Ottomans fight War with Holy League, treaty at Karlowitz (Carlowitz), 1699, 212
1700-1720
  Russia (Peter the Great) and Sweden fight the Great Northern War, 1700-1720, 205

1701-14
  War of Spanish Succession, 1701-14, 93, 95, 172
1714
  Treaty at Utrecht ends War of Spanish Succession, 1714, 173
1730S-40S
  America's Great Awakening 1730s-40s, 30
1756-63
  French and Indian War = Seven Years War ends with Treaty of Paris, 1756-63, 32, 173
1762-83
  Russia (Catherine the Great) war with Ottomans, annexes Crimea, peace treaty at Kuchuk Kaynarja, 1762-83, 206
1764
  Sugar Act and Currency Act 1764, 33
1765
  Stamp Act 1765, 33
1767
  Townshend Acts 1767, 34
1772-82
  American Revolutionary War 1772-82, 32
1772
  Alexander Fordyce and Panic of 1772, 122
  Ayr Bank of Scotland and Panic of 1772, 122
  English banking crisis and Panic of 1772, 34, 79, 122
1773-75
  Russia (Catherine the Great) Pugachev's Rebellion, 1773-75, 206

1773
  Russia's Pugachev Rebellion and Catherine the Great, 1773, 96
  Tea Act and Boston Tea Party, 1773, 34
1774
  Russia, Ottomans war, treaty at Kuchuk Kaynarja, 1774, 212
1789-1815
  French Revolution and Napoleonic Wars, 1789-1815, 173
1789
  Bankruptcy triggers French Revolution of 1789, 79, 93, 174
  French Revolution, 1789, 93
178
  Memorandum No. 178, 92
1798
  Thomas Roberts Malthus, Essay on Population, 1798, 245
1812
  Napoleon Bonaparte, French army invade Russia, 1812, 89
  Napoleon's invasion of Moscow, 1812, 100
  War of 1812, 93
1815
  Congress of Vienna ends Napoleonic wars, 1815, 179
1820S-30S
  American awakening of 1820s-30s, 37
1820
  Missouri Compromise - slavery 1820, 38
1825
  Lev Tolstoy, born 1825, fought in Crimean War in 1850s, 91

CONCEPT INDEX

1848
 Karl Marx, Communist Manifesto, 1848, 180
 Revolutions of 1848, 179
1850S
 Lev Tolstoy, born 1825, fought in Crimean War in 1850s, 91
1852
 Louis-Napoleon Bonaparte, Napoleon III, France, 1852, 182
1853-56
 Crimean War, 1853-56, 181
 Ottomans fight Crimean War, 1853-56, 213
1853-61
 Russia Crimean War and Emancipation Edict frees serfs, 1853-61, 206
1857
 Panic of 1857 and Civil War, 78
 Panic of 1857 and Ohio Life Insurance and Trust Company, 39, 123
1862
 Prussian Chancellor Otto von Bismarck, 1862, 182
1864
 Currency act of 1864, 122
1868
 Japan's imperialistic transformation after Meiji Restoration in 1868, 78
1871
 France cedes Alsace and Lorraine to Germany, 1871, 182
 French Commune civil war, 1871, 182
1879
 Thomas Edison, incandescent light bulb, 1879, 19, 249

1889-1908
 Ottoman Freedom Foundation, Committee of Union and Progress, Young Turks, 1889-1908, 213
1890-1920
 American awakening of 1890-1920, 43
1894-96
 Armenian uprising, Istanbul, 1894-96, 214
1905-27
 Russia's Bloody Sunday and Bolshevik (Communist) Revolution, 1905-27, 208
1908
 Young Turks rebellion against Ottomans, 1908, 68, 214
1910-45
 Japan colonizes Korea, 1910-45, 235
1917
 Russia's Communist transformation by World War I and Bolshevik Revolution in 1917, 78
1918-1990
 Kingdom of Yugoslavia, 1918-1990, 67
1922
 Mustafa Kemal, Attaturk, president of Turkey, 1922, 215
1930S-40S
 Stalin's Hitler's massacre of Ukraine and Crimean Tatars, 1930s-40s, 210
1930S
 European Jews flooding Palestine in 1930s, 72
 New 1930s style Great Depression, 114

1933
 Oil embargo against Japan in 1933, 79
1936-49
 Palestine versus Jews crisis war, 1936-49, 72, 149
1940S
 Jordan's King Abdullah opposing Jewish migration in 1940s, 72
1949
 Creation of Israel 1949, 72, 149
1960S-70S
 America's awakening 1960s-70s, 30
1964
 Moore's Law, transistors on integrated circuit, Gordon Moore, Intel Corporation, 1964, 253
1980S
 Iran / Iraq war in 1980s, 72
1984-2000
 Turkish civil war with PKK Kurds 1984-2000, 72
1990S
 Alan Greenspan and irrational exuberance of 1990s, 115
 Bosnian conflict in 1990s, 64
 Causes and timing of the 1990s Bosnian war, 67
 Securities Exchange Commission (SEC) failed to prevent 1990s bubble, 124
1993
 1993 bombing of World Trade Center, 21, 28
2000
 Nasdaq crash in 2000, 123
250
 Thousands of tribes merged to 250 nations and 9 major civilizations, 24

299

431BC
  Peloponnesian War between Athens and Sparta, 431BC, 133
500
  600 Indian tribes in America speaking 500 languages, 26
  Exponential growth: Standard & Poors 500 Stock Index (S&P), 265
563BC
  Hinduism and life of the Buddha, born 563BC, 150
600
  600 Indian tribes in America speaking 500 languages, 26
622
  Mohammed flees to Medina (Yathrib) in 622, 144
630
  Mohammed's conquest of Mecca and Quraish, 630, 149
711
  Muslim conquest of Spain in 711, 156
80-YEAR
  Length of 80-year cycle, 17
988
  Kiev Slav Vladimir adopts Orthodox religion, 988, 198
ABDULLAH
  Jordan's King Abdullah opposing Jewish migration in 1940s, 72
ABOLITION
  Abolitionist John Brown and Harper's Ferry insurrection, 39
ACCELERATE
  Ray Kurzweil, Law of Accelerating Returns, 296 (255)
ACCUSE
  Conversos accused of Judaizing as false Christians, 155

ACROPOLIS
  Ancient Greece: the Acropolis, the Parthenon, Pericles, Thucydides, Socrates, Aristophanes, Aeschylus, Sophocles and Euripides, 129
  Pericles commissions Parthenon and Acropolis, 132
ACT
  Currency act of 1864, 122
  Stamp Act 1765, 33
  Sugar Act and Currency Act 1764, 33
  Tea Act and Boston Tea Party, 1773, 34
  Townshend Acts 1767, 34
ADOPT
  Kiev Slav Vladimir adopts Orthodox religion, 988, 198
  Mohammed adopted Jewish rites, Jerusalem as holy city, 148
AESCHYLUS
  Ancient Greece: the Acropolis, the Parthenon, Pericles, Thucydides, Socrates, Aristophanes, Aeschylus, Sophocles and Euripides, 129
AFRICA
  Major civilizations: Western, Latin American, African, Islamic, Sinic, Hindu, Orthodox, Buddhist, Japanese, 24, 62
  Spread of humans and civilizations from north Africa, 187
AFTER
  Japan's imperialistic transformation after Meiji Restoration in 1868, 78
  Scapegoating after defeat, 84

AGAINST
  Luddite riots against intelligent computers, 276
  Oil embargo against Japan in 1933, 79
  Young Turks rebellion against Ottomans, 1908, 68, 214
AGE
  Golden Age of America, 159
  Golden Age of Ancient Athens Greece and Sparta (awakening), 129
  Golden age of Spain in 1500s, 156
AIRCRAFT
  Paul Martino, speed of combat aircraft, 296 (250)
  Speed of combat aircraft, 250
AL-ABBAS
  Al-Abbas, uncle of Mohammed, 192
ALAN
  Alan Greenspan and irrational exuberance of 1990s, 115
ALBERT
  Albert Hourani, 289 (144), 290 (150), 292 (191)
ALEXANDER
  Alexander Fordyce and Panic of 1772, 122
  Alexander Solzhenitsyn, The Gulag Archipelago, 210
  Alexander the Great of Macedonia, 188
  King Philip of Macedonia, Alexander the Great, 133
  Mike Alexander, Kondratieff Cycles and trends, 239
  Tsar Alexander I political reforms, 206
  Tsar Alexander of Russia, 92, 95

Concept Index

ALFRED
  Lord Alfred Tennyson poem, The Charge of the Light Brigade, Crimean War, 207

ALLAH
  There is no God except Allah, and Mohammed is the Messenger of Allah, 141, 193

ALSACE
  France cedes Alsace and Lorraine to Germany, 1871, 182

ALVAREZ
  Spain's sense of manifest destiny, Manuel Fernandez Alvarez, University of Salamanca, 291 (157)

AMBROSE
  Ambrose Bierce, 277

AMERICA
  600 Indian tribes in America speaking 500 languages, 26
  America's Great Awakening 1730s-40s, 30
  America's awakening 1960s-70s, 30
  America's manifest destiny: freedom and democracy, xiv
  American Revolutionary War 1772-82, 32
  American awakening of 1820s-30s, 37
  American awakening of 1890-1920, 43
  Deaths in major American wars, 44
  Golden Age of America, 159
  Major civilizations: Western, Latin American, African, Islamic, Sinic, Hindu, Orthodox, Buddhist, Japanese, 24, 62
  World War I not a crisis war for America, 44

AMOULDERING
  John Brown's Body Lies A'mouldering in the Grave, 39

ANCIENT
  Ancient Greece: the Acropolis, the Parthenon, Pericles, Thucydides, Socrates, Aristophanes, Aeschylus, Sophocles and Euripides, 129
  Delian League in ancient Greece, 131
  Golden Age of Ancient Athens Greece and Sparta (awakening), 129
  Persian War with ancient Greece, 131

ANDREW
  Andrew J Cherlin, Marriage and Divorce, 296 (257)

ANGLICAN
  Church of England and Anglican Church, 31

ANNEX
  Russia (Catherine the Great) war with Ottomans, annexes Crimea, peace treaty at Kuchuk Kaynarja, 1762-83, 206

ANTI-JEWISH
  David Nirenberg, anti-Jewish pogroms in Medieval Spain, 290 (155)
  Spain's anti-Jewish pogroms of 1390s and 1480s, 154, 155

ANXIETY
  Crisis wars: visceral feeling of anxiety, terror and fury, 3

ARAB
  Arab / Jewish fault line, 14
  Spread of Arabic language, 193

ARAFAT
  Ariel Sharon and Yasser Arafat cooperating to prevent major Mideast war, 73

ARCHIPELAGO
  Alexander Solzhenitsyn, The Gulag Archipelago, 210

ARIEL
  Ariel Sharon and Yasser Arafat cooperating to prevent major Mideast war, 73

ARISTOPHANES
  Ancient Greece: the Acropolis, the Parthenon, Pericles, Thucydides, Socrates, Aristophanes, Aeschylus, Sophocles and Euripides, 129

ARMADA
  England defeats Spain's Invincible Armada in 1588, 159

ARMENIA
  Armenian uprising, Istanbul, 1894-96, 214

ARMY
  Napoleon Bonaparte, French army invade Russia, 1812, 89

ARRANGE
  Pope arranges for Ivan III the Great to marry Sophia, 201

ARTIFICIAL
  Artificial light sources, 249
  Paul Martino, artificial light technologies, 296 (249)

ARTIST
  Artist Libby Chase, xxi

ASABIYA
  Asabiya (group solidarity), Ibn Khaldun, Peter Turchin, 288 (62)

ASIA
  Invasion of Seljuk Turks from Asia, 1000, 195

ASTRAKHAN
  Ivan the Terrible conquers Kazan, Astrakhan, 1552-56, 202
ATHENS
  Golden Age of Ancient Athens Greece and Sparta (awakening), 129
  Peloponnesian War between Athens and Sparta, 431BC, 133
ATTATURK
  Mustafa Kemal, Attaturk, president of Turkey, 1922, 215
AUGSBURG
  Civil war in Germany and Austria (Habsburg Empire), Peace at Augsburg in 1555, 167
AUSTERITY
  Austerity, awakening, and unraveling periods, 10
AUSTRIA
  Civil war in Germany and Austria (Habsburg Empire), Peace at Augsburg in 1555, 167
AVERAGE
  Exponential growth: Dow Jones Industrial Average (DJIA), 264
  Human lifespan: average versus maximum, 17
AWAKENING
  America's Great Awakening 1730s-40s, 30
  America's awakening 1960s-70s, 30
  American awakening of 1820s-30s, 37
  American awakening of 1890-1920, 43
  Austerity, awakening, and unraveling periods, 10

China's Tiananmen Square Awakening, 129, 232
Golden Age of Ancient Athens Greece and Sparta (awakening), 129
Jesus Christ and Christianity (awakening), 139
Teachings of Mohammed and Islam (awakening), 143
Vietnam War awakening, 128
AYR
  Ayr Bank of Scotland and Panic of 1772, 122
AZTECS
  Conquistador Hernando Cortes subdues the Aztecs in Mexico in 1519, 158
BADEN
  Prince Max von Baden on World War I, 289 (87)
BAGOT
  Sir John Bagot Glubb (Glubb Pasha), 289 (143)
BALBOA
  Vasco Nunez de Balboa reaches Pacific in 1513, 158
BALKAN
  Orthodox, Islamic and Western civilizations meet in the Balkans, 64
  World War I - crisis war for Balkans (Yugoslavia), Turkey (Ottoman Empire), Russia (Bolshevik Communist Revolution), 85
BALTIC
  Russia, Poland, Sweden, Denmark fight Livonian War on Baltic, 1557, 201
BANKRUPTCY
  Bankruptcy triggers French Revolution of 1789, 79, 93, 174

BANK
  Ayr Bank of Scotland and Panic of 1772, 122
  English banking crisis and Panic of 1772, 34, 79, 122
BANNER
  Francis Scott Key, Star Spangled Banner, 23
BAPTIZE
  I baptize thee in the name of the Father, and of the Son, and of the Holy Ghost, 141
BARBARIAN
  Barbarian hordes versus Roman Empire, 189
BARTHOLOMEW
  Charles IX, Massacre of St. Bartholomew, 102
  St. Bartholomew's Night Massacre by Catholics of Protestant Huguenots, France, 1572, 168
BASE
  Population based exponential growth trends, 242
  Technology based exponential growth trends, 248
BASSANO
  Duc de Bassano, 98
BATTLE
  Battle at Smolensk, 98
  Battle of Borodino, 99
BECOME
  Computers will become more intelligent than humans, 256, 274
  Russia becomes new Roman Empire, 201
BEDOUIN
  Nomadic Bedouin tribes - perpetual war as a way of life, 145

BELIEVER
Russian Orthodox Church Great Schism - Nikon and Old Believers, 1666, 204
BIERCE
Ambrose Bierce, 277
BIN
Osama bin Laden, 39
BIOGRAPHY
Life of Mohammed: Quran (Koran), biographies, Hadeeth (Traditions), 143
BIRTH
Exponential technology growth: Out of wedlock births, 263
BISMARCK
Prussian Chancellor Otto von Bismarck, 1862, 182
BLOOD
Russia's Bloody Sunday and Bolshevik (Communist) Revolution, 1905-27, 208
BLUE
IBM's Blue Gene project, 256
BODY
John Brown's Body Lies A'mouldering in the Grave, 39
BOLSHEVIK
Josef Stalin and Bolshevik (Communist) Revolution, 210

Nicolai Lenin and Bolshevik (Communist) Revolution, 208

Russia's Bloody Sunday and Bolshevik (Communist) Revolution, 1905-27, 208

Russia's Communist transformation by World War I and Bolshevik Revolution in 1917, 78

Russian Orthodox Church and Bolshevik (Communist) Revolution, 209

World War I - crisis war for Balkans (Yugoslavia), Turkey (Ottoman Empire), Russia (Bolshevik Communist Revolution), 85
BOMB
1993 bombing of World Trade Center, 21, 28
BONAPARTE
Louis-Napoleon Bonaparte, Napoleon III, France, 1852, 182

Napoleon Bonaparte, French army invade Russia, 1812, 89
BORN
Hinduism and life of the Buddha, born 563BC, 150

Lev Tolstoy, born 1825, fought in Crimean War in 1850s, 91
BORODINO
Battle of Borodino, 99
BOSNIA
Bosnian conflict in 1990s, 64

Causes and timing of the 1990s Bosnian war, 67
BOSTON
Tea Act and Boston Tea Party, 1773, 34
BOTTOM-UP
Top-down and bottom-up religions, 142
BOYAR
Ivan the Terrible versus wealthy landowners (boyars), 1564, 202
BRADFORD
William Bradford, 27
BRIGADE
Lord Alfred Tennyson poem, The Charge of the Light Brigade, Crimean War, 207

BRITISH
British General John Burgoyne, 36
BROWNS
John Brown's Body Lies A'mouldering in the Grave, 39
BROWN
Abolitionist John Brown and Harper's Ferry insurrection, 39
BUBBLE
Description of bubble, 120

Securities Exchange Commission (SEC) failed to prevent 1990s bubble, 124

Tulipomania market bubble panic in 1637, 79, 120, 171
BUDDHA
Hinduism and life of the Buddha, born 563BC, 150
BUDDHISM
Converting to Judaism, Christianity, Islam, Hinduism, Buddhism, 141
BUDDHIST
Major civilizations: Western, Latin American, African, Islamic, Sinic, Hindu, Orthodox, Buddhist, Japanese, 24, 62
BULB
Thomas Edison, incandescent light bulb, 1879, 19, 249
BUREAUCRACY
Crusty old bureaucracy theory, 125, in China 218
BURGOYNE
British General John Burgoyne, 36
BUSINESS
Jianping Mei of New York University's Stern School of Business, 296 (269)

Yasushi Hamao of the University of Southern California's Marshall School of Business, 296 (269)
BYZANTINE
Fall of Constantinople (Istanbul) ends Byzantine Empire, 1453, 199
BYZANTIUM
Byzantium to Constantinople to Istanbul, 190
CALIFORNIA
Yasushi Hamao of the University of Southern California's Marshall School of Business, 296 (269)
CAPITAL
Ottoman siege of Vienna, Habsburg capital, 1683, 211
CAPITULATE
Winston Churchill on German capitulation in World War I, 289 (87)
CAPTURE
Ivan the Great captures Novgorod territory, 1485, 201
Muslims capture Constantinople in 1453, 157
CARLOWITZ
Ottomans fight War with Holy League, treaty at Karlowitz (Carlowitz), 1699, 212
CARL
Effect of defeat - Carl von Clausewitz, 288 (83)
CATHERINE
Russia (Catherine the Great) Pugachev's Rebellion, 1773-75, 206
Russia (Catherine the Great) war with Ottomans, annexes Crimea, peace treaty at Kuchuk Kaynarja, 1762-83, 206

Russia's Pugachev Rebellion and Catherine the Great, 1773, 96
CATHOLIC
Catholic sacking of Constantinople, 1204, 197
Conversos - Jews converting to Catholicism, 155
Separation / Schism of Orthodox and Catholic Christianity, 190, 196
St. Bartholomew's Night Massacre by Catholics of Protestant Huguenots, France, 1572, 168
CAUSE
Cause versus timing of war, 13
Causes and timing of new Mideast war, 73
Causes and timing of the 1990s Bosnian war, 67
CEDE
France cedes Alsace and Lorraine to Germany, 1871, 182
CENTER
1993 bombing of World Trade Center, 21, 28
CHANCELLOR
Edward Chancellor, 289 (121)
Prussian Chancellor Otto von Bismarck, 1862, 182
CHARACTER
Character of a nation, 66
CHARGE
Lord Alfred Tennyson poem, The Charge of the Light Brigade, Crimean War, 207
CHARLES
Charles IX, Massacre of St. Bartholomew, 102
CHASE
Artist Libby Chase, xxi

Professor Gene Chase, Messiah College, 139
CHERLIN
Andrew J Cherlin, Marriage and Divorce, 296 (257)
CHIEF
Massasoit, chief of the Wampanoag Indians, 27
Muslim tribe chieftain Osman and Ottoman Empire, 199
CHINA
China's Tiananmen Square Awakening, 129, 232
Crusty old bureaucracy theory in China, 218
Genghis Kahn and Mongols (Tatars) defeated China, 1215, and Russia, 1227, 202
CHOSEN
Jewish law designed for Diaspora of chosen people, 136
CHRISTIANITY
Converting to Judaism, Christianity, Islam, Hinduism, Buddhism, 141
Eastern Europe: Islam versus Orthodox Christianity, 185
Jesus Christ and Christianity (awakening), 139
Separation / Schism of Orthodox and Catholic Christianity, 190, 196
CHRISTMAS
World War I Christmas truce, 86
CHRISTOPHER
Christopher Columbus discovers New World in 1492, 156
CHRIST
Jesus Christ and Christianity (awakening), 139

CONCEPT INDEX

CHURCHILL
  Winston Churchill on German capitulation in World War I, 289 (87)
CHURCH
  Church of England and Anglican Church, 31
  Russian Orthodox Church Great Schism - Nikon and Old Believers, 1666, 204
  Russian Orthodox Church and Bolshevik (Communist) Revolution, 209
CIRCUIT
  Moore's Law, transistors on integrated circuit, Gordon Moore, Intel Corporation, 1964, 253
CIRCUMNAVIGATE
  Ferdinand Magellan's expedition to circumnavigate the globe in 1522, 158
CITY
  Mohammed adopted Jewish rites, Jerusalem as holy city, 148
CIVILIZATION
  Major civilizations: Western, Latin American, African, Islamic, Sinic, Hindu, Orthodox, Buddhist, Japanese, 24, 62
  Orthodox, Islamic and Western civilizations meet in the Balkans, 64
  Rise of civilization consciousness, 63
  Samuel P. Huntington, Clash of Civilizations and fault line wars, 62
  Spread of humans and civilizations from north Africa, 187
  Thousands of tribes merged to 250 nations and 9 major civilizations, 24

CIVIL
  Civil war in Germany and Austria (Habsburg Empire), Peace at Augsburg in 1555, 167
  French Commune civil war, 1871, 182
  Panic of 1857 and Civil War, 78
  Revolutionary War to Civil War, 12
  Scottish rebellion and English civil war, 1638-60, 165
  Turkish civil war with PKK Kurds 1984-2000, 72
CLASH
  Samuel P. Huntington, Clash of Civilizations and fault line wars, 62
CLAUSEWITZ
  Effect of defeat - Carl von Clausewitz, 288 (83)
CLAY
  Unionist senators Henry Clay and Daniel Webster, 39
COIN
  Debasing of coins in Germany in early 1600s, 169
COLLEGE
  Professor Gene Chase, Messiah College, 139
  William and Mary College, 166
COLONIST
  King Philip's War: Colonists versus Indians 1675-78, 25
COLONIZE
  Japan colonizes Korea, 1910-45, 235
COLUMBUS
  Christopher Columbus discovers New World in 1492, 156

COMBAT
  Paul Martino, speed of combat aircraft, 296 (250)
  Speed of combat aircraft, 250
COMBINE
  Combined growth / cyclic trends, 241
COMMISSION
  Pericles commissions Parthenon and Acropolis, 132
  Securities Exchange Commission (SEC) failed to prevent 1990s bubble, 124
COMMITTEE
  Ottoman Freedom Foundation, Committee of Union and Progress, Young Turks, 1889-1908, 213
COMMUNE
  French Commune - internal revolution - Third Republic, 84
  French Commune civil war, 1871, 182
COMMUNIST
  Complexity Theory: Why Communism and Socialism must fail, 246
  Josef Stalin and Bolshevik (Communist) Revolution, 210
  Karl Marx, Communist Manifesto, 1848, 180
  Nicolai Lenin and Bolshevik (Communist) Revolution, 208
  Russia's Bloody Sunday and Bolshevik (Communist) Revolution, 1905-27, 208
  Russia's Communist transformation by World War I and Bolshevik Revolution in 1917, 78
  Russian Orthodox Church and Bolshevik (Communist) Revolution, 209

305

World War I - crisis war for Balkans (Yugoslavia), Turkey (Ottoman Empire), Russia (Bolshevik Communist Revolution), 85

COMPACT
Mayflower Compact, an early "declaration of independence", 26

COMPANY
Panic of 1857 and Ohio Life Insurance and Trust Company, 39, 123

COMPAQ
Compaq Computer Corporation, 118

COMPARE
Comparing Mohammed and Jesus, 144

COMPLEX
Complexity Theory: Why Communism and Socialism must fail, 246

COMPROMISE
Missouri Compromise - slavery 1820, 38
Revolutionary war and slavery compromise, 36
War processes: negotiation, compromise, containment, intensification, expansion, 63

COMPUTER
Compaq Computer Corporation, 118
Computers will become more intelligent than humans, 256, 274
Exponential technology growth: Computing power, 253
Luddite riots against intelligent computers, 276
Nanotechnology and DNA protein folding technology for computers, 256

Singularity: computers more intelligent than humans, 275

CONFLICT
Bosnian conflict in 1990s, 64
Jordan as mediator in Israeli versus Palestinian conflict, 63, 72

CONGRESS
Congress of Vienna ends Napoleonic wars, 1815, 179

CONQUEST
Ivan the Terrible conquers Kazan, Astrakhan, 1552-56, 202
Mohammed's conquest of Mecca and Quraish, 630, 149
Muslim conquest of Spain in 711, 156

CONQUISTADOR
Conquistador Hernando Cortes subdues the Aztecs in Mexico in 1519, 158

CONSCIOUSNESS
Rise of civilization consciousness, 63

CONSTANTINOPLE
Byzantium to Constantinople to Istanbul, 190
Catholic sacking of Constantinople, 1204, 197
Fall of Constantinople (Istanbul) ends Byzantine Empire, 1453, 199
Muslims capture Constantinople in 1453, 157

CONTAINMENT
War processes: negotiation, compromise, containment, intensification, expansion, 63

CONTINENTAL
Continental System, 92, 93

CONVERSO
Conversos - Jews converting to Catholicism, 155

Conversos accused of Judaizing as false Christians, 155

CONVERT
Conversos - Jews converting to Catholicism, 155
Converting to Judaism, Christianity, Islam, Hinduism, Buddhism, 141

COOPERATE
Ariel Sharon and Yasser Arafat cooperating to prevent major Mideast war, 73

CORPORATION
Compaq Computer Corporation, 118
Honeywell Corporation, 253
Lotus Development Corporation, 118
Moore's Law, transistors on integrated circuit, Gordon Moore, Intel Corporation, 1964, 253

CORTES
Conquistador Hernando Cortes subdues the Aztecs in Mexico in 1519, 158

COSSACK
Cossacks offer Moscow Crimean Tatar fortress, 1642, 203

COUNT
Count Lauriston, 98

CRASH
Nasdaq crash in 2000, 123

CREATE
Creation of Israel 1949, 72, 149

CRIMEA
Cossacks offer Moscow Crimean Tatar fortress, 1642, 203
Crimean War, 1853-56, 181
Florence Nightingale invents nursing in Crimean War, 206

CONCEPT INDEX

Lev Tolstoy, born 1825, fought in Crimean War in 1850s, 91

Lord Alfred Tennyson poem, The Charge of the Light Brigade, Crimean War, 207

Ottomans fight Crimean War, 1853-56, 213

Russia (Catherine the Great) war with Ottomans, annexes Crimea, peace treaty at Kuchuk Kaynarja, 1762-83, 206

Russia Crimean War and Emancipation Edict frees serfs, 1853-61, 206

Stalin's Hitler's massacre of Ukraine and Crimean Tatars, 1930s-40s, 210

CRISIS

Crisis Wars versus Mid-Cycle Wars, 80

Crisis war in Mexico, 57

Crisis wars and cultural memory, 81

Crisis wars: visceral feeling of anxiety, terror and fury, 3

English banking crisis and Panic of 1772, 34, 79, 122

Mideast crisis to Mideast crisis, 14

Palestine versus Jews crisis war, 1936-49, 72, 149

World War I - crisis war for Balkans (Yugoslavia), Turkey (Ottoman Empire), Russia (Bolshevik Communist Revolution), 85

World War I not a crisis war for America, 44

World War I not a crisis war for Germany, 86

CRUSTY

Crusty old bureaucracy theory, 125, in China 218

CULTURE

Crisis wars and cultural memory, 81

CURRENCY

Currency act of 1864, 122

Sugar Act and Currency Act 1764, 33

CYCLE

Combined growth / cyclic trends, 241

Cyclic trends: fashion, political economic, generational, 239

Length of 80-year cycle, 17

Mike Alexander, Kondratieff Cycles and trends, 239

Russia's mid-cycle wars with western Europe, 204

Technology cycle in economic growth, 271

CYPRUS

Cyprus - fault line between Greece and Turkey, 131

CZAR

Ivan the Terrible - Tsar (or Czar) of Russia, 201

DALLAS

Yexiao Xu of the School of Management at University of Texas at Dallas, 296 (269)

DANIEL-ROPS

Henri Daniel-Rops, 289 (136)

DANIEL

Unionist senators Henry Clay and Daniel Webster, 39

DAVID

David Nirenberg, anti-Jewish pogroms in Medieval Spain, 290 (155)

DEATH

Deaths in major American wars, 44

DEBASE

Debasing of coins in Germany in early 1600s, 169

DECLARATION

Mayflower Compact, an early "declaration of independence", 26

DEFEAT

Effect of defeat - Carl von Clausewitz, 288 (83)

England defeats Spain's Invincible Armada in 1588, 159

Genghis Kahn and Mongols (Tatars) defeated China, 1215, and Russia, 1227, 202

Scapegoating after defeat, 84

Timur defeats Ottomans, 1402, 199

Wolfgang Schivelbusch - transformation of defeated nation, 288 (82)

DELIAN

Delian League in ancient Greece, 131

DEMOCRACY

America's manifest destiny: freedom and democracy, xiv

DENMARK

Russia, Poland, Sweden, Denmark fight Livonian War on Baltic, 1557, 201

DEPRESSION

Federal Reserve using monetary policy to prevent depression, 124, 272

New 1930s style Great Depression, 114

DESCRIPTION

Description of bubble, 120

DESIGN

Jewish law designed for Diaspora of chosen people, 136

DESTINY

America's manifest destiny: freedom and democracy, xiv

Spain's sense of manifest destiny, Manuel Fernandez Alvarez, University of Salamanca, 291 (157)

DEVELOP
Lotus Development Corporation, 118

DE
Duc de Bassano, 98
Vasco Nunez de Balboa reaches Pacific in 1513, 158

DIASPORA
Jewish law designed for Diaspora of chosen people, 136

DISCOVER
Christopher Columbus discovers New World in 1492, 156

DIVORCE
Andrew J Cherlin, Marriage and Divorce, 296 (257)
Exponential technology growth: Divorce rate, 257

DJIA
Exponential growth: Dow Jones Industrial Average (DJIA), 264

DNA
Nanotechnology and DNA protein folding technology for computers, 256

DONALD
Donald Horowitz, 288 (61)

DOW
Exponential growth: Dow Jones Industrial Average (DJIA), 264

DR
Dr. Edip Yuksel, Islamic scholar, 147

DUC
Duc de Bassano, 98

DUKE
Duke of Oldenburg, 92

DUTCH
Dutch (Holland, Netherlands) invasion of England, 1688, 166

DYNAMICS
Generational Dynamics Forecasting Methodology, 76
Limitations of Generational Dynamics forecasting, xviii, 76
Peter Turchin, Historical Dynamics, 287 (60), 291 (162), 295 (219), 296 (242), 296 (243), 296 (244)

EARLY
Mayflower Compact, an early "declaration of independence", 26

EARNING
S&ampPP Price Earnings ratio, 266

EAST
Eastern Europe: Islam versus Orthodox Christianity, 185

ECONOMIC
Cyclic trends: fashion, political economic, generational, 239
Technology cycle in economic growth, 271

EDICT
Russia Crimean War and Emancipation Edict frees serfs, 1853-61, 206

EDIP
Dr. Edip Yuksel, Islamic scholar, 147

EDISON
Thomas Edison, incandescent light bulb, 1879, 19, 249

EDWARD
Edward Chancellor, 289 (121)
Edward Winslow, 27

EFFECT
Effect of defeat - Carl von Clausewitz, 288 (83)

EMANCIPATION
Russia Crimean War and Emancipation Edict frees serfs, 1853-61, 206

EMBARGO
Oil embargo against Japan in 1933, 79

EMPIRE
Barbarian hordes versus Roman Empire, 189
Civil war in Germany and Austria (Habsburg Empire), Peace at Augsburg in 1555, 167
Fall of Constantinople (Istanbul) ends Byzantine Empire, 1453, 199
Francisco Pizzaro overthrows Inca Empire in Peru in 1533, 158
Muslim tribe chieftain Osman and Ottoman Empire, 199
Rise and fall of Roman Empire, 187
Russia becomes new Roman Empire, 201
Turkey, Iraq, Jordan (Transjordan) from Ottoman Empire, 71
World War I - crisis war for Balkans (Yugoslavia), Turkey (Ottoman Empire), Russia (Bolshevik Communist Revolution), 85

END
Congress of Vienna ends Napoleonic wars, 1815, 179
Fall of Constantinople (Istanbul) ends Byzantine Empire, 1453, 199
French and Indian War = Seven Years War ends with

CONCEPT INDEX

Treaty of Paris, 1756-63, 32, 173

Peace of Westphalia ends Thirty Years' War in 1648, 171

Treaty at Utrecht ends War of Spanish Succession, 1714, 173

ENGLAND

Church of England and Anglican Church, 31

Dutch (Holland, Netherlands) invasion of England, 1688, 166

England defeats Spain's Invincible Armada in 1588, 159

Scottish rebellion and English civil war, 1638-60, 165

William and Mary named King and Queen of England, 1688, 166

ENGLISH

English banking crisis and Panic of 1772, 34, 79, 122

ESSAY

Thomas Roberts Malthus, Essay on Population, 1798, 245

EURIPIDES

Ancient Greece: the Acropolis, the Parthenon, Pericles, Thucydides, Socrates, Aristophanes, Aeschylus, Sophocles and Euripides, 129

EUROPE

Eastern Europe: Islam versus Orthodox Christianity, 185

European Jews flooding Palestine in 1930s, 72

Russia's mid-cycle wars with western Europe, 204

EXCEPT

There is no God except Allah, and Mohammed is the Messenger of Allah, 141, 193

EXCHANGE

Securities Exchange Commission (SEC) failed to prevent 1990s bubble, 124

Tokyo Stock Exchange / Japanese Nikkei Market Index, 268

EXPANSION

Identify Group Expansion principle in wars, 64

Principle of Localization versus Identify Group Expansion principle in wars, 69

War processes: negotiation, compromise, containment, intensification, expansion, 63

EXPEDITION

Ferdinand Magellan's expedition to circumnavigate the globe in 1522, 158

EXPEL

Mass expulsions of Muslims from Spain, 1568, 158

EXPONENTIAL

Exponential growth: Dow Jones Industrial Average (DJIA), 264

Exponential growth: Standard & Poors 500 Stock Index (S&P), 265

Exponential growth: forecasting stock trends, 263

Exponential technology growth: Computing power, 253

Exponential technology growth: Divorce rate, 257

Exponential technology growth: Out of wedlock births, 263

Population based exponential growth trends, 242

Technology based exponential growth trends, 248

EXUBERANCE

Alan Greenspan and irrational exuberance of 1990s, 115

FAIL

Complexity Theory: Why Communism and Socialism must fail, 246

Securities Exchange Commission (SEC) failed to prevent 1990s bubble, 124

FALL

Fall of Constantinople (Istanbul) ends Byzantine Empire, 1453, 199

Rise and fall of Roman Empire, 187

FALSE

Conversos accused of Judaizing as false Christians, 155

FASHION

Cyclic trends: fashion, political economic, generational, 239

FATHER

I baptize thee in the name of the Father, and of the Son, and of the Holy Ghost, 141

FAULT

Arab / Jewish fault line, 14

Cyprus - fault line between Greece and Turkey, 131

Fault line versus generation gap, 8

Kashmir fault line between Pakistan and India, 74

Samuel P. Huntington, Clash of Civilizations and fault line wars, 62

FEDERAL
  Federal Reserve using monetary policy to prevent depression, 124, 272
FEEL
  Crisis wars: visceral feeling of anxiety, terror and fury, 3
FERDINAND
  Ferdinand Magellan's expedition to circumnavigate the globe in 1522, 158
  Marriage of Isabella and Ferdinand, Spain 1469, 157
FERNANDEZ
  Spain's sense of manifest destiny, Manuel Fernandez Alvarez, University of Salamanca, 291 (157)
FERRY
  Abolitionist John Brown and Harper's Ferry insurrection, 39
FIGHT
  Lev Tolstoy, born 1825, fought in Crimean War in 1850s, 91
  Ottomans fight Crimean War, 1853-56, 213
  Ottomans fight War with Holy League, treaty at Karlowitz (Carlowitz), 1699, 212
  Russia (Peter the Great) and Sweden fight the Great Northern War, 1700-1720, 205
  Russia, Poland, Sweden, Denmark fight Livonian War on Baltic, 1557, 201
FLEE
  Mohammed flees to Medina (Yathrib) in 622, 144
FLOOD
  European Jews flooding Palestine in 1930s, 72

FLORENCE
  Florence Nightingale invents nursing in Crimean War, 206
FOLD
  Nanotechnology and DNA protein folding technology for computers, 256
FORDYCE
  Alexander Fordyce and Panic of 1772, 122
FORECAST
  Exponential growth: forecasting stock trends, 263
  Generational Dynamics Forecasting Methodology, 76
  Limitations of Generational Dynamics forecasting, xviii, 76
FORTRESS
  Cossacks offer Moscow Crimean Tatar fortress, 1642, 203
FOUNDATION
  Ottoman Freedom Foundation, Committee of Union and Progress, Young Turks, 1889-1908, 213
FRANCE
  Bankruptcy triggers French Revolution of 1789, 79, 93, 174
  France cedes Alsace and Lorraine to Germany, 1871, 182
  French Commune - internal revolution - Third Republic, 84
  French Revolution and Napoleonic Wars, 1789-1815, 173
  French Revolution, 1789, 93
  French and Indian War = Seven Years War ends with

Treaty of Paris, 1756-63, 32, 173
  Louis-Napoleon Bonaparte, Napoleon III, France, 1852, 182
  Napoleon Bonaparte, French army invade Russia, 1812, 89
  St. Bartholomew's Night Massacre by Catholics of Protestant Huguenots, France, 1572, 168
  War between France and Germany, 75
FRANCISCO
  Francisco Pizzaro overthrows Inca Empire in Peru in 1533, 158
FRANCIS
  Francis Scott Key, Star Spangled Banner, 23
FREEDOM
  America's manifest destiny: freedom and democracy, xiv
  Ottoman Freedom Foundation, Committee of Union and Progress, Young Turks, 1889-1908, 213
FREE
  Russia Crimean War and Emancipation Edict frees serfs, 1853-61, 206
  Russian freedom of religion, 211
FRENCH
  French Commune civil war, 1871, 182
FULANI-HAUSA
  Fulani-Hausa Nigerian tribes, 61
FURY
  Crisis wars: visceral feeling of anxiety, terror and fury, 3

GAP
Fault line versus generation gap, 8
Generation gap, 6

GENERAL
British General John Burgoyne, 36

GENERATIONAL
Cyclic trends: fashion, political economic, generational, 239
Generational Dynamics Forecasting Methodology, 76
Limitations of Generational Dynamics forecasting, xviii, 76

GENERATION
Fault line versus generation gap, 8
Generation gap, 6

GENE
IBM's Blue Gene project, 256
Professor Gene Chase, Messiah College, 139

GENGHIS
Genghis Kahn and Mongols (Tatars) defeated China, 1215, and Russia, 1227, 202

GEORGE
George Santayana, 2

GERMANY
Civil war in Germany and Austria (Habsburg Empire), Peace at Augsburg in 1555, 167
Debasing of coins in Germany in early 1600s, 169
France cedes Alsace and Lorraine to Germany, 1871, 182
War between France and Germany, 75
Wars of German and Italian Unification and Ottoman's and pan-Islamic movement, 213
Winston Churchill on German capitulation in World War I, 289 (87)
World War I not a crisis war for Germany, 86

GHOST
I baptize thee in the name of the Father, and of the Son, and of the Holy Ghost, 141

GLOBE
Ferdinand Magellan's expedition to circumnavigate the globe in 1522, 158

GLUBB
Sir John Bagot Glubb (Glubb Pasha), 289 (143)

GOD
There is no God except Allah, and Mohammed is the Messenger of Allah, 141, 193

GOLDEN
Golden Age of America, 159
Golden Age of Ancient Athens Greece and Sparta (awakening), 129
Golden age of Spain in 1500s, 156

GORDON
Moore's Law, transistors on integrated circuit, Gordon Moore, Intel Corporation, 1964, 253

GRAVE
John Brown's Body Lies A'moulderying in the Grave, 39

GREAT
Alexander the Great of Macedonia, 188
America's Great Awakening 1730s-40s, 30
Great Patriotic War, 210
Ivan the Great captures Novgorod territory, 1485, 201
King Philip of Macedonia, Alexander the Great, 133
New 1930s style Great Depression, 114
Pope arranges for Ivan III the Great to marry Sophia, 201
Russia (Catherine the Great) Pugachev's Rebellion, 1773-75, 206
Russia (Catherine the Great) war with Ottomans, annexes Crimea, peace treaty at Kuchuk Kaynarja, 1762-83, 206
Russia (Peter the Great) and Sweden fight the Great Northern War, 1700-1720, 205
Russia's Pugachev Rebellion and Catherine the Great, 1773, 96
Russian Orthodox Church Great Schism - Nikon and Old Believers, 1666, 204

GREECE
Ancient Greece: the Acropolis, the Parthenon, Pericles, Thucydides, Socrates, Aristophanes, Aeschylus, Sophocles and Euripides, 129
Cyprus - fault line between Greece and Turkey, 131
Delian League in ancient Greece, 131
Golden Age of Ancient Athens Greece and Sparta (awakening), 129
Persian War with ancient Greece, 131

GREENSPAN
Alan Greenspan and irrational exuberance of 1990s, 115

GROUP
  Asabiya (group solidarity), Ibn Khaldun, Peter Turchin, 288 (62)
  Identify Group Expansion principle in wars, 64
  Principle of Localization versus Identify Group Expansion principle in wars, 69
GROWTH
  Combined growth / cyclic trends, 241
  Exponential growth: Dow Jones Industrial Average (DJIA), 264
  Exponential growth: Standard & Poors 500 Stock Index (S&P), 265
  Exponential growth: forecasting stock trends, 263
  Exponential technology growth: Computing power, 253
  Exponential technology growth: Divorce rate, 257
  Exponential technology growth: Out of wedlock births, 263
  Growth trends, 239
  Population based exponential growth trends, 242
  Technology based exponential growth trends, 248
  Technology cycle in economic growth, 271
GULAG
  Alexander Solzhenitsyn, The Gulag Archipelago, 210
HABSBURG
  Civil war in Germany and Austria (Habsburg Empire), Peace at Augsburg in 1555, 167
  Ottoman siege of Vienna, Habsburg capital, 1683, 211

HADEETH
  Life of Mohammed: Quran (Koran), biographies, Hadeeth (Traditions), 143
HAMAO
  Yasushi Hamao of the University of Southern California's Marshall School of Business, 296 (269)
HARPER
  Abolitionist John Brown and Harper's Ferry insurrection, 39
HAUSA
  Fulani-Hausa Nigerian tribes, 61
HENRI
  Henri Daniel-Rops, 289 (136)
HENRY
  Unionist senators Henry Clay and Daniel Webster, 39
HERNANDO
  Conquistador Hernando Cortes subdues the Aztecs in Mexico in 1519, 158
HEROD
  King Herod, ruler of Judea, 138
HINDUISM
  Converting to Judaism, Christianity, Islam, Hinduism, Buddhism, 141
  Hinduism and life of the Buddha, born 563BC, 150
HINDU
  Major civilizations: Western, Latin American, African, Islamic, Sinic, Hindu, Orthodox, Buddhist, Japanese, 24, 62
HISTORICAL
  Peter Turchin, Historical Dynamics, 287 (60), 291 (162), 295 (219), 296 (242), 296 (243), 296 (244)

HITLER
  Stalin's Hitler's massacre of Ukraine and Crimean Tatars, 1930s-40s, 210
  World War II without Hitler, 50
HOLLAND
  Dutch (Holland, Netherlands) invasion of England, 1688, 166
HOLY
  I baptize thee in the name of the Father, and of the Son, and of the Holy Ghost, 141
  Mohammed adopted Jewish rites, Jerusalem as holy city, 148
  Ottomans fight War with Holy League, treaty at Karlowitz (Carlowitz), 1699, 212
HOMELAND
  Judea, a Jewish homeland, 138
HONEYWELL
  Honeywell Corporation, 253
HOPKINS
  Stephen Hopkins, 27
HORDE
  Barbarian hordes versus Roman Empire, 189
HOROWITZ
  Donald Horowitz, 288 (61)
HORSEPOWER
  Installed horsepower, 251
  Paul Martino, Installed technological horsepower, 296 (251)
HOURANI
  Albert Hourani, 289 (144), 290 (150), 292 (191)
HUGUENOT
  St. Bartholomew's Night Massacre by Catholics of Protestant Huguenots, France, 1572, 168

CONCEPT INDEX

HUMAN
  Computers will become more intelligent than humans, 256, 274
  Human lifespan: average versus maximum, 17
  Singularity: computers more intelligent than humans, 275
  Spread of humans and civilizations from north Africa, 187
HUNTINGTON
  Samuel P. Huntington, Clash of Civilizations and fault line wars, 62
IBM
  IBM's Blue Gene project, 256
IBN
  Asabiya (group solidarity), Ibn Khaldun, Peter Turchin, 288 (62)
IBO
  Owerri Ibo and Onitsha Ibo Nigerian tribes, 61
IDENTIFY
  Identify Group Expansion principle in wars, 64
  Principle of Localization versus Identify Group Expansion principle in wars, 69
III
  Louis-Napoleon Bonaparte, Napoleon III, France, 1852, 182
  Pope arranges for Ivan III the Great to marry Sophia, 201
II
  World War II without Hitler, 50
  World Wars I and II as "Thirty-one Years' War", 88
IMPARTIAL
  United States, impartial policeman of the world, 74

IMPERIALIST
  Japan's imperialistic transformation after Meiji Restoration in 1868, 78
IMPORTANT
  Social importance of polygamy, 149
INCANDESCENT
  Thomas Edison, incandescent light bulb, 1879, 19, 249
INCA
  Francisco Pizzaro overthrows Inca Empire in Peru in 1533, 158
INDEPENDENCE
  Mayflower Compact, an early "declaration of independence", 26
INDEX
  Exponential growth: Standard & Poors 500 Stock Index (S&P), 265
  Tokyo Stock Exchange / Japanese Nikkei Market Index, 268
INDIAN
  600 Indian tribes in America speaking 500 languages, 26
  French and Indian War = Seven Years War ends with Treaty of Paris, 1756-63, 32, 173
  King Philip's War: Colonists versus Indians 1675-78, 25
  Massasoit, chief of the Wampanoag Indians, 27
  Wampanoag, Narragansett, Mohawk Indian tribes, 26
INDIA
  Kashmir fault line between Pakistan and India, 74
  Russia with India versus Pakistan, 75

INDUSTRIAL
  Exponential growth: Dow Jones Industrial Average (DJIA), 264
INNOCENT
  Massacre of the Innocents in Matthew, 139
INQUISITION
  Spanish Inquisition, 155
INSTALL
  Installed horsepower, 251
  Paul Martino, Installed technological horsepower, 296 (251)
INSURANCE
  Panic of 1857 and Ohio Life Insurance and Trust Company, 39, 123
INSURRECTION
  Abolitionist John Brown and Harper's Ferry insurrection, 39
INTEGRATE
  Moore's Law, transistors on integrated circuit, Gordon Moore, Intel Corporation, 1964, 253
INTELLIGENT
  Computers will become more intelligent than humans, 256, 274
  Luddite riots against intelligent computers, 276
  Singularity: computers more intelligent than humans, 275
INTEL
  Moore's Law, transistors on integrated circuit, Gordon Moore, Intel Corporation, 1964, 253
INTENSIFICATION
  War processes: negotiation, compromise, containment, intensification, expansion, 63

INTERNAL
French Commune - internal revolution - Third Republic, 84
INVADE
Invasion of Seljuk Turks from Asia, 1000, 195
Napoleon Bonaparte, French army invade Russia, 1812, 89
INVASION
Dutch (Holland, Netherlands) invasion of England, 1688, 166
Napoleon's invasion of Moscow, 1812, 100
INVENT
Florence Nightingale invents nursing in Crimean War, 206
INVINCIBLE
England defeats Spain's Invincible Armada in 1588, 159
IRAN
Iran / Iraq war in 1980s, 72
IRAQ
Iran / Iraq war in 1980s, 72
Turkey, Iraq, Jordan (Transjordan) from Ottoman Empire, 71
IRRATIONAL
Alan Greenspan and irrational exuberance of 1990s, 115
ISABELLA
Marriage of Isabella and Ferdinand, Spain 1469, 157
ISLAM
Converting to Judaism, Christianity, Islam, Hinduism, Buddhism, 141
Dr. Edip Yuksel, Islamic scholar, 147

Eastern Europe: Islam versus Orthodox Christianity, 185
Major civilizations: Western, Latin American, African, Islamic, Sinic, Hindu, Orthodox, Buddhist, Japanese, 24, 62
Orthodox, Islamic and Western civilizations meet in the Balkans, 64
Shi'ite versus Sunni Islam, 192
Spread of Islam, 191
Teachings of Mohammed and Islam (awakening), 143
Wars of German and Italian Unification and Ottoman's and pan-Islamic movement, 213
ISRAEL
Creation of Israel 1949, 72, 149
Jordan as mediator in Israeli versus Palestinian conflict, 63, 72
Russia recognizes Israel, 210
Zionism and Israel, 215
ISTANBUL
Armenian uprising, Istanbul, 1894-96, 214
Byzantium to Constantinople to Istanbul, 190
Fall of Constantinople (Istanbul) ends Byzantine Empire, 1453, 199
ITALY
Wars of German and Italian Unification and Ottoman's and pan-Islamic movement, 213
IVAN
Ivan the Great captures Novgorod territory, 1485, 201
Ivan the Terrible - Tsar (or Czar) of Russia, 201

Ivan the Terrible conquers Kazan, Astrakhan, 1552-56, 202
Ivan the Terrible massacre in Novgorod, 1570, 202
Ivan the Terrible versus wealthy landowners (boyars), 1564, 202
Pope arranges for Ivan III the Great to marry Sophia, 201
IX
Charles IX, Massacre of St. Bartholomew, 102
JAPAN
Japan colonizes Korea, 1910-45, 235
Japan's imperialistic transformation after Meiji Restoration in 1868, 78
Major civilizations: Western, Latin American, African, Islamic, Sinic, Hindu, Orthodox, Buddhist, Japanese, 24, 62
Oil embargo against Japan in 1933, 79
Tokyo Stock Exchange / Japanese Nikkei Market Index, 268
JERUSALEM
Kingdom of Jerusalem, 196
Mohammed adopted Jewish rites, Jerusalem as holy city, 148
JESUS
Comparing Mohammed and Jesus, 144
Jesus Christ and Christianity (awakening), 139
JEWISH
David Nirenberg, anti-Jewish pogroms in Medieval Spain, 290 (155)
JEW
Arab / Jewish fault line, 14

CONCEPT INDEX

Conversos - Jews converting to Catholicism, 155
European Jews flooding Palestine in 1930s, 72
Jewish law designed for Diaspora of chosen people, 136
Jordan's King Abdullah opposing Jewish migration in 1940s, 72
Judea, a Jewish homeland, 138
Mohammed adopted Jewish rites, Jerusalem as holy city, 148
Palestine versus Jews crisis war, 1936-49, 72, 149
Spain's anti-Jewish pogroms of 1390s and 1480s, 154, 155

JIANPING
Jianping Mei of New York University's Stern School of Business, 296 (269)

JOHN
Abolitionist John Brown and Harper's Ferry insurrection, 39
British General John Burgoyne, 36
John Brown's Body Lies A'mouldering in the Grave, 39
John Wesley, Methodist religion, 31
Sir John Bagot Glubb (Glubb Pasha), 289 (143)

JONES
Exponential growth: Dow Jones Industrial Average (DJIA), 264

JONG-IL
Kim Jong-il, president of North Korea, 235

JORDAN
Jordan as mediator in Israeli versus Palestinian conflict, 63, 72
Jordan's King Abdullah opposing Jewish migration in 1940s, 72
Turkey, Iraq, Jordan (Transjordan) from Ottoman Empire, 71

JOSEF
Josef Stalin and Bolshevik (Communist) Revolution, 210

JOSEPH
Joseph Swan, 19

JUDAISM
Converting to Judaism, Christianity, Islam, Hinduism, Buddhism, 141

JUDAIZE
Conversos accused of Judaizing as false Christians, 155

JUDEA
Judea, a Jewish homeland, 138
King Herod, ruler of Judea, 138

KAHN
Genghis Kahn and Mongols (Tatars) defeated China, 1215, and Russia, 1227, 202

KARLOWITZ
Ottomans fight War with Holy League, treaty at Karlowitz (Carlowitz), 1699, 212

KARL
Karl Marx, Communist Manifesto, 1848, 180

KASHMIR
Kashmir fault line between Pakistan and India, 74

KAYNARJA
Russia (Catherine the Great) war with Ottomans, annexes Crimea, peace treaty at Kuchuk Kaynarja, 1762-83, 206
Russia, Ottomans war, treaty at Kuchuk Kaynarja, 1774, 212

KAZAN
Ivan the Terrible conquers Kazan, Astrakhan, 1552-56, 202

KEMAL
Mustafa Kemal, Attaturk, president of Turkey, 1922, 215

KEY
Francis Scott Key, Star Spangled Banner, 23

KHADIJA
Mohammed's wife Khadija, 144

KHALDUN
Asabiya (group solidarity), Ibn Khaldun, Peter Turchin, 288 (62)

KIEV
Kiev Slav Vladimir adopts Orthodox religion, 988, 198

KIM
Kim Jong-il, president of North Korea, 235

KINGDOM
Kingdom of Jerusalem, 196
Kingdom of Yugoslavia, 1918-1990, 67

KING
Jordan's King Abdullah opposing Jewish migration in 1940s, 72
King Herod, ruler of Judea, 138
King Philip of Macedonia, Alexander the Great, 133
King Philip's War: Colonists versus Indians 1675-78, 25
Martin Luther King, 19

315

Metacomet = King Philip, 27
William and Mary named King and Queen of England, 1688, 166

KONDRATIEFF
Mike Alexander, Kondratieff Cycles and trends, 239

KORAN
Life of Mohammed: Quran (Koran), biographies, Hadeeth (Traditions), 143

KOREA
Japan colonizes Korea, 1910-45, 235
Kim Jong-il, president of North Korea, 235

KUCHUK
Russia (Catherine the Great) war with Ottomans, annexes Crimea, peace treaty at Kuchuk Kaynarja, 1762-83, 206
Russia, Ottomans war, treaty at Kuchuk Kaynarja, 1774, 212

KURD
Turkish civil war with PKK Kurds 1984-2000, 72

KURGIN
Prince Kurgin, 98

KURZWEIL
Ray Kurzweil, Law of Accelerating Returns, 296 (255)

LADEN
Osama bin Laden, 39

LANDOWNER
Ivan the Terrible versus wealthy landowners (boyars), 1564, 202

LANGUAGE
600 Indian tribes in America speaking 500 languages, 26
Spread of Arabic language, 193

LATIN
Major civilizations: Western, Latin American, African, Islamic, Sinic, Hindu, Orthodox, Buddhist, Japanese, 24, 62

LAURISTON
Count Lauriston, 98

LAW
Jewish law designed for Diaspora of chosen people, 136
Moore's Law, transistors on integrated circuit, Gordon Moore, Intel Corporation, 1964, 253
Ray Kurzweil, Law of Accelerating Returns, 296 (255)
Ulozhenie, Russian law makes peasants into slaves, 1649, 204

LEAGUE
Delian League in ancient Greece, 131
Ottomans fight War with Holy League, treaty at Karlowitz (Carlowitz), 1699, 212

LENGTH
Length of 80-year cycle, 17

LENIN
Nicolai Lenin and Bolshevik (Communist) Revolution, 208

LEV
Lev Tolstoy, War and Peace, 89
Lev Tolstoy, born 1825, fought in Crimean War in 1850s, 91

LIBBY
Artist Libby Chase, xxi

LIBERTY
Sons of Liberty, 34

LIES
John Brown's Body Lies A'mouldering in the Grave, 39

LIFESPAN
Human lifespan: average versus maximum, 17

LIFE
Hinduism and life of the Buddha, born 563BC, 150
Life of Mohammed: Quran (Koran), biographies, Hadeeth (Traditions), 143
Nomadic Bedouin tribes - perpetual war as a way of life, 145
Panic of 1857 and Ohio Life Insurance and Trust Company, 39, 123

LIGHT
Artificial light sources, 249
Lord Alfred Tennyson poem, The Charge of the Light Brigade, Crimean War, 207
Paul Martino, artificial light technologies, 296 (249)
Thomas Edison, incandescent light bulb, 1879, 19, 249

LIMITATION
Limitations of Generational Dynamics forecasting, xviii, 76

LINE
Arab / Jewish fault line, 14
Cyprus - fault line between Greece and Turkey, 131
Fault line versus generation gap, 8
Kashmir fault line between Pakistan and India, 74
Samuel P. Huntington, Clash of Civilizations and fault line wars, 62

LIVONIA
  Russia, Poland, Sweden, Denmark fight Livonian War on Baltic, 1557, 201
LOCALIZATION
  Principle of Localization, 59, versus Identify Group Expansion principle in wars 69
LORD
  Lord Alfred Tennyson poem, The Charge of the Light Brigade, Crimean War, 207
LORRAINE
  France cedes Alsace and Lorraine to Germany, 1871, 182
LOTUS
  Lotus Development Corporation, 118
LOUIS-NAPOLEON
  Louis-Napoleon Bonaparte, Napoleon III, France, 1852, 182
LUDDITE
  Luddite riots against intelligent computers, 276
LUTHER
  Martin Luther King, 19
MACEDONIA
  Alexander the Great of Macedonia, 188
  King Philip of Macedonia, Alexander the Great, 133
MAGELLAN
  Ferdinand Magellan's expedition to circumnavigate the globe in 1522, 158
MAJOR
  Ariel Sharon and Yasser Arafat cooperating to prevent major Mideast war, 73
  Deaths in major American wars, 44
  Major civilizations: Western, Latin American, African, Islamic, Sinic, Hindu, Orthodox, Buddhist, Japanese, 24, 62
  Thousands of tribes merged to 250 nations and 9 major civilizations, 24
MAKE
  Ulozhenie, Russian law makes peasants into slaves, 1649, 204
MALTHUS
  Thomas Roberts Malthus, Essay on Population, 1798, 245
MANAGEMENT
  Yexiao Xu of the School of Management at University of Texas at Dallas, 296 (269)
MANIFESTO
  Karl Marx, Communist Manifesto, 1848, 180
MANIFEST
  America's manifest destiny: freedom and democracy, xiv
  Spain's sense of manifest destiny, Manuel Fernandez Alvarez, University of Salamanca, 291 (157)
MANUEL
  Spain's sense of manifest destiny, Manuel Fernandez Alvarez, University of Salamanca, 291 (157)
MARKET
  Tokyo Stock Exchange / Japanese Nikkei Market Index, 268
  Tulipomania market bubble panic in 1637, 79, 120, 171
MARRIAGE
  Andrew J Cherlin, Marriage and Divorce, 296 (257)
  Marriage of Isabella and Ferdinand, Spain 1469, 157
MARRY
  Pope arranges for Ivan III the Great to marry Sophia, 201
MARSHALL
  Yasushi Hamao of the University of Southern California's Marshall School of Business, 296 (269)
MARTINO
  Paul Martino, Installed technological horsepower, 296 (251)
  Paul Martino, artificial light technologies, 296 (249)
  Paul Martino, speed of combat aircraft, 296 (250)
MARTIN
  Martin Luther King, 19
MARX
  Karl Marx, Communist Manifesto, 1848, 180
MARY
  William and Mary College, 166
  William and Mary named King and Queen of England, 1688, 166
MASSACRE
  Charles IX, Massacre of St. Bartholomew, 102
  Ivan the Terrible massacre in Novgorod, 1570, 202
  Massacre of the Innocents in Matthew, 139
  St. Bartholomew's Night Massacre by Catholics of Protestant Huguenots, France, 1572, 168
  Stalin's Hitler's massacre of Ukraine and Crimean Tatars, 1930s-40s, 210
MASSASOIT
  Massasoit, chief of the Wampanoag Indians, 27

MASS
  Mass expulsions of Muslims from Spain, 1568, 158
MATTHEW
  Massacre of the Innocents in Matthew, 139
MAXIMUM
  Human lifespan: average versus maximum, 17
MAX
  Prince Max von Baden on World War I, 289 (87)
MAYFLOWER
  Mayflower Compact, an early "declaration of independence", 26
MECCA
  Mohammed threatened by Quraish of Mecca, 144
  Mohammed's conquest of Mecca and Quraish, 630, 149
MEDIATOR
  Jordan as mediator in Israeli versus Palestinian conflict, 63, 72
MEDIEVAL
  David Nirenberg, anti-Jewish pogroms in Medieval Spain, 290 (155)
MEDINA
  Mohammed flees to Medina (Yathrib) in 622, 144
MEET
  Orthodox, Islamic and Western civilizations meet in the Balkans, 64
MEIJI
  Japan's imperialistic transformation after Meiji Restoration in 1868, 78
MEI
  Jianping Mei of New York University's Stern School of Business, 296 (269)

MEMORANDUM
  Memorandum No. 178, 92
MEMORY
  Crisis wars and cultural memory, 81
MERGE
  Merger of timelines in Thirty Years' War, 1618-48, 168
  Merging timelines, 18
  Thousands of tribes merged to 250 nations and 9 major civilizations, 24
MESSENGER
  There is no God except Allah, and Mohammed is the Messenger of Allah, 141, 193
MESSIAH
  Professor Gene Chase, Messiah College, 139
METACOMET
  Metacomet = King Philip, 27
METHODIST
  John Wesley, Methodist religion, 31
METHODOLOGY
  Generational Dynamics Forecasting Methodology, 76
MEXICO
  Conquistador Hernando Cortes subdues the Aztecs in Mexico in 1519, 158
  Crisis war in Mexico, 57
MID-CYCLE
  Crisis Wars versus Mid-Cycle Wars, 80
  Russia's mid-cycle wars with western Europe, 204
MIDEAST
  Ariel Sharon and Yasser Arafat cooperating to prevent major Mideast war, 73
  Causes and timing of new Mideast war, 73

  Mideast crisis to Mideast crisis, 14
MIGRATE
  Jordan's King Abdullah opposing Jewish migration in 1940s, 72
MIKE
  Mike Alexander, Kondratieff Cycles and trends, 239
MISSOURI
  Missouri Compromise - slavery 1820, 38
MOHAMMED
  Al-Abbas, uncle of Mohammed, 192
  Comparing Mohammed and Jesus, 144
  Life of Mohammed: Quran (Koran), biographies, Hadeeth (Traditions), 143
  Mohammed / polygamy - multiple wives, 149
  Mohammed adopted Jewish rites, Jerusalem as holy city, 148
  Mohammed flees to Medina (Yathrib) in 622, 144
  Mohammed threatened by Quraish of Mecca, 144
  Mohammed's conquest of Mecca and Quraish, 630, 149
  Mohammed's wife Khadija, 144
  Teachings of Mohammed and Islam (awakening), 143
  There is no God except Allah, and Mohammed is the Messenger of Allah, 141, 193
MOHAWK
  Mohawk war, 1663-80, 28
  Wampanoag, Narragansett, Mohawk Indian tribes, 26
MONETARY
  Federal Reserve using monetary policy to prevent depression, 124, 272

MONGOL
  Genghis Kahn and Mongols (Tatars) defeated China, 1215, and Russia, 1227, 202
MOORE
  Moore's Law, transistors on integrated circuit, Gordon Moore, Intel Corporation, 1964, 253
MORE
  Computers will become more intelligent than humans, 256, 274
  Singularity: computers more intelligent than humans, 275
MOSCOW
  Cossacks offer Moscow Crimean Tatar fortress, 1642, 203
  Napoleon's invasion of Moscow, 1812, 100
MOVEMENT
  Wars of German and Italian Unification and Ottoman's and pan-Islamic movement, 213
MULTIPLE
  Mohammed / polygamy - multiple wives, 149
MUSLIM
  Mass expulsions of Muslims from Spain, 1568, 158
  Muslim conquest of Spain in 711, 156
  Muslim tribe chieftain Osman and Ottoman Empire, 199
  Muslims capture Constantinople in 1453, 157
  Reconquest of Spain from the Muslims in 1492, 156
MUSTAFA
  Mustafa Kemal, Attaturk, president of Turkey, 1922, 215

MUST
  Complexity Theory: Why Communism and Socialism must fail, 246
NAME
  I baptize thee in the name of the Father, and of the Son, and of the Holy Ghost, 141
  William and Mary named King and Queen of England, 1688, 166
NANOTECHNOLOGY
  Nanotechnology and DNA protein folding technology for computers, 256
NAPOLEON
  Congress of Vienna ends Napoleonic wars, 1815, 179
  French Revolution and Napoleonic Wars, 1789-1815, 173
  Louis-Napoleon Bonaparte, Napoleon III, France, 1852, 182
  Napoleon Bonaparte, French army invade Russia, 1812, 89
  Napoleon's invasion of Moscow, 1812, 100
  Russia and Napoleonic wars, 204, 206
NARRAGANSETT
  Wampanoag, Narragansett, Mohawk Indian tribes, 26
NASDAQ
  Nasdaq crash in 2000, 123
NATION
  Character of a nation, 66
  Thousands of tribes merged to 250 nations and 9 major civilizations, 24
  Wolfgang Schivelbusch - transformation of defeated nation, 288 (82)

NEGOTIATION
  War processes: negotiation, compromise, containment, intensification, expansion, 63
NETHERLANDS
  Dutch (Holland, Netherlands) invasion of England, 1688, 166
NEW
  Causes and timing of new Mideast war, 73
  Christopher Columbus discovers New World in 1492, 156
  Jianping Mei of New York University's Stern School of Business, 296 (269)
  New 1930s style Great Depression, 114
  Russia becomes new Roman Empire, 201
NICOLAI
  Nicolai Lenin and Bolshevik (Communist) Revolution, 208
NIGERIA
  Fulani-Hausa Nigerian tribes, 61
  Owerri Ibo and Onitsha Ibo Nigerian tribes, 61
NIGHTINGALE
  Florence Nightingale invents nursing in Crimean War, 206
NIGHT
  St. Bartholomew's Night Massacre by Catholics of Protestant Huguenots, France, 1572, 168
NIKKEI
  Tokyo Stock Exchange / Japanese Nikkei Market Index, 268

NIKON
  Russian Orthodox Church Great Schism - Nikon and Old Believers, 1666, 204
NIRENBERG
  David Nirenberg, anti-Jewish pogroms in Medieval Spain, 290 (155)
NIXON
  Vietnam War and resignation of Richard Nixon, 84
NOMAD
  Nomadic Bedouin tribes - perpetual war as a way of life, 145
NON-PROSELYTIZING
  Proselytizing and Non-Proselytizing religions, 141
NORTHERN
  Russia (Peter the Great) and Sweden fight the Great Northern War, 1700-1720, 205
NORTH
  Kim Jong-il, president of North Korea, 235
  Spread of humans and civilizations from north Africa, 187
NOVGOROD
  Ivan the Great captures Novgorod territory, 1485, 201
  Ivan the Terrible massacre in Novgorod, 1570, 202
NO
  There is no God except Allah, and Mohammed is the Messenger of Allah, 141, 193
NUNEZ
  Vasco Nunez de Balboa reaches Pacific in 1513, 158
NURSE
  Florence Nightingale invents nursing in Crimean War, 206

OFFER
  Cossacks offer Moscow Crimean Tatar fortress, 1642, 203
OHIO
  Panic of 1857 and Ohio Life Insurance and Trust Company, 39, 123
OIL
  Oil embargo against Japan in 1933, 79
OLDENBURG
  Duke of Oldenburg, 92
OLD
  Crusty old bureaucracy theory, 125, in China 218
  Russian Orthodox Church Great Schism - Nikon and Old Believers, 1666, 204
ONITSHA
  Owerri Ibo and Onitsha Ibo Nigerian tribes, 61
OPPOSE
  Jordan's King Abdullah opposing Jewish migration in 1940s, 72
ORTHODOX
  Eastern Europe: Islam versus Orthodox Christianity, 185
  Kiev Slav Vladimir adopts Orthodox religion, 988, 198
  Major civilizations: Western, Latin American, African, Islamic, Sinic, Hindu, Orthodox, Buddhist, Japanese, 24, 62
  Orthodox, Islamic and Western civilizations meet in the Balkans, 64
  Russian Orthodox Church Great Schism - Nikon and Old Believers, 1666, 204
  Russian Orthodox Church and Bolshevik (Communist) Revolution, 209

Separation / Schism of Orthodox and Catholic Christianity, 190, 196
OSAMA
  Osama bin Laden, 39
OSMAN
  Muslim tribe chieftain Osman and Ottoman Empire, 199
OTTOMAN
  Muslim tribe chieftain Osman and Ottoman Empire, 199
  Ottoman Freedom Foundation, Committee of Union and Progress, Young Turks, 1889-1908, 213
  Ottoman siege of Vienna, Habsburg capital, 1683, 211
  Ottomans fight Crimean War, 1853-56, 213
  Ottomans fight War with Holy League, treaty at Karlowitz (Carlowitz), 1699, 212
  Russia (Catherine the Great) war with Ottomans, annexes Crimea, peace treaty at Kuchuk Kaynarja, 1762-83, 206
  Russia, Ottomans war, treaty at Kuchuk Kaynarja, 1774, 212
  Timur defeats Ottomans, 1402, 199
  Turkey, Iraq, Jordan (Transjordan) from Ottoman Empire, 71
  Wars of German and Italian Unification and Ottoman's and pan-Islamic movement, 213
  World War I - crisis war for Balkans (Yugoslavia), Turkey (Ottoman Empire), Russia (Bolshevik Communist Revolution), 85

CONCEPT INDEX

Young Turks rebellion against Ottomans, 1908, 68, 214
OTTO
  Prussian Chancellor Otto von Bismarck, 1862, 182
OUT
  Exponential technology growth: Out of wedlock births, 263
OVERTHROW
  Francisco Pizzaro overthrows Inca Empire in Peru in 1533, 158
OWERRI
  Owerri Ibo and Onitsha Ibo Nigerian tribes, 61
PACIFIC
  Vasco Nunez de Balboa reaches Pacific in 1513, 158
PAKISTAN
  Kashmir fault line between Pakistan and India, 74
  Russia with India versus Pakistan, 75
PALESTINE
  European Jews flooding Palestine in 1930s, 72
  Jordan as mediator in Israeli versus Palestinian conflict, 63, 72
  Palestine versus Jews crisis war, 1936-49, 72, 149
PAN-ISLAMIC
  Wars of German and Italian Unification and Ottoman's and pan-Islamic movement, 213
PANIC
  Alexander Fordyce and Panic of 1772, 122
  Ayr Bank of Scotland and Panic of 1772, 122
  English banking crisis and Panic of 1772, 34, 79, 122

Panic of 1857 and Civil War, 78
Panic of 1857 and Ohio Life Insurance and Trust Company, 39, 123
Tulipomania market bubble panic in 1637, 79, 120, 171
PARIS
  French and Indian War = Seven Years War ends with Treaty of Paris, 1756-63, 32, 173
PARTHENON
  Ancient Greece: the Acropolis, the Parthenon, Pericles, Thucydides, Socrates, Aristophanes, Aeschylus, Sophocles and Euripides, 129
  Pericles commissions Parthenon and Acropolis, 132
PARTY
  Tea Act and Boston Tea Party, 1773, 34
PASHA
  Sir John Bagot Glubb (Glubb Pasha), 289 (143)
PATRIOTIC
  Great Patriotic War, 210
PAUL
  Paul Martino, Installed technological horsepower, 296 (251)
  Paul Martino, artificial light technologies, 296 (249)
  Paul Martino, speed of combat aircraft, 296 (250)
PEACE
  Civil war in Germany and Austria (Habsburg Empire), Peace at Augsburg in 1555, 167
  Lev Tolstoy, War and Peace, 89

Peace of Westphalia ends Thirty Years' War in 1648, 171
Russia (Catherine the Great) war with Ottomans, annexes Crimea, peace treaty at Kuchuk Kaynarja, 1762-83, 206
PEASANT
  Stephen Razin, Russia peasant revolt, 1669-71, 204
  Ulozhenie, Russian law makes peasants into slaves, 1649, 204
PELOPONNESIAN
  Peloponnesian War between Athens and Sparta, 431BC, 133
PEOPLE
  Jewish law designed for Diaspora of chosen people, 136
PERICLES
  Ancient Greece: the Acropolis, the Parthenon, Pericles, Thucydides, Socrates, Aristophanes, Aeschylus, Sophocles and Euripides, 129
  Pericles commissions Parthenon and Acropolis, 132
PERIOD
  Austerity, awakening, and unraveling periods, 10
PERPETUAL
  Nomadic Bedouin tribes - perpetual war as a way of life, 145
PERSIAN
  Persian War with ancient Greece, 131
PERU
  Francisco Pizzaro overthrows Inca Empire in Peru in 1533, 158

PETER
  Asabiya (group solidarity), Ibn Khaldun, Peter Turchin, 288 (62)
  Peter Turchin, Historical Dynamics, 287 (60), 291 (162), 295 (219), 296 (242), 296 (243), 296 (244)
  Russia (Peter the Great) and Sweden fight the Great Northern War, 1700-1720, 205
PHILIP
  King Philip of Macedonia, Alexander the Great, 133
  King Philip's War: Colonists versus Indians 1675-78, 25
  Metacomet = King Philip, 27
PIZZARO
  Francisco Pizzaro overthrows Inca Empire in Peru in 1533, 158
PKK
  Turkish civil war with PKK Kurds 1984-2000, 72
POEM
  Lord Alfred Tennyson poem, The Charge of the Light Brigade, Crimean War, 207
POGROM
  David Nirenberg, anti-Jewish pogroms in Medieval Spain, 290 (155)
  Spain's anti-Jewish pogroms of 1390s and 1480s, 154, 155
POLAND
  Russia, Poland, Sweden, Denmark fight Livonian War on Baltic, 1557, 201
POLICEMAN
  United States, impartial policeman of the world, 74
POLICY
  Federal Reserve using monetary policy to prevent depression, 124, 272

POLITICS,
  Cyclic trends: fashion, political economic, generational, 239
POLITICS
  Tsar Alexander I political reforms, 206
POLYGAMY
  Mohammed / polygamy - multiple wives, 149
  Social importance of polygamy, 149
POORS
  Exponential growth: Standard & Poors 500 Stock Index (S&P), 265
POPE
  Pope arranges for Ivan III the Great to marry Sophia, 201
POPULATION
  Population based exponential growth trends, 242
  Thomas Roberts Malthus, Essay on Population, 1798, 245
POWER
  Exponential technology growth: Computing power, 253
PRESIDENT
  Kim Jong-il, president of North Korea, 235
  Mustafa Kemal, Attaturk, president of Turkey, 1922, 215
PREVENT
  Ariel Sharon and Yasser Arafat cooperating to prevent major Mideast war, 73
  Federal Reserve using monetary policy to prevent depression, 124, 272
  Securities Exchange Commission (SEC) failed to prevent 1990s bubble, 124

PRICE
  S&ampPP Price Earnings ratio, 266
PRINCE
  Prince Kurgin, 98
  Prince Max von Baden on World War I, 289 (87)
PRINCIPLE
  Identify Group Expansion principle in wars, 64
  Principle of Localization, 59, versus Identify Group Expansion principle in wars 69
PROCESS
  War processes: negotiation, compromise, containment, intensification, expansion, 63
PROFESSOR
  Professor Gene Chase, Messiah College, 139
PROGRESS
  Ottoman Freedom Foundation, Committee of Union and Progress, Young Turks, 1889-1908, 213
PROJECT
  IBM's Blue Gene project, 256
PROSELYTIZE
  Proselytizing and Non-Proselytizing religions, 141
PROTEIN
  Nanotechnology and DNA protein folding technology for computers, 256
PROTESTANT
  St. Bartholomew's Night Massacre by Catholics of Protestant Huguenots, France, 1572, 168
PRUSSIA
  Prussian Chancellor Otto von Bismarck, 1862, 182

PUGACHEV
- Russia (Catherine the Great) Pugachev's Rebellion, 1773-75, 206
- Russia's Pugachev Rebellion and Catherine the Great, 1773, 96

QUEEN
- William and Mary named King and Queen of England, 1688, 166

QURAISH
- Mohammed threatened by Quraish of Mecca, 144
- Mohammed's conquest of Mecca and Quraish, 630, 149

QURAN
- Life of Mohammed: Quran (Koran), biographies, Hadeeth (Traditions), 143

RATE
- Exponential technology growth: Divorce rate, 257

RATIO
- S&ampPP Price Earnings ratio, 266

RAY
- Ray Kurzweil, Law of Accelerating Returns, 296 (255)

RAZIN
- Stephen Razin, Russia peasant revolt, 1669-71, 204

REACH
- Vasco Nunez de Balboa reaches Pacific in 1513, 158

REBELLION
- Russia (Catherine the Great) Pugachev's Rebellion, 1773-75, 206
- Russia's Pugachev Rebellion and Catherine the Great, 1773, 96
- Scottish rebellion and English civil war, 1638-60, 165
- Young Turks rebellion against Ottomans, 1908, 68, 214

RECOGNIZE
- Russia recognizes Israel, 210

RECONQUEST
- Reconquest of Spain from the Muslims in 1492, 156

REFORM
- Tsar Alexander I political reforms, 206

RELIGION
- John Wesley, Methodist religion, 31
- Kiev Slav Vladimir adopts Orthodox religion, 988, 198
- Proselytizing and Non-Proselytizing religions, 141
- Russian freedom of religion, 211
- Top-down and bottom-up religions, 142

REPUBLIC
- French Commune - internal revolution - Third Republic, 84

RESERVE
- Federal Reserve using monetary policy to prevent depression, 124, 272

RESIGN
- Vietnam War and resignation of Richard Nixon, 84

RESTORATION
- Japan's imperialistic transformation after Meiji Restoration in 1868, 78

RETURN
- Ray Kurzweil, Law of Accelerating Returns, 296 (255)

REVOLT
- Stephen Razin, Russia peasant revolt, 1669-71, 204

REVOLUTIONARY
- Revolutionary War to Civil War, 12

REVOLUTION
- American Revolutionary War 1772-82, 32
- Bankruptcy triggers French Revolution of 1789, 79, 93, 174
- French Commune - internal revolution - Third Republic, 84
- French Revolution and Napoleonic Wars, 1789-1815, 173
- French Revolution, 1789, 93
- Josef Stalin and Bolshevik (Communist) Revolution, 210
- Nicolai Lenin and Bolshevik (Communist) Revolution, 208
- Revolutionary war and slavery compromise, 36
- Revolutions of 1848, 179
- Russia's Bloody Sunday and Bolshevik (Communist) Revolution, 1905-27, 208
- Russia's Communist transformation by World War I and Bolshevik Revolution in 1917, 78
- Russian Orthodox Church and Bolshevik (Communist) Revolution, 209
- World War I - crisis war for Balkans (Yugoslavia), Turkey (Ottoman Empire), Russia (Bolshevik Communist Revolution), 85

RICHARD
- Vietnam War and resignation of Richard Nixon, 84

RIOT
- Luddite riots against intelligent computers, 276

RISE
  Rise and fall of Roman Empire, 187
  Rise of civilization consciousness, 63
RITE
  Mohammed adopted Jewish rites, Jerusalem as holy city, 148
ROBERTS
  Thomas Roberts Malthus, Essay on Population, 1798, 245
ROMAN
  Barbarian hordes versus Roman Empire, 189
  Rise and fall of Roman Empire, 187
  Russia becomes new Roman Empire, 201
RULE
  King Herod, ruler of Judea, 138
RUSSIA
  Genghis Kahn and Mongols (Tatars) defeated China, 1215, and Russia, 1227, 202
  Ivan the Terrible - Tsar (or Czar) of Russia, 201
  Napoleon Bonaparte, French army invade Russia, 1812, 89
  Russia (Catherine the Great) Pugachev's Rebellion, 1773-75, 206
  Russia (Catherine the Great) war with Ottomans, annexes Crimea, peace treaty at Kuchuk Kaynarja, 1762-83, 206
  Russia (Peter the Great) and Sweden fight the Great Northern War, 1700-1720, 205

Russia Crimean War and Emancipation Edict frees serfs, 1853-61, 206
Russia and Napoleonic wars, 204, 206
Russia becomes new Roman Empire, 201
Russia recognizes Israel, 210
Russia with India versus Pakistan, 75
Russia's Bloody Sunday and Bolshevik (Communist) Revolution, 1905-27, 208
Russia's Communist transformation by World War I and Bolshevik Revolution in 1917, 78
Russia's Pugachev Rebellion and Catherine the Great, 1773, 96
Russia's mid-cycle wars with western Europe, 204
Russia, Ottomans war, treaty at Kuchuk Kaynarja, 1774, 212
Russia, Poland, Sweden, Denmark fight Livonian War on Baltic, 1557, 201
Russian Orthodox Church Great Schism - Nikon and Old Believers, 1666, 204
Russian Orthodox Church and Bolshevik (Communist) Revolution, 209
Russian freedom of religion, 211
Stephen Razin, Russia peasant revolt, 1669-71, 204
Tsar Alexander of Russia, 92, 95
Ulozhenie, Russian law makes peasants into slaves, 1649, 204
World War I - crisis war for Balkans (Yugoslavia), Turkey (Ottoman Empire), Russia (Bolshevik Communist Revolution), 85

SACK
  Catholic sacking of Constantinople, 1204, 197
SAINT
  Charles IX, Massacre of St. Bartholomew, 102
  St. Bartholomew's Night Massacre by Catholics of Protestant Huguenots, France, 1572, 168
SALAMANCA
  Spain's sense of manifest destiny, Manuel Fernandez Alvarez, University of Salamanca, 291 (157)
SALEM
  Salem Witch Trials 1692, 29
SAMPPP
  S&ampPP Price Earnings ratio, 266
SAMUEL
  Samuel P. Huntington, Clash of Civilizations and fault line wars, 62
SANTAYANA
  George Santayana, 2
SCAPEGOAT
  Scapegoating after defeat, 84
SCHISM
  Russian Orthodox Church Great Schism - Nikon and Old Believers, 1666, 204
  Separation / Schism of Orthodox and Catholic Christianity, 190, 196
SCHIVELBUSCH
  Wolfgang Schivelbusch - transformation of defeated nation, 288 (82)
SCHOLAR
  Dr. Edip Yuksel, Islamic scholar, 147

SCHOOL
 Jianping Mei of New York University's Stern School of Business, 296 (269)
 Yasushi Hamao of the University of Southern California's Marshall School of Business, 296 (269)
 Yexiao Xu of the School of Management at University of Texas at Dallas, 296 (269)
SCOTLAND
 Ayr Bank of Scotland and Panic of 1772, 122
 Scottish rebellion and English civil war, 1638-60, 165
SCOTT
 Francis Scott Key, Star Spangled Banner, 23
SECURITIES
 Securities Exchange Commission (SEC) failed to prevent 1990s bubble, 124
SEC
 Securities Exchange Commission (SEC) failed to prevent 1990s bubble, 124
SELJUK
 Invasion of Seljuk Turks from Asia, 1000, 195
SENATOR
 Unionist senators Henry Clay and Daniel Webster, 39
SENSE
 Spain's sense of manifest destiny, Manuel Fernandez Alvarez, University of Salamanca, 291 (157)
SEPARATION
 Separation / Schism of Orthodox and Catholic Christianity, 190, 196
SERF
 Russia Crimean War and Emancipation Edict frees serfs, 1853-61, 206

SEVEN
 French and Indian War = Seven Years War ends with Treaty of Paris, 1756-63, 32, 173
SHARON
 Ariel Sharon and Yasser Arafat cooperating to prevent major Mideast war, 73
SHIITE
 Shi'ite versus Sunni Islam, 192
SIEGE
 Ottoman siege of Vienna, Habsburg capital, 1683, 211
SILIHDAR
 Silihdar Tarihi, 294 (212)
SINGULARITY
 Singularity: computers more intelligent than humans, 275
SINIC
 Major civilizations: Western, Latin American, African, Islamic, Sinic, Hindu, Orthodox, Buddhist, Japanese, 24, 62
SIR
 Sir John Bagot Glubb (Glubb Pasha), 289 (143)
SLAVE
 Missouri Compromise - slavery 1820, 38
 Revolutionary war and slavery compromise, 36
 Ulozhenie, Russian law makes peasants into slaves, 1649, 204
SLAV
 Kiev Slav Vladimir adopts Orthodox religion, 988, 198
SMOLENSK
 Battle at Smolensk, 98

SOCIALISM
 Complexity Theory: Why Communism and Socialism must fail, 246
SOCIAL
 Social importance of polygamy, 149
SOCRATES
 Ancient Greece: the Acropolis, the Parthenon, Pericles, Thucydides, Socrates, Aristophanes, Aeschylus, Sophocles and Euripides, 129
SOLIDARITY
 Asabiya (group solidarity), Ibn Khaldun, Peter Turchin, 288 (62)
SOLZHENITSYN
 Alexander Solzhenitsyn, The Gulag Archipelago, 210
SON
 I baptize thee in the name of the Father, and of the Son, and of the Holy Ghost, 141
 Sons of Liberty, 34
SOPHIA
 Pope arranges for Ivan III the Great to marry Sophia, 201
SOPHOCLES
 Ancient Greece: the Acropolis, the Parthenon, Pericles, Thucydides, Socrates, Aristophanes, Aeschylus, Sophocles and Euripides, 129
SOURCE
 Artificial light sources, 249
SOUTHERN
 Yasushi Hamao of the University of Southern California's Marshall School of Business, 296 (269)

SPAIN
  David Nirenberg, anti-Jewish pogroms in Medieval Spain, 290 (155)
  England defeats Spain's Invincible Armada in 1588, 159
  Golden age of Spain in 1500s, 156
  Marriage of Isabella and Ferdinand, Spain 1469, 157
  Mass expulsions of Muslims from Spain, 1568, 158
  Muslim conquest of Spain in 711, 156
  Reconquest of Spain from the Muslims in 1492, 156
  Spain's anti-Jewish pogroms of 1390s and 1480s, 154, 155
  Spain's sense of manifest destiny, Manuel Fernandez Alvarez, University of Salamanca, 291 (157)
  Spanish Inquisition, 155
  Treaty at Utrecht ends War of Spanish Succession, 1714, 173
  War of Spanish Succession, 1701-14, 93, 95, 172
SPANGLE
  Francis Scott Key, Star Spangled Banner, 23
SPARTA
  Golden Age of Ancient Athens Greece and Sparta (awakening), 129
  Peloponnesian War between Athens and Sparta, 431BC, 133
SPEAK
  600 Indian tribes in America speaking 500 languages, 26
SPEED
  Paul Martino, speed of combat aircraft, 296 (250)
  Speed of combat aircraft, 250

SPREAD
  Spread of Arabic language, 193
  Spread of Islam, 191
  Spread of humans and civilizations from north Africa, 187
SP
  Exponential growth: Standard & Poors 500 Stock Index (S&P), 265
SQUARE
  China's Tiananmen Square Awakening, 129, 232
STALIN
  Josef Stalin and Bolshevik (Communist) Revolution, 210
  Stalin's Hitler's massacre of Ukraine and Crimean Tatars, 1930s-40s, 210
STAMP
  Stamp Act 1765, 33
STANDARD
  Exponential growth: Standard & Poors 500 Stock Index (S&P), 265
STAR
  Francis Scott Key, Star Spangled Banner, 23
STATES
  United States, impartial policeman of the world, 74
STEPHEN
  Stephen Hopkins, 27
  Stephen Razin, Russia peasant revolt, 1669-71, 204
STERN
  Jianping Mei of New York University's Stern School of Business, 296 (269)
STOCK
  Exponential growth: Standard & Poors 500 Stock Index (S&P), 265

  Exponential growth: forecasting stock trends, 263
  Tokyo Stock Exchange / Japanese Nikkei Market Index, 268
STYLE
  New 1930s style Great Depression, 114
SUBDUE
  Conquistador Hernando Cortes subdues the Aztecs in Mexico in 1519, 158
SUCCESSION
  Treaty at Utrecht ends War of Spanish Succession, 1714, 173
  War of Spanish Succession, 1701-14, 93, 95, 172
SUGAR
  Sugar Act and Currency Act 1764, 33
SUNDAY
  Russia's Bloody Sunday and Bolshevik (Communist) Revolution, 1905-27, 208
SUNNI
  Shi'ite versus Sunni Islam, 192
SWAN
  Joseph Swan, 19
SWEDEN
  Russia (Peter the Great) and Sweden fight the Great Northern War, 1700-1720, 205
  Russia, Poland, Sweden, Denmark fight Livonian War on Baltic, 1557, 201
SYSTEM
  Continental System, 92, 93
TARIHI
  Silihdar Tarihi, 294 (212)

CONCEPT INDEX

TATAR
  Cossacks offer Moscow Crimean Tatar fortress, 1642, 203
  Genghis Kahn and Mongols (Tatars) defeated China, 1215, and Russia, 1227, 202
  Stalin's Hitler's massacre of Ukraine and Crimean Tatars, 1930s-40s, 210
TEACHING
  Teachings of Mohammed and Islam (awakening), 143
TEA
  Tea Act and Boston Tea Party, 1773, 34
TECHNOLOGY
  Exponential technology growth: Computing power, 253
  Exponential technology growth: Divorce rate, 257
  Exponential technology growth: Out of wedlock births, 263
  Nanotechnology and DNA protein folding technology for computers, 256
  Paul Martino, Installed technological horsepower, 296 (251)
  Paul Martino, artificial light technologies, 296 (249)
  Technology based exponential growth trends, 248
  Technology cycle in economic growth, 271
TENNYSON
  Lord Alfred Tennyson poem, The Charge of the Light Brigade, Crimean War, 207
TERRIBLE
  Ivan the Terrible - Tsar (or Czar) of Russia, 201

Ivan the Terrible conquers Kazan, Astrakhan, 1552-56, 202
Ivan the Terrible massacre in Novgorod, 1570, 202
Ivan the Terrible versus wealthy landowners (boyars), 1564, 202
TERRITORY
  Ivan the Great captures Novgorod territory, 1485, 201
TERROR
  Crisis wars: visceral feeling of anxiety, terror and fury, 3
TEXAS
  Yexiao Xu of the School of Management at University of Texas at Dallas, 296 (269)
THAN
  Computers will become more intelligent than humans, 256, 274
  Singularity: computers more intelligent than humans, 275
THEE
  I baptize thee in the name of the Father, and of the Son, and of the Holy Ghost, 141
THEORY
  Complexity Theory: Why Communism and Socialism must fail, 246
  Crusty old bureaucracy theory, 125, in China 218
THERE
  There is no God except Allah, and Mohammed is the Messenger of Allah, 141, 193
THIRD
  French Commune - internal revolution - Third Republic, 84
THIRTY-ONE
  World Wars I and II as "Thirty-one Years' War", 88

THIRTY
  Merger of timelines in Thirty Years' War, 1618-48, 168
  Peace of Westphalia ends Thirty Years' War in 1648, 171
THOMAS
  Thomas Edison, incandescent light bulb, 1879, 19, 249
  Thomas Roberts Malthus, Essay on Population, 1798, 245
THOUSAND
  Thousands of tribes merged to 250 nations and 9 major civilizations, 24
THREATEN
  Mohammed threatened by Quraish of Mecca, 144
THUCYDIDES
  Ancient Greece: the Acropolis, the Parthenon, Pericles, Thucydides, Socrates, Aristophanes, Aeschylus, Sophocles and Euripides, 129
TIANANMEN
  China's Tiananmen Square Awakening, 129, 232
TIMELINE
  Merger of timelines in Thirty Years' War, 1618-48, 168
  Merging timelines, 18
TIME
  Cause versus timing of war, 13
TIMING
  Causes and timing of new Mideast war, 73
  Causes and timing of the 1990s Bosnian war, 67
TIMUR
  Timur defeats Ottomans, 1402, 199

TOKYO
  Tokyo Stock Exchange / Japanese Nikkei Market Index, 268
TOLSTOY
  Lev Tolstoy, War and Peace, 89
  Lev Tolstoy, born 1825, fought in Crimean War in 1850s, 91
TOP-DOWN
  Top-down and bottom-up religions, 142
TOWNSHEND
  Townshend Acts 1767, 34
TRADE
  1993 bombing of World Trade Center, 21, 28
TRADITION
  Life of Mohammed: Quran (Koran), biographies, Hadeeth (Traditions), 143
TRANSFORM
  Japan's imperialistic transformation after Meiji Restoration in 1868, 78
  Russia's Communist transformation by World War I and Bolshevik Revolution in 1917, 78
  Wolfgang Schivelbusch - transformation of defeated nation, 288 (82)
TRANSISTOR
  Moore's Law, transistors on integrated circuit, Gordon Moore, Intel Corporation, 1964, 253
TRANSJORDAN
  Turkey, Iraq, Jordan (Transjordan) from Ottoman Empire, 71
TREATY
  French and Indian War = Seven Years War ends with Treaty of Paris, 1756-63, 32, 173
  Ottomans fight War with Holy League, treaty at Karlowitz (Carlowitz), 1699, 212
  Russia (Catherine the Great) war with Ottomans, annexes Crimea, peace treaty at Kuchuk Kaynarja, 1762-83, 206
  Russia, Ottomans war, treaty at Kuchuk Kaynarja, 1774, 212
  Treaty at Utrecht ends War of Spanish Succession, 1714, 173
TREND
  Combined growth / cyclic trends, 241
  Cyclic trends: fashion, political economic, generational, 239
  Exponential growth: forecasting stock trends, 263
  Growth trends, 239
  Mike Alexander, Kondratieff Cycles and trends, 239
  Population based exponential growth trends, 242
  Technology based exponential growth trends, 248
TRIAL
  Salem Witch Trials 1692, 29
TRIBE
  600 Indian tribes in America speaking 500 languages, 26
  Fulani-Hausa Nigerian tribes, 61
  Muslim tribe chieftain Osman and Ottoman Empire, 199
  Nomadic Bedouin tribes - perpetual war as a way of life, 145
  Owerri Ibo and Onitsha Ibo Nigerian tribes, 61
  Thousands of tribes merged to 250 nations and 9 major civilizations, 24
  Wampanoag, Narragansett, Mohawk Indian tribes, 26
TRIGGER
  Bankruptcy triggers French Revolution of 1789, 79, 93, 174
TRUCE
  World War I Christmas truce, 86
TRUST
  Panic of 1857 and Ohio Life Insurance and Trust Company, 39, 123
TSAR
  Ivan the Terrible - Tsar (or Czar) of Russia, 201
  Tsar Alexander I political reforms, 206
  Tsar Alexander of Russia, 92, 95
TULIPOMANIA
  Tulipomania market bubble panic in 1637, 79, 120, 171
TURCHIN
  Asabiya (group solidarity), Ibn Khaldun, Peter Turchin, 288 (62)
  Peter Turchin, Historical Dynamics, 287 (60), 291 (162), 295 (219), 296 (242), 296 (243), 296 (244)
TURKEY
  Cyprus - fault line between Greece and Turkey, 131
  Mustafa Kemal, Attaturk, president of Turkey, 1922, 215
  Turkey, Iraq, Jordan (Transjordan) from Ottoman Empire, 71
  Turkish civil war with PKK Kurds 1984-2000, 72

CONCEPT INDEX

World War I - crisis war for Balkans (Yugoslavia), Turkey (Ottoman Empire), Russia (Bolshevik Communist Revolution), 85

TURK
Invasion of Seljuk Turks from Asia, 1000, 195
Ottoman Freedom Foundation, Committee of Union and Progress, Young Turks, 1889-1908, 213
Young Turks rebellion against Ottomans, 1908, 68, 214

UKRAINE
Stalin's Hitler's massacre of Ukraine and Crimean Tatars, 1930s-40s, 210

ULOZHENIE
Ulozhenie, Russian law makes peasants into slaves, 1649, 204

UNCLE
Al-Abbas, uncle of Mohammed, 192

UNIFICATION
Wars of German and Italian Unification and Ottoman's and pan-Islamic movement, 213

UNION
Ottoman Freedom Foundation, Committee of Union and Progress, Young Turks, 1889-1908, 213
Unionist senators Henry Clay and Daniel Webster, 39

UNITED
United States, impartial policeman of the world, 74

UNIVERSITY
Jianping Mei of New York University's Stern School of Business, 296 (269)

Spain's sense of manifest destiny, Manuel Fernandez Alvarez, University of Salamanca, 291 (157)
Yasushi Hamao of the University of Southern California's Marshall School of Business, 296 (269)
Yexiao Xu of the School of Management at University of Texas at Dallas, 296 (269)

UNRAVELING
Austerity, awakening, and unraveling periods, 10

UPRISING
Armenian uprising, Istanbul, 1894-96, 214

UTRECHT
Treaty at Utrecht ends War of Spanish Succession, 1714, 173

VASCO
Vasco Nunez de Balboa reaches Pacific in 1513, 158

VIENNA
Congress of Vienna ends Napoleonic wars, 1815, 179
Ottoman siege of Vienna, Habsburg capital, 1683, 211

VIETNAM
Vietnam War and resignation of Richard Nixon, 84
Vietnam War awakening, 128

VISCERAL
Crisis wars: visceral feeling of anxiety, terror and fury, 3

VLADIMIR
Kiev Slav Vladimir adopts Orthodox religion, 988, 198

VON
Effect of defeat - Carl von Clausewitz, 288 (83)
Prince Max von Baden on World War I, 289 (87)

Prussian Chancellor Otto von Bismarck, 1862, 182

WAMPANOAG
Massasoit, chief of the Wampanoag Indians, 27
Wampanoag, Narragansett, Mohawk Indian tribes, 26

WAR
American Revolutionary War 1772-82, 32
Ariel Sharon and Yasser Arafat cooperating to prevent major Mideast war, 73
Cause versus timing of war, 13
Causes and timing of new Mideast war, 73
Causes and timing of the 1990s Bosnian war, 67
Civil war in Germany and Austria (Habsburg Empire), Peace at Augsburg in 1555, 167
Congress of Vienna ends Napoleonic wars, 1815, 179
Crimean War, 1853-56, 181
Crisis Wars versus Mid-Cycle Wars, 80
Crisis war in Mexico, 57
Crisis wars and cultural memory, 81
Crisis wars: visceral feeling of anxiety, terror and fury, 3
Deaths in major American wars, 44
Florence Nightingale invents nursing in Crimean War, 206
French Commune civil war, 1871, 182
French Revolution and Napoleonic Wars, 1789-1815, 173
French and Indian War = Seven Years War ends with

329

Treaty of Paris, 1756-63, 32, 173

Great Patriotic War, 210

Identify Group Expansion principle in wars, 64

Iran / Iraq war in 1980s, 72

King Philip's War: Colonists versus Indians 1675-78, 25

Lev Tolstoy, War and Peace, 89

Lev Tolstoy, born 1825, fought in Crimean War in 1850s, 91

Lord Alfred Tennyson poem, The Charge of the Light Brigade, Crimean War, 207

Merger of timelines in Thirty Years' War, 1618-48, 168

Mohawk war, 1663-80, 28

Nomadic Bedouin tribes - perpetual war as a way of life, 145

Ottomans fight Crimean War, 1853-56, 213

Ottomans fight War with Holy League, treaty at Karlowitz (Carlowitz), 1699, 212

Palestine versus Jews crisis war, 1936-49, 72, 149

Panic of 1857 and Civil War, 78

Peace of Westphalia ends Thirty Years' War in 1648, 171

Peloponnesian War between Athens and Sparta, 431BC, 133

Persian War with ancient Greece, 131

Prince Max von Baden on World War I, 289 (87)

Principle of Localization versus Identify Group Expansion principle in wars, 69

Revolutionary War to Civil War, 12

Revolutionary war and slavery compromise, 36

Russia (Catherine the Great) war with Ottomans, annexes Crimea, peace treaty at Kuchuk Kaynarja, 1762-83, 206

Russia (Peter the Great) and Sweden fight the Great Northern War, 1700-1720, 205

Russia Crimean War and Emancipation Edict frees serfs, 1853-61, 206

Russia and Napoleonic wars, 204, 206

Russia's Communist transformation by World War I and Bolshevik Revolution in 1917, 78

Russia's mid-cycle wars with western Europe, 204

Russia, Ottomans war, treaty at Kuchuk Kaynarja, 1774, 212

Russia, Poland, Sweden, Denmark fight Livonian War on Baltic, 1557, 201

Samuel P. Huntington, Clash of Civilizations and fault line wars, 62

Scottish rebellion and English civil war, 1638-60, 165

Treaty at Utrecht ends War of Spanish Succession, 1714, 173

Turkish civil war with PKK Kurds 1984-2000, 72

Vietnam War and resignation of Richard Nixon, 84

Vietnam War awakening, 128

War between France and Germany, 75

War of 1812, 93

War of Spanish Succession, 1701-14, 93, 95, 172

War processes: negotiation, compromise, containment, intensification, expansion, 63

Wars of German and Italian Unification and Ottoman's and pan-Islamic movement, 213

Winston Churchill on German capitulation in World War I, 289 (87)

World War I - crisis war for Balkans (Yugoslavia), Turkey (Ottoman Empire), Russia (Bolshevik Communist Revolution), 85

World War I Christmas truce, 86

World War I not a crisis war for America, 44

World War I not a crisis war for Germany, 86

World War II without Hitler, 50

World Wars I and II as "Thirty-one Years' War", 88

WAY

Nomadic Bedouin tribes - perpetual war as a way of life, 145

WEALTHY

Ivan the Terrible versus wealthy landowners (boyars), 1564, 202

WEBSTER

Unionist senators Henry Clay and Daniel Webster, 39

WEDLOCK

Exponential technology growth: Out of wedlock births, 263

WESLEY

John Wesley, Methodist religion, 31

WESTERN
Major civilizations: Western, Latin American, African, Islamic, Sinic, Hindu, Orthodox, Buddhist, Japanese, 24, 62

Orthodox, Islamic and Western civilizations meet in the Balkans, 64

Russia's mid-cycle wars with western Europe, 204

WESTPHALIA
Peace of Westphalia ends Thirty Years' War in 1648, 171

WIFE
Mohammed / polygamy - multiple wives, 149

Mohammed's wife Khadija, 144

WILLIAM
William Bradford, 27

William and Mary College, 166

William and Mary named King and Queen of England, 1688, 166

WINSLOW
Edward Winslow, 27

WINSTON
Winston Churchill on German capitulation in World War I, 289 (87)

WITCH
Salem Witch Trials 1692, 29

WITHOUT
World War II without Hitler, 50

WOLFGANG
Wolfgang Schivelbusch - transformation of defeated nation, 288 (82)

WORLD
1993 bombing of World Trade Center, 21, 28

Christopher Columbus discovers New World in 1492, 156

Prince Max von Baden on World War I, 289 (87)

Russia's Communist transformation by World War I and Bolshevik Revolution in 1917, 78

United States, impartial policeman of the world, 74

Winston Churchill on German capitulation in World War I, 289 (87)

World War I - crisis war for Balkans (Yugoslavia), Turkey (Ottoman Empire), Russia (Bolshevik Communist Revolution), 85

World War I Christmas truce, 86

World War I not a crisis war for America, 44

World War I not a crisis war for Germany, 86

World War II without Hitler, 50

World Wars I and II as "Thirty-one Years' War", 88

XU
Yexiao Xu of the School of Management at University of Texas at Dallas, 296 (269)

YASSER
Ariel Sharon and Yasser Arafat cooperating to prevent major Mideast war, 73

YASUSHI
Yasushi Hamao of the University of Southern California's Marshall School of Business, 296 (269)

YATHRIB
Mohammed flees to Medina (Yathrib) in 622, 144

YEAR
French and Indian War = Seven Years War ends with Treaty of Paris, 1756-63, 32, 173

Merger of timelines in Thirty Years' War, 1618-48, 168

Peace of Westphalia ends Thirty Years' War in 1648, 171

World Wars I and II as "Thirty-one Years' War", 88

YEXIAO
Yexiao Xu of the School of Management at University of Texas at Dallas, 296 (269)

YORK
Jianping Mei of New York University's Stern School of Business, 296 (269)

YOUNG
Ottoman Freedom Foundation, Committee of Union and Progress, Young Turks, 1889-1908, 213

Young Turks rebellion against Ottomans, 1908, 68, 214

YUGOSLAVIA
Kingdom of Yugoslavia, 1918-1990, 67

World War I - crisis war for Balkans (Yugoslavia), Turkey (Ottoman Empire), Russia (Bolshevik Communist Revolution), 85

YUKSEL
Dr. Edip Yuksel, Islamic scholar, 147

ZIONISM
Zionism and Israel, 215

Colophon

This book was created from standard ascii text files. A collection of software utility programs, written in Perl scripts and Microsoft Word macros, were developed. Using these programs, the text files could be transformed into either an online book (in HTML) or a Microsoft Word document.

The programs supported all the special features of the book, including cross-references, end notes, and the concept index. To support these features, the software generated URL hyperlinks for the online version and page number cross reference fields for the Microsoft Word version.

I believe that these features add a great deal of richness to a book, especially a technical book or any book as complex as this one is.

The web site for this book will be found at:

http://www.GenerationalDynamics.com/

John J. Xenakis